S0-BAI-163

NEW PERSPECTIVES SERIES

Computer
Concepts

SECOND EDITION

INTRODUCTORY

June Jamrich Parsons

University of the Virgin Islands

Dan Oja

GuildWare, Inc.

A Susan Solomon Book

CTI

A DIVISION OF COURSE TECHNOLOGY
ONE MAIN STREET, CAMBRIDGE MA 02142

an International Thomson Publishing company I(T)P

Albany • Bonn • Boston • Cincinnati • London • Madrid • Melbourne • Mexico City
New York • Paris • San Francisco • Singapore • Tokyo • Toronto • Washington

New Perspectives on Computer Concepts Second Edition—Introductory is published by CTI.

Managing Editor	Mac Mendelsohn
Series Consulting Editor	Susan Solomon
Product Manager	Susan Solomon
Production Editor	Debbie Masi
Art Direction and Design	Ella Hanna
Prepress Production and PhotoResearch	Hanna Design+Company
Interior Illustrators	Network Graphics and Tarragon Interactive, Inc.

© 1996 by CTI.
A Division of Course Technology - ITP.

For more information contact:

Course Technology
One Main Street
Cambridge, MA 02142

International Thomson Publishing Europe
Berkshire House 168-173
High Holborn
London WCIV 7AA, England

Thomas Nelson Australia
102 Dodds Street
South Melbourne, 3205
Victoria, Australia

Nelson Canada
1120 Birchmount Road
Scarborough, Ontario
Canada M1K 5G4

International Thomson Editores
Campos Eliseos 385, Piso 7
Col. Polanco
11560 Mexico D.F. Mexico

International Thomson Publishing GmbH
Kônigswinterer Strasse 418
53227 Bonn, Germany

International Thomson Publishing Asia
211 Henderson Road
#05-10 Henderson Building
Singapore 0315

International Thomson Publishing Japan
Hirakawacho Kyowa Building, 3F
2-2-1 Hirakawacho
Chiyoda-ku, Tokyo 102 Japan

All rights reserved. This publication is protected by federal copyright law. No part of this publication may be reproduced, stored in a retrieval system, or transmitted in any form or by any means, electronic, mechanical, photocopying, recording, or otherwise, or be used to make a derivative work (such as translation or adaptation), without prior permission in writing from Course Technology, Inc.

Trademarks
Course Technology and the open book logo are registered trademarks of Course Technology.
I(T)P The ITP logo is a trademark under license.
Microsoft and Windows 95 are registered trademarks of Microsoft Corporation.

Some of the product names and company names used in this book have been used for identification purposes only and may be trademarks or registered trademarks of their respective manufacturers and sellers.

Disclaimer
CTI reserves the right to revise this publication and make changes from time to time in its content without notice.

ISBN 0-7600-34397

Printed in the United States of America

10 9 8 7 6 5 4 3

From the

New Perspectives Series Team

We believe that technology is transforming the way people teach and learn, and we are excited about providing instructors and students with materials that use technology to teach about technology.

Our development process is unparalleled in the higher education publishing industry. Every product we create goes through an exacting process of design, development, review, and testing.

Reviewers give us direction and insight that shape our manuscripts and bring them up to the latest standards. Every manuscript is quality tested. Students whose backgrounds match the intended audience work through every keystroke, carefully checking for clarity and pointing out errors in logic and sequence. Together with our own technical reviewers, these testers help us ensure that everything that carries our name is error-free and easy to use.

We show both how and why technology is critical to solving problems in college and in whatever field you choose to teach or pursue. Our time-tested, step-by-step instructions provide unparalleled clarity. Examples and applications are chosen and crafted to motivate students.

As the New Perspectives Series team at Course Technology, our goal is to produce the most timely, accurate, creative, and technologically sound product in the entire college publishing industry. We strive for consistent high quality. This takes a lot of communication, coordination, and hard work. But we love what we do. We are determined to be the best. Write us and let us know what you think. You can also e-mail us at newperspectives@course.com.

The New Perspectives Series Team

Joseph Adamski	Kathy Finnegan	Harry Phillips
Judy Adamski	Robin Geller	Sandra Poindexter
Roy Ageloff	Roger Hayen	Mark Reimold
David Auer	Charles Hommel	Ann Shaffer
Rachel Bunin	Chris Kelly	Susan Solomon
Joan Carey	Terry Ann Kremer	Christine Spillett
Patrick Carey	Melissa Lima	Susanne Walker
Barbara Clemens	Nancy Ludlow	John Zeanchock
Kim Crowley	Mac Mendelsohn	Beverly Zimmerman
Kristin Duerr	Dan Oja	Scott Zimmerman
Jessica Evans	June Parsons	

Preface to the Instructor

An Integrated System of Instruction: Five Components

You hold in your hands a textbook that is one component of an integrated system of instruction. And what do we mean by an integrated system of instruction? We mean text, graphics, video, sound, animation, and simulations that are linked and that provide a flexible, unified, and interactive system to help you teach and to help your students learn. Specifically, the *New Perspectives Integrated System of Instruction* consists of five components: a Course Technology textbook (on computer concepts and/or microcomputer applications), Course Labs, Course Online, Course Presenter, and Course Test Manager. These components have been developed to work together to provide a complete, integrative teaching and learning experience.

The Textbook: The New Paradigm for Concepts Courses

This textbook–*New Perspectives on Computer Concepts*—is unique in many ways. It taps into the learning styles of today's students, and it empowers students to be self-sufficient computer users. It emphasizes the practical aspects of today's computing environment, such as the basics of installing software, expanding a computer system, defragmenting a disk, or decompressing a file. It contains SuperFigures—illustrations that students can read and that employ the well-known fact that people always look at the pictures first. And it includes a rich collection of end of chapter materials—Review, Projects, Resources, and Lab Assignments—that are thought-provoking and encourage critical thinking. Taken together these features propelled the first edition of *New Perspectives on Computer Concepts* to become the best-selling new first edition concepts book in over a decade.

The second edition of *New Perspectives on Computer Concepts* has retained all of the show-stopping features that made the first edition so popular. And now it includes more ways to choose your coverage, a reorganization of topics, new coverage, entirely new art and photographs, student notes, Internet Assignments, and much, much more. Here are *only a sampling* of the changes we've made to this feature-rich second edition:

- You can now choose the amount of coverage you want. Three editions are available—the Brief Edition (Chapters 1 through 5), the Introductory Edition (Chapters 1 through 8), or the Comprehensive Edition (Chapters 1 through 14). Also we are pleased to be the first computer concepts textbook to offer chapters (6 through 14) *available as separate modules* so you can order only the coverage you want. See below for more details about our Custom Editions and Course Kits.

- We've reorganized. The more technical topics have been delayed to Chapters 9 through 14. One example is how we moved coverage of topics formerly in Chapter 3 to Chapter 9.

- We've added new coverage. Obviously, we've updated our coverage to the latest technology; but we also now have two new chapters—one devoted entirely to buying a computer (Chapter 5) and one devoted entirely to the Internet and the information superhighway (Chapter 7). New *User Focus* sections—covering topics such as installing software, getting connected to the Internet, and setting up a modem—now conclude each chapter. We've beefed up our coverage of hardware, especially mainframes and peripheral devices.

■ We have all new art and photographs. Many of these new figures were developed using state-of-the-art object-oriented technology. See for example, Figures 1-20, 2-14, 2-21 and 5-7.

■ We've divided the chapters into numbered sections that always begin at the top of a page. This affords several tangible benefits, among them: Learning is broken up into more assimilatable chunks. You can more accurately allocate time in your syllabus. The numbers make it easier to navigate and communicate about the chapter. Look on pages 1-4 and 3-4 for examples.

■ We've added focus questions. Every major heading in each section is followed by new focus questions designed to engage students, to pique their interest, and to establish the relevance of the material that follows. Look for examples on pages 2-8, 4-12 and 4-13, 5-22 and 5-23.

■ We've put student notes in the margins. Throughout the text these notes direct students' attention to concepts and activities that maximize learning. You can find examples on pages 2-48, 6-8 and 7-19.

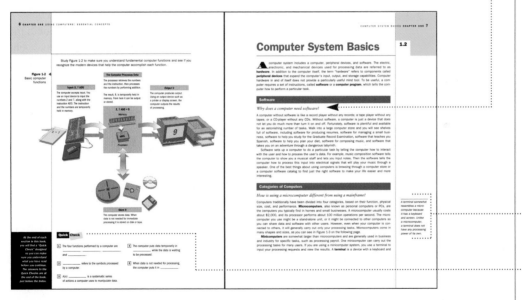

A terminal somewhat resembles a micro-computer because it has a keyboard and screen. Unlike a microcomputer, a terminal does not have any processing power of its own.

■ At the end of each Section we've added meaningful, conceptual questions–called Quick Checks–that test students' understanding of what they read in the section. Answers to Quick Check questions are at the back of the book preceding the Index. You can find examples of Quick Checks on pages 1-6, 5-16 and 8-15.

■ We now have Internet Projects. Icons in the Projects section designate those projects that have been carefully designed to require use of the Internet, or to permit use of the Internet and/or traditional library resources to complete the Project. Some representative examples are Project 4 in Chapter 1, Project 6 in Chapter 2, and Project 12 in Chapter 5, and Project 1 in Chapter 7.

Remember, this list includes only a few of the many changes and enhancements to this new second edition.

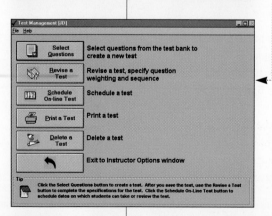

Course Labs: Now, Concepts Come to Life

Computer skills and concepts come to life with these New Perspectives Course Labs–25 highly interactive tutorials that combine illustrations, animation, digital images, and simulations. The Labs guide students step-by-step, present them with Quick Check questions, allow them to explore on their own, test them on their comprehension, and provide printed feedback. All of the Labs are either new or completely revised. *The Labs show students what textbooks can only talk about.* See pages xiv and xv for a complete list and brief description of the Labs.

Course Online: A Site Dedicated to Keeping You and Your Students Up-To-Date

Once again Course Technology ushers technology into the classroom by providing a dedicated site on the World Wide Web for users of *New Perspectives on Computer Concepts*. Instructors may visit the *password-protected* Faculty Online Companion for additional assignments with solutions, "Hot Tips" from other users, most commonly asked questions with answers, articles, content updates, and more. Students may visit the Student Online Companion where they'll find resources such as content updates to the text, links to interesting sites, additional graphics and exercises, and Internet Projects. Please see your Instructor's Manual or call your Course Technology customer service representative for more information.

Course Presenter: Ready-Made or Customized Dynamic Presentations

Course Presenter is a CD ROM-based presentation tool that provides you a wealth of resources for use in the classroom, replacing traditional overhead transparencies with computer generated screenshows. Presenter includes a structured presentation for each chapter of the textbook and also provides the flexibility to create your own custom presentations, complete with matching students notes and lecture notes pages.

Course Test Manager: Testing and Practice Online or On Paper

Course Test Manager is cutting edge Windows-based testing software that helps instructors design and administer pre-tests, practice tests, and actual examinations. The full-featured program allows students to randomly generate practice tests that provide immediate online feedback and detailed study guides for questions incorrectly answered. Online pre-tests help you assess student skills and plan instruction. You can use Course Test Manager to generate traditional paper tests. Also students can take tests at the computer that can be automatically graded and generate statistical information on student individual and group performance.

Integrating the Five Components: The Formula for Successful Teaching and Learning

The text, graphics, video, sound, animation, and simulations contained in the Textbook, Labs, Presenter, Test Manager and Web Pages are linked to provide a flexible, unified, and interactive system of instruction. How are they linked? The diagram here helps answer that question.

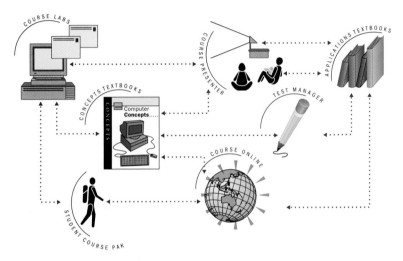

Start with the link between the Computer Concepts textbook and the Course Labs. The Labs teach skills and concepts that are introduced in the textbook. Each Lab is identified by an icon, and the icons appear throughout the text adjacent to the text material they reinforce. Quick Checks appears in both the textbook and the Labs. The textbook contains Lab Assignments that students complete using the Course Labs. These are only a few examples of how these two components are linked.

All of the components are linked in similar ways. Here are some examples. While using Course Presenter, you can click a button and launch a Lab. Presenter also contains Quick Checks that you can display for student interaction. Students see the same figures in Presenter that they see in the textbook and in Course Test Manager. The Practice Tests in the Test Manager generates a study guide of pages in the textbook to help students study the topics of those questions they incorrectly answered. Some of the Projects in the textbook require students to visit the *New Perspectives on Computer Concepts* Web page. And so on...

You can choose to integrate these components as much or as little as you like. Used in total this integration provides a powerful teaching and learning system.

Instructor's Manual: Your Help System

For each chapter the authors provide a chapter outline; suggestions for instruction on the chapter content, for integrating the Labs, and for using the Resources; answers to the Review, Projects, and Labs Assignments; Quick Quizes: and numerous teaching tips.

Student Course Pak: For Students With Computers and Distance Learners

We are pleased to present another Course Technology first–the Student Course Pak. It is available to students who have their own computers or who have access to computers with CD-ROM drives. It is also ideal for instructors and students in distance learning programs.

The Student Course Pak includes:
— the textbook *New Perspectives on Computer Concepts Second Edition* (Brief, Introductory, or Comprehensive Editions)
— a CD which contains:
  - the 25 Course Labs
  - the structured presentations from Course Presenter
  - the Practice Test component of Course Test Manager
— The Internet Student Survival Guide—a kit that provides students e-mail and World Wide Web access through a remote service provider.

These items are package together and discounted in price.

The New Perspectives Series: A Wide Selection of Application Software Texts

New Perspectives on Computer Concepts is part of the New Perspectives Series, which includes microcomputer applications textbooks. These applications textbooks are also part of the integrated system of instruction. For example, they include Quick Checks and Lab Assignments; they link to Course Presenter and Course Test Manager; and they have home pages.

The applications textbooks are available in different lengths, platforms, and releases. They are also available with the concepts textbooks in bound editions, in Course Kits, and in our new Custom Editions. Contact your CTI sales representative or customer service representative for the most up-to-date details. The following list shows the programs available in the New Perspectives Series.

dBASE	Microsoft PowerPoint	Paradox
Internet and World Wide Web	Microsoft Windows 3.1	Presentations
Lotus 1-2-3	Microsoft Windows 95	Quattro Pro
Microsoft Access	Microsoft Word	Microsoft Visual Basic
Microsoft Excel	Microsoft Works	WordPerfect
Microsoft Office Professional	Perfect Office	

Course Kits and Custom Editions: Exactly What You Want, the Way You Want It

If you want to customize your textbook to fit your course *exactly*, Course Technology offers you two ways to combine the materials you want and save students money. With Course Kits you can choose two or more New Perspectives or other Course Technology textbooks to use in one course; they will be packaged together in a box and sold to your students for a deeply discounted price. Or, if you want your New Perspectives course materials bound together in one volume, you can choose from our Custom Editions—select the materials and the binding (spiral or three-ring binder) and order at a discounted price. Contact your CTI sales representative or customer service representative for more details.

Acknowledgments

This integrated system of instruction works because of a powerful system of talented people. Many thanks to Mark Ciampa, Gail Miles, Cathy Moore, and Dave White, whose comments were invaluable. Sandi Poindexter and John Zeanchock deserve special recognition for their review of the instructional design. The extraordinary talent of Debbie Masi, Ella Hanna, and Kim Munsell are woven throughout this system of instruction. Coco and Claire hounded the team until everything was perfect. And still, no thanks to Marilyn.

Brief Contents

Table of Contents

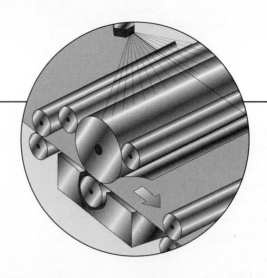

Course Labs

Course Labs offer the absolute best when it comes to interactive learning reinforcement. The newly designed Labs now offer:

- Steps, which guide students step-by-step as they learn/review basic concepts
- Quick Checks, which appear as students work through the Steps and which draw attention to key points
- Summary Reports, which automatically grade reports that can be printed as homework and as validation that students have completed the Steps
- Explore, in which students can experiment, practice skills, and complete the Lab Assignments at the end of each chapter.

CHAPTER ONE

Using a Mouse

This Lab guides students through basic mouse functions and operations.Interactive exercises using dialog boxes allow students to practice mouse skills by creating posters.

Using a Keyboard

Students learn the parts of the keyboard and basic keyboard operations.They practice basic keyboarding with interactive typing exercises, including a self-paced typing tutor that helps improve speed and accuracy.

User Interfaces

Students are presented with user interfaces on a general/conceptual level, and then have the opportunity to interact with menu driven, prompted dialog, command line, graphical, and combination interfaces.

DOS Command-Line Interface

This Lab presents students with concepts and basic skills associated with the DOS command line, and provides hands-on practice entering commands at a live DOS prompt.

Peripheral Devices

Descriptions, drawings, and animations explain the functions of many popular peripheral devices.

CHAPTER TWO

Word Processing

This Lab guides students through essential word processing skills, such as typing and editing text, formatting, saving, and opening a document. They interact with a word processing program, specially designed for this Lab, that offers a hands-on introduction to word processors.

Spreadsheets

Students are introduced to essential spreadsheet skills. A spreadsheet program, specially designed for this Lab, allows students to practice and explore these skills on their own.

Databases

After learning essential database concepts, students learn to use query by example to search a visual database for specific records.

Computer History Hypermedia

This dynamic Lab contains descriptions, drawings and photos related to the history and development of computing devices. Students learn to use hypertext links to research historical events and trends.

CHAPTER THREE

Using Files
Students see what happens on the screen, in RAM, and on disk when they save, open, revise, and delete files.

Defragmentation and Disk Operations
In this Lab, students interact with simulated disks, files, and FATs to discover how the computer physically stores files. The Lab demonstrates how files become fragmented and how defragmentation utilities work.

Windows Directorie, Folders, and Files
Students work with a directory tree to learn basic concepts of directory hierarchies and file types.

DOS Directories and File Management
Students learn the basics of DOS file managment, including subdirectories, copying, and moving files.

CHAPTER FOUR

Troubleshooting
Students use a simulated computer to step through the boot process. They learn to identify and troubleshoot the most common boot-related problems.

Binary Numbers
This Lab introduces students to binary numbers, demonstrates how data is stored electronically using ones and zeroes, and provides practice converting between binary and decimal.

CPU Simulator
Students use a microprocessor simulation to see what happens in the ALU, control unit, and register during execution of simple assembly language programs. They can run prepared programs or write their own to see how a microprocessor actually works.

CHAPTER FIVE

Buying a Computer
In this Lab an online glossary helps students interpret the technical specifications and advertisements to compare features and make purchase decisions.

CHAPTER SIX

E-mail
Students use a simple e-mail simulation to learn essential e-mail skills including creating, sending , forwarding, replying, printing and saving mail.

CHAPTER SEVEN

The Internet: World Wide Web
Students interact with a simulated Web browser to explore home pages, URLs, linking, and hypertext. You can assign this Lab even if an Internet connection is not available.

CHAPTER EIGHT

Data Backup
Using a simulated business environment, this Lab teaches basic backup procedures.Students experience data loss, attempt to restore lost data, and learn first-hand the value of regular backup procedures.

Credits

Chapter One Opener: Photofest. Figure 1-1: UPI/Bettmann. Figure 1-3 a-c: Courtesy of International Business Machines Corporation. Figure 1-3d: ©Frank Pryor/Courtesy of Apple Computer, Inc. Figure 1-4 and 1-5: Courtesy of International Business Machines Corporation. Figure 1-6: ©Charles Thatcher/Tony Stone Images. **Chapter Two** Opener: AP/Wide World Photos. Figure 2-2 and 2-5: Courtesy of Microsoft Corporation. Photographed by Durvin & Co. Figure 2-11a: Courtesy of International Business Machines Corporation. Figure 2-11b: Courtesy of Apple Computer, Inc. Figure 2-17: Courtesy of Berkeley Systems, Inc. Figure 2-22: Courtesy of Creative Labs, Inc. ©1995. Figure 2-24: Compliments of Microsoft Corporation. Photographed by Durvin & Co. **Chapter Three** Opener: ©Dilip Meta/Contact Press Images, Inc. **Chapter Four** Opener: James Kaczman **Chapter Five** Opener: Bonnie Kamin Photography. Figure 5-1: Courtesy Midwest Micro, Fletcher Ohio. Figure5-7a-b: Courtesy EPSON Americas, Inc. Figure 5-7c: Courtesy Hewlett-Packard Company. Figure 5-8: PC-3050 Courtesy of Sharp Electronics Corporation. Figure 5-9: Mobile Communications Division of U.S. Robotics. Figure 5-10, 5-11 and 5-12a: Courtesy of International Business Machines Corporation. Figure 5-12b: PC-3050 Courtesy of Sharp Electornics Corporation. Figure 5-12c: Toshiba America Information Systems, Inc. Figure 5-13a: James P. Dawson/NYT Pictures. Figure 5-13b-c: Images reprinted with permission from Microsoft Corporation. Figure 5-15: Micron Electronics, Inc. Figure 5-19: Reprinted by permission of Wall Street Journal. ©1995 Dow Jones & Company, Inc. All Rights Reserved Worldwide. **Chapter Six** Opener: Spencer Jones 1995/FPG International. Figure 6-14a: Courtesy of International Business Machines Corporation. Figure 6-14b (Lotus Notes): Courtesy of Lotus Development Corporation. Figure 6-14c (ProshareVideo 200): Courtesy of Intel Corporation. Figure 6-14d: (Collabra Share): Courtesy of Netscape Communications Corporations. Figure 6-14e: ©Steven Peters/Tony Stone Images. **Chapter Seven** Opener: Created by Dan Oja, Guildware, Inc. Figure 7-6 and 7-7: Prodigy Services Company. Figure 7-20: Drawing by P. Steiner, ©1993 The New Yorker Magazine, Inc. Figure 7-21: ©1990 Peter Menzel Photography. **Chapter Eight** Opener: Ducal Palace, Mantua/Mauro Magliani/SuperStock, Inc. Figure 8-11: Source: *Understanding Computers: Computer Security*. Alexandria, VA: Time-Life Books, 1986. Figure 8-14: I. Essa, T. Darrell, A. Pentland, ©MIT, Medial Library 1994.

Using Computers: Essential Concepts

Using Computers:

Essential Concepts

In the classic science-fiction film *2001: A Space Odyssey*, astronaut Dave Bowman and four crew members depart on a mission to Jupiter. The mission objective: to discover the source of a mysterious object from space. Midway through the mission, the onboard computer, named HAL, begins to exhibit strange behavior. Dave leaves the spacecraft to make some external repairs. When he is ready to reboard, he speaks to the computer, "Open the pod bay door, HAL." HAL's reply is chilling, "I'm sorry, Dave, I'm afraid I can't do that."

This dialog between a human and a computer raises some intriguing questions. How realistic is it? Can humans and computers communicate this fluently? What went wrong with the communication? Why won't the computer let Dave back into the spaceship?

To use a computer effectively, you must communicate tasks to the computer and accurately interpret the information the computer provides to you. The means by which humans and computers communicate is referred to as the *user interface*, and this is the central theme of Chapter 1.

In this chapter you will learn which computer components are necessary for communication between humans and computers. You will also learn about the user interfaces typically found on today's computer systems and how to respond to what you see on the computer screen. The chapter concludes with a discussion about manuals, reference guides, and tutorials that will help you learn how to interact with a specific computer system or software package.

CHAPTER**PREVIEW**

This chapter is a practical introduction to computers that you can immediately apply in the Lab component of this course: starting a computer, logging into a network, starting programs, and using a variety of user interfaces. When you have completed this chapter you should be able to:

- Define the term "computer"

- Describe the relationship between computer hardware and software

- Identify the parts of a typical microcomputer system

- List the peripheral devices that are typically found on microcomputer systems

- Define the term "user interface"

- Describe how you use interface elements such as prompts, commands, menus, and graphical objects

- Describe the resources you can use to learn how to use computers and software

LABS

Peripheral Devices

User Interfaces

DOS Command-Line User Interface

Using a Mouse

Using a Keyboard

1.1 Computers: Mind Tools

Computers have been called "mind tools" because they enhance our ability to perform tasks that require mental activity. Computers are adept at performing activities such as making calculations quickly, sorting large lists, and searching through vast information libraries. Humans can do all these activities, but a computer can often accomplish them much faster and more accurately. Our ability to use a computer complements our mental capabilities and makes us more productive. The key to making effective use of the computer as a tool is to know what a computer does, how it works, and how you can use it. That is the focus of this book.

Von Neumann's Definition

What is a computer?

If you look in a dictionary printed before 1940, you might be surprised to find a computer defined as a *person* who performs calculations! Machines also performed calculations back then, but they were referred to as calculators, not computers. The modern definition and use of the term "computer" emerged in the 1940s when the first electronic computing devices were developed as a response to World War II military needs.

In 1945, a team of engineers began working on a secret military project to construct the Electronic Discrete Variable Automatic Computer, referred to by the acronym EDVAC. At the time, only one other functioning computer had been built in the United States. Plans for the EDVAC were described in a report by the eminent mathematician John von Neumann, pictured in Figure 1-1.

Figure 1-1
John von Neumann

When this photo was published in 1947, the caption read, "Dr. John von Neumann stands in front of a new Electronic 'Brain,' the fastest computing machine for its degree of precision yet made. The machine which can do 2,000 multiplications in one second and add or subtract 100,000 times in the same period was displayed today for the first time at the Institute for Advanced Study. Its fabulous memory can store 1,024 numbers of 12 decimal places each. Dr. von Neumann was one of the designers of the wonder machine."

Von Neumann's report has been described as "the most influential paper in the history of computer science." It was one of the earliest documents to specifically define the components of a computer and describe their functions. In the report, von Neumann used the term "automatic computing system." Today, popular usage has abandoned this cumbersome terminology in favor of the shorter terms "computer" or "computer system." Based on the concepts presented in von Neumann's paper, we can define a **computer** as a device that accepts input, processes data, stores data, and produces output. Let's look more closely at the elements of this definition.

A Computer Accepts Input

What kinds of input can a computer use?

Computer **input** is whatever is put into a computer system. "Input" is also used as a verb that means to feed information into a computer. Input can be supplied by a person, by the environment, or by another computer. Some examples of the kinds of input a computer can process are the words and symbols in a document, numbers for a calculation, instructions for completing a process, pictures, audio signals from a microphone, and temperatures from a thermostat.

An **input device** gathers and translates input into a form that the computer can process. As a computer user you will probably use the keyboard as your main input device.

A Computer Processes Data

In what ways can a computer process data?

Data refers to the symbols that describe people, events, things, and ideas. Computers manipulate data in many ways, and we call this manipulation "processing." In the context of computers, then, we can define a **process** as a systematic series of actions a computer uses to manipulate data. Some of the ways a computer can process data include performing calculations, sorting lists of words or numbers, modifying documents and pictures according to user instructions, and drawing graphs. A computer processes data in a device called the **central processing unit** or **CPU**.

You will get a more technical perspective on data in Chapter 3 and learn more about the way the central processing unit works in Chapter 4.

A Computer Stores Data

Why does a computer store data?

A computer must store data so it is available for processing. The places a computer puts data are referred to as **storage**. Most computers have more than one location for storing data. The place where the computer stores data depends on how the data is being used. The computer puts data in one place while it is waiting to be processed and another place when it is not needed for immediate processing. **Memory** is an area that holds data that is waiting to be processed. **Storage** is the area where data can be left on a permanent basis while it is not needed for processing.

A Computer Produces Output

What kinds of output does a computer produce?

Computer **output** is the results produced by a computer. "Output" is also used as a verb that means the process of producing output. Some examples of computer output include reports, documents, music, graphs, and pictures. An **output device** displays, prints, or transfers the results of processing from the computer memory.

The distinction between memory and storage is particularly useful for understanding how computers work. Make sure you understand that "memory" is a holding area used while the data is waiting to be processed. "Storage" is a more permanent location for data when it is not needed for processing.

Study Figure 1-2 to make sure you understand fundamental computer functions and see if you recognize the modern devices that help the computer accomplish each function.

Figure 1-2
Basic computer functions

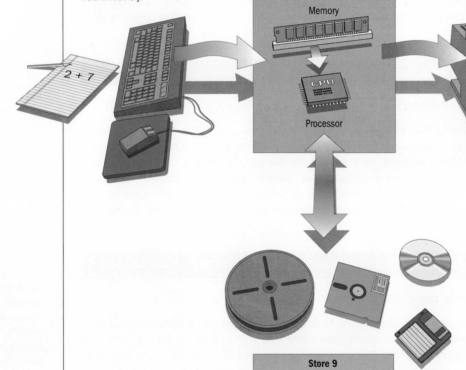

The Computer Processes Data

The processor retrieves the numbers and the instruction, then processes the numbers by performing addition.

The result, 9, is temporarily held in memory. From here it can be output or stored.

Input: 2, 7 ADD

The computer accepts input. You use an input device to input the numbers 2 and 7, along with the instruction ADD. The instruction and the numbers are temporarily held in memory.

Output 9

The computer produces output. Using an output device such as a printer or display screen, the computer outputs the results of processing.

2, 7 ADD = 9

Memory

CPU

Processor

Store 9

The computer stores data. When data is not needed for immediate processing it is stored on disk or tape.

At the end of each section in this book, you will find a "Quick Check" designed so you can make sure you understand what you have read before you continue. The answers to the Quick Checks are at the end of the book, just before the Index.

Quick Check

1. The four functions performed by a computer are _____, _____, _____, and _____.

2. _____ refers to the symbols processed by a computer.

3. A(n) _____ is a systematic series of actions a computer uses to manipulate data.

4. The computer puts data temporarily in _____ while the data is waiting to be processed.

5. When data is not needed for processing, the computer puts it in _____.

Computer System Basics

A computer system includes a computer, peripheral devices, and software. The electric, electronic, and mechanical devices used for processing data are referred to as **hardware**. In addition to the computer itself, the term "hardware" refers to components called **peripheral devices** that expand the computer's input, output, and storage capabilities. Computer hardware in and of itself does not provide a particularly useful mind tool. To be useful, a computer requires a set of instructions, called **software** or a **computer program**, which tells the computer how to perform a particular task.

Software

Why does a computer need software?

A computer without software is like a record player without any records; a tape player without any tapes; or a CD-player without any CDs. Without software, a computer is just a device that does not let you do much more than turn it on and off. Fortunately, software is plentiful and available for an astonishing number of tasks. Walk into a large computer store and you will see shelves full of software, including software for producing resumes, software for managing a small business, software to help you study for the Graduate Record Examination, software that teaches you Spanish, software to help you plan your diet, software for composing music, and software that takes you on an adventure through a dangerous labyrinth.

Software sets up a computer to do a particular task by telling the computer how to interact with the user and how to process the user's data. For example, music composition software tells the computer to show you a musical staff and lets you input notes. Then the software tells the computer how to process this input into electrical signals that will play your music through a speaker. One of the best things about using computers is browsing through a computer store or a computer software catalog to find just the right software to make your life easier and more interesting.

Categories of Computers

How is using a microcomputer different from using a mainframe?

Computers traditionally have been divided into four categories, based on their function, physical size, cost, and performance. **Microcomputers**, also known as personal computers or PCs, are the computers you typically find in homes and small businesses. A microcomputer usually costs about $2,000, and its processor performs about 100 million operations per second. The microcomputer you use might be a stand-alone unit, or it might be connected to other computers so you can share data and software with other users. However, even when your computer is connected to others, it will generally carry out only your processing tasks. Microcomputers come in many shapes and sizes, as you can see in Figure 1-3 on the following page.

Minicomputers are somewhat larger than microcomputers and are generally used in business and industry for specific tasks, such as processing payroll. One minicomputer can carry out the processing tasks for many users. If you are using a minicomputer system, you use a terminal to input your processing requests and view the results. A **terminal** is a device with a keyboard and

A terminal somewhat resembles a microcomputer because it has a keyboard and screen. Unlike a microcomputer, a terminal does not have any processing power of its own.

Figure 1-3
Microcomputers

A standard **desktop microcomputer** fits on a desk and runs on power from an electrical outlet. The display screen is usually placed on top of the horizontal "desktop" case.

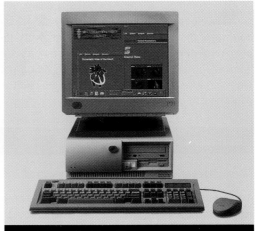

Desktop Microcomputer

Microcomputer with Tower Case

A microcomputer with a **tower case** contains the same basic components as a standard desktop microcomputer, but the vertically-oriented case is large and allows more room for expansion. The tower unit can be placed on the floor to save desk space.

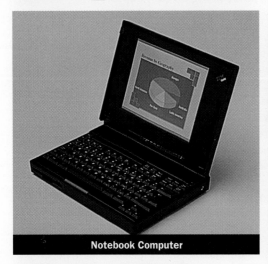

Notebook Computer

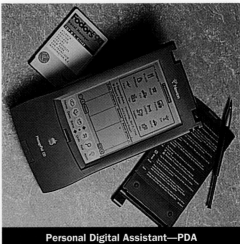

Personal Digital Assistant—PDA

A **notebook computer** is small and light, giving it the advantage of portability that a standard desktop computer does not have. A notebook computer can run on power from an electrical outlet or batteries.

To achieve even more portability, a **personal digital assistant** (PDA) eliminates the size and weight of a keyboard. PDAs accept input written with a special stylus.

A minicomputer handles processing tasks for multiple users. This minicomputer can handle up to 20 users, but only three terminals are currently connected.

Terminals act as each user's main input and output device. The terminal has a keyboard for input and a display screen for output, but it does not process the user's data. Instead, processing requests must be transmitted from the terminal to the minicomputer.

The minicomputer stores data for all the users in one centralized location.

screen used for input and output, but not for processing. Your terminal transmits your processing request to the minicomputer. The minicomputer sends back results to your terminal when the processing is complete. The minicomputer system with three terminals in Figure 1-4 is fairly typical and carries a price tag of $68,000.

Mainframes are large, fast, and fairly expensive computers, generally used by business or government to provide centralized storage, processing, and management for large amounts of data. As with a minicomputer, one mainframe computer carries out processing tasks for multiple users who input processing requests using a terminal. However, a mainframe generally services more users than a minicomputer. To process large amounts of data, mainframes often include more than one processing unit. One of these processing units directs overall operations. A second processing unit handles communication with all the users requesting data. A third processing unit finds the data requested by users.

When you use a mainframe, your processing requests are transmitted from your terminal to the computer. At the same time, other users may also transmit requests. The computer processes each request in turn and transmits back the results. Mainframes service user requests quickly. Even though there might be 200 people submitting processing requests, the speed of the computer's response makes it seem as if you are the only user.

Mainframes remain the computer of choice in situations where reliability, data security, and centralized control are necessary. The price of a mainframe computer system is typically several hundred thousand dollars. A mainframe computer is housed in a closet-size cabinet, and its peripheral devices are contained in separate cabinets, as shown in Figure 1-5 on the following page.

Supercomputers are the largest, fastest, and most expensive type of computer. Unlike minicomputers and mainframes, supercomputers are not designed to optimize processing for multiple users. Instead, supercomputers use their significant processing power to solve a few very difficult problems such as predicting the weather and modeling nuclear reactions. The speed of a supercomputer can reach one trillion instructions per second. The cost of a supercomputer, like the one in Figure 1-6 on the following page, tops out at about $35 million.

If you were a scientific researcher using a supercomputer, you would probably need to make an appointment and provide an estimate of the time needed to complete your processing task.

Both mainframes and supercomputers are large, expensive, and powerful. However, a mainframe usually supports many users doing relatively simple processing tasks, whereas a supercomputer supports only a few users who have complex processing tasks.

Figure 1-5 ◄
IBM mainframe
computer

The mainframe processor and storage
units are housed in the large cabinets.
The four terminals in the foreground
are used for computer maintenance.
Additional terminals are located in other
areas of the building.

Figure 1-6 ◄
A Cray
supercomputer

The processing unit of this Cray computer
is just over six feet tall. The terminals are
located in other areas of the building.

When your appointment arrives, you input your problem from a terminal. While the supercomputer works on your problem, other users have to wait.

Today the lines that divide the different computer categories are fuzzy and tend to shift as more powerful computers become available. For example, the definition of minicomputers in technical dictionaries published in the early 1980s specified performance features that more accurately describe today's microcomputers. Because the characteristics of each computer category shift and change as technology advances, it is difficult to categorize a particular computer unless you have up-to-date technical expertise. So, if you want to know whether a particular computer is a micro, a mini, a mainframe, or a supercomputer, look at the sales literature to find out how the manufacturer classifies it.

This book focuses on microcomputers because that is the category of computers you are likely to use. Although the focus is on microcomputers, most of the concepts you will learn apply to the other categories of computers as well.

Computer System Components

When I use a computer system, what hardware components will it include?

Microcomputer, minicomputer, mainframe, and supercomputer systems include devices to input, output, process, and store data. Study Figure 1-7 to learn about the hardware components you are likely to use on a typical microcomputer system.

The primary output device on a microcomputer is the **monitor**; a display device that converts electrical signals from the computer into points of colored light on the screen to form an image.

Figure 1-7
Microcomputer
system
components

The **system unit** is the case or box that contains the main circuit board of the computer system. In a typical micro-computer, the system unit contains the power supply, storage devices, and the main circuit board with the computer's main processor and memory.

A **floppy disk drive** is a storage device that writes data on floppy disks. A typical microcomputer system has a 3¹/₂-inch floppy disk drive that stores up to 1.44 million characters of data on a single floppy disk. Some micro-computer systems also have a 5¹/₄-inch drive to accommodate programs supplied on 5¹/₄-inch disks. A light indicates when the floppy disk drive is in use—a warning not to remove your disk until the light goes out.

A **CD-ROM** is a high-capacity storage medium with a capacity of up to 680 million characters. Most CD-ROMs contain informa-tion when you purchase them and do not allow you to add or change the information they contain.

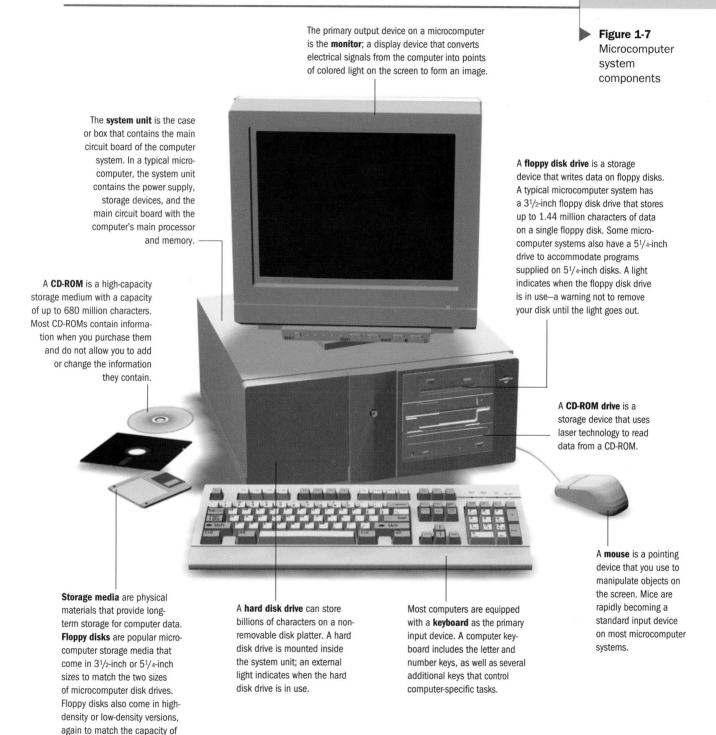

A **CD-ROM drive** is a storage device that uses laser technology to read data from a CD-ROM.

A **mouse** is a pointing device that you use to manipulate objects on the screen. Mice are rapidly becoming a standard input device on most microcomputer systems.

Storage media are physical materials that provide long-term storage for computer data. **Floppy disks** are popular micro-computer storage media that come in 3¹/₂-inch or 5¹/₄-inch sizes to match the two sizes of microcomputer disk drives. Floppy disks also come in high-density or low-density versions, again to match the capacity of the disk drive.

A **hard disk drive** can store billions of characters on a non-removable disk platter. A hard disk drive is mounted inside the system unit; an external light indicates when the hard disk drive is in use.

Most computers are equipped with a **keyboard** as the primary input device. A computer key-board includes the letter and number keys, as well as several additional keys that control computer-specific tasks.

Microcomputer Compatibility

Because about two-thirds of the microcomputers in use today are IBM-compatible, the examples in this book focus on the IBM platform.

Can all computers use the same software?

Hundreds of companies manufacture microcomputers, but there are only a small number of microcomputer designs or **platforms**. Today there are two major microcomputer platforms: IBM-compatibles and Macintosh-compatibles. **IBM-compatible computers**, also referred to as **PC-compatibles**, are based on the architecture of the first IBM microcomputer. IBM-compatible computers are manufactured by Compaq, Dell, Gateway, and hundreds of other companies. The second major microcomputer platform is based on the Macintosh computer, manufactured by Apple Computer, Inc.

Computers that operate in essentially the same way are said to be **compatible**. Two computers are compatible if they can communicate with each other, share the same software, share data, and use the same peripheral devices.

Not all microcomputers are compatible with each other. The IBM platform and the Macintosh platform are not regarded as compatible because they cannot use the same hardware devices or

Figure 1-8 ◀
Peripheral devices

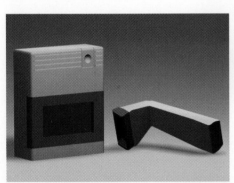

A **bar code reader** gathers input data by reading bar codes, such as the universal product codes on supermarket products. Bar code readers are also used at library circulation desks to track books.

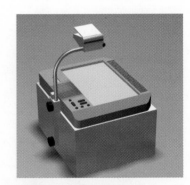

An **LCD projection display panel** is placed on an overhead projector to produce a large display of the information shown on the computer screen.

A **hand scanner** converts a 4–6″ section of text or graphics into electronic format. To use the scanner, you pull it over the text you want to convert.

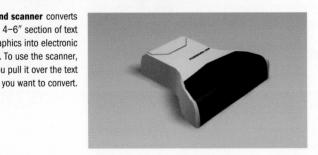

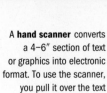

A **modem** transfers data from one computer to another over telephone lines. External modems have their own case. Internal modems are installed inside the computer system unit.

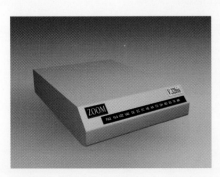

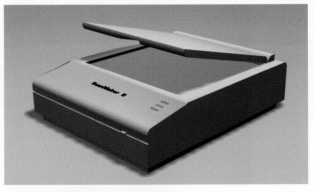

A **scanner** converts text or images on paper documents into an electronic format that the computer can display, print, and store.

use the same programs without hardware or software to translate between them. Apple is trying to overcome compatibility problems with a new platform called the **PowerPC** that uses a built-in translation process to run both IBM and Macintosh software.

Peripheral Devices

Is it possible to expand or modify a basic computer system?

The term "peripheral device" designates equipment that is used with a computer, but is not a necessary or integral part of it. For example, a printer is a popular peripheral device used with micro, mini, and mainframe computers, but the computer can function without one. Keyboards, monitors, mice, and disk drives are peripheral devices, even though they are included with most basic computer systems. Figure 1-8 shows some of the more popular peripheral devices used with microcomputers.

Peripheral devices allow you to expand and modify your basic computer system. For example, you might purchase a computer that includes a mouse, but you might prefer to use a trackball,

Lab

Peripheral Devices

A **monitor** is an output device the computer uses to display the results of processing.
A **touch sensitive screen** displays options you can select by touching them on the screen.

A **sound card** can be installed inside the system unit to give a computer the capability to accept audio input from a **microphone**, play sound files stored on disks or CD-ROMs, and produce audio output through **speakers** or earphones.

A **trackball** is a pointing device that you might use as an alternative to a mouse. You roll the ball to position the pointer on the screen. Unlike a mouse, a trackball doesn't move on the desk and therefore requires less space.

A **keyboard** is the main input device for most computer systems.

A **mouse** is a pointing device you use to manipulate on-screen objects.

Figure 1-8
Peripheral devices
continued

A **laser printer** uses the same technology as a photocopier to print professional-quality text and graphics. Heat fuses a fine dark powder, called toner, onto paper to create text and images.

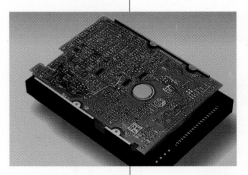

A **disk drive** stores data.

A **dot matrix printer** creates characters and graphics by printing a fine pattern of dots using a 9-pin or 24-pin print mechanism. A 9-pin printer creates a coarser image than a 24-pin printer.

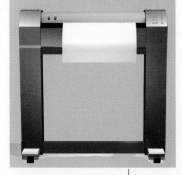

A **plotter** uses pens to draw an image on paper. Plotters are often used by architects and engineers to produce multicolor line drawings.

A **computer projector** generates a large image of what's on the computer screen suitable for conference and lecture presentations.

or you might want to expand your computer's capabilities by adding a scanner so you can input photographs.

What's the difference between the terms computer *and* computer system*? A computer does not include peripheral devices, but a computer system does.*

Most microcomputer peripheral devices are designed for installation by users without technical expertise. When you buy a peripheral device it usually comes with installation instructions and specially designed software. You should carefully follow the instructions to install the device. Also make sure the computer is turned off before you attempt to connect a peripheral device so you don't damage your computer system. The instructions will also give you directions on how to install any software that might be necessary to use the peripheral device.

Computer Networks

Our school has a computer network. Is using a network going to be difficult?

A **computer network** is a collection of computers and other devices connected to share data, hardware, and software. A network can connect microcomputers, minicomputers, and mainframes. A network has advantages for an organization and its users. For example, if users share a printer on a network, the organization saves money because it does not have to purchase a printer for every user. Network users can send messages to others on the network and retrieve data from a centralized storage device. Using a computer on a network is not much different from using a stand-alone computer, except that you usually have access to more data and software. On a network you might also have to be more aware of security.

Networks must be secured against unauthorized access to protect the data they store. Most organizations restrict access to the software and data on a network by requiring users to log in. To **log in** you enter a unique user ID and password. A **user ID** is a combination of letters and numbers that serve as your "call sign" or "identification." You can let people know your user ID so they can send you messages over the network, but you don't want to reveal your password. A **password** is a special set of symbols known only to you and the person who supervises the network. You should not reveal your password because it would violate your responsibility to help maintain network security. Also, you should understand that if someone logs into a network using your user ID and sends offensive messages or erases important files, it will look as if you did it. In addition to logging into a network, you might have to log in to use some software; the login procedure is similar. Figure 1-9 shows you what to do when a computer asks you to log in.

If your school has a computer network, Project 3 at the end of this chapter will help you learn how to use it.

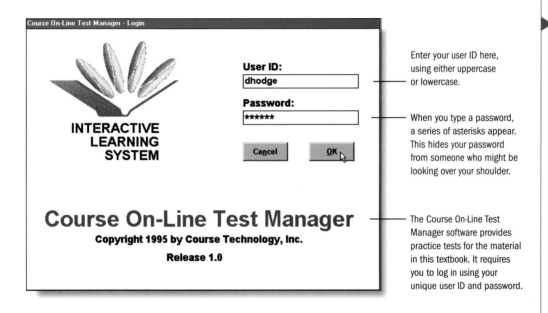

▶ **Figure 1-9**
Entering a user ID and password

Enter your user ID here, using either uppercase or lowercase.

When you type a password, a series of asterisks appear. This hides your password from someone who might be looking over your shoulder.

The Course On-Line Test Manager software provides practice tests for the material in this textbook. It requires you to log in using your unique user ID and password.

Quick Check

1. Most microcomputers are equipped with a(n) _____ as the primary input device and a(n) _____ as the primary output device.

2. A(n) _____ is generally devoted to carrying out the processing tasks of only one user, even when it is connected to other computers.

3. A(n) _____ is a device that resembles a microcomputer but does not have any processing capability.

4. What two types of computers are designed to perform processing tasks for many users?

5. If an organization wants to provide processing for more than 200 users and reliability, security, and centralized control are necessary, a(n) _____ computer would best meet its needs.

6. An IBM computer is _____ with a Compaq computer because it operates in essentially the same way.

7. A computer _____ allows you to send messages to other computer users and access data from a centralized storage device.

The User Interface

To effectively use the computer as a mind tool, you must communicate with it; you must tell the computer what tasks to perform, and you must accurately interpret the information the computer provides to you. The means by which humans and computers communicate is referred to as the **user interface**. Through the user interface, the computer accepts your input and presents you with output. This output provides you with the results of processing, confirms the completion of the processing, or indicates that data was stored.

The user interface is a combination of software and hardware. The software that controls the user interface defines its characteristics. For example, software controls whether you accomplish tasks by manipulating graphical objects or typing commands. The hardware controls the way you physically manipulate the computer to establish communication, for example, whether you use a keyboard or your voice to input commands. After you have a general understanding of user interfaces, you will be able to figure out quickly how to make the computer do what you want it to do.

Lab

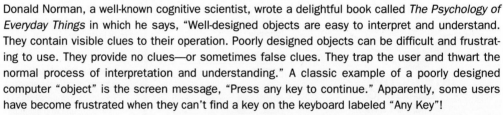

User Interfaces

Interacting with the Computer

What kinds of user interfaces are typically found on computers?

Donald Norman, a well-known cognitive scientist, wrote a delightful book called *The Psychology of Everyday Things* in which he says, "Well-designed objects are easy to interpret and understand. They contain visible clues to their operation. Poorly designed objects can be difficult and frustrating to use. They provide no clues—or sometimes false clues. They trap the user and thwart the normal process of interpretation and understanding." A classic example of a poorly designed computer "object" is the screen message, "Press any key to continue." Apparently, some users have become frustrated when they can't find a key on the keyboard labeled "Any Key"!

User interfaces have changed and evolved in response to the needs of a rapidly growing community of computer users. Yet interface design and development are still in an early stage. Using computers can be enjoyable. However, as with many objects in everyday life, some computer user interfaces are not well conceived, and using them is frustrating.

A user interface is constructed using hardware and software interface elements, such as a mouse, menus, and graphics. In this section of the chapter you are going to look at several basic interface elements, so you will recognize them and understand how to use them. With this background, you can make some intelligent guesses about how to proceed when you use an unfamiliar computer or a new software package.

In Project 5 at the end of this chapter, you have a chance to make your own evaluation of a user interface.

As you read the descriptions of the interface elements, consider not only how to use them, but also the positive and negative aspects of each design. Which interface elements are easy to interpret and understand? Which provide clues about what to do and how to do it? If you have used computers, you should remember using some or all of these user interface elements, and you might recall your own reaction to them.

Prompts

Why is it sometimes hard for me to figure out what the computer wants me to do?

A **prompt** is a message displayed by the computer that asks for input from the user. In response to a computer prompt, you enter the requested information or follow the instruction. Some prompts, such as "Enter your name:," are helpful and easy to understand, even for beginners. Other prompts, like A:\>, are less helpful.

A sequence of prompts is sometimes used to develop a user interface called a **prompted dialog**. In a prompted dialog, a sort of conversation takes place between the computer and user. Here is an example of a prompted dialog that tells you how much money will accumulate in your savings account. The computer's prompts are in uppercase. The user's responses are in bold.

HOW MUCH MONEY IS CURRENTLY IN YOUR ACCOUNT?
1000
HOW MUCH MONEY WILL YOU DEPOSIT EACH MONTH?
100
WHAT IS THE YEARLY INTEREST RATE PERCENT?
6
WHAT IS THE LENGTH OF THE SAVINGS PERIOD IN MONTHS?
36
O.K. AFTER 36 MONTHS YOU WILL HAVE $5149.96 IN YOUR SAVINGS ACCOUNT.

A prompted dialog is rarely found in commercial software packages. There are two reasons why. First, the process of interacting with such a dialog is very linear. You must start at the beginning of the dialog and respond sequentially to each prompt. It is difficult to back up if you make an error.

The second reason that a prompted dialog is difficult to use is due to the ambiguity of human language. If a prompt is not clear and you respond to it with something unexpected, the dialog will not function correctly. In Figure 1-10 you can see an example of this difficulty in the dialog with a computer-based library card catalog system.

Do Project 6 to apply what you know about user interfaces to an evaluation of your school's library card catalog.

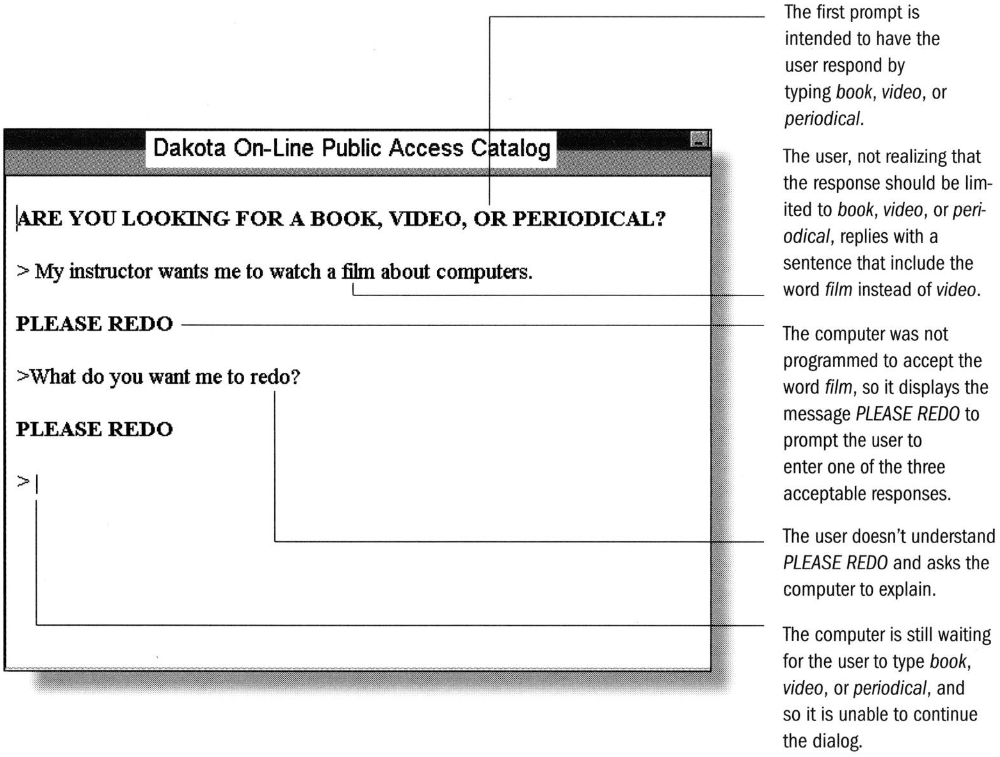

The first prompt is intended to have the user respond by typing *book*, *video*, or *periodical*.

The user, not realizing that the response should be limited to *book*, *video*, or *periodical*, replies with a sentence that include the word *film* instead of *video*.

The computer was not programmed to accept the word *film*, so it displays the message *PLEASE REDO* to prompt the user to enter one of the three acceptable responses.

The user doesn't understand *PLEASE REDO* and asks the computer to explain.

The computer is still waiting for the user to type *book*, *video*, or *periodical*, and so it is unable to continue the dialog.

Figure 1-10
An unsuccessful dialog

Dakota On-Line Public Access Catalog

ARE YOU LOOKING FOR A BOOK, VIDEO, OR PERIODICAL?

> My instructor wants me to watch a film about computers.

PLEASE REDO

>What do you want me to redo?

PLEASE REDO

>|

The difficulty with the dialog in Figure 1-10 is not necessarily the fault of the user. The prompts should have provided more specific instructions, and the computer program should have accepted a wider vocabulary. Unfortunately, if this were the interface on your on-line library card catalog, you would need to learn how to work within its limitations.

Today's commercial software tends to use "wizards" instead of prompted dialogs. A **wizard** is a sequence of screens that direct you through multi-step software tasks such as creating a graph, a list of business contacts, or a fax cover sheet. Wizards, like the one in Figure 1-11, use graphics to help explain the prompts and allow users to back up and change their responses.

Figure 1-11
Using a wizard
to make a list of
business clients

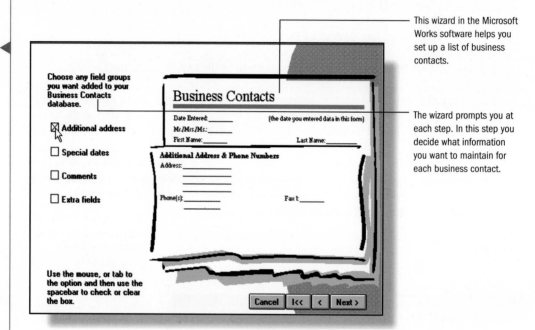

This wizard in the Microsoft Works software helps you set up a list of business contacts.

The wizard prompts you at each step. In this step you decide what information you want to maintain for each business contact.

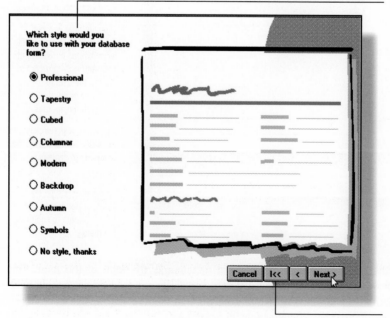

In the next step, the wizard helps you decide how you want the list to look— you can select from several professionally designed styles.

The wizard lets you move forward or backup and change your responses until the business contacts list is set up to your satisfaction.

Commands

Is it true that I have to memorize lots of commands to use a computer?

A **command** is an instruction you input to tell the computer to carry out a task. When you use many older microcomputer interfaces and many mainframe interfaces, you must type commands, then press the Enter key to indicate that the computer should now carry out the command. Each word in a command results in a specific action by the computer. Command words are often English words, such as *print, begin, save,* and *erase,* but command words can also be more cryptic and might even use special symbols. Some examples of cryptic command words include *ls,* which means list; *cls,* which means clear the screen; and *!,* which means quit. Figure 1-12 shows how you might use a command to find out what is on your disk.

The phrases "enter a command" and "enter data" probably originated because pressing the Enter key signals the end of the input data.

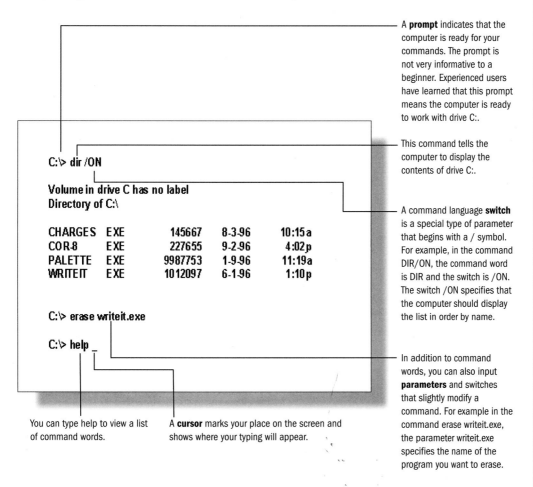

A **prompt** indicates that the computer is ready for your commands. The prompt is not very informative to a beginner. Experienced users have learned that this prompt means the computer is ready to work with drive C:.

This command tells the computer to display the contents of drive C:.

A command language **switch** is a special type of parameter that begins with a / symbol. For example, in the command DIR/ON, the command word is DIR and the switch is /ON. The switch /ON specifies that the computer should display the list in order by name.

In addition to command words, you can also input **parameters** and switches that slightly modify a command. For example in the command erase writeit.exe, the parameter writeit.exe specifies the name of the program you want to erase.

You can type help to view a list of command words.

A **cursor** marks your place on the screen and shows where your typing will appear.

Figure 1-12
Using commands

The commands you input must conform to a specific syntax. **Syntax** specifies the sequence and punctuation for command words, parameters, and switches. If you misspell a command word, leave out required punctuation, or type the command words out of order, you will get an **error message** or **syntax error.** When you get an error message or syntax error, you must figure out what is wrong with the command and retype it correctly.

An interface that requires the user to type in commands is referred to as a **command-line user interface.** Some people like to use command-line interfaces. They believe that once you have become fluent with the command words and syntax, the commands are easy to construct, quick

Lab

DOS Command- Line User Interface

to type, and have the versatility to accomplish a wide variety of tasks. Learning to use a command line user interface is not easy. You must memorize the command words and know what they mean. To make the situation even more difficult, there is no single set of commands that you can use for every computer and every software package. Instead, there are many different sets of commands.

If you forget the correct command word or punctuation, or if you find yourself using an unfamiliar command-line user interface, you should type HELP and press the Enter key. With some command-line user interfaces, the HELP command provides you with a list of commands. If on-line help is not available, you need to use a reference manual to find out how to proceed.

Menus

Are menus easier to use than commands?

Menus were developed as a response to the difficulties many people experienced trying to remember the command words and syntax for command-line user interfaces. A **menu** displays a list of commands or options. Each line of the menu is referred to as a **menu option** or a **menu item**. Figure 1-13 shows you how to use a menu.

Figure 1-13
Using a menu

To use this **pull-down** menu, you first select which menu you want to use from a menu bar. The menu bar for this software package includes File, Edit, View, Insert, Format, and Help menus.

When you click the menu title, the menu appears and shows you a list of menu options.

You can select the option you want using the mouse or keyboard.

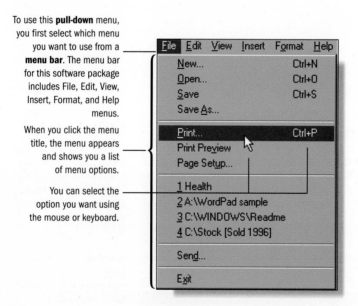

Menus are popular because when you use them, you do not have to remember command words. You just choose the command you want from a list. Also, because all the commands on the list are valid commands, it is not possible to make syntax errors.

You might wonder how a menu can present all the commands you might want to input. Obviously, there are many possibilities for combining command words, so there could be hundreds of menu options. Two methods are generally used to present a reasonably sized list of menu options. One method uses a menu hierarchy. The other method uses a dialog box.

A **hierarchy** is an organization of things ranked one above the other. For example, an organizational chart shows the hierarchy of the people in a business. As the name implies, a **menu hierarchy** arranges menus in a hierarchical structure. After you make a selection from one menu, a submenu appears, and you can make additional choices by selecting an option from the submenu. Some software has a fairly complex menu hierarchy, making it difficult to remember how to find a particular menu option. Visualizing the menus as a hierarchy, as shown in Figure 1-14, makes a complex menu structure easier to use.

If you choose the
Worksheet option
from this menu...

...you can make
a choice from
this submenu.
Then, if you
choose the
Delete option
from the
submenu...

...you can choose whether
you want to delete
a column or a row.

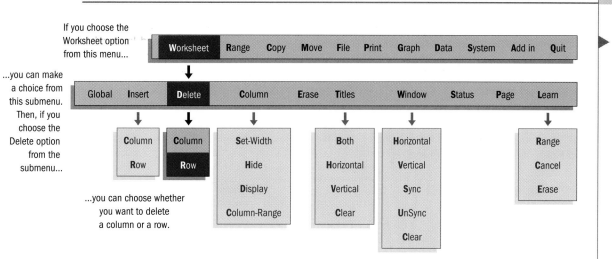

Figure 1-14
A menu hierarchy

*Although a dialog
box appears in
conjunction with
a menu, it is really
a different type
of user interface
element. It combines
the characteristics
of both menus and
prompts.*

Instead of leading to a submenu, some menu options lead to a dialog box. A **dialog box** displays the options associated with a command. You fill in the dialog box to indicate specifically how you want the command carried out, as shown in Figure 1-15.

When you select Print, the Print
dialog box appears. The dialog box
prompts you to enter specifications
about how the computer should
carry out the Print task.

Click this button to display a list
of printers you can use.

Change the number of copies
by clicking these buttons.

The Print option
displays three dots to
indicate that this menu
leads to a dialog box.

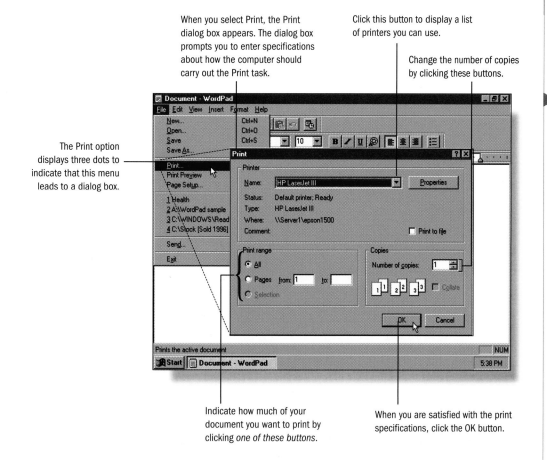

Figure 1-15
Using a dialog box

Indicate how much of your
document you want to print by
clicking *one of these buttons*.

When you are satisfied with the print
specifications, click the OK button.

Graphical Objects

Why are GUIs so popular?

A **graphical object** is a small picture on the screen that you can manipulate using a mouse or other input device. Each graphical object represents a computer task, command, or a real-world object. You show the computer what you want it to do by manipulating an object instead of entering commands or selecting menu options. Graphical objects include icons, buttons, tools, and windows, as explained in Figure 1-16.

Mainframe computers have been slow to incorporate GUIs. You will find out why when you read about monitors at the end of Section 1.3.

Figure 1-16
Graphical objects

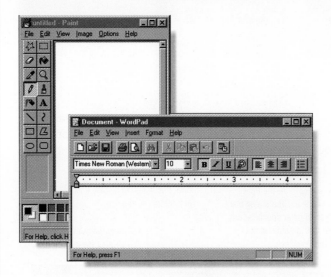

A **window** usually contains a specific piece of work. For example, a window might contain a document you are typing or a picture you are drawing. You can think of windows as work areas, analogous to different documents and books that you might have on your desk. Just as you switch between the documents and books you have on your desk, you can switch between windows on the computer screen to work on different tasks.

A **button** helps you make a selection. When you select a button, its appearance changes to indicate that it has been activated. The button labeled "Document-WordPad" is selected and it appears to be pushed in. The button labeled "untitled-Paint" is not selected so it does not appear to be pushed in.

People generally communicate with each other using what we might call a "speech" or "verbal" user interface. The use of voice input and output to communicate with computers, however, has taken a back seat to the development of graphical user interfaces. You'll discover some of the problems with verbal interfaces if you do Project 9 at the end of this chapter.

An **icon** is a small picture that represents an object. When you select an icon, you indicate to the computer that you want to manipulate the object. A selected icon is highlighted. The My Computer icon on the right is selected, so it is highlighted with dark blue.

Some buttons are labeled with pictures. These buttons are often referred to as **tools**.

An example of manipulating on-screen objects is the way you delete a document using Windows 95. The documents you create are represented by icons that look like sheets of paper. A Recycle Bin represents the place where you put documents you no longer want. Suppose you used your computer to write a report named "Sport Statistics," but you no longer need the report stored on your computer system. You use the mouse to drag the Sport Statistics icon to the Recycle Bin and erase the report from your computer system, as shown in Figure 1-17.

The Sport Statistics document is no longer needed.

Using the mouse, you can drag the Sport Statistics document icon to the Recycle Bin.

Once in the Recycle Bin, the document will no longer appear in the My Document window. Periodically, you can empty the Recycle Bin to permanently get rid of the documents it contains.

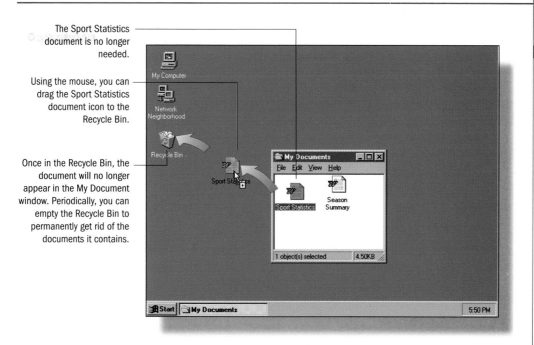

▶ **Figure 1-17**
Directly manipulating on-screen objects

Graphical objects are a key element of **graphical user interfaces** or **GUIs** (pronounced "gooies") found on most of today's microcomputers. GUIs are based on the philosophy that people can use computers intuitively—that is, with minimal training—if they can manipulate on-screen objects that represent tasks or commands.

Graphical user interfaces often contain menus and prompts in addition to graphical objects because graphical user interface designers found it difficult to design icons and tools for every possible task. Figure 1-18 shows how a graphical user interface incorporates menus and prompts in addition to graphical objects.

For more information on the design principles for graphical user interfaces, refer to the Schneiderman article listed in the Resources section at the end of this chapter.

The **menu bar**, usually at the top of the screen, displays menu titles. Selecting a menu title displays its pull-down menu.

Tool bars display buttons or tools that provide shortcuts to the commands on the menus.

This **wizard** appears when you click the ChartWizard button. The ChartWizard prompts you through the steps to create a chart or graph.

The **ChartWizard** button starts a wizard.

The **window** in the background contains the data for the chart.

The **status bar** gives you brief help about what you're doing.

The **task bar** contains buttons that show you which software programs you are using.

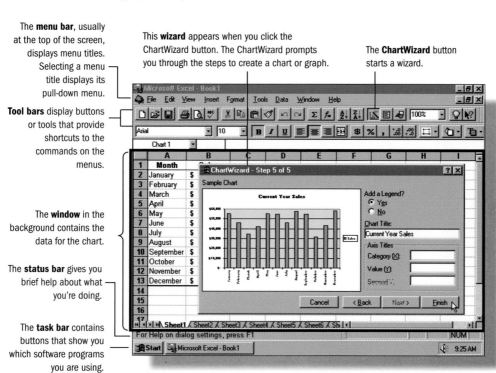

▶ **Figure 1-18**
Graphical user interface elements for Windows 95 software

Most graphical user interfaces are based on a metaphor in which computer components are represented by real-world objects. For example, a user interface with a **desktop metaphor** might represent documents as file folders and storage as a filing cabinet. Metaphors are intended to make the tasks you perform with computers more concrete, easier to explore, and more intuitive.

Pointing Devices

Some mice have three buttons, while others have only one or two—why?

A **pointing device** such as a mouse, trackball, or lightpen helps you manipulate objects and select menu options. The most popular pointing device is the mouse. The mouse was developed by Douglas Engelbart in the early 1970s to provide an input method more efficient than the keyboard. Englebart's work coincided with efforts to construct graphical user interfaces. The popularity of the mouse and graphical user interfaces grew slowly, until Apple Computer, Inc. produced the Macintosh computer in 1983. Now virtually every computer is equipped with a mouse.

When you move the mouse on your desk, a **pointer**—usually shaped like an arrow—moves on the screen in a way that corresponds to how you move the mouse. You select an object on the screen by pressing the left mouse button a single time. This is referred to as **clicking**. Some operations require you to click the mouse twice in rapid succession. This is referred to as **double-clicking**. You can also use the mouse to **drag** objects from one screen location to another by clicking the object, holding down the mouse button, and moving the mouse to the new location for the object. When the object is in its new location, you release the mouse button. Figure 1-19 shows you how to hold a mouse and use it to manipulate graphical objects.

The mouse moves the pointer only when the mouse is in contact with a hard surface like a desk. If you pick up the mouse and move it, the pointer will not move. This is handy to know. Suppose you are dragging an object, but your mouse runs into an obstacle on your desk. You can just pick up the mouse, move it to a clear space, and continue dragging.

The mouse you use with a Macintosh computer only has one button. IBM-compatible computers use either a two- or three-button mouse. A two-button mouse allows you to **right click** an object and provides another way of manipulating it. For example, if clicking the left button selects an object, clicking the right button might bring up a menu of actions you can do with the object. On a three-button mouse you rarely use the third button.

Lab

Using a Mouse

Figure 1-19
Using a mouse

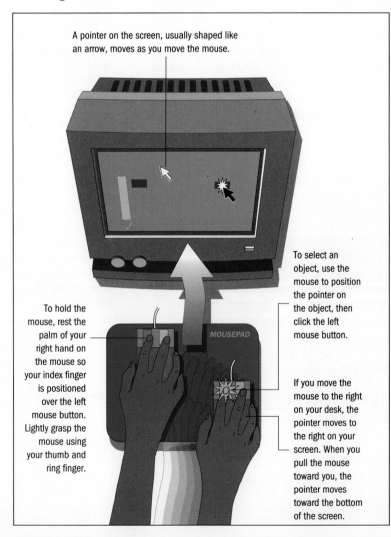

A pointer on the screen, usually shaped like an arrow, moves as you move the mouse.

To hold the mouse, rest the palm of your right hand on the mouse so your index finger is positioned over the left mouse button. Lightly grasp the mouse using your thumb and ring finger.

MOUSEPAD

To select an object, use the mouse to position the pointer on the object, then click the left mouse button.

If you move the mouse to the right on your desk, the pointer moves to the right on your screen. When you pull the mouse toward you, the pointer moves toward the bottom of the screen.

Some three-button mice, however, allow you to click the middle button once instead of double-clicking the left mouse button. This feature is useful for people who have trouble double-clicking. It also helps prevent some muscular stress injuries that result from excessive clicking.

Keyboard

Do I need to be a good typist to use a computer?

Virtually every computer user interface requires you to use a keyboard. You don't have to be a great typist, but to use a computer effectively you should be familiar with the computer keyboard because it contains special keys to manipulate the user interface. Study Figure 1-20 on the following page before you read the rest of this section.

You use the typing keys to input commands, respond to prompts, and type the text of documents. A cursor or an insertion point indicates where the characters you type will appear. The **cursor** appears on the screen as a flashing underline. The **insertion point** appears on the screen as a flashing vertical bar. You can change the location of the cursor or insertion point using the arrow keys or the mouse.

The **numeric keypad** provides you with a calculator-style input device for numbers and arithmetic symbols. You can type numbers using either the set of number keys at the top of the typing keypad or the keys on the numeric keypad. However, notice that some keys on the numeric keypad contain two symbols. When the Num Lock key is activated, the numeric keypad produces numbers. When the Num Lock key is not activated, the keys on the numeric keypad move the cursor in the direction indicated by the arrows on the keys.

The Num Lock key is an example of something called a toggle key. A **toggle key** switches back and forth between two modes. The Caps Lock key is also a toggle. When you press the Caps Lock key you switch or "toggle" into uppercase mode. When you press the Caps Lock key again you toggle back into lowercase mode.

Now here's an interesting problem that faced the designers for word processors that use command-line interfaces. Suppose someone is typing in the text of a document and wants to issue a command to save the document on a disk. If the user types SAVE, it will just appear as another word in the document. How does the computer know that SAVE is supposed to be a command and not just part of a sentence such as "Save your money." Interface designers solved this problem by introducing function keys, control keys, and Alt keys.

Function keys, like those numbered F1 through F12, are located at the top of your keyboard. They do not exist on the keyboard of a standard typewriter but were added to computer keyboards to initiate commands. For example, with many software packages F1 is the key you press to get help. The problem with function keys is that they are not standardized. In one program, you press F7 to save a document, but in another program, you press F5.

There are 12 function keys, but you usually need more than 12 commands to control software. Therefore, you can use the Ctrl, Alt, and Shift keys in conjunction with the function keys to expand the repertory of available commands. For example, if you hold down the Ctrl key while you press F1, instead of issuing the command to get help, you might issue the command to change margins. If you see <Alt F1>, Alt+F1, [Alt F1], Alt-F1, or Alt F1 on the screen or in an instruction manual, it means to hold down the Alt key and press F1. You might see similar notation for using the Ctrl or Shift keys.

If you are left handed, you can hold the mouse in your left hand and click the right mouse button after selecting the left-handed mouse option in your software.

Lab

Using a Keyboard

Ctrl+C rarely works in today's graphical user interfaces, but the Esc key often cancels your last command.

The Alt and Ctrl keys also work in conjunction with the letter keys. For example, Ctrl+C has been used since the early days of computing to tell the computer to stop what it is doing. Even in a graphical user interface, you can use Ctrl and Alt key "shortcuts" instead of using menus. For example, when you use the Windows 95 software, Ctrl+X is a shortcut for clicking the Edit menu and then clicking the Cut option. Or, if you see an underlined menu title such as Edit, you can open the menu using Alt+E instead of clicking Edit.

Figure 1-20
The computer keyboard

COLOR KEY

- **Typing Keypad**
- **Function Key Array**
- **Editing Keypad**
- **Numeric Keypad**

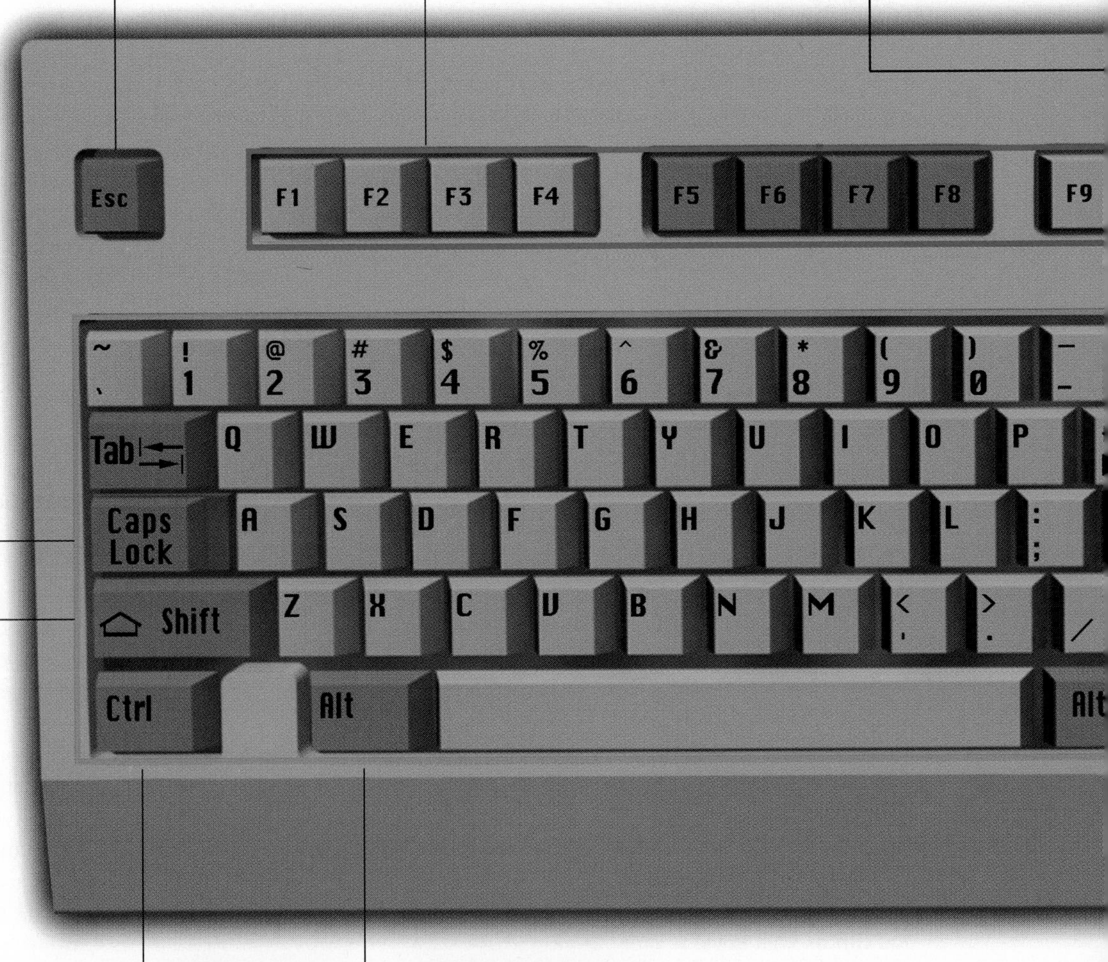
The **Esc** or "escape" key cancels an operation.
The **function keys** execute commands, such as centering a line of text or boldfacing text. The command associated with each function key depends on the software you are using.
Each time you press the **Backspace** key, one character to the left of the cursor is deleted. If you hold down the backspace key, multiple characters to the left are deleted one by one until you release it.
The **Caps Lock** key capitalizes all the letters you type when it is engaged, but does not produce the top symbol on keys that contain two symbols. This key is a **toggle key**, which means that each time you press it, you switch between uppercase and lowercase modes. There is usually an indicator light on the keyboard to show which mode you are in.
You hold down the **Shift** key while you press another key. The Shift key capitalizes letters and produces the top symbol on keys that contain two symbols.
You hold down the **Ctrl** key while you press another key. The result of Ctrl key combinations depends on the software you are using.
You hold down the **Alt** key while you press another key. The result of Alt key combinations depends on the software you are using.
Esc
F1 F2 F3 F4 F5 F6 F7 F8 F9
Tab
Caps Lock
Shift
Ctrl
Alt
Alt

Monitor

How are the monitor and user interface related?

A monitor is a required output device for just about every computer user interface. Whereas you manipulate the keyboard and mouse to communicate with the computer, the monitor is what the computer manipulates to communicate with you by displaying results, prompts, menus, and

The **Print Screen** key prints the contents of the screen when you use some software. With other software, the Print Screen key stores a copy of your screen in memory that you can manipulate or print with draw or paint software.

The function of the **Scroll Lock** key depends on the software you are using. This key is rarely used with today's software.

The **Pause** key stops the current task your computer is performing. You might need to hold down both the Ctrl key and the Pause key to stop the task.

Indicator lights show you the status of each toggle key: Num Lock, Caps Lock, and Scroll Lock. The Power light indicates whether the computer is on or off.

Home takes you to the beginning of a line or the beginning of a document, depending on the software you are using.

The **Num Lock** key is a toggle key that switches between number keys and cursor keys on the numeric keypad.

Page Up displays the previous screen of information. **Page Down** displays the next screen of information.

The **cursor keys** move your position on the screen up, down, right, or left.

End takes you to the end of the line or the end of a document, depending on the software you are using.

In the context of computers, the term "legacy" refers to equipment, systems, or software that is handed down, inherited, or old. A "legacy system" usually means an older mainframe system that is still in use in a business or organization.

graphical objects. Monitor display technology determines whether the interface designer can include color and graphical objects.

The first microcomputer monitors and the displays on many terminals still in use today were character-based. A **character-based display** divides the screen into a grid of rectangles, which can each display a single character. The set of characters that the screen can display is not modifiable; therefore, it is not possible to display different sizes or styles of characters. The only graphics possible on character-based displays are those composed of underlines, exclamation points, and other symbols that already exist in the character set. One of the reasons that mainframes rarely support graphical user interfaces is because of the legacy of character-based terminals connected to mainframe systems.

Character-based displays use only one color to display text on a black background. Green is probably the most frequently used color, followed by amber and white. Even though there appears to be "color" on the screen of a character-based display, it is technically classified as a monochrome display.

A **graphics display** or **bit-map display** divides the screen into a matrix of small dots called **pixels**. Any characters or graphics the computer displays on the screen must be constructed of dot patterns within the screen matrix. The more dots your screen displays in the matrix, the higher the **resolution**. A high-resolution monitor can produce complex graphical images and text that is easier to read than a low-resolution monitor. Most of the monitors on microcomputers have bit-map display capabilities. This provides the flexibility to display characters in different sizes and styles as well as the graphical objects needed for GUIs.

Monochrome or gray-scale monitors display text and graphics in shades of gray. Color monitors allow the interface designer to use the impact of color to create pleasing screen designs and use color as a cue to direct the user's attention to important screen elements.

A User Interface Comparison: Starting Programs

Now that you have learned about user-interface elements, let's see how they work for a typical computer activity. One of the most frequent computer activities is starting a program. Figure 1-21 illustrates the different ways you could start a program—using commands, using graphical objects, and using a menu.

`C:>works`

To start Microsoft Works using the DOS command-line user interface, you need to know the name the computer has given the program. In this case, the computer calls Microsoft Works "Works." At the C:> prompt, type **works** then press the Enter key.

To start Microsoft Works using the Windows 3.1 user interface, you must move the pointer to the Microsoft Works graphical object and double-click the left mouse button.

2. Next, you move the pointer to the Programs menu item to display a list of program folders.

3. Select the Microsoft Works for Windows folder from the menu.

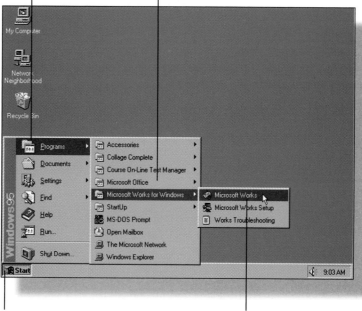

Figure 1-21
Starting programs with different types of user interfaces

1. To start Microsoft Works using the Windows 95 interface, you click the Start button to view a menu of categories.

4. Use the mouse to click Microsoft Works.

Quick Check

1 A(n) _____, such as "Enter your name:," is one way a computer can tell the user what to do.

2 Instead of prompted dialogs, today's software tends to use _____ to direct a user through multi-step software tasks, such as creating a graph or creating a fax cover sheet.

3 When you use a command-line interface, you press _____ when you are done typing a command.

4 If you type a command, but leave out a required space, you have made a _____ error.

5 When you make a menu selection, a(n) _____ or a(n) _____ might appear to let you enter more details on how you want the computer to do a task.

6 Most _____ are based on a metaphor, such as a desktop metaphor in which documents are represented by folder icons.

7 The flashing underline that marks your place on the screen is called the _____; the flashing vertical bar is called the _____.

8 You can use the _____ key and the _____ key in conjunction with letter keys instead of using the mouse to control menus.

9 _____ are work areas on the screen analogous to different documents and books you might have open on your desk. (Hint: Don't forget to read the figure captions!)

10 A(n) _____ display cannot be used in conjunction with a GUI.

User Focus:

1.4

Help, Tutorials, and Manuals

Many resources are available to help you learn how to use computers; look for those that suit your budget, time, and learning style.

No class can ever teach you all you need to know about using computers or every-thing about one software package. You should not feel frustrated if you don't "know" how something on your computer works. One of the most important skills you can develop as a computer user is the ability to figure out how to do new computing tasks. But don't expect to figure things out in a flash of inspiration! You usually have to get some additional information.

You can find information about installing computer hardware and using computer software in books, on your computer screen, on videotapes, and on audio cassettes. We can refer to these books, tapes, and so forth as "resources." To use these resources effectively, you need to know they exist, you need to know where to find them, and you need to develop some strategies for applying the information they contain. Let's take a look at some of the resources you can use to do this.

On-line Help

If I'm using a program and I "get stuck," what help can I get from the computer?

The term "on-line" refers to resources that are immediately available on your computer screen. Reference information is frequently available as on-line Help, accessible from a Help menu or by typing HELP at a command-line prompt. Figure 1-22 shows how you access on-line Help for the Microsoft Windows 95 software.

Figure 1-22
Using on-line Help for the Windows 95 software

In Windows 95 software. Help is available on the menu bar or from the Start button. Help appears in a help window.

Help has three sections: Contents, Index, and Find. To select the section you want, click one of the tabs.

If you are using the Contents section of help, look through the list of "books." Each book covers a help subject.

Once you open a Help book, you will see a list of specific Help topics. Click the topic you want, then click the Display button.

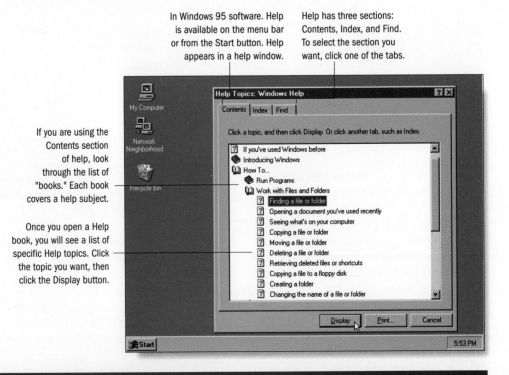

Tutorials

How can I get the most out of a tutorial?

A **tutorial** is a guided, step-by-step learning experience. Usually this learning experience teaches you the generic skills you need to use specific hardware or software. For example, suppose you purchase CorelDRAW software, and the first thing you want to draw is your company logo. When you use a tutorial that teaches you how to use CorelDRAW, you learn how to do such things as draw straight lines and wavy lines, use color in the drawing, and change the sizes of the pictures you draw. The tutorial does not teach you exactly how to draw your company logo. To get the most out of a tutorial, therefore, you need to think about how you can *generalize* the skills you are learning so you can apply them to other tasks.

When you use a tutorial, don't try to cover too much ground at once. Two 60-minute sessions each day are probably sufficient. As you work on a tutorial, take notes on those techniques you expect to apply to your own projects. When you have completed enough of the tutorial to do your own project, put the tutorial aside. You can complete the rest of the tutorial later if you need to learn more. Tutorials come in a variety of forms, as shown in Figure 1-23.

Computer-based tutorials display a simulation of the hardware or software and display tutorial instructions in boxes or windows on the screen. Computer-based tutorials have an advantage over their printed counterparts because they can demonstrate procedures using computer animation.

Figure 1-23
Tutorials and reference resources

Video tutorials on videotape visually illustrate how the software or hardware works. Some video tutorials are designed so that you watch them, take notes, then try the steps on the computer later. Other video tutorials are designed to be used while you are sitting at the computer. As with audio tutorials, you can stop and rewind video tutorials if you miss something.

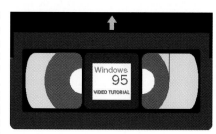

Printed tutorials are very popular. To use a printed tutorial, you read how to do a step, then you try to do it on the computer.

Audio tutorials on cassette verbally walk you through the steps of the tutorial. An advantage to this type of tutorial is that you do not have to read instructions. However, you must stop the tutorial and rewind, if you do not hear or understand the instructions. You might like audio tutorials if you easily retain information presented in lectures.

Reference Manuals

When should I use a reference manual instead of a tutorial?

Reference manuals are usually printed books or on-line resources that describe each feature of a hardware device or software package. They might also include examples of how to use these features. A reference manual is organized by features, rather than in the lesson formats.

Think of reference manuals as encyclopedias, containing descriptions of all features of the software and how to use them. You can do Project 7 to become more familiar with reference manuals.

Do not assume that you should read a reference manual from cover to cover. Instead, leaf through it to get a quick overview of all the features. A reference manual can be quite long, sometimes thousands of pages.

You should use a reference manual to find out if a feature exists or to find out how to use a feature. When you use a reference manual, you should first check the table of contents or index to locate the information you need, then turn to the appropriate section and read it carefully.

Reference manuals are usually included with the hardware or software that you buy. Most often, reference manuals are printed documents, but a recent trend is to provide computer-based reference manuals that you can read on the computer screen. Computer-based reference manuals are extensive and are often distributed on CD-ROMs.

You can usually find independent publishers who produce reference manuals for popular hardware and, particularly, for popular software. You might want to purchase one of these reference manuals if it is easier to understand or better organized than the manual included with the hardware or software you purchased.

Other Sources of Information

Although it is sometimes possible to dispense with manuals to learn software, you should not throw aside your hardware installation manual. You could damage equipment if you do not install it correctly, so read and follow the manual carefully whenever you are installing hardware.

Who needs a manual?

If you like reading and easily remember the things you read in books, you will probably like using printed reference manuals and tutorials. If you are a visual learner, you will probably like video tutorials. If you are an adventurous learner, you might enjoy exploring software applications without referring to printed materials or video tutorials. Graphical and menu-driven user interfaces make this sort of exploration possible, as do interfaces that include on-line Help.

Another approach to learning how to use computers is to take a course. Because you're reading this book, you are probably enrolled in an introductory computer course. Courses are available from schools, manufacturers, and private training firms and might last from several hours to several months. Courses about software packages tend to be laboratory-based with an instructor leading you through steps. Some courses might be lecture only, however; you might want to ask about the course format before you register.

If you run into a problem and are pressed for time, the best course of action might be to ask an expert. You might have a friend who knows a lot about computers, or on the job you might know a computer "guru." These are both good sources of information, as long as you don't overuse them.

You might also seek help from the support line of a software or hardware company. A **support line** is a service offered over the phone by a hardware manufacturer or software publisher to customers who have questions about how to use a software or hardware product. Sometimes these support line calls are toll-free; sometimes they are not. In addition to paying for the phone call, you might also pay a fee for the time it takes the support person to answer your question.

End Note Learning to use computers is a challenging activity, heightened by the fact that computer hardware and software change rapidly. Just when you master one software package, a better one appears. You then face the challenge of learning something new. Happily, you will discover that many concepts you learned previously carry over to new hardware and software technologies. To maintain a good attitude about computers, it is important to view the learning process itself as an interesting challenge. Approach this challenge as if you were a detective—gather information, make hypotheses, explore and test your hypotheses, and when you've solved one case, look forward to the challenge of the next.

Review

1. Using your own words, write out the answers to the questions in italics below each heading in the chapter.

2. List each of the boldface terms used in the chapter, then use your own words to write a short definition of each term. If you would like clarification of one or more terms, refer to a computer dictionary or a computer science encyclopedia such as those listed in the Resources section of this chapter. You can also refer to the Glossary/Index at the back of this book.

3. At the top of a sheet of paper write "Definition of the term *computer*," then make a list of important words, names, and phrases that are related to your list.

4. Use lines to divide a sheet of paper into four equal sections. In the top left corner write "microcomputer." Write "minicomputer" in the top right corner, "mainframe" in the bottom left corner, and "supercomputer" in the bottom right corner. Place words, phrases, and definitions in each section that describe and differentiate each type of computer.

5. Draw a sketch of a microcomputer system, without referring to the book. Then label as many components as you can. When you have finished, look at Figure 1-7 to see if you omitted anything.

6. List as many peripheral devices as you can, without referring to the book. Indicate whether each peripheral is an input device, an output device, or both. When you have finished, refer to Figure 1-8 and review any devices you omitted.

7. Make a list of the user interface elements covered in this chapter. Write at least three terms or phrases associated with each. For example, User interface element: Prompt. Associated terms and phrases: (a) prompted dialog, (b) wizards, (c) can be ambiguous or confusing.

8. Make a list of information resources that might help you install hardware and learn to use software. Write a one-sentence description of each resource.

Projects

1. Your Computer Draw a sketch of a computer system in your computer lab, home, or office and do the following:

   a. Title the sketch appropriately, for example, "My Computer at Home."

   b. List its brand name and model number, for example, "Dell 486/50."

   c. Label the following parts, if applicable:

monitor	screen
keyboard	3½-inch disk drive
5¼-inch disk drive	hard drive light
CD-ROM drive	power switch
power light	system unit
mouse	printer

2. Microcomputers: Input and Output Devices Look in a computer magazine and photocopy one ad for each of the following types of microcomputers: desktop, tower, notebook, and PDA. On the computer in each ad, label each component and indicate if it is an input, output, processing, or storage device.

3. Getting Started on Your Network Do this project only if your school has a computer network for student use. If the network requires a user ID and password, get them. Learn how to log in. Your school might have a short tutorial that teaches you how to use the network, or your instructor might provide a demonstration. Write a one- to two-page step-by-step tutorial on how to log into the network. Your tutorial should include the following:

   a. A title

   b. An introductory paragraph explaining where the network is located, who can access it, and how students can get a user ID and password

   c. Numbered steps to log into the network (if your lab policy requires that you turn on the computer each time you log in, you should include instructions for doing this in your tutorial)

   d. Numbered steps for logging out of the network

4. Research Tool: The Internet Do this project only if your school provides you with access to the Internet. The Internet is a worldwide computer network that provides access to a wealth of information including a World Wide Web site designed to accompany this textbook. Using the Internet can come in handy right from the start of this course. Several of the end-of-chapter projects refer you to information resources on the Internet. If you would like to use the Internet for these projects, this is a good time to get started.

There are several software tools to help you use the Internet, such as Mosaic, Netscape, and Lynx. It is not possible to cover all these software tools here. Therefore, this is an exploratory project that you can accomplish with the help of your instructor or with a tutorial prepared by your school. Find out how to use the Internet at your school and then answer the following questions:

a. What is the name of the software tool you use to access the Internet?

b. How do you access the "home page" for your school?

c. Use your Internet software to access the World Wide Web site *http://www.vmedia.com/ cti/concepts2*. How can the information at this site help you with the end-of-chapter Projects in this textbook?

d. List at least five other locations or "sites" that are available from your home page. How do you get to these other sites?

e. How can you keep track of where you have been on the Internet? (In other words, is there a way to backtrack to sites?)

f. When you are finished browsing on the Internet, how do you quit?

5. Evaluate a User Interface Select a computer inter-face with which you are familiar. For example, you might select your bank's ATM machine or your favorite arcade game. Using the terminology you learned in this chapter, write a complete description of the user interface and its features. Your description might answer questions such as: Does the interface use menus? If so, what type? What hardware elements are required for the user interface? Is the interface intuitive? Does the interface use a metaphor? If so, what? Don't limit yourself to answering just these questions.

6. Your Library Card Catalog Find out if your library has a computerized card catalog. If it does, use it to answer the following questions:

a. What is the name of the software your library uses for its computerized card catalog?

b. What type of user interface does it have?

c. Explain the steps you would take to find the call number for the book *War and Peace*.

d. Is the computerized card catalog efficient to use, or do you need to enter a lot of extra information to find a book?

e. What kind of on-line help is available?

f. Is the computerized card catalog easy to learn to use?

g. How much had you used the computerized card catalog before this assignment?

7. Reference Manuals Locate a software reference manual in your computer lab, home, or library; then answer the following questions:

a. What is the title of the reference manual?

b. How many pages does it have?

c. What are the titles of each section of the manual? For example, there might be a "Getting Started" section or an "Installation" section, and so on.

d. Does the reference manual include an index? If so, does it look complete? You should be suspicious of a large reference manual with a short index—it might be difficult to find the information you need.

e. Does the reference manual contain a list of fea-tures? If so, is this list arranged alphabetically? If not, how is it arranged?

f. Read a few pages of the reference manual. Write one or two sentences describing what you read. Does the reference manual seem to be well written and easy to follow? Why or why not?

8. Identify Your Learning Style In this chapter, you learned that you can take many approaches to learning how to use hardware and software. For this project, think about your own learning style and how it might affect the resources you select for learning about computers and software. Write a one-page paper and include the following:

a. Describe the way you like to learn things in general—do you like to read about them, take a class, listen to a cassette, watch a video, think about them, do library research, or take a different approach?

b. If you had to learn how to use a new software application, which approach would you like best: working through a tutorial, using a reference manual, exploring on your own, taking a class, or asking an expert? Why?

c. How does this relate to the way you like to learn other things?

9. Why Not Just Talk to It? Computer scientists have discovered that it is quite difficult to develop a "conver-sational" user interface that you could use to simply "talk" to a computer. One of the stumbling blocks is the ambiguity of human speech. For example, if someone tells you "My friend was looking at a bicycle in the store window, and she wanted it," you assume that "it" refers to the bicycle, not the *store window*. But English grammar does not make the meaning of "it" explicit, so a com-

Resources

puter would have a hard time understanding what you mean. Hurbert Dreyfus discusses this problem in the video *The Machine That Changed the World* and in the book entitled *What Computers Can't Do*. To pursue this topic, do one or more of the following activities:

a. With a small group of other students, try to think of other examples of ambiguity in human conversation that a computer would probably have difficulty understanding. You can share your list with the rest of the class or turn it in to your instructor.

b. Watch Episode IV of the video *The Machine That Changed the World*, if it is available, and use your library to research this topic so you more fully understand the problem. Write a term paper summarizing your research.

10. Super Fast, Major Price Tag
In 1995, the NEC Corp. announced technology for the fastest super-computer in the world, capable of one trillion calculations per second. However, the *Communications of the ACM* reported that the supercomputer would "sell for more than $100 million, virtually guaranteeing it will never be built." Is this price exorbitant compared to other supercomputers? How much does the average supercomputer cost? Who owns them? What tasks do supercomputers perform that make them cost effective? Write a two-page paper addressing these questions about supercomputers. You can use books and periodicals in your library or, if you have access to the Internet, a list of supercomputing resources is at *http://www.yahoo.com/Computers/ Supercomputing_and_Parallel_Computing*.

- **Clarke, A.C.** *2001: A Space Odyssey*. New York: New American Library, 1968. *2001* is a science-fiction classic that takes a bold perspective on how computers might develop in the future. Perhaps Clarke's writing is so powerful because of his strong background in science and research. Clarke is well known for his contribution to the invention of the communications satellite.

- *Computer Dictionary,* 2nd ed. Redmond, WA: Microsoft Press, 1994. It is useful to have a dictionary of computer terms when you read articles in computer magazines. Microsoft Press publishes this up-to-date dictionary that will help you make sense of computer jargon.

- **Dreyfus, H.** *What Computers Can't Do: the limits of artificial intelligence*. Rev. ed. New York: Harper & Row, 1979. *What Computers Can't Do* is a classic contribution to the ongoing discussion about computer intelligence. Dreyfus updated his arguments against computer intelligence in the 1992 book, *What Computers Still Can't Do: a critique of artificial reason*, published by MIT Press.

- **Graham, N.** *The Mind Tool: Computers and Their Impact on Society*, 5th ed. St. Paul, MN: West Publishing, 1989. This well-respected text provides broad coverage of the history of computing, how computers work, and the impact computers have on society.

- **Norman, D.** *The Psychology of Everyday Things*. New York: Basic Books, 1988. Donald Norman says, "This is the book I have always wanted to write, but I didn't know it." The book is an entertaining account of the predicaments caused by poor engineering of everyday objects, such as stoves and revolving doors, as well as more technological devices, such as computer interfaces and nuclear power plants.

- **Ralston, A., and E. D. Reilly.** *Encyclopedia of Computer Science and Engineering*, 3rd ed. New York: Van Nostrand Reinhold, 1993. A definitive reference work on computer concepts, this single-volume encyclopedia is arranged alphabetically by topic and is extensively indexed. You can find information on the first computers, biographies of people who made key contributions to the computer industry, and explanations of many simple and complex computer concepts. Check your library to find this book or a similar computer reference resource.

- **Reinhardt, A.** "Your Next Mainframe." *Byte Magazine*, May 1995, pp. 48-58. Reinhardt points out that "the blurring of computer architectures is erasing the relevance of terms like *mainframe, minicomputer,* and *microcomputer,*" and supports this thesis by comparing microcomputer and mainframe specifications. He suggests some alternative ways of categorizing computers, for example, by the software they run or by the functions they perform within a system. Particularly interesting are his charts "What PCs have that mainframes don't" and "Where mainframes still excel."

- **Schneiderman, B.** "Direct Manipulation: A Step Beyond Programming Languages." *Computer*, August 1983, IEEE publication. Ben Schneiderman, one of the gurus of computer interface design, summarized four principles of direct manipulation interfaces, now popularized as GUIs: (1) continuous representation of available objects, (2) physical actions replace typed commands, (3) manipulation of an object results in immediate feedback, and (4) users can explore the environment and learn to use features gradually.

- *The Machine That Changed the World.* (video) Boston: WGBH Television in cooperation with the British Broadcasting Corp., 1991. An excellent collection of five videos about computers. Episode IV, "The Thinking Machine," focuses on research in the field of artificial intelligence. It presents both sides of the controversy over whether computers can ever be intelligent.

- **von Neumann, J.** "First Draft of a Report on the EDVAC" [unpublished report written in 1945] in Stern, N. B. *From ENIAC to UNIVAC: An Appraisal of the Eckert-Mauchly Computers.* Bedford, MA: Digital Press, 1981. John von Neumann's report on the EDVAC computer is printed in full as an appendix to Nancy Stern's well-researched book about the earliest efforts to build a working electronic computer. The book contains some fascinating photos of one-of-a-kind computing equipment, as well as detailed circuit diagrams showing how these machines worked.

Lab Assignments

The New Perspectives Labs are designed to help you master some of the key computer concepts and skills presented in each chapter of the text. If you are using your schoolís lab computers, your instructor or technical support person should have installed the Labs software for you. If you want to use the Labs on your home computer, ask your instructor for the appropriate software.

Each Lab has two parts: Steps and Explore. Use Steps first to learn and review concepts. Read the information on each page and do the numbered steps. As you work through the Lab, you will be asked to answer Quick Check questions about what you have learned. At the end of the Lab, you will see a Summary Report of your answers to the Quick Checks. If your instructor wants you to turn in this Summary Report, click the Print button on the Summary Report screen.

When you have completed Steps, you can click the Explore button to complete the Lab Assignments. You can also use Explore to practice the skills you learned and to explore concepts on your own.

The instructions for starting the Labs depend on whether your computer has Windows 3.1 or Windows 95. Use the appropriate set of steps for your computer system. Your instructor or technical support person might help you get started.

To begin the Lab from Windows 3.1 Program Manager:

1. Double-click the Course Labs group icon to open the Course Labs window.

2. Double-click the New Perspectives Course Labs Concepts icon to open a window containing icons for all the Labs.

3. Click the icon for the Lab you want to use.

4. Follow the instructions on the screen to enter your name and class section.

5. Read the instructions for using the Lab by clicking the Instructions button.

6. When you are ready to begin the Lab, click the Steps button.

To begin the Lab from Windows 95:

1. Click the Start button.

2. Point to Programs.

3. Point to Course Labs.

4. Click New Perspectives Concepts to open a window containing icons for all the Labs.

5. Click the name of the Lab you want to use.

6. Read the instructions for using the Lab by clicking the Instruction button.

7. When you are ready to begin the Lab, click the Steps button.

Peripheral Devices

 A wide variety of peripheral devices provide expandability for computer systems and provide users with the equipment necessary to accomplish tasks efficiently. In the Peripheral Devices Lab you will use an on-line product catalog of peripheral devices.

1. Complete the Steps to find out how to use the on-line product catalog. Click the Steps button and begin the Steps. As you work through the Steps, answer all of the Quick Check questions that appear. When you complete the Steps, you will see a Summary Report that summarizes your performance on the Quick Checks. Follow the directions on the screen to print the Summary Report.

2. After you know how to use the product catalog to look up products, features, and prices, use Explore to:

   a. List the characteristics that differentiate printers.

   b. List the factors that differentiate monitors.

   c. Describe the factors that determine the appropriate type of scanner for a task.

   d. List the peripheral devices in the catalog that are specially designed for notebook computers.

3. Suppose that the company that produces the peripheral devices catalog selected your name from its list of customers for a free scanner. You can select any one of the scanners in the catalog. Assume that you own a notebook computer to which you could attach any one of the scanners. Click the Explore button and use the catalog to help you write a one-page paper explaining which scanner you would select, why you would select it, and how you would use it.

4. Suppose you are in charge of information systems in a metropolitan hospital. Twenty nursing stations need printers. The printers will be used for a variety of reports. High print quality is not essential; but, of course, the reports must be readable. Some reports require more than one copy. Because they will be situated near patients, the printers must be quiet. Use the catalog in the Explore portion of the Lab to write a one-page paper in which you recommend a printer from the catalog for the nursing stations. Support your recommendation by explaining the advantages of the printer you selected and the disadvantages of the other printers available.

5. Suppose you own a basic computer system, such as the one in Figure 1-7 of this text book. You have an idea that you can earn the money for your college tuition by using your computer to help other students produce spiffy reports with color graphs and scanned images. Your parents have agreed to "loan" you $1,000 to get started. Click the Explore button and look through the on-line peripheral devices catalog. List any of the devices that might help you with this business venture. Write a one-page paper explaining how you would spend your $1,000 to get the equipment you need to start the business.

User Interfaces

 You have learned that the hardware and software for a user interface determine how you interact and communicate with the computer. In the User Interfaces Lab, you will try five different user interfaces to accomplish the same task—creating a graph.

1. Begin with the Steps to find out how each interface works. Click the Steps button and begin the Steps. As you work through the Steps, answer all of the Quick Check questions that appear. When you complete the Steps, you will see a Summary Report that summarizes your performance on the Quick Checks. Follow the directions on the screen to print the Summary Report.

2. In Explore, use each interface to make a 3-D pie graph using data set 1. Title your graphs "Bike U.S. Sales." Use the percent style to show the percent of each slice of the pie. Print each of the five graphs (one for each interface).

3. In Explore, select one of the user interfaces. Write a step-by-step set of instructions for how to produce a line graph using data set 3. This line graph should show lines and symbols, and have the title "Home Budget."

4. Using the user interface terminology you learned in this Lab and in Chapter 1 of the text book, write a description of each of the interfaces you used in the Lab. Then, suppose you worked for a software publisher and you were going to create a software package for producing line, bar, column, and pie graphs. Which user interface would you use for the software? Why?

DOS Command-Line User Interface

 The DOS command-line user interface provides a typical example of the advantages and disadvantages of command-line user interfaces. DOS was included with the original IBM PC computers to provide users with a way to accomplish system tasks such as listing, moving, and deleting files on disk. Although todayís typical computer user prefers to use a graphical user interface such as Windows, DOS commands still function on most IBM-compatible computers.

1. Begin with Steps to learn how to use the DOS command-line interface. Click the Steps button and begin the Steps. As you work through the Steps, answer all of the Quick Check questions that appear. When you complete the Steps, you will see a Summary Report that summarizes your performance on the Quick Checks. Follow the directions on the screen to print the Summary Report.

2. In Explore, write out your answers to a through d.

a. Explain the different results you get when you use the commands DIR, DIR /p, and DIR /w.

b. What happens if you make a typing error and enter the command DUR instead of DIR? What procedure must you follow to correct your error?

c. Enter the command, DIR /? and explain what happens. Enter the command VER /? and explain what happens. What generalization can you make about the /? command parameter?

d. Enter the command VER /p. Why do you think /p does not work with the VER command word, but it works with DIR?

3. Write a one-page paper summarizing what you know about command line user interfaces and answering the following questions:

a. Which DOS commands do you now know how to use?

b. How do you know which commands to use to accomplish a task?

c. How do you know what parameters work with each command?

d. What kinds of mistakes can you make that will produce an error message?

e. Can you enter valid commands that don't produce the results you want?

Using a Mouse

 A mouse is a standard input device on most of today's computers. You need to know how to use a mouse to manipulate graphical user interfaces and to use the rest of the Labs.

1. The Steps for the Using a Mouse Lab show you how to click, double-click, and drag objects using the mouse. Click the Steps button and begin the Steps. As you work through the Steps, answer all of the Quick Check questions that appear. When you complete the Steps, you will see a Summary Report that summarizes your performance on the Quick Checks. Follow the directions on the screen to print the Summary Report.

2. In Explore, demonstrate your ability to use a mouse and to control a Windows program by creating a poster. To create a poster, select a graphic, type the caption for the poster, then select a font, font styles, and a border. Print your completed poster.

Using a Keyboard

 To become an effective computer user, you must be familiar with your primary input device—the keyboard.

1. The Steps for the Using a Keyboard Lab provide you with a structured introduction to the keyboard layout and the function of special computer keys. Click the Steps button and begin the Steps. As you work through the Steps, answer all of the Quick Check questions that appear. When you complete the Steps, you will see a Summary Report that summarizes your performance on the Quick Checks. Follow the directions on the screen to print the Summary Report.

2. In Explore, start the typing tutor. You can develop your typing skills using the typing tutor in Explore. Take the typing test and print out your results.

3. In Explore, try to improve your typing speed by 10 words per minute. For example, if you currently type 20 words per minute, your goal would be 30 words per minute. Practice each typing lesson until you see a message that indicates you can proceed to the next lesson. Create a Practice Record as shown on page 1-39 to keep track of how much you practice. When you have reached your goal, print out the results of a typing test to verify your results.

Practice Record

Name: _____

Section: _____

Start Date: _____ Start Typing Speed: _____ wpm

End Date: _____ End Typing Speed: _____ wpm

Lesson #: _____ Date Practiced/Time Practiced _____

Quick Check

Answers

1.1

1. accepts input, processes data, stores data, produces output

2. data

3. process

4. memory

5. storage

1.2

1. keyboard, monitor

2. microcomputer

3. terminal

4. minicomputers, mainframes

5. mainframe

6. compatible

7. network

1.3

1. prompt

2. wizards

3. Enter

4. syntax

5. submenu, dialog box

6. graphical user interfaces

7. cursor, insertion point

8. Ctrl, Alt

9. Windows

10. character-based

Glossary/Index

Special Characters

/ (slash), 1-19

A

Alt key A key that you hold down with another key. The result of the Alt key combinations depend on the software used, 1-25, 1-26

Apple Computer, Inc., 1-12, 1-13. *See also* Macintosh computers

architecture. *See* memory

audio tutorials A cassette that verbally walks you through the steps of a tutorial, 1-31

B

Backspace key A key that when pressed deletes one character to the left of the cursor, 1-26

bar code reader A device that gathers input data by reading bar codes, 1-12, 1-12–1-13

bit-map displays, 1-28

button An object that helps you make a selection, 1-22
    commands, 1-22
    mouse, 1-24–25

C

Caps Lock key A key that when engaged, capitalizes all the letters you type, but does not produce the top symbol on keys that display two symbols, 1-25, 1-26

CD-ROM A high capacity storage medium with a capacity of up to 680 million characters. Most CD-ROMs do not allow you to add or change the information on them, 1-11

CD-ROM drive A storage device that uses laser technology to read data from a CD-ROM, 1-11

central processing unit (CPU) The circuitry in a computer that performs arithmetic and logic operations and executes instructions. Also called the CPU or processor, 1-5 *See also* microprocessor.

ChartWizard button A button that when pressed starts a wizard, 1-23

character-based display A screen display in which the screen is divided into a grid of rectangles, which each display a single character; the characters cannot be modified, 1-28

clicking Pressing the left mouse button once to select an object on the screen, 1-24

command A combination of words, parameters, and punctuation that tells the computer what you want it to do, 1-19, 1-20

errors
command syntax, 1-19
syntax, 1-19

Esc key When pressed, this key cancels an operation, 1-26

experts, 1-32

files. *See* software; storage

fixed disks, 1-11

floppies. *See* floppy disks

floppy disks Storage media that come in 3½-inch or 5¼-inch sizes to match the two sizes of microcomputer disk drives. Floppy disks also come in high-density or low-density versions, 1-11

floppy disk drive A storage device that writes data on floppy disks, 1-11

function keys Twelve keys, numbered F1 through F12, used to initiate commands, 1-25, 1-26

Gateway, 1-12

graphical object A small picture on the screen that can be manipulated using an input device, 1-22, 1-22-1-24

graphical user interface (GUI) A type of user interface in which you manipulate on-screen objects to activate commands, 1-23, 1-23-1-24
metaphors, 1-24

graphics display A screen display in which the screen is divided into a matrix of pixels; any characters or graphics the matrix displays must be constructed of dot patterns within the screen matrix, 1-28

hand scanner A scanning device used by hand that converts a section of text or graphics into electronic format, 1-12, 1-12-1-13

hard disk drive A storage device that is mounted inside a system unit. This drive can store billions of characters on a non-removable disk platter, 1-11

hardware, 1-7
installation manuals, 1-32

Help, 1-30

HELP command, 1-20

hierarchy An organization of things ranked one above the other, 1-20

Home key When pressed, this key takes you to the beginning of a line or the document, depending on the software being used, 1-27, 1-27-1-28

IBM-compatible computer Computer systems based on the architecture of the first IBM microcomputers. Also called PC-compatibles, 1-12

IBM platform, 1-12-13

icon A picture used by a graphical user interface to represent an object, 1-22

indicator lights, 1-27-28

input The words, symbols, and numbers put into a computer for processing, 1-5, 1-6

input device Transfers into the computer memory the words and numbers to be processed. The keyboard and the mouse are the most commonly used input devices, 1-5

insertion point A flashing vertical bar that indicates where the characters you type will appear, 1-25

installing hardware, manuals, 1-32

Internet, 1-33

keyboard Input device that includes letter, number, and computer-specific task keys, 1-11, 1-13, 1-25-1-27

keyboard shortcuts, 1-26

laser printer A printer that uses heat to fuse a fine dark powder, called toner, onto paper to create text and images, 1-14

LCD projection display panel A piece of equipment that is placed on an overhead projector to produce a large display of the information shown on a computer screen, 1-12, 1-12-1-13

learning styles, 1-32

legacy systems, 1-28

login process The process you use to access network resources, including entering your user ID and password, 1-15

Macintosh compatible computers, 1-12-13

Macintosh computers, 1-12
mouse, 1-24-25

Computer Files and Data Storage

Software
and **Multimedia**
Applications

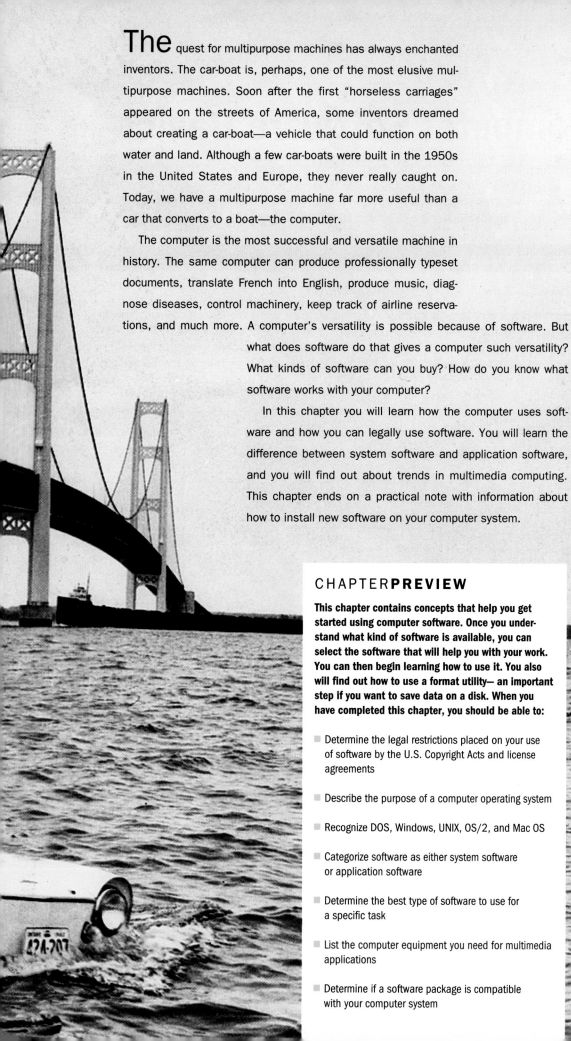

The quest for multipurpose machines has always enchanted inventors. The car-boat is, perhaps, one of the most elusive multipurpose machines. Soon after the first "horseless carriages" appeared on the streets of America, some inventors dreamed about creating a car-boat—a vehicle that could function on both water and land. Although a few car-boats were built in the 1950s in the United States and Europe, they never really caught on. Today, we have a multipurpose machine far more useful than a car that converts to a boat—the computer.

The computer is the most successful and versatile machine in history. The same computer can produce professionally typeset documents, translate French into English, produce music, diagnose diseases, control machinery, keep track of airline reservations, and much more. A computer's versatility is possible because of software. But what does software do that gives a computer such versatility? What kinds of software can you buy? How do you know what software works with your computer?

In this chapter you will learn how the computer uses software and how you can legally use software. You will learn the difference between system software and application software, and you will find out about trends in multimedia computing. This chapter ends on a practical note with information about how to install new software on your computer system.

CHAPTER**PREVIEW**

This chapter contains concepts that help you get started using computer software. Once you understand what kind of software is available, you can select the software that will help you with your work. You can then begin learning how to use it. You also will find out how to use a format utility— an important step if you want to save data on a disk. When you have completed this chapter, you should be able to:

- Determine the legal restrictions placed on your use of software by the U.S. Copyright Acts and license agreements

- Describe the purpose of a computer operating system

- Recognize DOS, Windows, UNIX, OS/2, and Mac OS

- Categorize software as either system software or application software

- Determine the best type of software to use for a specific task

- List the computer equipment you need for multimedia applications

- Determine if a software package is compatible with your computer system

LABS

Word Processing

Spreadsheets

Databases

Computer History Hypermedia

2.1

Computer Software Basics

Computer magazines are a great source of information about the rich variety of computer software available. Project 4 at the end of this chapter helps you learn how to use this information resource.

Computer software determines what a computer can do. In a sense, software transforms a computer from one kind of machine to another—from a drafting station to a typesetting machine, from a flight simulator to a calculator, from a filing system to a music studio.

Computer Programs

Do I need to write programs for my computer?

A **computer program** is a set of detailed, step-by-step instructions that tells a computer how to solve a problem or carry out a task. Some computer programs handle simple tasks, such as converting feet and inches to centimeters. Longer and more complex computer programs handle very complicated tasks, such as reconstructing photographs sent back from a spacecraft flyby of Jupiter.

The steps in a computer program are written in a language that the computer can interpret and process. As you read through the simple computer program in Figure 2-1, notice the number of steps required to perform a relatively simple calculation.

Figure 2-1
A computer program that converts feet and inches to centimeters

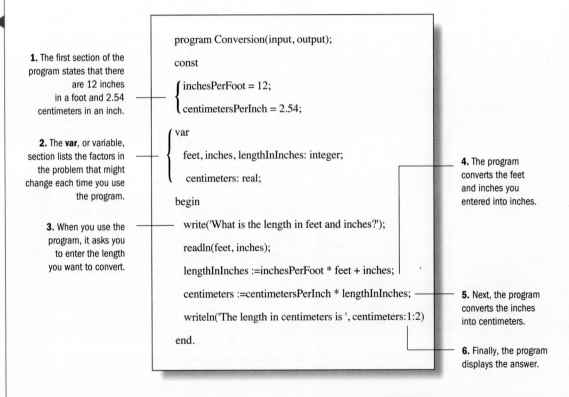

1. The first section of the program states that there are 12 inches in a foot and 2.54 centimeters in an inch.

2. The **var**, or variable, section lists the factors in the problem that might change each time you use the program.

3. When you use the program, it asks you to enter the length you want to convert.

4. The program converts the feet and inches you entered into inches.

5. Next, the program converts the inches into centimeters.

6. Finally, the program displays the answer.

```
program Conversion(input, output);

const
{ inchesPerFoot = 12;
{ centimetersPerInch = 2.54;

{ var
{    feet, inches, lengthInInches: integer;
{    centimeters: real;

begin

    write('What is the length in feet and inches?');

    readln(feet, inches);

    lengthInInches :=inchesPerFoot * feet + inches;

    centimeters :=centimetersPerInch * lengthInInches;

    writeln('The length in centimeters is ', centimeters:1:2)

end.
```

Although most computer users do not write computer programs, computer programming is a challenging career. Project 9 at the end of this chapter helps you discover more about computer programming careers.

At one time organizations and individuals had to write most of the computer programs they wanted to use. A team of programmers might have spent several years writing a program for a task such as billing clients for insurance premiums. A program like that could easily contain more than 100,000 steps.

Today many organizations purchase commercially written programs to avoid the time and expense of writing their own programs. Individuals rarely write computer programs for their personal computers, preferring to select from thousands of commercially written programs. Most computer users are not computer programmers.

Computer Software

Are computer programs, data, and software the same thing?

Software is a basic part of a computer system, but "software" is a term that has more than one definition. In the early days of the computer industry, it became popular to use the term "software" for all the non-hardware components of a computer. In this context, software referred to computer programs and to the data used by the programs.

The U.S. Copyright Act of 1980 defines software as "a set of statements or instructions to be used directly or indirectly in a computer in order to bring about a certain result." This definition implies that computer software is essentially the same as a computer program. It also implies that a collection of data, such as a list of dictionary words, is not software.

In practice, the term "software" is usually used to describe a commercial product, which might include more than a single program and might also include data, as shown in Figure 2-2.

As you read articles about computers, scan computer ads, and listen to people talk about computers, you will begin to understand the different shades of meaning associated with computer terms such as "software." A good computer dictionary helps, too.

The disks contain one or more **programs**, and possibly some data. For example, the Microsoft Windows 95 software includes programs that help you draw graphics, write documents, and keep track of what's on your disks. The software also includes some data, such as information on time zones that you can use to set your computer's clock.

▶ **Figure 2-2**
Software products

A **software package** contains disks and a reference manual.

In this textbook, we define **software** as instructions and associated data, stored in electronic format, that direct the computer to accomplish a task. Under this definition, computer software may include more than one computer program, if those programs work together to carry out a task; software also can include data, but data alone is not software. For example, word processing software might include the data for a dictionary, but the data *you create* using a word processor is not called software. Suppose you write a report using a software package, then store the report on a disk. Your report consists of data rather than instructions for the computer to carry out. Because your report does not contain instructions, it is not software.

"Software" is a plural noun, so there is no such thing as "softwares" or "one software." How, then, do we talk about software in the singular? We often use the term "software package" when we want to talk about a particular example of software.

The distinction between software, programs, and data is important. Try Quick Check Questions 1 through 3 to see if you can use these terms correctly.

Copyrighted Software

Is it illegal to copy software?

Just because you can copy software doesn't make it legal to do so. Like books and movies, most computer software is protected by a copyright. A **copyright** is a form of legal protection that grants certain exclusive rights to the author of a program or the owner of the copyright. The owner of the copyright has the exclusive right to copy the software, to distribute or sell the software, and to modify the software. If you are not the owner of the copyright, it is illegal for you to copy, distribute, or sell the software unless you obtain permission from the copyright owner.

When you purchase copyrighted software, you do not become the owner of the copyright. Instead, you own only a copy of the software. Your purchase allows you to use the software on your computer, but you cannot make additional copies to give away or sell. People who illegally copy, distribute, or modify software are sometimes called **software pirates**, and the illegal copies they create are referred to as **pirated software**.

The restrictions stated by the Copyright Act apply only to the programs and data included as part of the original software. The data you enter—the documents, files, and graphics you create—can be copied without restriction.

Copyrighted materials such as software display a copyright notice that contains the word "Copyright" (or the © symbol), the year of publication, and the name of the copyright holder. For example, the copyright notice on the software that accompanies this book is "Copyright 1996

The Software Publisher's Association provides public service information on copyright issues in an effort to educate the public about the legal use of software. Learn more about this organization in the Resources section at the end of this chapter.

Figure 2-3
Sections 106 and 117 of the 1980 Copyright Act

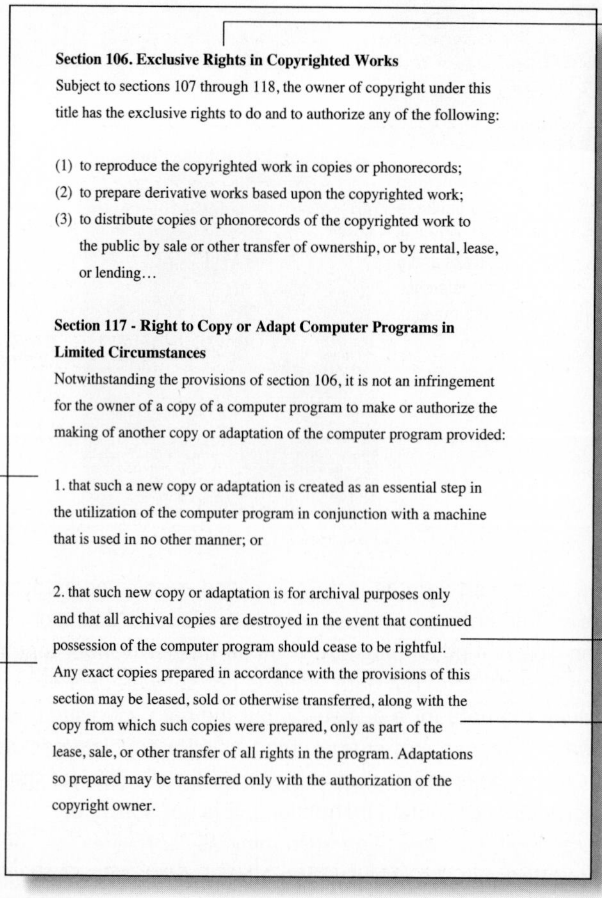

Section 106. Exclusive Rights in Copyrighted Works
Subject to sections 107 through 118, the owner of copyright under this title has the exclusive rights to do and to authorize any of the following:

(1) to reproduce the copyrighted work in copies or phonorecords;
(2) to prepare derivative works based upon the copyrighted work;
(3) to distribute copies or phonorecords of the copyrighted work to the public by sale or other transfer of ownership, or by rental, lease, or lending...

Section 117 - Right to Copy or Adapt Computer Programs in Limited Circumstances
Notwithstanding the provisions of section 106, it is not an infringement for the owner of a copy of a computer program to make or authorize the making of another copy or adaptation of the computer program provided:

1. that such a new copy or adaptation is created as an essential step in the utilization of the computer program in conjunction with a machine that is used in no other manner; or

2. that such new copy or adaptation is for archival purposes only and that all archival copies are destroyed in the event that continued possession of the computer program should cease to be rightful. Any exact copies prepared in accordance with the provisions of this section may be leased, sold or otherwise transferred, along with the copy from which such copies were prepared, only as part of the lease, sale, or other transfer of all rights in the program. Adaptations so prepared may be transferred only with the authorization of the copyright owner.

Only the copyright owner can reproduce, sell, or distribute the copyrighted software. Note that this section was written before computer software copyright became an issue, thus the reference to phonorecords, but not to software.

It is legal to copy the software from the distribution disks to the hard disk of your computer system so you can access the software from the hard disk.

It is legal to make an extra copy of the software in case the copy you are using becomes damaged.

If you give away or sell the software, you cannot legally keep a copy.

You cannot legally sell or give away modified copies of the software without permission.

Course Technology, Inc." When you start a computer program, the copyright notice usually appears on the first screen; it is also usually printed in the reference manual. The Copyright Acts of 1976 and 1980 address software copyright issues and allow you to copy or modify software only under certain circumstances. If you read the sections of the Copyright Act shown in Figure 2-3, you will discover under what circumstances you can and cannot legally copy copyrighted software.

Licensed Software

Do I need to read the small print before I buy software?

In addition to copyright protection, computer software is often protected by the terms of a software license. A **software license** is a legal contract that defines the ways in which you may use a computer program. For microcomputer software, you will find the license on the outside of the package, on a separate card inside the package, or in the reference manual. Mainframe software licenses are usually a separate legal document, negotiated between the software publisher and a corporate buyer.

Software licenses are often lengthy and written in "legalese," but they are generally divided into manageable sections that you can understand by reading them carefully. To become familiar with a typical license agreement, you can read through the "No-Nonsense License Statement" used for software published by Borland International, shown in Figure 2-4.

▶ **Figure 2-4**
A software license

The book analogy explained here is a useful way to think about software use.

This section explains how you are allowed to use the software.

These sections make provisions for multiple users.

Here, Borland essentially says that you use this software at your own risk.

This software is protected by both United States copyright law and international copyright treaty provisions. Therefore, you must treat this software just like a book, except that you may copy it onto a computer to be used and you may make archival copies of the software for the sole purpose of backing-up our software and protecting your investment from loss.

By saying "just like a book," Borland means, for example, that this software may be used by any number of people, and may be freely moved from one computer location to another, so long as there is no possibility of it being used at one location while it's being used at another or on a computer network by more than one user at one location. Just like a book can't be read by two different people in two different places at the same time, neither can the software be used by two different people in two different places at the same time. (Unless, of course, Borland's copyright has been violated or the use is on a computer network by up to the number of users authorized by additional Borland licenses as explained below.)

LAN PACK MULTIPLE-USE NETWORK LICENSE

If this is a LAN Pack package, it allows you to increase the number of authorized users of your copy of the software on a single computer network by up to the number of users specified in the LAN Pack package (per LAN Pack — see LAN Pack serial number).

USE ON A NETWORK

A "computer network" is any electronically linked configuration in which two or more users have common access to software or data. If more than one user wishes to use the software on a computer network at the same time, then you may add authorized users either by (a) paying for a separate software package for each additional user you wish to add or (b) if a LAN Pack is available for this product, paying for the multiple-use license available in the LAN Pack. You may use any combination of regular software packages or LAN Packs to increase the number of authorized users on a computer network. (In no event may the total number of concurrent users on a network exceed one for each

software package plus the number of authorized users installed from the LAN Pack(s) that you have purchased. Otherwise, you are not using the software "just like a book.") The multiple-use network license for the LAN Pack may only be used to increase the number of concurrent permitted users of the software logged onto the network, and not to download copies of the software for local workstation use without being logged onto the network. You must purchase an individual copy of the software for each workstation at which you wish to use the software without being logged onto the network.

FURTHER EXPLANATION OF COPYRIGHT LAW PROVISIONS AND THE SCOPE OF THIS LICENSE STATEMENT

You may not download or transmit the software electronically (either by direct connection or telecommunication transmission) from one computer to another, except as may be specifically allowed in using the software on a computer network. You may transfer all of your rights to use the software to another person, provided that you transfer to that person

(or destroy) all of the software, diskettes and documentation provided in this package, together with all copies, tangible or intangible, including copies in RAM or installed on a disk, as well as all back-up copies. Remember, once you transfer the software, it may only be used at the single location to which it is transferred and, of course, only in accordance with the copyright laws and international treaty provisions. Except as stated in this paragraph, you may not otherwise trans-

fer, rent, lease, sub-license, time-share, or lend the software, diskettes, or documentation. Your use of the software is limited to acts that are essential steps in the use of the software on your computer or computer network as described in the documentation. You may not otherwise modify, alter, adapt, merge, decompile or reverse-engineer the software, and you may not remove or obscure Borland copyright or trademark notices.

LIMITED WARRANTY

Borland International, Inc. ("Borland") warrants the physical diskette(s) and physical documentation enclosed herein (but not any diskettes or documentation distributed by the Paradox Runtime Licensee) to be free of defects in materials and workmanship for a period of sixty days from the purchase date. If Borland receives notification within the warranty period of defects in materials or workmanship, and such notification is determined by Borland to be correct, Borland will replace the defective diskette(s) or documentation. DO NOT RETURN ANY PRODUCT UNTIL YOU HAVE CALLED THE BORLAND CUSTOMER SERVICE DEPARTMENT AND OBTAINED A RETURN AUTHORIZATION NUMBER.

The entire and exclusive liability and remedy for breach of the Limited Warranty shall be limited to replacement of defective diskette(s) or documentation and shall not include or extend to any claim for or right to recover any other damages, including but not limited to, loss of profit, data, or use of the software, or special, incidental, or consequential damages or other similar claims, even if Borland has been specifically advised of the possibility of such damages. In no event will Borland's liability for any damages to you or any other

person ever exceed the lower of suggested list price or actual price paid for the license to use the software, regardless of any form of the claim.

BORLAND INTERNATIONAL, INC. SPECIFICALLY DISCLAIMS ALL OTHER WARRANTIES, EXPRESS OR IMPLIED, INCLUDING BUT NOT LIMITED TO, ANY IMPLIED WARRANTY OF MERCHANTABILITY OR FITNESS FOR A PARTICULAR PURPOSE. Specifically, Borland makes no representation or warranty that the software is fit for any particular purpose and any implied warranty of merchantability is limited to the sixty-day duration of the Limited Warranty covering the physical diskette(s) and physical documentation only (and not the software) and is otherwise expressly and specifically disclaimed.

This limited warranty gives you specific legal rights; you may have others which may vary from state to state. Some states do not allow the exclusion of incidental or consequential damages, or the limitation on how long an implied warranty lasts, so some of the above may not apply to you.

BUSINESS PRODUCTS (With Network Provisions): NO-NONSENSE LICENSE STATEMENT

BUSINESS PRODUCTS (With Network Provisions): NO-NONSENSE LICENSE STATEMENT

This section restates the basic copyright restrictions about transferring software.

Not all software licenses allow you to buy one copy of the software and install it on your home and work computers. You must read your license agreement to find out.

Although you pay for a software license, your legal right to use the software continues only as long as you abide by the terms of the software license. Therefore, reading the terms of the software license agreement included with any software package you use is important. The software license agreement explains whether you may make copies, modify the software, or transfer it to another person. A software license often extends the rights given to you by the U.S. Copyright Act. For example, although the Copyright Act makes it illegal to copy software for use on more than one computer, the license for Claris Works software allows you to buy one copy of the software and install it on your home computer and your office computer as long as you are the primary user of both computers.

It is important to distinguish the concept of licensing from that of purchasing a copy of software. When you pay for licensed software, you do not buy and then own a copy of the software. Instead, you buy permission to use the software. You can think of it as renting software, rather than buying it.

Shrink Wrap Licenses

Do I have to sign a software license for it to be valid?

Signing and submitting a license agreement every time you purchase software would be inconvenient, so the computer industry makes extensive use of **shrink wrap licenses**. When you purchase computer software, the disks or CD-ROM in the package are usually sealed in an envelope or plastic shrink wrapping. A notification, such as the one in Figure 2-5, states that opening the wrapping signifies your agreement to the terms of the software license.

Figure 2-5
A typical shrink wrap license

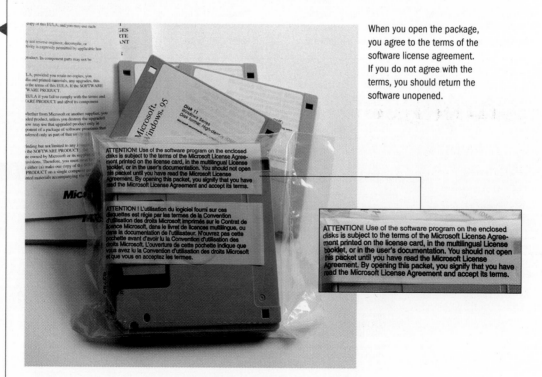

When you open the package, you agree to the terms of the software license agreement. If you do not agree with the terms, you should return the software unopened.

ATTENTION! Use of the software program on the enclosed disks is subject to the terms of the Microsoft License Agreement printed on the license card, in the multilingual License booklet, or in the user's documentation. You should not open this packet until you have read the Microsoft License Agreement. By opening this packet, you signify that you have read the Microsoft License Agreement and accept its terms.

With a shrink wrap license, the software publisher avoids the lengthy process of negotiating the terms of the license and obtaining your signature. It is essentially a "take it or leave it" approach to licensing. Although the courts have yet to provide a definitive ruling on its validity, shrink wrap licensing is one of the most frequently used methods for providing legal protection for computer software.

Licenses for More Than One User

If my company has a computer network, does it still have to pay for a license for each user?

Most software publishers offer a variety of license options; some are designed for a single user, others for more than one user. A **single-user license** limits the use of the software to one user at a time. Most commercial software is distributed under a single-user license.

A **multiple-user license** allows more than one person to use a particular software package. This type of license is useful in cases where users each have their own personalized version of the software. An electronic mail program would typically have a multiple-user license because users each have their own mailbox. Multiple-user licenses are generally priced per user, but the price for each user is typically less than the price of a single-user license.

A **concurrent-use license** allows a certain number of copies of the software to be used at the same time. For example, if an organization with a computer network has a concurrent-use license for five copies of a word processor, at any one time as many as five employees may use the software. Concurrent-use licenses are usually priced in increments. For example, a company might be able to purchase a concurrent-use license for up to 50 users for $2,500, or up to 250 users for $10,000.

A **site license** generally allows the software to be used on any and all computers at a specific location, such as within a corporate office building or on a university campus. A site license is priced at a flat rate, for example, $5,000 per site.

Public Domain Software

Isn't some software free?

Sometimes an author abandons all rights to a particular software title and places it in the public domain, making the program available without restriction. Such software, referred to as **public domain software**, is owned by the public rather than by the author.

Public domain software may be freely copied, distributed, and even resold. The primary restriction on public domain software is that you are not allowed to apply for a copyright on it. Public domain software is fairly rare. It is frequently confused with shareware because it is legal to copy and distribute both public domain software and shareware.

What's the difference between a multiple-user license and a concurrent-use license? With a multiple-user license, each individual who uses the software must be assigned a license. If five employees use mail software under a multiple-user license, a five-user license is required even if they are not all using the software at the same time. With a concurrent-use license for five users, any five employees can use the software at the same time even if there are hundreds of employees in the firm.

Shareware

My friend gave me a copy of something called "shareware." Was that illegal?

Shareware is copyrighted software marketed under a "try before you buy" policy. Shareware usually includes a license that allows you to use the software for a trial period. If you want to continue to use it, you must send in a registration fee. Take a look at the shareware license in Figure 2-6 and notice the rights it includes.

Figure 2-6
A typical shareware license

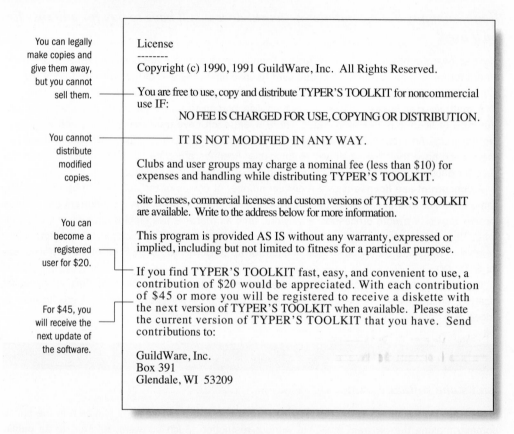

You can legally make copies and give them away, but you cannot sell them.

You cannot distribute modified copies.

You can become a registered user for $20.

For $45, you will receive the next update of the software.

License

Copyright (c) 1990, 1991 GuildWare, Inc. All Rights Reserved.

You are free to use, copy and distribute TYPER'S TOOLKIT for noncommercial use IF:
    NO FEE IS CHARGED FOR USE, COPYING OR DISTRIBUTION.

    IT IS NOT MODIFIED IN ANY WAY.

Clubs and user groups may charge a nominal fee (less than $10) for expenses and handling while distributing TYPER'S TOOLKIT.

Site licenses, commercial licenses and custom versions of TYPER'S TOOLKIT are available. Write to the address below for more information.

This program is provided AS IS without any warranty, expressed or implied, including but not limited to fitness for a particular purpose.

If you find TYPER'S TOOLKIT fast, easy, and convenient to use, a contribution of $20 would be appreciated. With each contribution of $45 or more you will be registered to receive a diskette with the next version of TYPER'S TOOLKIT when available. Please state the current version of TYPER'S TOOLKIT that you have. Send contributions to:

GuildWare, Inc.
Box 391
Glendale, WI 53209

To avoid problems, be sure you're clear on your rights to copy, use, and distribute software. Many programs provide this information when you click Help and then select the Help About menu option.

When you send in the fee to become a registered shareware user, you are granted a license to use the software beyond the trial period. You might also receive a free copy of the latest version of the software or printed documentation for the program.

When you read the shareware license in Figure 2-6, you might have noticed that you are allowed to make copies of the software and distribute them to others. This is a typical shareware policy and a fairly effective marketing strategy that provides low-cost advertising. Unfortunately, registration fee payment relies on the honor system, so many shareware authors collect only a fraction of the payment they deserve for their programming efforts.

Software Categories

What's the difference between system software and application software?

Because there are so many software titles, categorizing software as either system software or application software is useful. **System software** helps the computer carry out its basic operating tasks. **Application software** helps the human user carry out a task.

System software and application software are further divided into subcategories. As you continue to read this chapter, use Figure 2-7 to help you understand the differences between system and application software and to help you distinguish among the various subcategories of system and application software.

Remember the key difference between system software and application software: system software helps the computer, application software helps you.

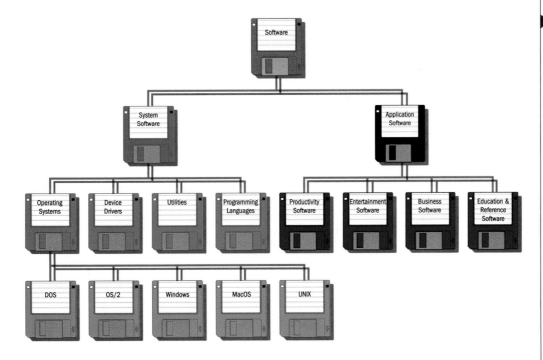

▶ **Figure 2-7**
Software categories

Quick Check

1 If you use a computer to write a report, the report is considered software. True or false?

2 When you type a report or enter the information for a mailing list, you are creating _____.

3 The instructions that tell a computer how to convert inches to centimeters are a computer _____.

4 To use a computer to write and edit documents, you need word processing _____.

5 The "try before you buy" policy refers to _____ licenses.

6 A(n) _____ for microcomputer or mainframe software is a contract by which the software publisher grants the buyer permission to use the software.

7 _____ software helps the *computer* carry out its basic operating tasks.

2.2 | System Software

System software is the category of software containing programs that perform tasks essential to the efficient functioning of computer hardware. System software includes the programs that direct the fundamental operations of a computer, such as displaying information on the screen, storing data on disks, sending data to the printer, interpreting commands typed by users, and communicating with peripheral devices.

Let's look at some of the specific functions of the four subcategories of system software: operating systems, utilities, device drivers, and computer programming languages.

Operating Systems

Why does a computer need an operating system?

An **operating system** is the software that controls the computer's use of its hardware resources such as memory and disk storage space. An operating system works like an air traffic controller to coordinate the activities within the computer. Just as an airport cannot function without air traffic controllers, a computer cannot function without an operating system. When you purchase a microcomputer, the operating system is usually pre-installed on the hard disk and ready to use. You "see" the operating system each time you turn on your computer, and the operating system helps you start the application software you want to use.

If you envision computer hardware as the core of your computer system, then the operating system provides the next layer of functionality by assisting the computer with its basic hardware operations. The operating system also interacts with the next layer—application software—to carry out application tasks such as printing and saving data. Figure 2-8 helps you envision the relationship between your computer hardware, the operating system, and application software.

You might be familiar with the names of the most popular microcomputer operating systems: DOS, Microsoft Windows, OS/2, and Mac OS. You are less likely to be familiar with the names of minicomputer and mainframe operating systems such as UNIX, VMS, and MVS. Operating systems for micro, mini, and mainframe computers perform many similar tasks. An operating system helps you start an application, then works "behind the scenes" while application software is running to perform tasks essential to the computer system's efficient functioning. It controls input and output, allocates system resources, manages the storage space for programs and data, maintains security, and detects equipment failure. Study Figure 2-9 to discover more about what an operating system does.

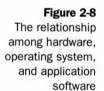

Figure 2-8
The relationship among hardware, operating system, and application software

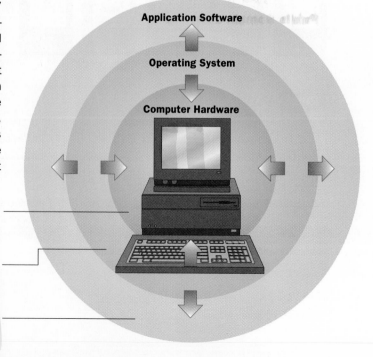

Application Software

Operating System

Computer Hardware

The **computer hardware** is the core of the system, but the hardware cannot function without an operating system.

The **operating system** acts as a liason between the computer hardware and application software.

Application software requires the operating system to carry out hardware related tasks such as printing reports and storing data on disks.

Figure 2-9
Operating system functions

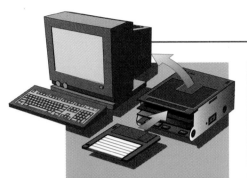

Control Basic Input and Output

An operating system controls the flow of data into and out of the computer, as well as the flow of data to and from peripheral devices. It routes input to areas of the computer where it can be processed and routes output to the screen, a printer, or any other output device you request.

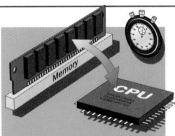

Allocate System Resources

A **system resource** is any part of a computer system, such as a disk drive, memory, printer, or processor time, that can be used by a computer program. The operating system allocates system resources so programs run properly.

For example, each program instruction takes up space inside the computer and each instruction requires a certain amount of time to complete. The operating system ensures that adequate space is available for each program that is running and makes sure the processor quickly performs each program instruction.

The operating system also manages the additional resources required for using multiple programs or for providing services to more than one user at the same time. For example, if you want to run two or more programs at the same time, a process called **multitasking**, the operating system ensures that each program has adequate space and that the computer devotes an appropriate amount of time to the tasks prescribed by each program.

To accommodate more than one user at a time, an operating system must have multiuser capabilities. You typically find **multiuser** operating systems on mainframe and minicomputer systems, where users each have their own terminal but share the processing capability of a single main computer. Multiuser operating systems typically provide speedy service so users each think they are the only ones using the computer.

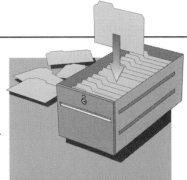

Manage Storage Space

The operating system keeps track of the data stored on disks and CD-ROMs. Think of your disks as filing cabinets, your data as papers stored in file folders, and the operating system as a filing clerk. The filing clerk takes care of filing a folder when you finish using it. When you need something from your filing cabinet, you ask the filing clerk to get it. The filing clerk knows where to find your folder. On your computer system, the operating system stores your data at some location on a disk. Although you might not know exactly where your data is stored on the disk, when you need the data again, you only need to ask the operating system to retrieve it.

Detect Equipment Failure

The operating system monitors the status of critical computer components to detect failures that affect processing. When you turn on your computer, the operating system checks each of the electronic components and takes a quick inventory of the storage devices. For example, if an electrical component inside your computer fails, the operating system displays a message identifying the problem and does not let you continue with the computing session until the problem is fixed.

Maintain Security

The operating system also helps maintain security for the data on the computer system. For example, the operating system might not allow you to access the computer system unless you have a user ID and password.

Let's look at a specific example of how the operating system works as a liaison between the computer hardware and application software. The operating system provides a foundation so that application software operates correctly and uses peripheral devices properly. For example, suppose you use application software to write a letter and then you want to print it. The operating system helps the application software communicate with your computer's printer, as shown in Figure 2-10.

Figure 2-10 ◄
The operating system: a liaison between the computer hardware and application software

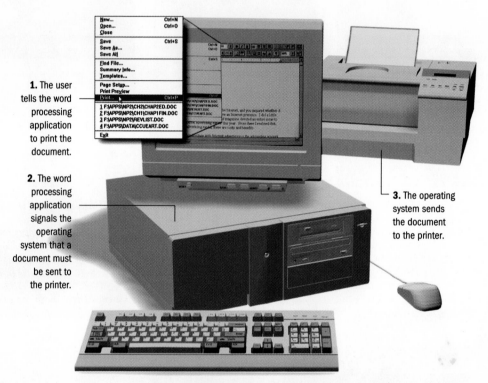

1. The user tells the word processing application to print the document.

2. The word processing application signals the operating system that a document must be sent to the printer.

3. The operating system sends the document to the printer.

Microcomputer Operating Systems

As a computer user, why is it important for me to know which operating system is on my computer?

Microsoft Windows 3.1 is sometimes referred to as an "operating environment," rather than an operating system; newer versions of Windows such as Windows NT and Windows 95 are generally classified as operating systems.

Today's popular operating systems for IBM-compatible microcomputers include DOS, Windows, and OS/2. The Macintosh operating system is called Mac OS. UNIX is available for both IBM-compatible and Macintosh computers. Versions of UNIX and Windows are also available for some minicomputers and mainframes.

You interact directly with your computer's operating system to start programs and manage the data on your disks. You need to know which operating system your computer uses so you can enter the appropriate instructions to accomplish these tasks. How can you tell which operating system your computer uses? Many microcomputer users can recognize an operating system by looking at the first screen that appears when they turn the computer on or by recognizing the operating system prompt. If you study Figure 2-11, you can identify the DOS, Mac OS, Windows 3.1, Windows 95, UNIX, and OS/2 operating systems when you encounter them in the future.

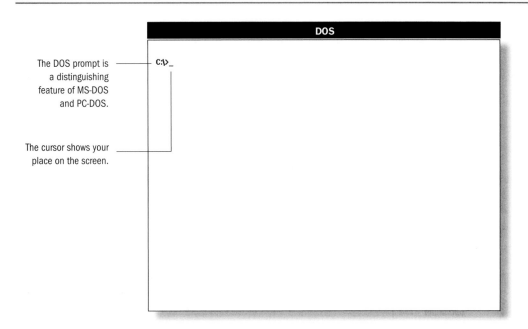

Figure 2-11
Microcomputer
operating systems

The DOS prompt is a distinguishing feature of MS-DOS and PC-DOS.

The cursor shows your place on the screen.

DOS, which stands for Disk Operating System, is marketed under the trade names PC-DOS and MS-DOS. Both PC-DOS and MS-DOS were developed primarily by Microsoft Corporation and are essentially the same operating system. DOS was introduced in 1981 with IBM's first personal computer. Since the first version of DOS appeared, this operating system has gone through six major versions.

Early versions of DOS provided only a command-line user interface, but more recent versions include a menu-driven user interface called the DOS Shell. The DOS Shell provides menu access to the most frequently used operating system features, so you do not have to memorize the DOS commands.

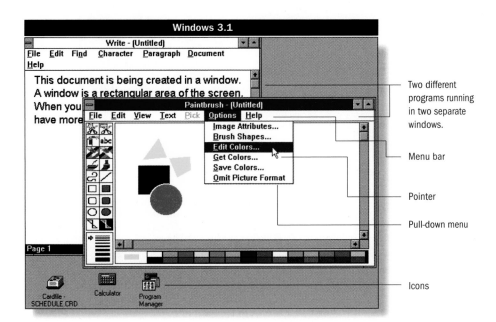

Two different programs running in two separate windows.

Menu bar

Pointer

Pull-down menu

Icons

Microsoft took a more graphical approach to operating systems when it designed Windows.

Microsoft Windows 3.1 provides icons that you can directly manipulate on the screen using a pointing device, and pull-down menus you can use to easily issue a command. The applications you use with Windows 3.1 all have a consistent look, so it is easy to learn how to use new software. Windows 3.1 also lets you run more than one program at a time in separate windows on the screen, and lets you easily transfer data between them. While using Windows 3.1, you can still run DOS software.

Figure 2-11
Microcomputer
operating systems
continued

My Computer icon

Disk drive icon

Windows

The Start button is a unique feature of Windows 95.

Title bar
Menu Bar
Document icon
Task bar

Microsoft introduced a new version of Windows in 1995 that offers better operating efficiency than Windows 3.1. The user interface design for Windows 95 is based on extensive usability testing by both novice and expert computer users.

Windows 95 has a graphical user interface that uses icons to represent objects such as computers, disk drives, and documents.

In addition to programs designed specially for Windows 95, the operating system also runs software designed for Windows 3.1 and DOS. Windows 95 support multitasking, networking, and electronic mail.

Icons

Windows

Menu bar

OS/2 was designed jointly by Microsoft and IBM. Their goal was to create an operating system that would take advantage of newer, more powerful computers, plus offer a graphical user interface while retaining the ability to run DOS

programs. As with other graphical user interfaces, OS/2 allows you to manipulate objects on the screen to perform tasks and select commands from menus. As with Microsoft Windows, OS/2 lets you work with more than one

application at a time and easily transfer data between them. If your computer uses OS/2, you can run most DOS and Windows software, as well as software designed specifically for OS/2.

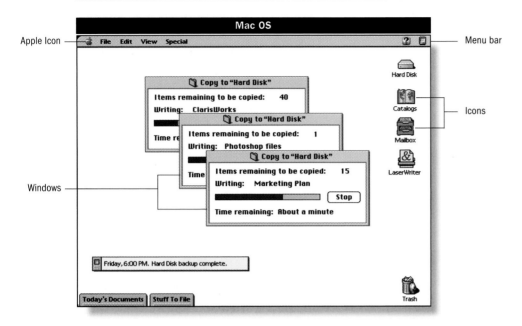

Apple Icon — Menu bar

Icons

Windows

Figure 2-11
Microcomputer
operating systems
continued

In 1984, Apple Computer, Inc. took a revolutionary step when it introduced the Apple Lisa computer with a new operating system based on a graphical user interface featuring pull-down menus, icons, and a mouse. The Lisa computer was not a commercial success, but Apple's next product, the Macintosh computer, was very successful and defined a new direction in operating system user interfaces that became an industry standard.

The **Macintosh Operating System** is usually referred to by its version number. For example, version eight of the operating system is called System 8. The Macintosh operating system has multitasking capability and offers network support.

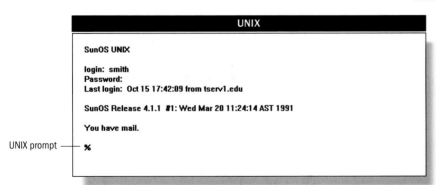

UNIX prompt

UNIX is an operating system that was developed at AT&T's Bell Laboratories in 1969. UNIX was originally designed for minicomputers, but is now also available for microcomputers and mainframes. Many versions of UNIX exist, such as AIX from IBM, XENIX from Microsoft, and ULTRIX from Digital Equipment Corporation, but these other versions are essentially the same operating system adapted for different computers. UNIX features a command-line user interface, but you can purchase add-on software that provides a graphical user interface with direct object manipulation and pull-down menus. UNIX is a multi-user operating system, which means that many users can run programs on a single computer at the same time. UNIX also supports multitasking.

Utilities

Does the operating system include all the system software I need?

Utilities are a subcategory of system software designed to augment the operating system by providing a way for a computer user to control the allocation and use of hardware resources. Some utilities are included with the operating system; they perform tasks such as preparing disks to

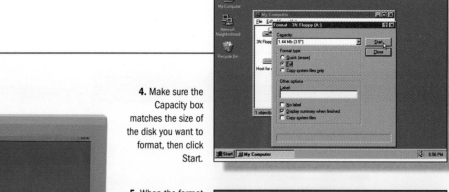

Figure 2-12
Using the Windows
95 format utility

1. Insert the disk
you want to
format and click
the **My Computer**
icon to select it,
then press **Enter**.

4. Make sure the
Capacity box
matches the size of
the disk you want to
format, then click
Start.

5. When the format
is complete, the
computer displays
this window. Click
the **Close** button.

2. Click the
3¹/₂ **Floppy
(A:)** icon in the
My Computer
window.

3. Click **File**
on the menu
bar, then click
Format to open
the Format
window.

hold data, providing information about the files on a disk, and copying data from one disk to another. Additional utilities can be purchased separately from software publishers and vendors. For example, Norton Utilities, published by Symantec, is a very popular collection of utility software. It retrieves data from damaged disks, makes your data more secure by encrypting it, and helps you troubleshoot problems with your computer's disk drives.

One of the important tasks performed by an operating system utility is formatting a disk. Each disk must be formatted before you can store data on it. Think of formatting as creating the electronic equivalent of storage shelves. Before you can put things on the shelves, you must assemble the shelves. In a similar way, before you can store data on a disk, you must make sure the disk is formatted.

You can buy preformatted disks, but you still might need a disk format utility if you use a disk that has not been preformatted or a disk that was formatted previously for a different type of computer. To run a format utility, you either type the name of the utility or select the format option from a menu. Figure 2-12 shows how to use the format utility for Windows 95.

Device Drivers

How do I use a device driver?

In Chapter 1, you learned that when you purchase a new peripheral device, such as a CD-ROM drive or a mouse, you often need to install software that tells your computer how to use the device. The system software that helps the computer control a peripheral device is called a **device driver**.

When you purchase a new peripheral device, its installation instructions usually tell you how to install both the device and the necessary device drivers. The way you "use" a device driver is to install it according to the instructions. Once the device driver is installed correctly, the computer uses it to communicate with the device.

Computer Programming Languages

Is a computer programming language part of the system software included with a basic computer system?

As you know, a computer program is a series of instructions that the computer follows to perform a task. However, the list of instructions written by a human programmer is quite different from the instructions that the computer actually follows. The programmer's instructions must be translated into electrical signals that the computer can manipulate and process.

A **computer programming language** allows a programmer to write programs using English-like instructions, such as those you saw in Figure 2-1. The programming language then translates the instructions created by a programmer into a format the computer can interpret and directly process.

As mentioned earlier in this chapter, most computer users do not need to write programs. Therefore, most computers do not include a computer programming language. If you want to write programs, you must purchase programming language software. Today some of the most popular programming languages are BASIC, Visual Basic, C, C++, COBOL, Ada, and FORTRAN.

If you have followed the instructions for installing a new device and its device driver, but the device does not work, check with the manufacturer. You might need an updated version of the device driver.

Quick Check

1. If you want to run more than one program at a time, you must use an operating system with _____ capability.

2. _____ is a multiuser operating system.

3. The DOS, Windows, Mac OS, and OS/2 operating systems are typically used on _____ computer systems.

4. _____ software helps the computer accomplish such tasks as preparing a disk for data, providing information about the files on a disk, copying data from one disk to another, and retrieving data from damaged disks.

5. You install a(n) _____ to tell the computer how to use a new peripheral device.

6. A(n) _____ translates a programmer's instructions into instructions the computer can interpret and directly process.

2.3 Application Software

Now let's return to the idea presented at the beginning of this chapter—that the computer is a multipurpose machine. Although system software handles internal computer functions and helps the computer use peripheral devices, it doesn't transform the computer into the different kinds of machines you need to write reports, "crunch" numbers, learn how to type, or draw pictures. It is application software that enables the computer to become a multipurpose machine and to perform many different tasks.

Software categorized as **application software** helps you accomplish a specific task using the computer. Application software helps you produce documents, perform calculations, manage financial resources, create graphics, compose music, play games, maintain files of information, and so on. Application software packages are sometimes referred to simply as **applications**.

The vast amount of application software makes classifying it convenient. Keep in mind, though, that the categories are neither formal nor standard. You might see word processing software categorized as business software in one software catalog, but as productivity software in another.

One way to classify application software is to use four categories: productivity, business, education and reference, and entertainment. Figure 2-13 shows you an expanded view of the application software branch of the software hierarchy chart you saw in Figure 2-7.

Figure 2-13
Application
software

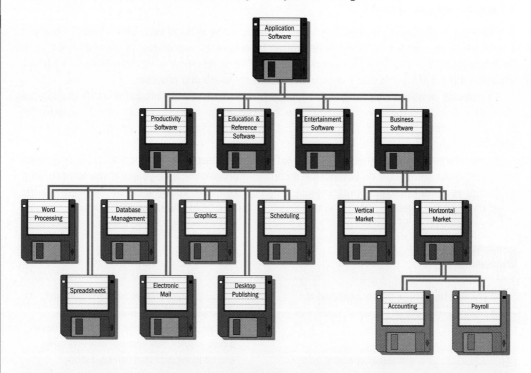

Productivity Software

What productivity software is right for me?

As you might expect from its name, **productivity software** helps you work more effectively. The most popular types of productivity software are word processing, spreadsheet, and database management. We'll look at these first, then take a look at some additional types of productivity software. As you read the descriptions, consider which types would be most useful for you.

Word processing software helps you produce documents such as reports, letters, papers, and manuscripts. Word processing is the most popular type of application software. Individuals use word processing software for correspondence, students use it to write reports and papers, writers use it for novels, reporters use it to compose news stories, and scientists use it to write research reports.

Lab

Word Processing

Word processing software gives you the ability to create, spell check, edit, and format your document on the screen before you commit it to paper. Therefore, when you begin typing the text of a document, you can let your ideas flow without worrying about making typing errors. After you have entered your first draft, word processing software gives you the flexibility to improve the quality of your document by changing the wording or rearranging topics. When you are satisfied with the content of your document, you can use formatting and page layout features of your word processing software to create a professional-looking printout.

Word processing software also gives you the ability to easily reuse documents. For example, if you have a resume that you send out periodically, it is easy to retrieve it, make necessary updates, and print it. In a law office, many standard documents such as wills, rental agreements, and premarital agreements are created using word processing software. These documents can be modified and reused for many clients.

Most word processing software has **mail merge**—the capability to merge a list of names and addresses with a form letter, then print a personalized version of the letter. Corporations use mail merge on a large scale to produce mass mailings about their services, new products, and latest sweepstakes. On a smaller scale, individuals can use mail merge to send out job applications, holiday letters, announcements, and invitations. Figure 2-14 on pages 60 and 61 explains how word processing software helps you write, edit, format, and print documents.

Spreadsheet software helps you work with numbers. The software displays a grid of rows and columns on the screen. You enter numbers and mathematical formulas in the grid and the computer automatically calculates the result. To visualize how this works, think about a simple hand held calculator. Suppose you need to add five numbers: 10234, 77654, 23411, 765487, and 341112. You enter the first number, press the + key, enter the second number, and so on. But when the calculation is complete, how do you know if you entered all the numbers correctly? You can't go back and check. Now, suppose the numbers you entered were somehow displayed in a column on a computer screen and the computer automatically added up the column and displayed the result. By looking at the numbers, you could be sure they were entered correctly. You could even change a number if you had made a mistake when you entered it.

Lab

Spreadsheets

Let's look at another example. Suppose you are buying a car and you have narrowed the choice to two cars. One car is less expensive, but the interest rate is higher. The other car is more expensive, but the interest rate is lower. Which car is the better deal? With a hand-held calculator, you have to do the entire calculation twice—once for each car. But, if you could type the formula for the calculation so it would appear on a computer screen, you could first plug in the numbers for one car. After you see the result, you could plug in the numbers for the second car.

When you use your spreadsheet software you can set up your own formulas for calculation or you can use built-in formulas, called functions, similar to the square root and log functions built into a hand-held calculator. You can use a spreadsheet function just by plugging in numbers—you don't have to know the details of the formula.

Figure 2-14
Word processing
software

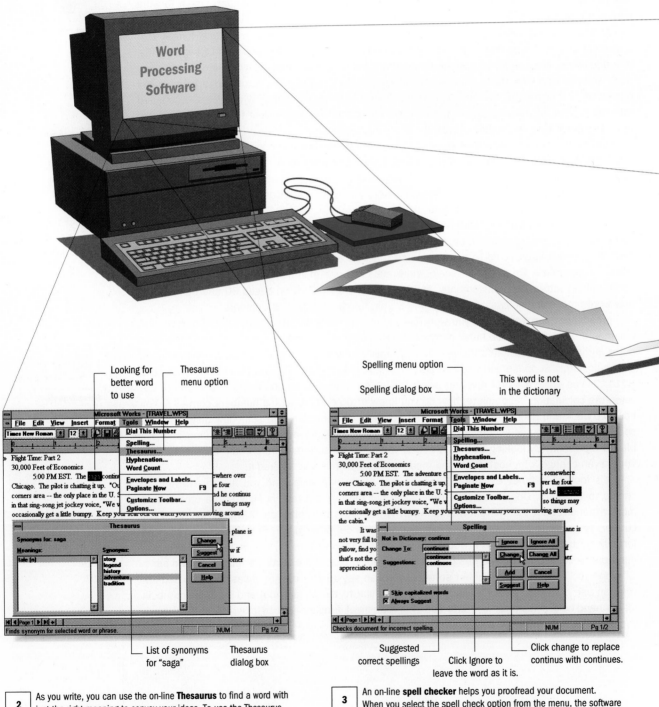

Looking for better word to use

Thesaurus menu option

Spelling menu option

Spelling dialog box

This word is not in the dictionary

List of synonyms for "saga"

Thesaurus dialog box

Suggested correct spellings

Click Ignore to leave the word as it is.

Click change to replace continus with continues.

2 As you write, you can use the on-line **Thesaurus** to find a word with just the right meaning to convey your ideas. To use the Thesaurus, click the word you want to change and then select the Thesaurus options from the menu. You can then select the word you want from a list of synonyms.

3 An on-line **spell checker** helps you proofread your document. When you select the spell check option from the menu, the software compares each word in your document to the words in the software's dictionary. Words that can't be found in the dictionary are highlighted so you can change them to the correct spelling. Some words, such as proper names, are not in the dictionary. When the spell checker highlights one of these words in your document, you can skip the word.

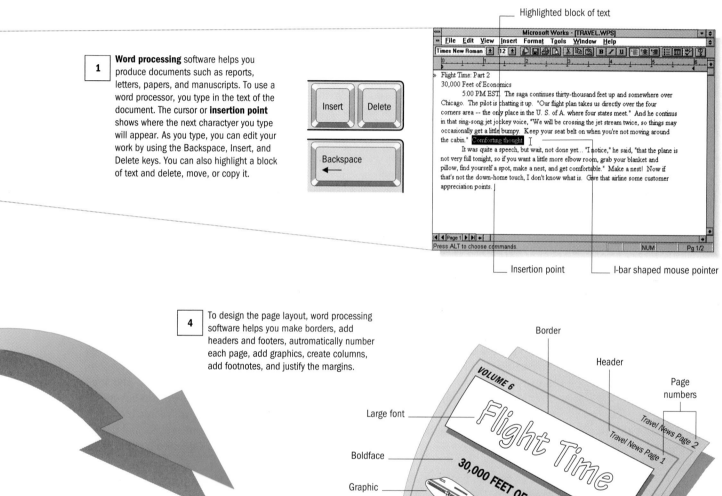

Highlighted block of text

1 **Word processing** software helps you produce documents such as reports, letters, papers, and manuscripts. To use a word processor, you type in the text of the document. The cursor or **insertion point** shows where the next charactyer you type will appear. As you type, you can edit your work by using the Backspace, Insert, and Delete keys. You can also highlight a block of text and delete, move, or copy it.

Insert   Delete

Backspace

Insertion point   I-bar shaped mouse pointer

4 To design the page layout, word processing software helps you make borders, add headers and footers, autromatically number each page, add graphics, create columns, add footnotes, and justify the margins.

Border

Header

Page numbers

Large font

Boldface

Graphic

5 Word processing software has many formatting features to help you design the appearance of your printed document. You can use formatting features to adjust the line spacing, boldface text, italicize text, center text, change the font, and change the font size.

Columns

Justified margins

Footnote

Lab

Databases

Figure 2-15 on pages 64 and 65 explains more about spreadsheet software.

Spreadsheet software is frequently used by financial analysts to examine investment opportunities, by managers to create budgets, by entrepreneurs to create business plans, and even by educators to keep track of student grades. Individuals use spreadsheet software to track household budgets, calculate retirement investments, calculate loan payments, and compare investment opportunities.

Database management software helps you store, find, update, organize, and report information. Usually, this information is stored as **records** similar to the file cards or Rolodex cards you might use to store names and addresses. When information is in a computerized database, it is easy to search through it—even in a database containing thousands of records. To find information in a database, you enter a **query** that tells the computer exactly what you want to find. For example, when you use a library card catalog database, you can enter a query to find all the books written by Mark Twain.

You can also easily update the information in a record. For example, a computerized library card catalog keeps track of which books are checked out, by placing "out" in the Status field. When the book Tom Sawyer is checked out, its status field is updated to "out."

One of the most useful features of database management software is its ability to organize information by sorting it alphabetically or numerically. For example, if you have a database of all the names and birth dates of your friends, you can enter a query to find all your friends who have birthdays this month.

You can easily update the information in a record. For example, Latisha Smith gets married and changes her last name to Billings. When you give your database management software a command such as "update Latisha for Lastname—Billings" the software searches for Latisha's record, then changes her last name to Billings.

One of the most useful features of database management software is its ability to organize information by sorting it alphabetically or numerically. For example, suppose your insurance company requires an inventory of your household possessions, their date of purchase, and their value. You find it easy to make a list of the items one room at a time. However, your insurance company requires an *alphabetized* list of items in the entire house. After you enter the items room by room, you can have the database management software quickly alphabetize your list for the insurance company. You could even create a list of your possessions organized by their value or date of purchase.

Database management software also has sophisticated reporting features that help you produce professional-looking printouts. Usually reports are organized in a column or table format. You can print a report containing all the records in the database or just selected records. Most database management software will automatically calculate totals for your reports, such as the entire value of your household inventory.

Database management software helps hospitals and doctors keep track of patient records. The IRS uses database management software to keep track of tax payments. The phone company keeps track of names, addresses, and phone numbers using database software. Record clubs and book clubs keep track of members and sales using database software. Figure 2-16 on pages 66 and 67 explains more about using database management software to store, find, update, organize, and report information.

Although word processing, spreadsheet, and database management software are the most popular productivity software, you might find that other types of productivity software are also useful—electronic mail, desktop publishing, graphics, and scheduling.

Electronic mail software provides you with a computerized mailbox that collects documents or "mail" you receive electronically from other computer users. You can send electronic mail messages, read your electronic mail on your computer screen, save or throw away your electronic mail after you read it, and compose electronic replies to the mail you receive.

Graphics software helps you draw pictures, 3-D images, and animations. If you have limited artistic ability, you can use graphics software to retrieve predrawn images called **clip art**, which you can use as-is or modify. **Presentation graphics software** helps you present business information using screen-based slide shows of bulleted lists, graphs, and charts.

Desktop publishing software provides you with computerized tools for page layout and design that combine text and graphics. Although many desktop publishing features are available in today's sophisticated word processing software, desktop publishing software provides additional features to help you produce professional, quality output for newspapers, newsletters, and brochures.

Scheduling software helps you keep track of appointments, due dates, and special dates such as birthdays and holidays. You can use scheduling software to print a daily, weekly, or monthly calendar.

A software publisher sometimes combines several productivity software applications into a single package called **integrated software**. Typically, integrated software includes word processing, spreadsheet, database, and presentation graphics applications. Electronic mail is also included in some integrated software. The applications in an integrated software package are sometimes referred to as **modules**. Integrated software is often called a **suite**, **office**, or **works**. Some popular integrated software packages include Microsoft Works, Claris Works, Lotus Smart-Suite, Novell Perfect Office, and Microsoft Office.

Integrated software makes it easy to cut and paste data between applications. For example, you can easily incorporate budget figures from a spreadsheet module into a document you are writing using a word processing module. Another handy feature of integrated software is that the modules have a consistent user interface, so it is more like using one large application than using several smaller ones.

Business Software

What's the difference between horizontal-market and vertical-market software?

A second major category of application software, called **business software**, helps organizations efficiently accomplish routine tasks. Software in the business category is different from productivity software because its emphasis is on organization-wide tasks such as accounting, personnel management, and inventory control. Often, business software is divided into two categories: horizontal-market software and vertical-market software.

A horizontal market is a group of different types of businesses that, despite their differences, have some of the same software needs. **Horizontal-market software** refers to generic software packages that can be used by many different kinds of businesses. Accounting and payroll applications are good examples of horizontal-market software. Every business needs to maintain a set of books to track income and expenses and generate financial reports. Accounting software is designed to computerize the bookkeeping and financial reporting tasks typically required in most businesses. Almost every business has employees and needs to maintain payroll records. Payroll software keeps track of employee hours and produces the reports required by the government for income tax reporting.

A vertical market is a group of similar businesses—travel agencies, for example—that need specialized software. **Vertical-market software** is designed for specialized tasks in a specific market or business. Tasks in the construction industry include estimating the cost of labor and materials for a new building and providing the customer with a bid or estimate of the price for the finished building. Vertical-market software, such as estimating software designed specifically for construction businesses, can automate the task of gathering labor and materials costs and perform the calculations needed to arrive at an estimate. Other examples of vertical market software include the software that handles billing and insurance for medical practices and software that tracks the amount of time attorneys spend on each case.

Some productivity software, such as word processing applications, can also be categorized as horizontal-market software because they can be used in virtually any business.

Figure 2-15
Spreadsheet
software

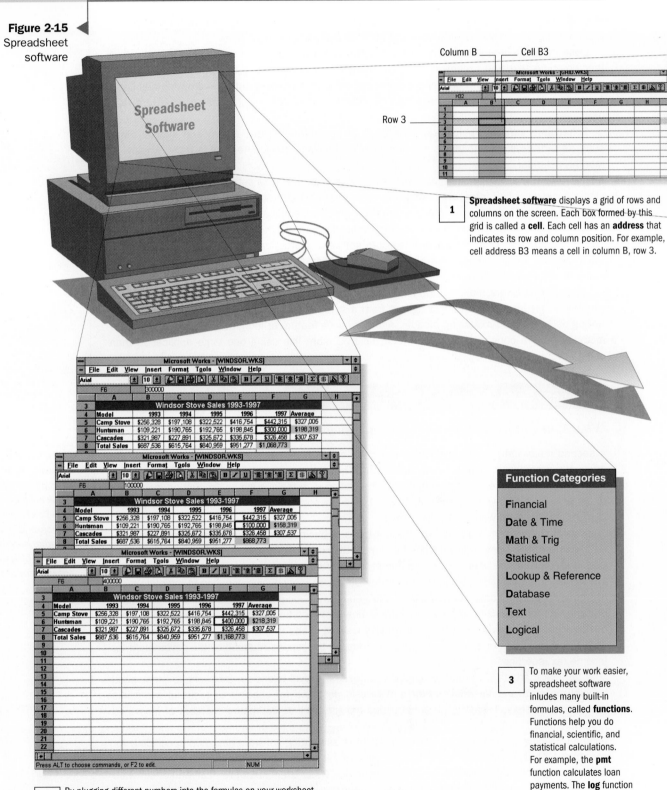

Column B — Cell B3

Row 3

1 Spreadsheet software displays a grid of rows and columns on the screen. Each box formed by this grid is called a **cell**. Each cell has an **address** that indicates its row and column position. For example, cell address B3 means a cell in column B, row 3.

Function Categories

Financial

Date & Time

Math & Trig

Statistical

Lookup & Reference

Database

Text

Logical

3 To make your work easier, spreadsheet software inludes many built-in formulas, called **functions**. Functions help you do financial, scientific, and statistical calculations. For example, the **pmt** function calculates loan payments. The **log** function calculates logarithms. The **stdev** function calculates standard deviations.

4 By plugging different numbers into the formulas on your worksheet, you can examine the outcome of different **"what if" scenarios**, such as "What if 1997 sales of the Huntsman stoves are $300,000?" or "What if they are $100,000 or $400,000?" A spreadsheet automatically calculates the results for each scenario, so you don't have to do the calculations over and over again by hand.

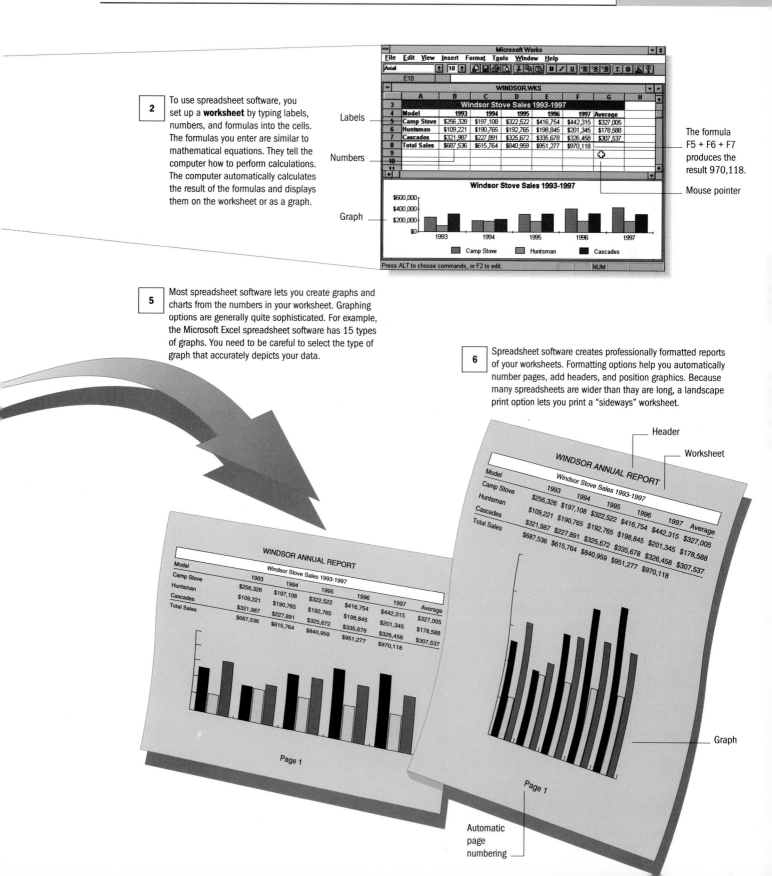

2 To use spreadsheet software, you set up a **worksheet** by typing labels, numbers, and formulas into the cells. The formulas you enter are similar to mathematical equations. They tell the computer how to perform calculations. The computer automatically calculates the result of the formulas and displays them on the worksheet or as a graph.

Labels

Numbers

Graph

The formula F5 + F6 + F7 produces the result 970,118.

Mouse pointer

5 Most spreadsheet software lets you create graphs and charts from the numbers in your worksheet. Graphing options are generally quite sophisticated. For example, the Microsoft Excel spreadsheet software has 15 types of graphs. You need to be careful to select the type of graph that accurately depicts your data.

6 Spreadsheet software creates professionally formatted reports of your worksheets. Formatting options help you automatically number pages, add headers, and position graphics. Because many spreadsheets are wider than thay are long, a landscape print option lets you print a "sideways" worksheet.

Header

Worksheet

Graph

Automatic page numbering

Figure 2-16
Database
management
software

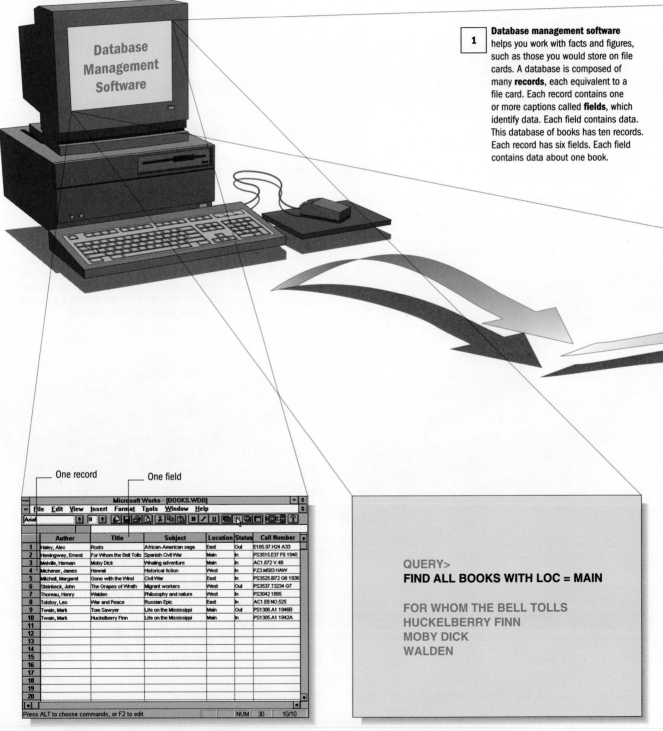

1 **Database management software**
helps you work with facts and figures,
such as those you would store on file
cards. A database is composed of
many **records**, each equivalent to a
file card. Each record contains one
or more captions called **fields**, which
identify data. Each field contains data.
This database of books has ten records.
Each record has six fields. Each field
contains data about one book.

One record — One field

Microsoft Works - [BOOKS.WDB]
File Edit View Insert Format Tools Window Help

Arial

	Author	Title	Subject	Location	Status	Call Number
1	Haley, Alex	Roots	African-American saga	East	Out	E185.97.H24 A33
2	Hemingway, Ernest	For Whom the Bell Tolls	Spanish Civil War	Main	In	PS3515.E37 F6 1940
3	Melville, Herman	Moby Dick	Whaling adventure	Main	In	AC1.672 V.48
4	Michener, James	Hawaii	Historical fiction	West	In	PZ3.M583 HAW
5	Mitchell, Margaret	Gone with the Wind	Civil War	East	In	PS3525.I972 G6 1936
6	Steinbeck, John	The Grapes of Wrath	Migrant workers	West	Out	PS3537.T3234 G7
7	Thoreau, Henry	Walden	Philosophy and nature	West	In	PS3042 1895
8	Tolstoy, Leo	War and Peace	Russian Epic	East	In	AC1.E8 NO.525
9	Twain, Mark	Tom Sawyer	Life on the Mississippi	Main	Out	PS1306.A1 1946B
10	Twain, Mark	Huckelberry Finn	Life on the Mississippi	Main	In	PS1305.A1 1942A
11						
12						
13						
14						
15						
16						
17						
18						
19						
20						

Press ALT to choose commands, or F2 to edit.   NUM   30   10/10

QUERY>
FIND ALL BOOKS WITH LOC = MAIN

FOR WHOM THE BELL TOLLS
HUCKELBERRY FINN
MOBY DICK
WALDEN

3 Another way to visualize a database is as a list or table. Each
row of the table is a record. Each column of the table is a field.

4 You can make a **query** to find one or more records. For example,
a query to "find all the books where Location = Main" produces
four titles.

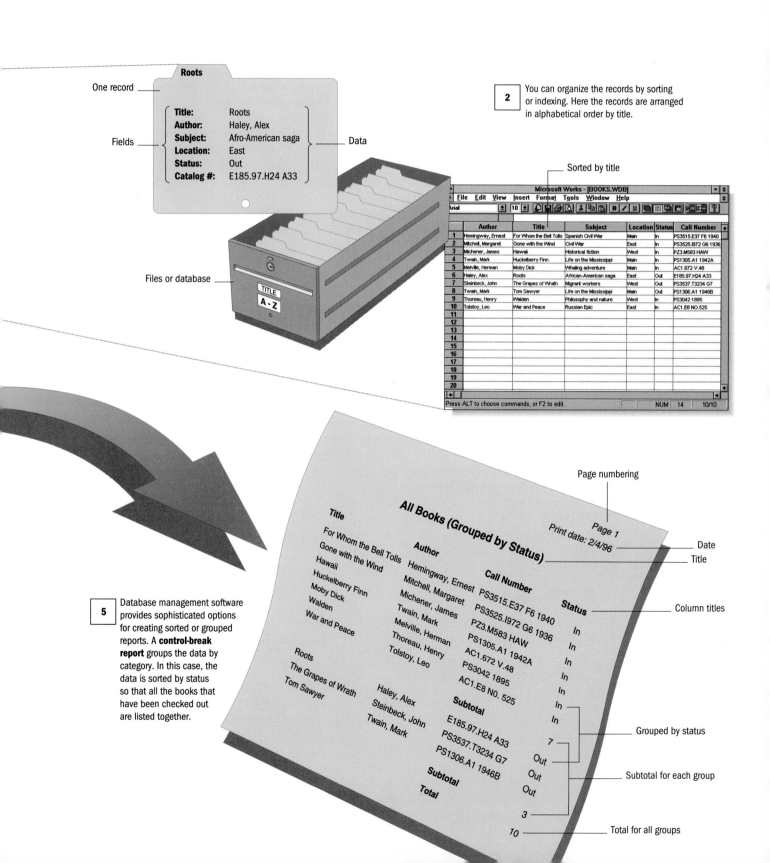

One record

Roots

Title:	Roots
Author:	Haley, Alex
Subject:	Afro-American saga
Location:	East
Status:	Out
Catalog #:	E185.97.H24 A33

Fields

Data

Files or database

TITLE
A - Z

2 You can organize the records by sorting or indexing. Here the records are arranged in alphabetical order by title.

Sorted by title

Microsoft Works - [BOOKS.WDB]

File Edit View Insert Format Tools Window Help

Arial 10

	Author	Title	Subject	Location	Status	Call Number
1	Hemingway, Ernest	For Whom the Bell Tolls	Spanish Civil War	Main	In	PS3515.E37 F6 1940
2	Mitchell, Margaret	Gone with the Wind	Civil War	East	In	PS3525.I972 G6 1936
3	Michener, James	Hawaii	Historical fiction	West	In	PZ3.M583 HAW
4	Twain, Mark	Huckelberry Finn	Life on the Mississippi	Main	In	PS1305.A1 1942A
5	Melville, Herman	Moby Dick	Whaling adventure	Main	In	AC1.672 V.48
6	Haley, Alex	Roots	African-American saga	East	Out	E185.97.H24 A33
7	Steinbeck, John	The Grapes of Wrath	Migrant workers	West	Out	PS3537.T3234 G7
8	Twain, Mark	Tom Sawyer	Life on the Mississippi	Main	Out	PS1306.A1 1946B
9	Thoreau, Henry	Walden	Philosophy and nature	West	In	PS3042 1895
10	Tolstoy, Leo	War and Peace	Russian Epic	East	In	AC1.E8 NO.525
11						
12						
13						
14						
15						
16						
17						
18						
19						
20						

Press ALT to choose commands, or F2 to edit.   NUM   14   10/10

Page numbering

All Books (Grouped by Status)

Print date: 2/4/96   Page 1

Date
Title

Title	Author	Call Number	Status
For Whom the Bell Tolls	Hemingway, Ernest	PS3515.E37 F6 1940	In
Gone with the Wind	Mitchell, Margaret	PS3525.I972 G6 1936	In
Hawaii	Michener, James	PZ3.M583 HAW	In
Huckelberry Finn	Twain, Mark	PS1305.A1 1942A	In
Moby Dick	Melville, Herman	AC1.672 V.48	In
Walden	Thoreau, Henry	PS3042 1895	In
War and Peace	Tolstoy, Leo	AC1.E8 NO. 525	In
		Subtotal	7
Roots	Haley, Alex	E185.97.H24 A33	Out
The Grapes of Wrath	Steinbeck, John	PS3537.T3234 G7	Out
Tom Sawyer	Twain, Mark	PS1306.A1 1946B	Out
		Subtotal	3
		Total	10

Column titles

Grouped by status

Subtotal for each group

Total for all groups

5 Database management software provides sophisticated options for creating sorted or grouped reports. A **control-break report** groups the data by category. In this case, the data is sorted by status so that all the books that have been checked out are listed together.

Figure 2-17
Software toys

Screen saver software such as *After Dark* puts a moving image on the screen when you are not using your computer. On older monitors, screen savers prevented an image from "burning" into the screen if it was left on too long. Newer monitors are not so susceptible to burned images, but many users still have fun watching screen saver images such as these flying toasters.

If you are using the New Perspectives Labs that accompany this text book, you will have a first-hand experience with computer-aided instruction.

Entertainment Software

Are computers changing the way we spend our spare time?

Entertainment software included games and software designed for entertainment. Using entertainment software, you can fly a simulated jet, play 18 holes of golf, solve a Sherlock Holmes mystery, battle monsters, or explore new worlds. Although games are plentiful, not all entertainment software is in game format. With "software toys" there is no competition, no score, no winner, no loser. Software toys have a certain appeal to computer users who are looking for low-stress diversions. One software toy is a computerized fish tank application that lets you catch, breed, and watch a collection of brilliantly realistic tropical fish inside the glass "tank" of your computer monitor. Another is "Paper Planes," software that shows you how to construct several types of paper airplanes. Figure 2-17 shows some examples of software toys.

In 1993, entertainment software generated more than $500 million in sales. Considering that about 37% of U.S. households have one or more personal computers, you might expect to see significant changes in the pattern of leisure-time activity. The average person, however, spends about 2 hours a week using entertainment software, but spends about 17 hours watching television. Clearly, the computer industry has some work to do to make inroads on television's appeal.

Education and Reference Software

Can I use educational and reference software to improve my grades?

Education and reference software is designed to help you learn more about a particular topic. One subcategory of education software is called **CAI** or **tutorial software**. CAI stands for "computer-aided instruction." CAI software can help you learn how to type, fix your car, use your word processor, speak French, or prepare for the GMAT exam.

Educational simulations let you work with a computerized model of something in the real world, manipulate it, and see what happens. Some students use computerized simulations in introductory chemistry classes so they can experiment with chemical reactions without using real, and sometimes dangerous, chemicals.

Reference software, such as an electronic encyclopedia, helps you look up facts on any topic. Other reference software includes collections of classic literary works, electronic dictionaries, the phone directories for every city in the United States, a trip planner with maps of the entire United States, and medical reference guides.

Quick Check

1. The three most popular types of productivity software are _____, _____, and _____.

2. When several productivity software modules are sold as a package, it is referred to _____.

3. Personnel management software designed to be used in businesses as varied as hospitals, schools, and restaurants would be considered _____ market software.

4. Simulators and tutorials would be classified as _____ software.

5. Although word processing software helps you produce documents, _____ software is often used to produce professional-looking brochures and newsletters.

Multimedia

In the 1960s, a group of mop-haired musicians called the Beatles burst onto the music scene. Millions of screaming fans sent "I Want to Hold Your Hand" rocketing to the top of the charts. The Beatles formed their own record company called Apple Corps, Ltd.

In 1976, two young Californians, Steve Jobs and Steve Wozniak, started a computer company in a garage. Before the decade was out, their company had one of the most successful public stock offerings in history. Both Wozniak and Jobs became instant millionaires. Unfortunately, they named their company Apple Computer, Inc. According to the lawyers who represented Apple Corps, Ltd., that was a problem. The computer makers were charged with copyright infringement for using the Apple name.

In 1981, after lengthy negotiations, Apple Corps agreed to let Wozniak and Jobs use the Apple name. In return, Wozniak and Jobs agreed not to manufacture musical products. At the time, this arrangement seemed perfectly reasonable because computer technology and record companies had very little in common.

Today, however, the distinction between computer technology and record companies is not so clear. Consumer electronic inventions—radio, telephone, photography, sound recording, television, video recording, and computers—are merging and creating a new technology called multimedia.

Multimedia's Roots

Is multimedia the same as CD-ROM?

The term "multimedia" isn't really anything new—it refers to the integrated use of multiple media, such as slides, videotapes, audiotapes, records, CD-ROMs, and photos. School children sometimes still watch multimedia presentations that synchronize a tape-recorded sound track with a series of slides. As you can imagine, coordinating such a multimedia presentation is not easy. The teacher typically has difficulty getting the slides to synchronize with the sound track. If one slide is out of order or upside down, the teacher has to stop the tape, fix the slide, then restart the tape. The technology is cumbersome, and it is virtually impossible to go back to review segments of the presentation that students did not understand.

Today, the computer is replacing or controlling many of the technologies and media previously used for multimedia presentations. Advances in computer technology have made it possible to combine text, photo images, speech, music, animated sequences, and video into a single interactive computer presentation. A new definition of multimedia has emerged from this blend of technology. Today, **multimedia** is defined as an integrated collection of computer-based media including text, graphics, sound, animation, photo images, and video.

Envision a multimedia encyclopedia, for example. Like a traditional encyclopedia, it contains articles and pictures on a wide range of topics. But a multimedia encyclopedia has more. Suppose you're writing a research paper that explains the reasons for the European conflict in the country formerly known as Yugoslavia. You can pull up an article about Yugoslavia on your screen, listen to the Yugoslav national anthem, and view a map of eastern Europe. As you read the article, you can instantly access a cross-reference to an article about the Bosnia-Herzegovina conflict. A narrated video segment gives you some background on the causes of the conflict. A multimedia encyclopedia provides you with a rich selection of text, graphics, sound, animation, and video, as shown in Figure 2-18 on the next page.

Most multimedia applications are shipped on a CD-ROM because the graphics, sound, and video require large amounts of storage space. However, not everything shipped on CD-ROM is multimedia. Many software publishers distribute large data files and non-multimedia software on CD-ROM because one CD-ROM is more convenient and more cost-effective than 20 or 30 floppy disks. For example, one software company sells a CD-ROM that contains more than 200 classic works of literature—but only the text of the classics, not any graphics or sound. In this case, the CD-ROM contains data, not a multimedia application.

Figure 2-18
Compton's
multimedia
encyclopedia

To initially find information, you can use the Menu,
Contents list, Idea Search, Info Plot, or Topic Tree.

You control the
video clip of
the Bosnia-
Herzegovina
conflict using
on-screen
controls
modeled
after a VCR.

Topics related
to the main
article are listed
here. You jump
to a related
topic by clicking
here.

This status bar
tells you how to
use the
controls.

Click here
to see a map
of Yugoslavia.

Click here
to listen to
the Yugoslav
national
anthem.

Articles
explain
topics.

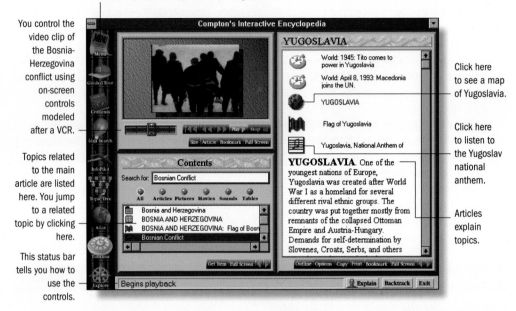

*There are many more
multimedia applica-
tions than we can
describe in this
chapter. Project 7 at
the end of this chap-
ter helps you find out
what's available,
what's popular,
and what's useful
in multimedia.*

Multimedia Applications

Are multimedia applications better than plain old software?

Multimedia technology adds pizzazz to all types of computer applications: productivity, business, entertainment, and education and reference. You can use a multimedia scheduler to remind you of appointments and due dates. Instead of flashing a message on your screen, the multimedia scheduler reminds you of appointments by displaying a video image of a "personal assistant." "Excuse me," your personal assistant might say, "but I believe you have an appointment in five minutes."

You can use a multimedia presentation application to create a motivational business presentation that includes a short video message from the company president, pictures of a new product line, graphs of projected sales, sound effects of cheering crowds, and text that lists the features and benefits of the new products.

You can use multimedia entertainment applications to have an animated adventure in the far reaches of space. You control the animated instrument panel of your spacecraft from your computer keyboard, discuss tactics with video images of your crew members, and hear the sounds of your engines, instrument warnings, and weapons.

You can use multimedia computer-aided instruction to learn a foreign language. You can watch and listen to a short foreign-language video segment and view a synchronized translation. Then you can practice your pronunciation by speaking into a microphone so the computer can compare your pronunciation with a native speaker's.

Many "plain old" software applications can be improved by adding multimedia features. Multimedia technology also opens possibilities for new and creative applications. However, all multimedia products do not necessarily make effective use of multimedia technology. Multimedia product designers have not always considered which technologies would actually enhance their product.

Some multimedia products can be faulted for an incomplete use of multimedia technology. For example, one multimedia product was criticized for including "photos with brief titles but no explanatory text...sketchy text, discontinuity, and almost total lack of sound." On the other hand, overuse of multimedia elements can sometimes detract from the contents. A reviewer pans one multimedia encyclopedia as "big on photos and animations, small on info." So, multimedia has the *potential* to improve an application, if the multimedia product is well designed.

Hypertext and Hypermedia

How do hypertext and hypermedia help me use multimedia applications?

Hypertext, a key element of many multimedia products, has been used effectively in non-multimedia products as well. Because you are likely to use hypertext with many computer applications, it is useful to learn what it's all about. The term **hypertext** was coined by Ted Nelson in 1965 to describe the idea of documents that could be linked to each other. Linked documents make it possible for a reader to jump from a passage in one document to a related passage in another document. Figure 2-19 will help you visualize a hypertext.

Lab

Computer History Hypermedia

▶ **Figure 2-19**
A hypertext of linked documents

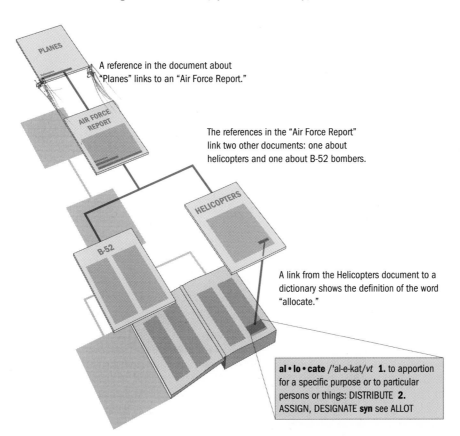

A reference in the document about "Planes" links to an "Air Force Report."

The references in the "Air Force Report" link two other documents: one about helicopters and one about B-52 bombers.

A link from the Helicopters document to a dictionary shows the definition of the word "allocate."

al•lo•cate /'al-e-kat/vt **1.** to apportion for a specific purpose or to particular persons or things: DISTRIBUTE **2.** ASSIGN, DESIGNATE **syn** see ALLOT

Nelson wanted to create a giant hypertext that encompassed virtually every document on library shelves. His goal was not achievable with the technology of the sixties, and little was heard about hypertext for about 20 years. Then in 1987 Apple shipped a software product called Hypercard. It provided users a way to create the electronic equivalent of a stack of note cards. Each card could contain text, graphical images, or sounds; the cards could be linked to each other. Users jumped from one card to another by clicking buttons or specially marked *hot spots* in the text or graphics. The Hypercard-style implementation of hypertext developed over the next 10 years and became an important element of on-line Help, computer-based learning systems, and multimedia applications.

To try hypermedia, and follow links between text, graphics, and sounds, use the Computer History Hypermedia Lab.

The links in today's applications often involve graphics, sound, and video, as well as text. This type of multimedia hypertext is referred to as **hypermedia**. Hypertext and hypermedia are important computer-based tools because they help you easily follow a path that makes sense to you through a large selection of text, graphical, audio, and video information. Figure 2-20 shows you how to use hypermedia links to view film clips, compare critical reviews, and listen to sections of dialog with Microsoft's Cinemania application.

Figure 2-20 ◀
Using hypermedia

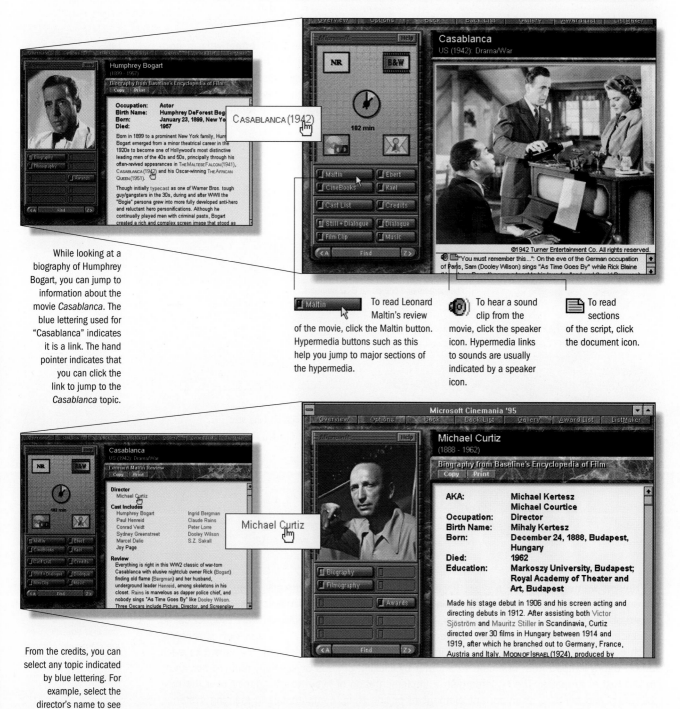

While looking at a biography of Humphrey Bogart, you can jump to information about the movie *Casablanca*. The blue lettering used for "Casablanca" indicates it is a link. The hand pointer indicates that you can click the link to jump to the *Casablanca* topic.

To read Leonard Maltin's review of the movie, click the Maltin button. Hypermedia buttons such as this help you jump to major sections of the hypermedia.

To hear a sound clip from the movie, click the speaker icon. Hypermedia links to sounds are usually indicated by a speaker icon.

To read sections of the script, click the document icon.

From the credits, you can select any topic indicated by blue lettering. For example, select the director's name to see his biography.

Multimedia Equipment

How do I know if my computer can use multimedia applications?

Today's multimedia applications require a computer system that can display graphic images, run video clips, and play sounds. Because most multimedia applications are shipped on a CD-ROM disk, your computer needs to have a CD-ROM drive. Your computer system must be able to quickly manipulate and transfer large amounts of data so you need a fast computer with a lot of memory. To display realistic graphical and video images, your computer system must have a high-resolution monitor capable of displaying a wide range of colors. To play realistic sounds, your computer needs a sound card and speakers. Figure 2-21 shows a computer well equipped for multimedia.

Just about every computer has a built-in internal speaker, but its sound capabilities are very primitive. Even though your computer can "beep" through the internal speaker, you need an additional sound card for multimedia applications.

A fast processor and lots of memory can speedup searches and video displays.

A high-resolution color monitor displays graphics, animations, and videos.

Figure 2-21
A multimedia PC

Earphones can be used as an alternative to speakers.

Speakers are attached to a sound card for audio playback.

A CD-ROM drive plays the multimedia software.

CD-ROMs contain multimedia software.

Most computer companies produce one or more computer models equipped for multimedia applications. If you are in the market for a new computer, it makes sense to get one equipped for multimedia because of the many excellent multimedia applications available today. If you already have a computer, but it is not equipped for multimedia, you can add multimedia capabilities by purchasing a multimedia kit that contains a CD-ROM drive and sound card. A multimedia kit, like the one shown in Figure 2-22, is designed for non-technical users and usually can be installed in a few hours. Instead of using a multimedia kit, you can purchase a CD-ROM drive and sound card individually, but installing these individual components usually requires more technical expertise.

Figure 2-22
A multimedia kit

Speakers

Sound card

Disk containing
device drivers

CD-ROM drive

In Chapter 5 you will learn technical terminology that will let you compare the capability of computer systems, including those equipped for multimedia.

The Multimedia PC Marketing Council publishes what is known as the MPC standard, which specifies the computer equipment you need to successfully use multimedia applications on your computer system. You will sometimes see the MPC logo on the box of multimedia applications, along with a description of the computer hardware required. The MPC logo is shown in Figure 2-23.

Figure 2-23
MPC Logo

Multimedia applications are available for both the Macintosh and IBM-compatible platforms. When you purchase a multimedia CD-ROM, read the package to make sure it will work with your computer. You might be surprised that Apple Computers, Inc. is active in the multimedia market after promising Apple Records that it would not manufacture musical products. In fact, Apple is an industry leader in multimedia technology. Considering past disagreements, it is somewhat ironic that the multimedia version of the Beatles' 1964 movie *A Hard Day's Night* is available exclusively for Macintosh computers.

Quick Check

1. Multimedia applications combine media such as _____, _____, _____, _____, _____, and _____.

2. Multimedia is the same as CD-ROM. True or false?

3. _____ and _____ are important computer-based tools because they help you easily navigate through a large selection of text, graphical, audio, and video information by following a path you choose.

4. The _____ standard specifies the minimum hardware requirements you need to successfully use multimedia applications on your computer system.

5. Most multimedia applications require equipment such as _____, _____, _____, _____, and _____.

6. You can add multimedia capability to your computer by purchasing a(n) _____ designed to be installed in a few hours by a non-technical user.

User **Focus:**

Installing Software

Many microcomputers are sold with pre-installed system and application software, but eventually most computer users want to install additional software.

Software Compatibility

How do I know what software will work on my computer?

Before you install software or a multimedia application, you must make sure it is compatible with your computer system. To be compatible, the software must be written for the type of computer you use and for the operating system installed on your computer. You must also make sure your computer meets or exceeds the system requirements specified by the software. **System requirements** specify the minimum hardware and operating system requirements needed for a software product to work correctly. The system requirements are usually listed on the outside of a software package, as shown in Figure 2-24. They might also be explained in more detail in the software reference manual.

▶ **Figure 2-24**
System requirements

You need multimedia hardware that complies with the basic MPC standard.

Your computer must have DOS version 3.1 or later.

To run Encarta, your computer must have Microsoft Windows version 3.1 or later.

Determining Compatibility

Does the version of my computer's operating system affect compatibility?

Suppose you want to purchase software for your IBM-compatible computer. First, you need to make sure the software is written for IBM-compatible computers, rather than for the Apple Macintosh. Sometimes the same software title is available for more than one type of computer. For example, Microsoft Word is available for both IBM-compatible and Apple Macintosh computers, but these are two distinct versions of the software. You cannot use the Macintosh version of Microsoft Word on your IBM-compatible.

Once you know the software is compatible with your computer, you must make sure the software will work with your operating system. If your IBM-compatible computer uses the DOS operating system, you must select DOS software. If your computer uses the Microsoft Windows operating system, you can select DOS or Windows software because Windows can run software designed for both of these operating systems. If your computer uses OS/2, you can select OS/2, DOS, or Windows software because OS/2 can run software designed for all three operating systems.

Operating systems go through numerous revisions. A higher version number indicates a more recent revision; for example, DOS 6.0 is a more recent version than DOS 5.0. Windows 95 is a more recent version than Windows 3.1. Operating systems are usually **downwardly compatible**, which means that you can use application software designed for earlier versions of the operating system, but not those designed for later versions. For example, if Windows 95 is installed on your computer, you can generally use software designed for earlier versions of Windows, such as Windows 3.1. However, your software might not work correctly if it requires Windows 95 but you have Windows 3.1 on your computer. If you want to use software that requires a newer version of your operating system, you must first purchase and install an operating system upgrade. Figure 2-25 on the next page summarizes the concept of downward compatibility.

Figure 2-25
Downward
compatibility

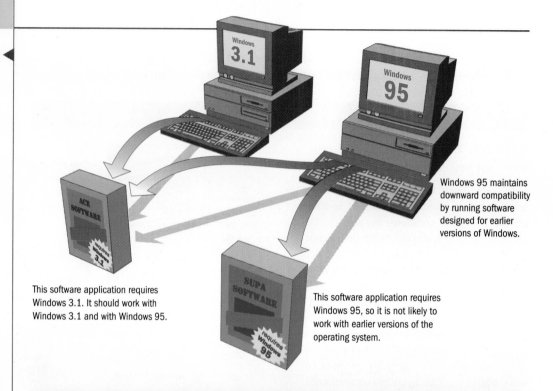

Windows 95 maintains
downward compatibility
by running software
designed for earlier
versions of Windows.

This software application requires
Windows 3.1. It should work with
Windows 3.1 and with Windows 95.

This software application requires
Windows 95, so it is not likely to
work with earlier versions of the
operating system.

Software Setup

When I purchase software, what do I do with the disks?

Computer software is usually shipped on floppy disks, called **distribution disks**, or on CD-ROMs. In the years when personal computers first appeared on the market, you could often use the software directly from the distribution disk. Now that is rarely possible because the programs are so large they take up many disks. Today, instead of using software directly from the distribution disk, you usually install it on your hard disk. During the installation process, programs and data for the software are copied to the hard disk of your computer system.

When you install software using a command-line operating system, such as DOS, you should carefully follow the installation instructions provided in the reference manual. There is no consistent installation procedure for DOS software, so each software application might require different steps. On the other hand, for Microsoft Windows applications, the installation process is more consistent and usually much easier. Figure 2-26 shows you how to install Windows applications.

Installing software from a CD-ROM frequently differs from the installation process for software shipped on floppy disks. Software shipped on a CD-ROM is usually too large to fit on a hard disk. As you learned in Chapter 1, a CD-ROM stores up to 680 million characters of data, but a typical hard disk stores approximately 500 million characters of data. Because of the large size of CD-ROM software, you generally access the CD-ROM programs and data directly from the CD-ROM instead of from a hard disk. In this case, a very limited amount of information must be copied to your hard disk during the installation process. As with any software, you should read the installation instructions to find out how to install software distributed on a CD-ROM.

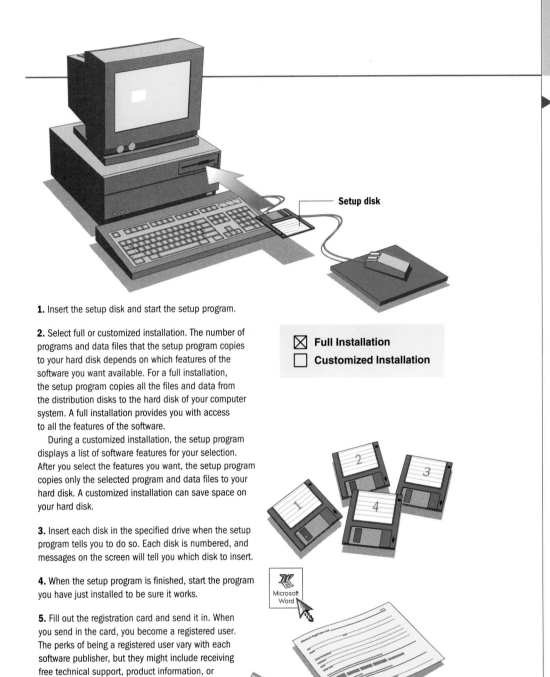

▶ **Figure 2-26**
The installation
process

1. Insert the setup disk and start the setup program.

2. Select full or customized installation. The number of programs and data files that the setup program copies to your hard disk depends on which features of the software you want available. For a full installation, the setup program copies all the files and data from the distribution disks to the hard disk of your computer system. A full installation provides you with access to all the features of the software.

    During a customized installation, the setup program displays a list of software features for your selection. After you select the features you want, the setup program copies only the selected program and data files to your hard disk. A customized installation can save space on your hard disk.

3. Insert each disk in the specified drive when the setup program tells you to do so. Each disk is numbered, and messages on the screen will tell you which disk to insert.

4. When the setup program is finished, start the program you have just installed to be sure it works.

5. Fill out the registration card and send it in. When you send in the card, you become a registered user. The perks of being a registered user vary with each software publisher, but they might include receiving free technical support, product information, or discounts on new versions of the software.

☒ **Full Installation**
☐ **Customized Installation**

End Note
Software is the key to the computer's versatility. System software and application software work together to help you accomplish an incredible variety of tasks. You might think it is "corny" to follow copyright laws and license restrictions, but ethical software use benefits everyone. Software publishers use revenues from software sales to improve current software, provide technical support, and develop new applications. By resisting the temptation to use illegal copies of software, you can help provide software publishers with the resources they need to develop more of the software that makes the computer such a versatile machine.

Review

1. Write a sentence or two explaining the most important concept you learned from this chapter.

2. Below each heading in this chapter, there is a question. Look back through this chapter and answer each of these questions using your own words.

3. Select 10 terms in this chapter that you believe are most important, then use your own words to write a definition of each term.

4. Under U.S. copyright law, what are the two major rights granted to the copyright holder? What are the three rights granted to the user of copyrighted materials?

5. Complete the following "legal" matrix to clarify the difference between copyrighted software, licensed software, shareware, and public domain software.

Suppose you are not the author of a software package. Is it...	Copyrighted Software	Licensed Software	Shareware	Public Domain Software
Legal to make a backup copy?				
Legal to sell a copy?				
Legal to give a copy to a friend?				
Protected by U.S. Copyright Law?				

6. For each of the following descriptions, indicate whether the software is copyrighted, licensed, shareware, or public domain. For some descriptions, there is more than one answer.

   a. The software does not have a copyright notice

   b. You must send in money to become a registered user

   c. The software is shrink wrapped and there is a message about your rights and responsibilities

   d. When you start the software you see a message "©1994 Course Technology, Inc."

   e. When you start the program you see a message, "Copyright 1986, 1987 SupRSoft, Inc. All Rights Reserved. You are free to use, copy, and distribute this software for non-commercial use if no fee is charged for use, copying, or distribution, and if the software is not modified in any way."

7. Create a sentence outline of Section 2.2 System Software. Your outline should have at least three levels. You can use I., A., and 1. for the outline levels. Be sure that the sentence you write for each outline level focuses on a single, important point.

8. Fill in the following table by using a check mark to indicate which operating systems are available for each type of computer.

Operating System	IBM Compatible	Macintosh	Minicomputer	Mainframe
DOS				
WINDOWS				
OS/2				
MVS				
VMS				
UNIX				

9. At the top of a sheet of paper, write "Productivity Software." Next, list all the terms you associate with productivity software. You can include terms that are not in the chapter; for example, if you use a productivity software package that is not mentioned in the chapter, you might still list it.

10. Review Section 2.3 on software applications. Then make a list of what you think are the three most important features of word processing, spreadsheet, and database software.

11. For each of the following applications, indicate what software tool would be the best to use—word processing, spreadsheet, database, graphics, electronic mail, desktop publishing, or scheduling.

   a. Working with numbers and examining "what-if" scenarios

   b. Producing documents

c. Working with facts and figures, such as customer names and addresses

d. Drawing pictures, 3-D images, and animations

e. Sending electronic messages between two computers

f. Producing professional-looking brochures and newsletters

g. Creating pie charts, line graphs, and bar graphs

h. Determining times for meetings, tracking special events, and maintaining a to-do list

12. Make a two-column list to summarize multimedia. The left column of the list should include multimedia features such as sound, animation, and so on. The right column should indicate the computer equipment that is needed to implement the features you listed in the left column.

13. Suppose you're thinking of purchasing spreadsheet software, and you read a very favorable review of Microsoft Excel for Windows. The article indicates that the software requires "an IBM-PC/AT, PS/2, or compatible; graphics compatible with Microsoft Windows version 3.0 or later; MS-DOS version 3.1 or later; optional printer; a mouse or compatible pointing device is recommended." You have a Compaq computer with Windows 95, a Hewlett-Packard printer, and a Microsoft mouse. Explain whether you can expect the Microsoft Excel spreadsheet software to work on your computer after you install it.

Projects

1. Format a Disk In this chapter you learned how utility software helps you direct the operating system to accomplish tasks such as formatting a disk. This is a good time to try it out. If your lab computers have the Windows 95 operating system, you can do this project on your own by referring to Figure 2-12. Otherwise, your instructor will need to help you.

2. The Operating System in Your School's Lab In this chapter you learned how to identify microcomputer operating systems by looking at the main screen and prompt. In this project you will explore more about the operating system in your school computer lab. If you have more than one lab or your computer uses more than one operating system, your instructor should tell you which one to use for the project.

Find out which operating system is used in your school computer lab. Be sure you find out the type and version. You can go into the lab and obtain this information from one of the computers. If you see a command-line user

interface, try typing "ver" and then pressing the Enter key. If you see a graphical user interface, try clicking the Apple menu, or click the Help menu, then select Help About. Once you know the operating system used in your school lab, use the operating system reference manual and library resources to answer the following questions:

a. Which operating system and version are used in your school lab?

b. What company publishes the operating system software?

c. When was the first version of this operating system introduced?

d. Does this operating system have a command-line user interface or a graphical user interface?

e. Does this operating system support multitasking?

f. Do you need a password to use the computers in your school lab? Even if you do not need to use a password, does the operating system provide some way to secure access to the computers?

g. What is the anticipated arrival date for the next version of this operating system?

h. How much does the publisher of this operating system usually charge for upgrades if you are a registered user?

3. The Legal Beagle: Analyzing a License Agreement When you use a software package, it is important to understand the legal restrictions on its use. In this project you have an opportunity to practice reading a real software license agreement and making decisions based on how you interpret what it says. You can do this project on your own or discuss it in a small group, as specified by your instructor. To extend this project, you can locate another license agreement, answer the same questions, then write a short paper about which license is better for the software user.

Read the IBM Program License Agreement in Figure 2-27 on the next page, then answer the questions in a through h that follow:

a. Is this a "shrink wrap" license? Why or why not?

b. After you pay your computer dealer for the program this license covers, who owns the program?

c. Can you legally have one copy of the program on your computer at work and another copy of the program on your computer at home if you use the software only in one place at a time?

d. Can you legally sell the software? Why or why not?

e. Under what conditions can you legally transfer possession of the program to someone else?

f. If you were the owner of a software store, could you legally rent the program to customers if you were sure they did not keep a copy after the rental period was over?

g. Can you legally install this software on one computer, but give more than one user access to it?

h. If you use this program for an important business decision and you later find out that a mistake in the program caused you to lose $500,000, what legal recourse is provided by the license agreement?

4. Software Applications: What's Available? There are so many software packages that it is difficult to get an idea of what's available unless you take a look through current computer magazines and software catalogs. This project has two parts.

Figure 2-27 ◀

You can do either one or both as your instructor assigns. Part A helps you discover the variety of available software applications. Part B helps you research an application or operating system in more depth. You will be able to find the information for this project in the computer magazines listed in the Resources section at the end of the chapter. If you have access to the Internet, check out Computer Express at *http://www.cexpress.com*.

Part A. Find an ad for a computer vendor that sells a large variety of software. Jot down the name of the vendor and where you found the ad. List the categories the vendor uses to classify software and the number of software packages in each category.

Part B. Select one type of software from the following categories: operating systems, disk utilities, word processing, graphics, presentation graphics, electronic mail, desktop publishing, spreadsheets, database, accounting, or scheduling. Read a comparison review of software packages in the category you select. Next try to locate and photocopy ads for each of the products in the review. Look through the software vendor ads to find the best price for each product. Finally, write a one- or two-page summary explaining your purchase recommendation.

5. What Software Tool Would You Recommend? Folk wisdom tells us to use the appropriate tool for a job. This is true for software tools, too. In this project you decide what software tool is most appropriate for a task. You can do this project on your own or discuss it in a small group.

For each of the scenarios that follow, decide if word processing, spreadsheet, database, desktop publishing, graphics, scheduling, electronic mail, or accounting software is the best tool.

International Business Machines Corporation   *Armonk, New York 10504*

IBM Program License Agreement

BEFORE OPENING THIS PACKAGE, YOU SHOULD CAREFULLY READ THE FOLLOWING TERMS AND CONDITIONS. OPENING THIS PACKAGE INDICATES YOUR ACCEPTANCE OF THESE TERMS AND CONDITIONS. IF YOU DO NOT AGREE WITH THEM, YOU SHOULD PROMPTLY RETURN THE PACKAGE UNOPENED AND YOUR MONEY WILL BE REFUNDED.

This is a license agreement and not an agreement for sale. IBM owns, or has licensed from the owner, copyrights in the Program. You obtain no rights other than the license granted you by this Agreement. Title to the enclosed copy of the Program, and any copy made from it, is retained by IBM. IBM licenses your use of the Program in the United States and Puerto Rico. You assume all responsibility for the selection of the Program to achieve your intended results and for the installation of, use of, and results obtained from, the Program.

The Section in the enclosed documentation entitled "License Information" contains additional information concerning the Program and any related Program Services.

LICENSE
You may:
1) use the Program on only one machine at any one time, unless permission to use it on more than one machine at any one time is granted in the License Information (Authorized Use);
2) make a copy of the Program for backup or modification purposes only in support of your Authorized Use. However, Programs marked "Copy Protected" limit copying;
3) modify the Program and/or merge it into another program only in support of your Authorized Use; and
4) transfer possession of copies of the Program to another party by transferring this copy of the IBM Program License Agreement, the License Information, and all other documentation along with at least one complete, unaltered copy of the Program. You must, at the same time, either transfer to such other party or destroy all your other copies of the Program, including modified copies or portions of the Program merged into other programs. Such transfer of possession terminates your license from IBM. Such other party shall be licensed, under the terms of this Agreement, upon acceptance of the Agreement by its initial use of the Program.

You shall reproduce and include the copyright notice(s) on all such copies of the Program, in whole or in part.
You shall not:
1) use, copy, modify, merge, or transfer copies of the program except as provided in this Agreement;
2) reverse assemble or reverse compile the Program; and/or
3) sublicense, rent, lease, or assign the Program or any copy thereof.

LIMITED WARRANTY
Warranty details and limitations are described in the Statement of Limited Warranty which is available upon request from IBM, its Authorized Dealer or its approved supplier and is also contained in the License Information. IBM provides a three-month limited warranty on the media for all Programs. For selected Programs, as indicated on the outside of the package, a limited warranty on the Program is available. The applicable Warranty Period is measured from the date of delivery to the original user as evidenced by a receipt.

Certain Programs, as indicated on the outside of the package, are not warranted and are provided "AS IS."
Z125-3301-02 4/87

SUCH WARRANTIES ARE IN LIEU OF ALL OTHER WARRANTIES, EXPRESS OR IMPLIED, INCLUDING, BUT NOT LIMITED TO, THE IMPLIED WARRANTIES OF MERCHANTABILITY AND FITNESS FOR A PARTICULAR PURPOSE.

Some states do not allow the exclusion of implied warranties, so the above exclusion may not apply to you.

LIMITATION OF REMEDIES
IBM's entire liability and your exclusive remedy shall be as follows:
1) IBM will provide the warranty described in IBM's Statement of Limited Warranty. If IBM does not replace defective media or, if applicable, make the Program operate as warranted or replace the Program with a functionally equivalent program, all as warranted, you may terminate your license and your money will be refunded upon the return of all your copies of the Program.
2) For any claim arising out of IBM's limited warranty, or for any other claim whatsoever related to the subject matter of this Agreement, IBM's liability for actual damages, regardless of the form of action, shall be limited to the greater of $5,000 or the money paid to IBM, its Authorized Dealer or its approved supplier for the license for the Program that caused the damages that is the subject matter of, or is directly related to, the cause of action. This limitation will not apply to claims for personal injury or damages to real or tangible personal property caused by IBM's negligence.
3) In no event will IBM be liable for any lost profits, lost savings, or any incidental damages or other consequential damages, even if IBM, its Authorized Dealer or its approved supplier has been advised of the possibility of such damages, or for any claim by you based on a third party claim.

Some states do not allow the limitation or exclusion of incidental or consequential damages so the above limitation or exclusion may not apply to you.

GENERAL
You may terminate your license at any time by destroying all your copies of the Program or as otherwise described in this Agreement.

IBM may terminate your license if you fail to comply with the terms and conditions of this Agreement. Upon such termination, you agree to destroy all your copies of the Program.

Any attempt to sublicense, rent, lease or assign, or, except as expressly provided herein, to transfer any copy of the Program is void.

You agree that you are responsible for payment of any taxes, including personal property taxes, resulting from this Agreement.

No action, regardless of form, arising out of this Agreement may be brought by either party more than two years after the cause of action has arisen except for the breach of the provisions in the Section entitled "License" in which event four years shall apply.

This agreement will be construed under the Uniform Commercial Code of the State of New York.

a. You want to keep track of your monthly expenses and try to figure out ways to save some money.

b. As the leader of an international team of researchers studying migration patterns of Canadian geese, you want all the team members to communicate their findings to each other quickly.

c. You are the office manager for a department of a large Fortune 500 company. One of your responsibilities is to arrange meetings and schedule facilities for the employees in your department.

d. As a partner in a law firm, you need to draft and modify legal briefs.

e. You are in charge of a fund-raising campaign and you need to track the names, addresses, phone numbers, and donations made by contributors.

f. You are going to design and produce the printed program for a community theater play listing the actors, director, lighting specialists, and so on.

g. A sales manager for a cosmetics company wants to motivate the sales force by graphically showing the increases in consumer spending in each of the past five years.

h. The marketing specialist for a new software company wants to send out announcements to 150 computer magazines.

i. The owners of five golf courses in Jackson County want to design a promotional brochure that can be distributed to tourists in restaurants and hotels.

j. The owner of a small business wants to keep track of ongoing income and expenses and print out monthly profit and loss statements.

k. The superintendent of a local school system wants to prepare a press release explaining why student test scores were 5% below the national average.

l. A contractor wants to calculate his cost for materials needed to build a new community center.

m. A college student wants to send out customized letters addressed to 20 prospective employers.

n. The parents of three children want to decide whether they should invest money for their children's education in the stock market or whether they should buy into their state's prepaid tuition plan.

o. The director of fund-raising for a large nonprofit organization wants to keep a list of prospective donors.

6. Where's the Shareware? You learned in this chapter that shareware can be less expensive than commercial software; it also lets you try the software before you buy it. But is shareware as available as commercial software? In this project you will find out.

Use computer magazines and/or Internet sites to find a shareware program and a commercial program for each of the categories in the table below. For each shareware package, indicate the program name, the name of the retailer or vendor, and the selling price. In the reference column, indicate the name, date, and page of the magazine, or the Internet site, where you found the information. Shareware vendors frequently advertise in the back pages of computer magazines. If you have access to the Internet, you might try the Virtual Software Library at *http://www.acs.oakland.edu/oak.html.*

Software Type	Title	Price	Vendor	Reference
Shareware productivity				
Commercial productivity				
Shareware system utility				
Commercial system utility				
Shareware education				
Commercial education				
Shareware games				
Commercial games				

7. Multimedia "Top 10" In the last two years the multimedia market has exploded. For this project, create your own list of "top 10" multimedia titles. Look in recent editions of computer magazines and select the 10 multimedia applications that are most interesting or useful to you. For each multimedia application you select, list its title, publisher, and a short description of what it does. Also list the name of the computer magazine you used and the page on which you found the information about each multimedia application.

8. The Great Scheduler Problem Using a computer to maintain your schedule—what could be better? The computer warns you if you try to make two appointments at the same time, gives you advance notice of your appointments, and keeps track of your "To Do" list by bringing forward the tasks you didn't complete yesterday. Well, one slight problem—where is your computer when you see a friend in the "caf" and you set up a date, or when your colleague stops you in the hall to let you know about the sales meeting next Tuesday? Better switch to one of those pocket schedulers, right? No, too limiting—not enough memory and a small screen. Why not carry around a small device that communicates to your computer using an infrared beam? Is this the solution? What other solutions have been tried? Can you think of a better one?

This project is suitable for a term paper. You will need to research the software packages that give you scheduling capabilities, along with some of the hardware innovations that give you the option of running scheduling software on something other than a desktop computer. When you write your paper, be sure to include references to the resources you use.

9. Programming as a Career You learned in this chapter that most people do not need to write programs to use their computers. You also learned that computer programming is a challenging career field. In this project you will find out more about computer programming careers.

Computer programming jobs are often listed in the back pages of computer magazines, in professional journals, and on career bulletin boards on the Internet. Some of the best sources of information are the following:

InfoWorld magazine

The professional journal *Communications of the ACM*

The newspaper *San Jose Mercury News*, and its Internet site *http://www.sjmercury.com*

The Internet Monster Board *http://www.monster.com*

The Internet Career Mosaic *http://www.careermosaic.com*

To complete this project first locate three advertisements for computer programming jobs. Photocopy or print out a copy of the ads. Create a table like the one that follows, and fill it in for each of the three job openings you found.

Programming Jobs	Job 1	Job 2	Job 3
Educational requirements			
Work experience required			
Programming languages required			
Mainframe, mini, or microcomputer			
Company name			
Starting salary			

Resources

- *A Hard Day's Night*, The Voyager Co., 1351 Pacific Coast Highway, Santa Monica, CA 90401, 310-451-1383, $39.95. This CD-ROM contains the entire 90-minute Beatles film, *A Hard Day's Night*, along with an annotated script.

- **Nelson, T.** *Literary Machines*. Southbend, MI: The Distributors, 1981. Nelson describes project Xanadu as "the most audacious and specific plan for knowledge, freedom, and a better world yet to come out of computerdom: the original (and perhaps the ultimate) hypertext system." The details are here in Nelson's book, *Literary Machines*. You might also look for these other books by Nelson: *Computer Lib* (1987 edition published by Microsoft Press) and *The Home Computer Revolution* (published by the author in 1977).

- **Software Publishers Association** The Software Publishers Association provides public information on the legal use of software. SPA estimates that one-third of the software currently in use is pirated; its goal is to make software piracy a major issue in the computer industry. It publicizes its campaign slogan "Don't copy that floppy" in magazines, pamphlets, and videotapes. You can contact the organization at 1-800-388-7478 to obtain information or to report copyright violations.

- **White, R.** *How Software Works*. Emeryville, CA: Ziff-Davis Press, 1993. Browse through this book if you would like to look "under the hood" to see how a computer runs software, but you don't want to get lost in technical detail. Some of the topics related to the chapter you just finished include how Windows runs more than one program at a time, how programming languages translate ideas into software, and how spreadsheet formulas work.

■ **Wodaski, R.** *Multimedia Madness.* Carmel, IN: Sams Publishing, 1992. This 616-page book provides a good background in multimedia applications and hardware. The book includes a disk and CD-ROM containing hundreds of multimedia samples.

Computer Magazines

It's a good idea to become familiar with computer magazines, journals, and newsletters because they carry the most current information about the fast-moving computer industry. Although computer books are excellent for explaining concepts and history, computer magazines contain more up-to-date information on the latest hardware and software.

■ **Byte**
One of the oldest and most respected computer publications, *Byte*'s main focus is on computer hardware, although it also contains software reviews and a variety of regular columns. Jerry Pournelle, a science fiction writer and venerable computer columnist, provides product reviews and opinions in a column called "Chaos Manor."

■ **Computer Select**
If your library has CD-ROM databases, it might also have the *Computer Select* CD. Published quarterly, *Computer Select* contains abstracts and articles from many computer magazines. It is easy to search the entire CD for all articles on a specific topic.

■ **Computer Shopper**
If nothing else, this magazine must be the largest monthly computer publication! Each edition is about 800 pages. The articles are somewhat overshadowed by the numerous and lengthy (some up to 10 pages) computer ads. If you are going to buy a computer via mail order, this is the definitive resource.

■ **InfoWorld**
This weekly publication in tabloid format reports the latest industry news and is required reading for all computer "gurus."

■ **Macworld**
Macintosh users like the hardware and software reviews they find in this monthly magazine, which is dedicated to the Apple Macintosh computer.

■ **PC Computing**
The focus of this magazine is on IBM-compatible computers and software. Featured columnist John Dvorak usually presents an interesting perspective on new developments in the computer industry.

■ **PC World**
Similar in focus to *PC Computing*, *PC World* is distinguished by its "Consumer Watch" column, which acts as an industry watchdog and consumer advocate. "Consumer Watch" answers reports on product bugs, clarifies deceptive advertising, and prints consumer complaints.

■ **Windows**
This publication is especially for Microsoft Windows users. Each issue contains hardware and software reviews, as well as hints and tips on customizing the Microsoft Windows operating environment.

Lab Assignments

Word Processing

 Word processing software is the most popular computerized productivity tool. In this Lab you will learn how word processing software works. When you have completed this Lab, you should be able to apply the general concepts you learned to any word processing package you use at home, at work, or in your school lab.

1. Click the Steps button to learn how word processing software works. As you proceed through the Steps, answer all of the Quick Check questions that appear. After you complete the Steps, you will see a Quick Check Summary Report. Follow the instructions on the screen to print this report.

2. Click the Explore button to begin. Click File, then click Open to display the Open dialog box. Click the file **Timber.Doc**, then press the Enter key to open the letter to Northern Timber Company. Make the following modifications to the letter, then print it out. You do not need to save the letter.

    a. In the first and last lines of the letter, change "Jason Kidder" to your name.

    b. Change the date to today's date.

    c. The second paragraph begins "Your proposal did not include..." Move this paragraph so it is the last paragraph in the text of the letter.

    d. Change the cost of a permanent bridge to $20,000.

    e. Spell check the letter.

3. In Explore, open the file **Stars.Doc**. Make the following modifications to the document, then print it out. You do not need to save the document.

   a. Center and boldface the title.

   b. Change the title font to size 16 Arial.

   c. Boldface the DATE, SHOWER, and LOCATION.

   d. Move the January 2-3 line to the top of the list.

   e. Number the items in the list 1., 2., 3., etc.

   f. Add or delete tabs to re-align the columns.

   g. Double-space the entire document.

4. In Explore, compose a one-page double-spaced letter to your parents or to a friend. Make sure you date the letter and check your spelling. Print the letter and sign it. You do not need to save your letter.

Spreadsheets

 Spreadsheet software is used extensively in business, education, science, and humanities to simplify tasks that involve calculations. In this Lab you will learn how spreadsheet software works. You will use spreadsheet software to examine and modify worksheets, as well as to create your own worksheets.

1. Click the Steps button to learn how spreadsheet software works. As you proceed through the Steps, answer all of the Quick Check questions that appear. After you complete the Steps, you will see a Quick Check Summary Report. Follow the instructions on the screen to print this report.

2. Click the Explore button to begin this assignment. Click OK to display a new worksheet. Click File, then click Open to display the Open dialog box. Click the file **Income.Xls**, then press the Enter key to open the **Income and Expense Summary** worksheet. Notice that the worksheet contains labels and values for income from consulting and training. It also contains labels and values for expenses such as rent and salaries. The worksheet does not, however, contain formulas to calculate Total Income, Total Expenses, or Profit. Do the following:

   a. Calculate the Total Income by entering the formula =sum(C4:C5) in cell C6.

   b. Calculate the Total Expenses by entering the formula =sum(C9:C12) in C13.

   c. Calculate Profit by entering the formula =C6-C13 in cell C15.

   d. Manually check the results to make sure you entered the formulas correctly.

   e. Print your completed worksheet showing your results.

3. You can use a spreadsheet to keep track of your grade in a class. Click the Explore button to display a blank worksheet. Click File, then click Open to display the Open dialog box. Click the file **Grades.Xls** to open the Grades worksheet. This worksheet contains all the labels and formulas necessary to calculate your grade based on four test scores.

Suppose you receive a score of 88 out of 100 on the first test. On the second test, you score 42 out of 48. On the third test, you score 92 out of 100. You have not taken the fourth test yet. Enter the appropriate data in the **Grades.Xls** worksheet to determine your grade after taking three tests. Print out your worksheet.

4. Worksheets are handy for answering "what if" questions. Suppose you decide to open a lemonade stand. You're interested in how much profit you can make each day. What if you sell 20 cups of lemonade? What if you sell 100? What if the cost of lemons increases?

In Explore, open the file **Lemons.Xls** and use the worksheet to answer questions a through d, then print the worksheet for question e:

   a. What is your profit if you sell 20 cups a day?

   b. What is your profit if you sell 100 cups a day?

   c. What is your profit if the price of lemons increases to $.07 and you sell 100 cups?

   d. What is your profit if you raise the price of a cup of lemonade to $.30? (Lemons still cost $.07 and assume you sell 100 cups.)

   e. Suppose your competitor boasts that she sold 50 cups of lemonade in one day and made exactly $12.00. On your worksheet adjust the cost of cups, water, lemons, and sugar, and the price per cup to show a profit of exactly $12.00 for 50 cups sold. Print this worksheet.

5. It is important to make sure the formulas in your worksheet are accurate. An easy way to test this is to enter 1's for all the values on your worksheet, then check the calculations manually. In Explore, open the worksheet **Receipt.Xls**, which calculates sales receipts. Enter 1 as the value for Item 1, Item 2, Item 3, and Sales Tax %. Now, manually calculate what you would pay for three items that cost $1.00 each in a state where sales tax is 1% (.01). Do your manual calculations match those of the worksheet? If not, correct the formulas in the worksheet and print out a *formula report* of your revised worksheet.

6. In Explore, create your own worksheet showing your household budget for one month. You may use real or made up numbers. Make sure you put a title on the worksheet. Use formulas to calculate your total income and your total expenses for the month. Add another formula to calculate how much money you were able to save. Print a formula report of your worksheet. Also, print your worksheet showing realistic values for one month.

Databases

The Database Lab demonstrates the essential concepts of file and database management systems. You will use the Lab to search, sort, and report the data contained in a file of classic books.

1. Click the Steps button to review basic database terminology and to learn how to manipulate the classic books database. As you proceed through the Steps, answer the Quick Check questions that appear. After you complete the Steps, you will see a Quick Check Summary Report. Follow the instructions on the screen to print this report.

2. Click the Explore button. Make sure you can apply basic database terminology to describe the classic books database by answering the following questions:

    a. How many records does the file contain?

    b. How many fields does each record contain?

    c. What are the contents of the Catalog # field for the book written by Margaret Mitchell?

    d. What are the contents of the Title field for the record with Thoreau in the Author field?

    e. Which field has been used to sort the records?

3. In Explore, manipulate the database as necessary to answer the following questions:

    a. When the books are sorted by title, what is the first record in the file?

    b. Use the Search button to search for all books in the West location. How many do you find?

    c. Use the Search button to search for all books in the Main location that are checked in. What do you find?

4. In Explore, use the Report button to print out a report that groups the books by Status and sorted by title. On your report, circle the four field names. Put a box around the summary statistics showing which books are currently check in and which books are currently checked out.

Computer History Hypermedia

The Computer History Hypermedia Lab is an example of a multimedia hypertext, or hypermedia that contains text, pictures, and recordings that trace the origins of computers. This Lab provides you with two benefits: first, you learn how to use hypermedia links, and second, you learn about some of the events that took place as the computer age dawned.

1. Click the Steps button to learn how to use the Computer History Hypermedia Lab. As you proceed through the Steps, answer all the Quick Check questions that appear. After you complete the Steps, you will see a Quick Check Summary Report. Follow the instructions on the screen to print this report.

2. Click the Explore button. Find the name and date for each of the following:

    a. First automatic adding machine.

    b. First electronic computer.

    c. First fully electronic stored-program computer.

    d. First widely used high-level programming language.

    e. First microprocessor.

    f. First microcomputer.

    g. First word processing program.

    h. First spreadsheet program.

3. Select one of the following computer pioneers and write a one-page paper about that person's contribution to the computer industry: Grace Hopper, Charles Babbage, Augusta Ada, Jack Kilby, Thomas Watson, or J. Presper Eckert.

4. Use this Lab to research the history of the computer. Based on your research, write a paper explaining how you would respond to the question, "Who invented the computer?"

Quick Check

Answers

2.1

1. false

2. data

3. program

4. software

5. shareware

6. license

7. system

2.2

1. multitasking

2. UNIX

3. micro

4. Utility

5. device driver

6. programming language

2.3

1. word processing, spreadsheet, database management

2. integrated software

3. horizontal market software

4. education software

5. desktop publishing

2.4

1. text, graphics, sound, animation, photo images, video

2. false

3. hypertext, hypermedia

4. MPC

5. speakers, sound card, CD-ROM drive, high-resolution color monitor, fast processor (high memory capacity is also acceptable)

6. multimedia kit

Glossary/Index

computer hardware The electric, electronic, and mechanical devices used for processing data. This hardware is the core of the system unit, but cannot function without an operating system, 2-12

computer program A set of detailed, step-by-step instructions that tell a computer how to solve a problem or carry out a task. *See also* application software; system software, 2-4

computer programming language A language that allows the programmer to use English-like instructions, then translates the instructions into a format the computer can interpret and directly process, 2-14, 2-19

computer-aided instruction (CAI) Education software that helps you learn how to do something, 2-30

computers, software. *See* application software; system software

concurrent-use license A software license that allows a certain number of copies of a software package to be used at the same time, 2-9

control-break report A report generated by database management software that groups the data by category, 2-29

copying, software, 2-6–2-7, 2-8, 2-10

Copyright Act of 1976, 2-7

Copyright Act of 1980, 2-5, 2-6, 2-7, 2-8

copyright notices, 2-6–2-7

copyright A form of legal protection that grants certain exclusive rights to the author of a program or the owner of the copyright, 2-6, 2-6–2-7

cost, free software, 2-9

cursor, word processing software, 2-23

customized installation, 2-39

D

data On disk, the words, numbers, and graphics that describe people, events, things, and ideas, 2-5

data, updating, 2-24

database management software A type of productivity software that helps you work with facts and figures comparable to those that might be stored on file cards or in a Rolodex, 2-24, 2-28–2-29

desktop publishing software Application software that provides you with computerized tools for page layout and design, 2-25

device driver A type of system software that tells the computer how to use a peripheral device, 2-19

Digital Equipment Corporation, 2-17

disks Media that contains data, 2-5
   formatting, 2-18
   setup, 2-39

distribution disks The floppy disks or CD-ROMs on which software is shipped, 2-38

documents, linked, 2-33

DOS (Disk Operating System) An operating system developed by Microsoft Corporation for IBM PCs and compatible computers. Early versions of DOS provided only a command-line user interface, but more recent versions include a menu-driven user interface, 2-15

DOS, installing software, 2-38

DOS prompt, 2-15

DOS Shell, 2-15

downwardly compatible A feature of operating systems that allow you to use software designed for earlier versions of the operating system, 2-37, 2-37–2-38

E

earphones, multimedia, 2-35

educational simulation A computerized model of a real world experience that can be manipulated with different outcomes, 2-30

education and reference software, 2-30

electronic mail software Software that maintains electronic mailboxes and sends messages from one computer to another, 2-24

encyclopedias, multimedia, 2-31, 2-32

entertainment software Games and software designed for entertainment, 2-30
   multimedia, 2-32

F

field Caption within a database record that identifies data, 2-28

floppy disks, software packages, 2-38

Format button, 2-18

formatting
   disks, 2-18
   word processing software, 2-23

FORTRAN, 2-19

free software, 2-9

full installation, 2-39

functions Built-in formulas in spreadsheet software, 2-26

G

graphical user interfaces (GUIs)
   Windows 3.1, 2-15
   Windows 95, 2-16

graphics software Application software that helps you draw pictures, 3-D images, and animation, 2-24, 2-24–2-25

graphs, spreadsheet software, 2-27

H

hardware
   multimedia, 2-35–2-36
   operating systems, 2-12, 2-13
   software requirements, 2-37

operating system A set of programs that manages the resources of a computer, including controlling input and output, allocating system resources, managing storage space, maintaining security, and detecting equipment failure, 2-8, 2-12

    identifying, 2-14
    interaction with application software, 2-12, 2-14
    interaction with hardware, 2-12, 2-14
    Mac OP, 2-17
    microcomputers, 2-14–17
    multiuser, 2-13
    MVS, 2-12
    OS/2, 2-16
    revisions, 2-37–2-38
    software requirements, 2-37–2-38
    UNIX, 2-17
    VMS, 2-12

OS/2 An operating system designed jointly by Microsoft and IBM. This system takes advantage of newer, more powerful computers, plus offers a graphical user interface while retaining the ability to run DOS programs, 2-16

P

page layout, word processing software, 2-23
PC-DOS, 2-15
peripheral devices, device drivers, 2-19
pirated software Illegal copies of software, 2-6
platforms, software compatibility, 2-37
presentation graphics software Application software that helps you represent business information using screen-based slide shows of bulleted lists, graphs, and charts, 2-25
    multimedia, 2-32
printing, landscape orientation, 2-27
processors, multimedia, 2-35
productivity software A category of application software that helps you work more effectively. Types of productivity software include word processing, spreadsheet, and database management, 2-20, 2-20–2-25
programs A set of detailed, step-by-step instructions that tell a computer how to solve a problem or carry out a task. Usually contained on disks, 2-5
programming languages, 2-19
prompts, DOS, 2-15
public domain software Software that is available for use without restriction and may be freely copied, distributed, and even resold, 2-9

Q

query A request you make to the database for records that meet specific criteria, 2-24, 2-28

R

record A group of fields containing information about a single person, place, or thing. A record in a database is equivalent to a card in a card file, 2-24, 2-28
    sorting, 2-24
reference software Software such as an electronic encyclopedia that lets you look up facts, 2-30
registration cards, 2-39
reports
    database management software, 2-24, 2-29
    spreadsheet software, 2-27
resources, system, 2-13
revisions, operating systems, 2-37–2-38

S

setup disk, 2-39
scheduling software Software that helps you keep track of important dates, 2-25
shareware Copyrighted software marketed under a "try-before-you-buy" policy that allows you to use a software package for a trial period. After the trial period, you should send in a registration fee, 2-10
shrink wrap license A software license that is visible in the back of a software product shrink wrapped in plastic. Opening the wrapping indicates the user agrees to the terms of the software license, 2-8, 2-8–2-9
simulations, educational, 2-30
single-user license A software license that limits the use of software to one user at a time, 2-9
site license A software license that allows a software package to be used on any and all computers at a specific location, 2-9
software One or more computer programs and associated data that exist in electronic form on a storage medium, 2-5, 2-4–2-30
    application. *See* application software
    business, 2-25, 2-29
    CAI, 2-30
    categories, 2-11
    commercial, 2-5–2-9
    compatibility, 2-37–2-38
    copying, 2-6–2-7, 2-8, 2-10
    copyrighted, 2-6–2-7
    database management, 2-24, 2-28–2-29
    desktop publishing, 2-25
    education and reference, 2-30
    e-mail, 2-24
    entertainment. *See* entertainment software
    graphics, 2-24–2-25
    horizontal-market, 2-25
    installing. *See* installing software
    integrated, 2-25
    licensed, 2-7–2-9
    multimedia. *See* multimedia
    operating systems, 2-16, 2-17

X

CHAPTER THREE

Computer Files
and **Data** Storage

How much data can you pack into a small area? In 1968, Frederick Watts hand-printed 9,452 characters on a piece of paper the size of a postage stamp. In 1983, Tsutomu Ishii of Tokyo, Japan wrote the Japanese characters for *Tokyo, Japan* on a human hair. A few years later, Surendra Apharya of Jaipur, India managed to squeeze 241 characters on a single grain of rice.

That seems like a lot of data packed into a small area, but a computer can store hundreds of times as much data in the same area. For example, an entire encyclopedia, complete with illustrations, can fit on a single CD-ROM disk.

Of course, a computer does not achieve such storage capability by making letters smaller! How, then, can computers store so much data in such a small area? How can you search through all that data to find what you want? Can you change data once it is stored? What happens if you run out of space on a disk?

In this chapter you will learn the answers to these and many more questions. First, you'll learn the definitions of the terms *file*, *data*, and *information*. You will learn that there are different types of files, and you will find out how to use each type. This chapter explains how computers store and retrieve data.

You will find out that the operating system provides you with a metaphor to help visualize and manipulate files. But you will see that this metaphor is quite different from the way the computer itself actually stores and keeps track of files.

This chapter also provides information about the speed, cost, and storage capacity of popular microcomputer storage media. With this information, you can make decisions about the storage devices that are right for your computing needs.

CHAPTER**PREVIEW**

The information in this chapter provides you with a practical foundation for using a computer to manage your own data. You will find out which disk drive to use when you store data and how to create a valid filename that the computer will accept. You will learn how to use DOS, Windows 3.1, or Windows 95 to organize the files on your disk so they are easy to locate. You will also learn what happens in the computer when you save, retrieve, or modify a file, so you will know what to do when the computer asks if you want to "Replace file?" After you have completed this chapter you should be able to:

■ Correctly use the terms *data* and *information*

■ Determine if a file is an executable file, data file, or source file

■ Create valid filenames under DOS, Windows 3.1, and Windows 95

■ Explain how file extensions and wildcards simplify file access

■ Describe the difference between logical and physical file storage

■ Discuss how the directory and the FAT help you access files

■ Select a storage device based on characteristics such as its capacity and access speed

■ Understand the process of saving, retrieving, revising, deleting, and copying files

LABS

DOS Directories and File Management

Windows Directories, Folders, and Files

Defragmentation and Disk Operations

Using Files

Data, Information, and Files

Computer professionals have special definitions for the terms *data*, *information*, and *file*. Although we might refer to these as technical definitions, they are not difficult to understand. Knowing these technical definitions will help you communicate with computer professionals and understand phrases such as "data in, information out."

Data and Information: Technically Speaking

Aren't data and information the same thing?

In everyday conversation, people use the terms *data* and *information* interchangeably. However, some computer professionals make a distinction between the two terms. **Data** is the words, numbers, and graphics that describe people, events, things, and ideas. Data becomes information when you use it as the basis for initiating some action or for making a decision. **Information**, then, is defined as the words, numbers, and graphics used as the basis for human actions and decisions.

To understand the distinction between data and information, consider the following: AA 4199 ORD 9:59 CID 11:09. These letters, numbers, and symbols, which describe an event—a flight schedule—are typical of the data stored in a computer system. Along with other flight schedules, this data can be sorted or transmitted to other computers.

Now, let's say that you decide to take a trip from Chicago (ORD) to Cedar Rapids, Iowa (CID). You ask your travel agent to make your reservation. Your agent requests information on flights from Chicago to Cedar Rapids and sees the following on the computer screen:

Carrier	Flight Number	From	Departs	To	Arrives
AA	4199	ORD	9:59	CID	11:09

Here, the letters, numbers, and symbols displayed on the screen are considered *information* because your travel agent is using them to make your reservation.

The distinction between data and information might seem somewhat elusive, because "AA 4199 ORD 9:59 CID 11:09" can be both data and information. Remember that the distinction is based on usage. Usually, if letters, numbers, and symbols are stored in a computer, they are referred to as data. If letters, numbers, and symbols are being used by a person to complete an action or make a decision, they are referred to as information.

Incidentally, in Latin, the word *data* is the plural for *datum*. According to this usage, it would be correct to say "The January and February rainfall *data* are stored on the disk," and "The March *datum* is not yet available." Most English dictionaries accept the use of *data* as either singular or plural. In this text *data* is used with the singular verb, as in "The *data is* stored on the disk."

Computer Files

What kinds of files will I have on my computer?

A **file** is a named collection of program instructions or data that exists on a storage medium such as a hard disk, a floppy disk, or a CD-ROM. Suppose you use a computer to write a memo to your employer. The words contained in the memo are stored on a disk in a file. The file has a name to distinguish it from other files on your disk.

Although there are several kinds of files, a typical computer user deals mainly with two kinds of files: executable files and data files. Executable files contain the commands that the computer follows to perform tasks. Data files contain data. Understanding the difference between these two kinds of files is important because you use them in different ways. Let's take a closer look at the differences between executable files and data files.

To differentiate between data and information, remember this: Data is used by computers; information is used by humans.

This definition of the term file is serviceable for most of the work you do with applications software. If you work with databases or write computer programs, however, you will find that there are some variations to this definition.

Executable Files

How do I use executable files?

An **executable file** contains the instructions that tell a computer how to perform a specific task. For example, the word processing program that tells your computer how to display and print text is stored on disk as an executable file. Other executable files on your computer system include the operating system, utilities, and application software programs.

To use an executable file, you *run* it. In Chapter 1 you learned how to run programs. In DOS you type the name of the program, in Windows 3.1 you double-click a program icon, and in Windows 95 you select the program from a menu. The programs you run are one type of executable file.

Your computer also has executable files that you cannot run. These files are executed at the request of a computer program, not the user. For example, a word processing program may request that the computer use an executable file called **Grammar.Dll** to check the grammar in a document.

Most operating systems help you identify the executable files you can run. DOS uses part of the filename to indicate an executable file. You will learn more about this later in the section "Filenaming Conventions." Windows 3.1 and Windows 95 use icons to indicate which files you can run. Figure 3-1 shows how Windows 95 uses icons to indicate which files you can run.

There are two types of executable files: some that you can run and some that you cannot run.

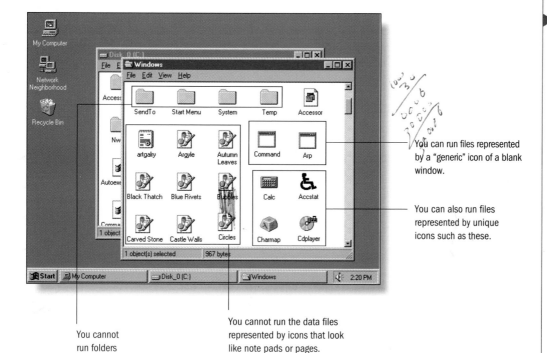

You can run files represented by a "generic" icon of a blank window.

You can also run files represented by unique icons such as these.

You cannot run folders

You cannot run the data files represented by icons that look like note pads or pages.

▶ **Figure 3-1**
Program icons

The instructions in an executable file are directly executed by the computer. The instructions are stored in a format that the computer can interpret, but this format is not designed to be readable to humans. If you try to look at the contents of an executable file using word processing software, the file will appear to contain meaningless symbols such as ☺□¬%□□.

You can try to look at the contents of an executable file and compare it to the contents of a data file. Project 6 helps you do this.

Data Files

How do I use data files?

A **data file** contains words, numbers, and pictures that you can view, edit, save, send, and print. Typically, you create data files when you use application software. For example, you create a data file when you store a document you have written using word processing software or a picture you have drawn using graphics software. You also create a data file when you store the numbers for a spreadsheet, a statistical analysis, or a graph. When you store a list using database software, a sound clip, or a video, you also create a data file. Once you create a data file and store it on a disk, you can later view it, modify it, copy it to another disk, print it, erase it, or save it again.

You probably won't create all the data files you use. You might receive data files as part of a software package you purchase. For example, word processing software often includes a dictionary data file that contains a list of words the software uses to check spelling.

You can also purchase specific data files that contain information you need. Suppose you own a business and want to mail product information to prospective customers. You could purchase a data file that contains the names and addresses of people in your geographical area who fit the age and income profile of consumers who are likely to buy your product.

Whether you create or purchase a data file, you typically use it in conjunction with application software. The application software helps you manipulate the data in the file. You usually view, revise, and print a data file using the same software you used to create it. For example, if you create a data file using word processing software such as Microsoft Word, you would usually use Microsoft Word to edit the file.

If you purchase a data file, how do you know what application software to use it with? Usually, a software product that contains data files will also contain the program you need to manipulate the data. If the program that manipulates the data is not included, the user manual indicates which program you can use. For example, if you purchase a collection of data files that contain graphical images, the user manual might indicate that you need a program such as Microsoft Paintbrush to view and modify the images.

Source Files

Is **Autoexec.Bat** *an executable file or a data file?*

If you look at the files on most DOS or Windows computers, you will see a file named **Autoexec.Bat**. This is an example of a batch file. A **batch file** is a series of operating system commands that you use to automate tasks you want the operating system to perform.

When you first turn on an IBM-compatible computer, it looks for a batch file called **Autoexec.Bat**. If it finds this file, the computer automatically executes any instructions the file contains. Usually the **Autoexec.Bat** file contains instructions that customize your computer configuration. For example, **Autoexec.Bat** might tell your computer that you have a CD-ROM drive or that the computer should establish connection with a network.

Because batch files contain instructions, you might assume that they are executable files. However, unlike most executable files, a batch file does not contain instructions in a format that the computer can directly carry out. Instead, a batch file contains instructions that computer users can read and modify. The commands in a batch file must go through a translation process before they can be executed.

Batch files belong to a third category of files called source files. A **source file** contains instructions that must be translated before a computer can execute them. The computer does the translation, so it seems as if the source file is being executed just like an executable file. But this is not the case; behind the scenes, a translation program converts the source file into commands

Think of data files as passive: The data does not instruct or direct the computer to do anything. Think of executable files as active: The instructions stored in the file cause the computer to do something.

*The **Autoexec.Bat** file is important, so don't delete it! Project 6 helps you learn more about the **Autoexec.Bat** file on the computers you use.*

the computer can execute. When you use a computer language such as BASIC to write a computer program, you create a source file that must be translated into executable instructions.

The Documentcentric Approach to Files

How important is it for me to distinguish between executable files, data files, and source files?

Understanding the difference between executable, data, and source files helps you understand how a computer works. Once you understand the characteristics of these file types, you understand that the computer performs the instructions in executable files to help you create data files. It follows, then, that the way you use a computer is to run an application program and use it to create data files. For example, you run the WordPerfect word processing program, then you use it to create a report.

The problem with this model is that to revise a document, you must remember what software you used to create it. Suppose you create a list of people who contributed to your organization's 1995 fund-raising campaign. The next year, you want to use this list again. You remember you called the file Contributors 95, but what program did you use to create it? Did you use Microsoft's Excel spreadsheet or Access database? Or did you use a word processing program such as Microsoft Word?

An alternative approach to using files is referred to by the term *documentcentricity*. The term is derived from two words: document and centric. **Documentcentricity** means that the *document* is *central* to the way you use a computer. Under the documentcentric model, once you indicate the document you want to revise, the computer automatically starts the appropriate application program. For example, if you are using Windows 95, when you click the Contributors 95 document, the computer starts the Microsoft Word application, then retrieves the data file Contributors 95, as shown in Figure 3-2.

Under the documentcentric approach, you select the data file you want to revise and the computer automatically runs the appropriate application program. Under the traditional model, you run an application program first, then select the file you want to revise.

Clicking the document starts the appropriate program.

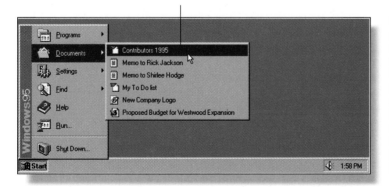

Windows 95 supports a documentcentric approach, as well as the traditional approach to using files. With the documentcentric approach, you select the *data* file you want to revise. The operating system automatically starts the appropriate application software and opens the data file you selected.

▶ **Figure 3-2**
Using the documentcentric approach

The operating system on your computer determines whether you can use the documentcentric approach. The trend with the latest versions of Windows and the Mac OS is to provide the tools you need to use the documentcentric approach. However, many people will continue with the traditional approach for using programs and files even with these new operating systems.

Filenaming Conventions

*When you study
Figure 3-4, pay
particular attention to
the naming
conventions for the
operating system you
use. You should learn
those filenaming
conventions so you
can create filenames
the computer will
accept.*

May I use any name I want when I create my own files?

A **filename** is a unique set of letters and numbers that identifies a file and usually describes the file contents. For example, **Excel** is the name of one of the main files for the Microsoft Excel spreadsheet software.

The filename might be followed by a **filename extension** that further describes the file contents. Filename extensions are also referred to as *file extensions* or *extensions*. The filename **Excel.Exe**, with the **.Exe** extension, indicates it is an executable file. The extension is separated from the filename with a period, called a *dot*. So, if you were to tell someone the name of this file, you would say "Excel dot E-x-e."

As a computer user, you are not usually responsible for naming executable files. These files are included with the application software you purchase, and the files are named by the programmers who write them. It is useful to know, however, that the executable files you can run generally have either a **.Com** (for *command*) extension or **.Exe** (for *executable)* extension. Executable files that you cannot run have extensions such as **.Sys**, **.Dll**, **.Drv**, and **.Vbx**. When you look through a list of files on a disk, you can quickly identify executable files by their file extensions. See Figure 3-3.

Figure 3-3
Executable file
extensions

File Type	File Extension
Files you can run	.EXE, .COM
Files you cannot run	.SYS, .DLL, .DRV, .VBX

On the other hand, you get to name the data files you create. When you create a data file or rename an existing file, you must assign it a valid filename. A **valid filename** is created by following specific rules. The rules for creating a valid filename are referred to as **filenaming conventions**. Each operating

Figure 3-4
Filenaming
conventions

system has a unique set of filenaming conventions; the filenaming conventions of several operating systems are listed in Figure 3-4. Can you determine why **Aux**, **My File.Doc**, and **Bud93/94.Txt** are not valid filenames under some operating systems?

	DOS and Windows 3.1	Windows 95	MacOS	UNIX
Maximum length of filename	8 character filename plus 3 character extension	255 character filename including the 3 character extension	32 characters No extensions used	14 characters (depends on the version of UNIX), including an extension of any length
Character to separate filename from extension	. (period)	. (period)	No extensions	. (period)
Spaces allowed	No	Yes	Yes	No
Numbers allowed	Yes	Yes	Yes	Yes
Characters not allowed	/[];="\:,|*?	\?:"<>|	None	!@#$%^&*()[]{}""\/|;<>
Reserved words	AUX, COM1, COM2, COM3, COM4, CON, LPT1, LPT2, LPT3, PRN, or NUL	AUX, COM1, COM2, COM3, COM4, CON, LPT1, LPT2, LPT3, PRN, or NUL	None	Depends on version of UNIX
Case sensitive	No	No	Yes	Yes—use lower case

Using DOS or Windows 3.1 filenaming conventions, **Aux** is not a valid filename because it is a reserved word. **My File.Doc** is not valid because it contains a space between My and File. The filename **Bud93/94.Txt** is not valid because it contains a slash. Filenames such as **Session**, **Report.Doc**, **Budget1.Wks**, and **Form.1** are valid under all the operating systems listed in Figure 3-4.

It is sometimes difficult to select a DOS or Windows 3.1 filename that is unique and descriptive within the eight-character limit. You should try, however, to choose filenames that help you remember what is in the file. When DOS was originally introduced, many computer users added a three-letter extension to each filename to further describe the file contents. For example, **.Mem** was a popular extension to use for data files that contained memos.

Some file extensions do not tell you what application was used to create the file; instead they tell you a general file category. For example, a **.Txt** extension tells you that the file is in the general category of text data files. A **.Bmp** extension tells you that that file contains a graphic.

Figure 3-5 lists some of the extensions that indicate the general category or type of data file.

File Type	File Extension
Text	.Txt
Sound	.Wav, .Mid, .Voc
Graphics	.Bmp, .Pcx, .Tif, .Wmf, .Pic
Animation	.Flc, .Fli, .Avi

▶ **Figure 3-5**
Extensions that indicate a general category or type of data file

Increasingly, however, software automatically assigns a file extension. For example, when you create a file with the word processing software Microsoft Word for Windows, the software assigns a **.Doc** extension to your filename. By automatically assigning an extension, the application helps you identify the files you created using that application. Suppose that you had many files on a disk—some created using Word and others created using a spreadsheet program and a graphics program. Now you want to view or edit one of the files you created using Microsoft Word. The Word software searches through all the files on your disk and shows you a list of only those filenames that have a **.Doc** extension. Because you see only the files you created using Word, you do not have to wade through a long list of files that include your spreadsheets and graphics. Figure 3-6 on the following page lists some of the file extensions automatically assigned to data files by application software.

When you create files using Windows applications, don't add a filename extension. The application software will automatically add the appropriate extension for you.

Figure 3-6 ◄
Extensions used
by application
software

Application Category	Application Software	File Extension
Database	Lotus Approach	.Apr
	Microsoft Cardfile	.Crd
	Microsoft Access	.Mdb
	Microsoft Works	.Wdb
	Paradox	.Db
	dBase V	.Dbf
Spreadsheet	Lotus 1-2-3	.Wk4
	Microsoft Excel	.Xls
	Microsoft Works	.Wks
	Quattro Pro	.Wb1
Word Processing	WordPerfect	.Wrd
	Microsoft Word and Wordpad	.Doc
	Microsoft Write	.Wri
	Microsoft Works	.Wps
	Lotus Ami Pro	.Sam

Wildcards

Wildcards provide a handy shortcut for managing many files at once. Exercise 7 in the Chapter Review will help you practice using wildcards.

What's *.* ?

Files have unique names, but sometimes you want to refer to more than one file. For example, suppose you want to list all the files on your disk with an .Exe extension. You can specify *.Exe (pronounced "star dot e-x-e"). The asterisk is a **wildcard character** used to represent a group of characters. *.Exe means all the files with an .Exe extension. Suppose your disk contains the files: **Excel.Exe**, **Spell.Exe**, **Excel.Cfg**, and **Budget.Dat.** You could use *.Exe to represent **Excel.Exe** or **Spell.Exe** and **Excel.*** to represent **Excel.Exe** and **Excel.Cfg**.

. (pronounced "star dot star") means all files. When you use DOS, the command DEL *.* will delete all the files in a directory. Be careful if you use this command!

Most operating systems use wildcards to make it easier to manipulate a collection of files. For example, using wildcards, you can delete all the files on a disk in one operation, instead of deleting each file individually. You will use wildcards even with a graphical user interface such as Windows 3.1, as shown in Figure 3-7.

When you want to retrieve a file in Microsoft Word, the Open dialog box appears.

The *.doc in the File Name box means that the files list displays any file with a .doc extension.

Only those files with the .doc extension appear.

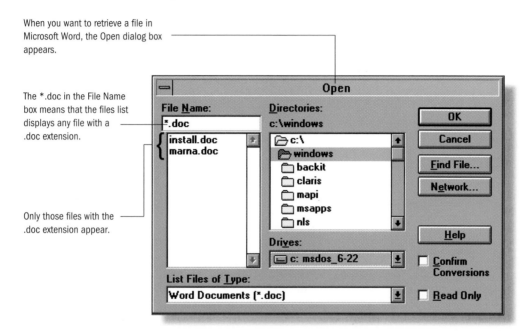

Figure 3-7
Wildcards help you locate files in Microsoft Word for Windows

Logical File Storage

How do I keep track of all the files on my disks?

Your computer system might contain hundreds, even thousands, of files stored on disks and storage devices. To keep track of all these files, the computer has a filing system that is maintained by the operating system. Once you know how the operating system manages your computer's filing system, you can use it effectively to store and retrieve files.

Most computers have more than one storage device that the operating system uses to store files. Each storage device is identified by a letter and a colon. Floppy disk drives are usually identified as A: and B:. The hard disk drive is usually identified as C:. Additional storage devices can be assigned letters from D: through Z:. Figure 3-8 on the following page shows some microcomputer configurations and the letters typically assigned to their storage devices. Does one of these match the configuration for the computer you use?

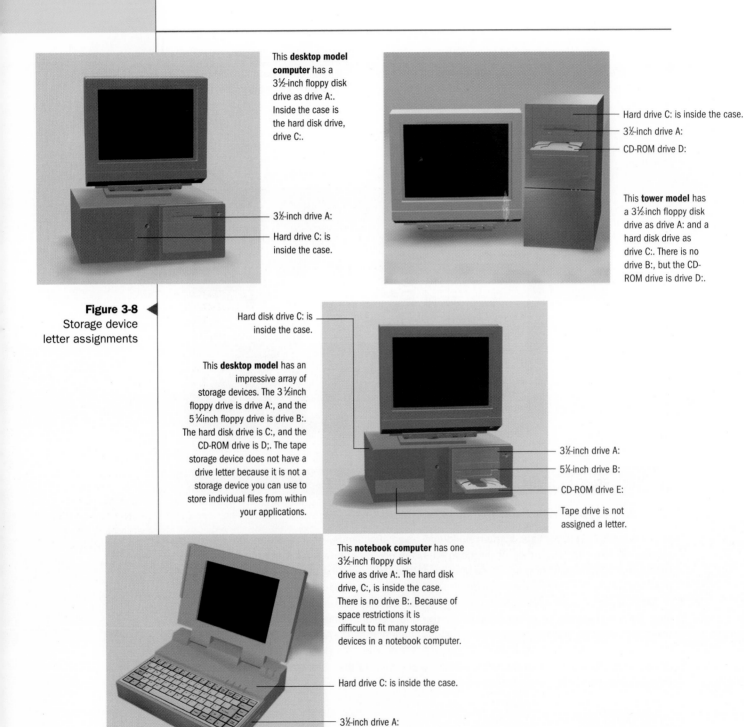

This **desktop model computer** has a 3½-inch floppy disk drive as drive A:. Inside the case is the hard disk drive, drive C:.

Hard drive C: is inside the case.
3½-inch drive A:
CD-ROM drive D:

This **tower model** has a 3½-inch floppy disk drive as drive A: and a hard disk drive as drive C:. There is no drive B:, but the CD-ROM drive is drive D:.

3½-inch drive A:
Hard drive C: is inside the case.

Figure 3-8
Storage device letter assignments

Hard disk drive C: is inside the case.

This **desktop model** has an impressive array of storage devices. The 3½-inch floppy drive is drive A:, and the 5¼-inch floppy drive is drive B:. The hard disk drive is C:, and the CD-ROM drive is D;. The tape storage device does not have a drive letter because it is not a storage device you can use to store individual files from within your applications.

3½-inch drive A:
5¼-inch drive B:
CD-ROM drive E:
Tape drive is not assigned a letter.

This **notebook computer** has one 3½-inch floppy disk drive as drive A:. The hard disk drive, C:, is inside the case. There is no drive B:. Because of space restrictions it is difficult to fit many storage devices in a notebook computer.

Hard drive C: is inside the case.

3½-inch drive A:

The operating system maintains a list of files called a **directory** for each disk or CD-ROM. The directory contains information about the files such as the filename, the file extension, the date and time the file was created, and the size of every file on a storage device. You can use the operating system to view the directory of a disk. Study Figure 3-9 on the next two pages to learn how a directory looks in DOS, Windows 3.1, and Windows 95.

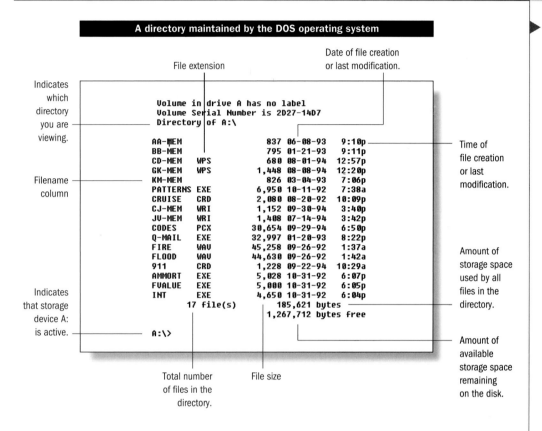

A directory maintained by the DOS operating system

File extension

Date of file creation or last modification.

Indicates which directory you are viewing.

```
      Volume in drive A has no label
      Volume Serial Number is 2D27-14D7
      Directory of A:\

      AA-MEM              837 06-08-93    9:10p
      BB-MEM              795 01-21-93    9:11p
      CD-MEM     WPS      680 08-01-94   12:57p
      GK-MEM     WPS    1,448 08-08-94   12:20p
      KM-MEM              826 03-04-93    7:06p
      PATTERNS   EXE    6,950 10-11-92    7:38a
      CRUISE     CRD    2,080 08-20-92   10:09p
      CJ-MEM     WRI    1,152 09-30-94    3:40p
      JU-MEM     WRI    1,408 07-14-94    3:42p
      CODES      PCX   30,654 09-29-94    6:50p
      Q-MAIL     EXE   32,997 01-20-93    8:22p
      FIRE       WAV   45,258 09-26-92    1:37a
      FLOOD      WAV   44,630 09-26-92    1:42a
      911        CRD    1,228 09-22-94   10:29a
      AMMORT     EXE    5,028 10-31-92    6:07p
      FVALUE     EXE    5,000 10-31-92    6:05p
      INT        EXE    4,650 10-31-92    6:04p
          17 file(s)       185,621 bytes
                         1,267,712 bytes free

      A:\>
```

Filename column

Indicates that storage device A: is active.

Time of file creation or last modification.

Amount of storage space used by all files in the directory.

Amount of available storage space remaining on the disk.

Total number of files in the directory.

File size

▶ **Figure 3-9**
Directories

When you type directory names, don't confuse the backslash \ with the regular slash /.

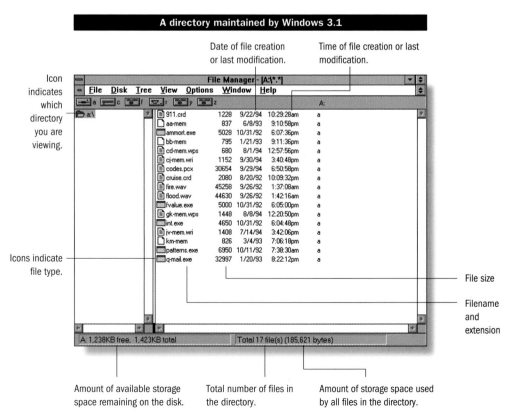

A directory maintained by Windows 3.1

Date of file creation or last modification.

Time of file creation or last modification.

Icon indicates which directory you are viewing.

```
File Manager - [A:\*.*]
 File  Disk  Tree  View  Options  Window  Help
   a    c    f    r    y    z                      A:

 a:\          911.crd       1228   9/22/94  10:29:28am   a
              aa-mem         837    6/8/93   9:10:58pm   a
              ammort.exe    5028  10/31/92   6:07:36pm   a
              bb-mem         795   1/21/93   9:11:36pm   a
              cd-mem.wps     680    8/1/94  12:57:56pm   a
              cj-mem.wri    1152   9/30/94   3:40:48pm   a
              codes.pcx    30654   9/29/92   6:50:58pm   a
              cruise.crd    2080   8/20/92  10:09:32pm   a
              fire.wav     45258   9/26/92   1:37:08am   a
              flood.wav    44630   9/26/92   1:42:16am   a
              fvalue.exe    5000  10/31/92   6:05:00pm   a
              gk-mem.wps    1448    8/8/94  12:20:50pm   a
              int.exe       4650  10/31/92   6:04:48pm   a
              iv-mem.wri    1408   7/14/94   3:42:06pm   a
              km-mem         826    3/4/93   7:06:18pm   a
              patterns.exe  6950  10/11/92   7:38:30am   a
              q-mail.exe   32997   1/20/93   8:22:12pm   a

A: 1,238KB free, 1,423KB total        Total 17 file(s) (185,621 bytes)
```

Icons indicate file type.

File size

Filename and extension

Amount of available storage space remaining on the disk.

Total number of files in the directory.

Amount of storage space used by all files in the directory.

Figure 3-9
Directories
(continued)

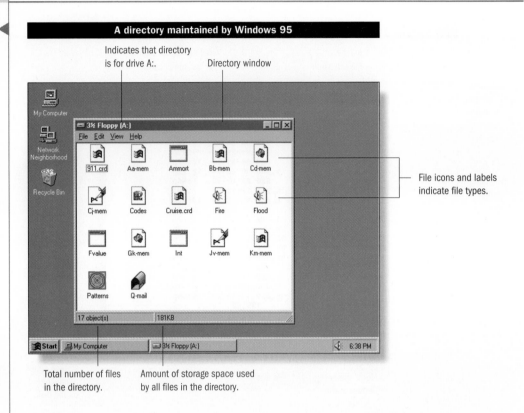

A directory maintained by Windows 95

Indicates that directory is for drive A:.

Directory window

File icons and labels indicate file types.

Total number of files in the directory.

Amount of storage space used by all files in the directory.

Lab

**Windows
Directories,
Folders, and Files**

The main directory of a disk, sometimes referred to as the **root directory**, provides a useful list of files. It could be difficult, however, to find a particular file if your directory contains several hundred files. To help you organize a large number of files, most operating systems allow you to divide your directory into smaller lists called **subdirectories**. For example, you can create one subdirectory to hold all your files that contain documents and another subdirectory to hold all your files that contain graphical images.

A subdirectory name is separated from a drive letter and a filename by a special symbol. In DOS and Microsoft Windows, this symbol is the backslash \. For example, the root directory of drive C: might have a subdirectory called **Graphics**, written as **C:\Graphics**.

A **file specification** is the drive letter, subdirectory, and filename that identifies a file. Suppose you create a subdirectory on drive A: named Word for your word processing documents. Now suppose you want to create a list of things to do called **To-do.Doc** and put it on drive A: in the Word subdirectory. The file specification is:

Drive letter → **A:\Word\To-do.Doc** ← Extension
Subdirectory   Filename

Subdirectories can be further divided into what you might think of as *sub-subdirectories.* As you create more and more subdirectories on a disk, it becomes important to pay attention to the structure of the directories. Metaphors, such as those shown in Figure 3-10 can help you visualize this structure.

Metaphors of directory structures are sometimes called *logical models* because they represent the way you logically conceive of them. **Logical storage** is a conceptual model of the way data is stored on your disk. This logical view of storage is a convenient mental model that helps you understand the computer's filing system; however, it is not how the data is actually stored. **Physical storage** refers to how data is actually stored on the physical disk. To find out more about how computers physically store data, it is useful to understand a bit about storage media and storage devices. That is the topic of Section 3.2.

Figure 3-10
Metaphors of
directory structures

You can mentally visualize the directory of a disk as a tree on its side. The trunk and branches are directories and the leaves are files.

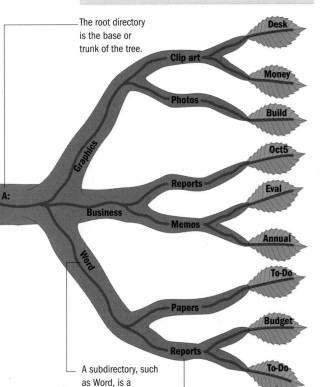

The root directory is the base or trunk of the tree.

A subdirectory, such as Word, is a branch of the tree. It is called A:\Word.

Reports is a subdirectory of Word, written as A:\Word\Reports.

Files, such as To-Do and Budget, are the leaves of the tree. To-Do and Budget are in the Reports subdirectory. The file specification for To-Do is A:\Word\Reports\To-Do.

Windows 3.1 displays the directory as a hierarchical structure of file folders.

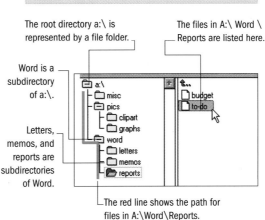

The root directory a:\ is represented by a file folder.

Word is a subdirectory of a:\.

Letters, memos, and reports are subdirectories of Word.

The files in A:\ Word \ Reports are listed here.

The red line shows the path for files in A:\Word\Reports.

When you use Windows 95 you can visualize the directory of a disk as boxes within boxes. Here, nested windows show the files and directories on A:\.

The root directory is the title for a window that holds the file folders representing files and subdirectories in A:.

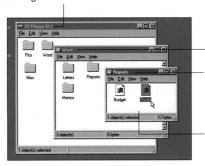

By clicking the Word file folder, you open the window for the

By clicking the Reports folder, you open the window for the Reports directory.

The files in A:\Word\Reports are shown here.

Quick Check

1 To differentiate between data and information, use the rule: _____ is used by computers; _____ is used by humans.

2 Name each part of the file specification A:\Research\Primates\Jan5.Dat.

↑   ↑   ↑   ↑ ↑
__ _____ _____ ___ ___

3 Executable files that you can run have _____ or _____ extensions.

4 When you use software designed for Windows 3.1 to create a data file, why don't you add a file extension?

5 Nested file folders and directory trees are ways of representing _____ storage.

6 The main directory for a disk is called the _____ directory.

7 **Autoexec.Bat** is an example of a(n) _____ file that needs to be translated by the computer before its instructions are executed.

| # Storage Technologies

The terms reading and writing make sense if you imagine you are the computer. As the computer you write a note and save it for later. You retrieve the note and read it when you need the information it contains.

When it comes to computer storage, users have two questions: How much data can I store? How fast can I access it? The answers to these questions depend on the storage medium and the storage device. A **storage medium** (storage *media* is the plural) is the disk, tape, paper, or other substance that contains data. A **storage device** is the mechanical apparatus that records and retrieves the data from the storage medium. When we want to refer to a storage device and the media it uses, we can use the term **storage technology**.

The process of storing data is often referred to as **writing data** or **saving a file** because the storage device *writes* the data on the storage medium to *save* it for later use. The process of retrieving data is often referred to as **reading data**, **loading data**, or **opening a file**. The terms *reading data* and *writing data* are often associated with mainframe applications. The terms *save* and *open* are standard Windows terminology.

Storage Specifications

How do I compare storage technologies?

Knowing the characteristics of a storage device or storage medium helps you determine which one is best for a particular task. Storage technology comparisons are often based on storage capacity and speed.

A byte is a unit of information equivalent to a single character—a letter, punctuation mark, space, or numeral.

Data is stored as bytes—each **byte** usually represents one character. The phrase "profit margin" requires 13 bytes of storage space because the phrase contains 12 characters and the space between the two words requires an additional byte of storage space. **Storage capacity** is the maximum amount of data that can be stored on a storage medium and is usually measured in kilobytes, megabytes, or gigabytes. A **kilobyte** (KB) is 1,024 bytes, but this is often rounded to one thousand bytes. A **megabyte** (MB) is approximately one million bytes. A **gigabyte** is approximately one billion bytes. When you read that the storage capacity of a computer is 850 MB, it means the hard disk on that computer can store up to 850 million bytes of information. This is equivalent to approximately 225,000 single-spaced pages of text.

In addition to storage capacity, users are concerned with access time. **Access time** is the average time it takes a computer to locate data on the storage medium and read it. Access time for a microcomputer storage device, such as a disk drive, is measured in milliseconds. One **millisecond** (ms) is a thousandth of a second. When you read, for example, that disk access time is 11 ms, it means that on average, it takes the computer eleven thousandths of a second to locate and read data from the disk.

It is fairly easy to compare two storage technologies based on storage capacity and access time; these specifications are usually included in advertisements and product descriptions. However, additional characteristics of storage technologies must be considered. The durability and access methods of a storage technology are also important characteristics to compare.

Magnetic or Optical Storage?

Will the metal detector in an airport erase the data on my disks?

Magnetic and optical storage technologies are used for the majority of today's micro, mini, and mainframe computers. Each of these technologies has advantages and disadvantages.

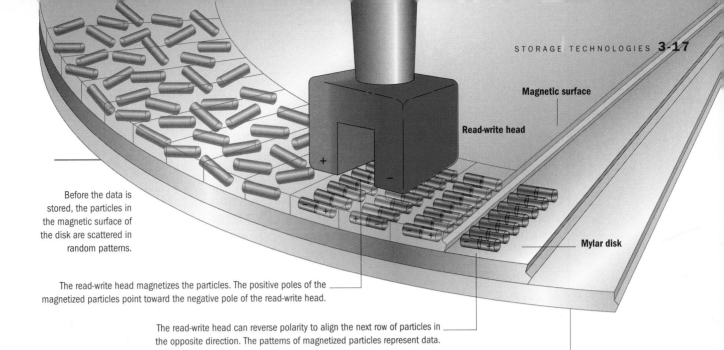

Magnetic surface

Read-write head

Mylar disk

Before the data is stored, the particles in the magnetic surface of the disk are scattered in random patterns.

The read-write head magnetizes the particles. The positive poles of the magnetized particles point toward the negative pole of the read-write head.

The read-write head can reverse polarity to align the next row of particles in the opposite direction. The patterns of magnetized particles represent data.

With **magnetic storage** the computer stores data on disks and tape by magnetizing selected particles of an oxide-based surface coating. The particles retain their magnetic orientation until that orientation is changed, thereby making disks and tape fairly permanent but modifiable storage media. Figure 3-11 shows how a computer stores data on magnetic media.

You can intentionally change or erase files stored on magnetic media. If you run out of storage space on a disk, you can erase files you no longer need to make more space available.

Data stored on magnetic media such as floppy disks can also be unintentionally altered by the environment and by device or media failure.

In the environment, magnetic fields, dust, mold, smoke particles, and heat are the primary culprits causing data loss. Placing a magnet on your disk is a sure way of losing data. The metal detectors in an airport use a magnetic field, but the field is not strong enough to disrupt the data on your floppy or hard disks. The x-ray machine on the conveyer belt is even less disruptive—x-rays do not affect the magnetic particles. You are more likely to damage your disks by leaving them on the dashboard of your car in the sun or carrying them around in your backpack where they will pick up dust and dirt. At many mainframe installations, magnetic media are stored in climate-controlled vaults to protect against environmental hazards such as dust, extreme temperatures, smoke, and mold.

Media failure is a problem with the storage media that results in data loss. Magnetic media gradually lose their magnetic charge, resulting in lost data. Some experts estimate that the reliable life span of data stored on magnetic media is about three years, and they recommend that you refresh your data every two years by recopying it.

A device failure can damage a disk and result in data loss. A **device failure** is a problem with a mechanical device such as a disk drive. Storage devices fail as a result of power or circuitry problems.

With **optical storage**, data is burned into the storage medium using beams of laser light. The burns form patterns of small pits in the disk surface to represent data. The pits on optical media are permanent, so the data cannot be changed. Optical media are very durable—the useful life of

Figure 3-11
Storing data on magnetic media

The data stored on optical media cannot be changed, but the data stored on magnetic media can.

a CD-ROM is estimated to exceed 500 years. Optical media do not, however, give you the flexibility of magnetic media for changing the data once it is stored. CD-ROMs are the most popular type of optical storage. Figure 3-12 shows how a laser burns pits onto an optical disk.

Figure 3-12
Storing data on
an optical disk

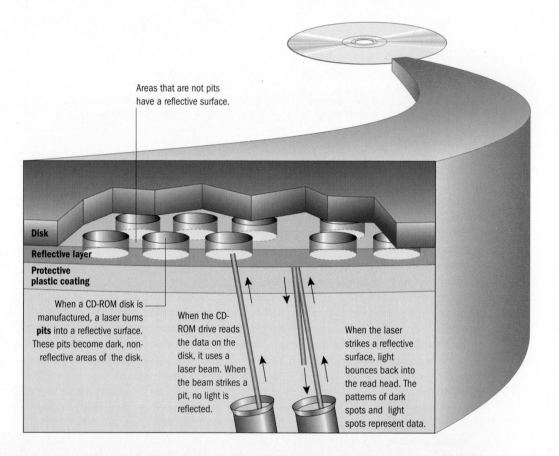

Areas that are not pits
have a reflective surface.

Disk

Reflective layer

**Protective
plastic coating**

When a CD-ROM disk is
manufactured, a laser burns
pits into a reflective surface.
These pits become dark, non-
reflective areas of the disk.

When the CD-
ROM drive reads
the data on the
disk, it uses a
laser beam. When
the beam strikes a
pit, no light is
reflected.

When the laser
strikes a reflective
surface, light
bounces back into
the read head. The
patterns of dark
spots and light
spots represent data.

Floppy Disks

Why is it called a floppy disk?

*A common
misconception
is that a 3½-inch
disk is a "hard disk"
because it has a hard
plastic case. A 3½-
inch disk is a floppy
disk, not a hard disk.*

A **floppy disk** is a flexible mylar plastic disk covered with a thin layer of magnetic oxide. Floppy disks get their name from this thin mylar disk. If you cut open the disk casing (something you should never do unless you want to ruin the disk), you would see that the mylar disk inside is thin and, well, floppy. Floppy disks are also called **floppies** or **diskettes**.

Floppy disks come in several sizes: 3½ inch, 5¼ inch, and 8 inch. The disk size most commonly used on today's microcomputers is 3½ inch. A 3½-inch circular disk made of flexible mylar is housed inside a protective case of rigid plastic. When the disk is inserted in the disk drive, the spring-loaded access cover slides to the side to expose the disk surface for reading and writing data. Figure 3-13 shows the construction of a 3½-inch disk.

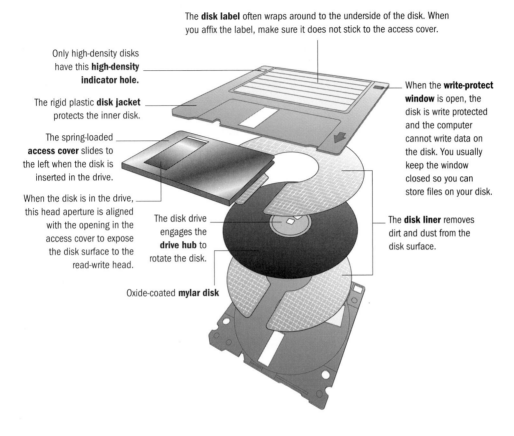

The **disk label** often wraps around to the underside of the disk. When you affix the label, make sure it does not stick to the access cover.

Only high-density disks have this **high-density indicator hole.**

The rigid plastic **disk jacket** protects the inner disk.

The spring-loaded **access cover** slides to the left when the disk is inserted in the drive.

When the disk is in the drive, this head aperture is aligned with the opening in the access cover to expose the disk surface to the read-write head.

The disk drive engages the **drive hub** to rotate the disk.

Oxide-coated **mylar disk**

When the **write-protect window** is open, the disk is write protected and the computer cannot write data on the disk. You usually keep the window closed so you can store files on your disk.

The **disk liner** removes dirt and dust from the disk surface.

Figure 3-13
3½-inch floppy disk

In the past, floppy disks stored data only on one side; but today most store data on both sides. As you might guess, a **double-sided disk**, sometimes abbreviated as DS, stores twice as much data as a single-sided disk.

The amount of data a computer can store on each side of a disk depends on the way the disk is formatted. In Chapter 2 you learned that a disk must be formatted before you can store data on it. The formatting process creates a series of concentric **tracks** on the disk, and each track is divided into smaller segments called **sectors**, as shown in Figure 3-14.

Figure 3-14
A formatted disk

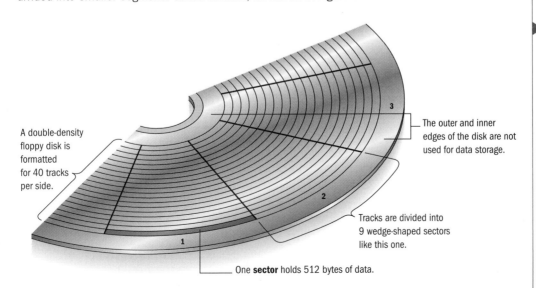

A double-density floppy disk is formatted for 40 tracks per side.

The outer and inner edges of the disk are not used for data storage.

Tracks are divided into 9 wedge-shaped sectors like this one.

One **sector** holds 512 bytes of data.

A double-sided disk that is formatted with 40 tracks per side and 9 sectors per track has 720 sectors. On IBM-compatible computers, each sector of a track holds 512 bytes of data. A file that is 512 bytes or less fits in a single sector. Larger files are stored in more than one sector.

In addition to being doubled-sided, floppy disks are available in both double-density and high-density versions. **Disk density** refers to the size of the magnetic particles on the disk surface. The disk density limits the amount of data you can reliably store on the disk. **Double-density disks**, abbreviated as DD, are also referred to as *low-density* disks. A double-density 3½-inch disk is usually formatted with 80 tracks per side and 9 sectors per track; it stores 720 kilobytes. A **high-density disk**, abbreviated as HD, stores more data than a double-density disk. A high-density 3½-inch disk is usually formatted for 80 tracks and 18 sectors per side, for a storage capacity of 1.44 megabytes. Figure 3-15 summarizes floppy disk capacities by size and density.

Figure 3-15
Floppy disk
capacities

Disk Size	3½ Inch		5¼ Inch	
Density	High	Low	High	Low
Capacity	1.44 MB	720 KB	1.2 MB	360 KB
Sectors per side	18	9	18	9
Tracks per side	80	40	80	40

The higher the disk density, the smaller the magnetic particles it stores, and the more data it can store. Think of it this way: Just as you can put more lemons than grapefruit in a basket, you can store more data on a disk coated with smaller magnetic particles than with larger magnetic particles.

When you purchase and use floppy disks, you must make sure the disk size and storage density match the capacity of your disk drive. You can tell the size of the disk drive by looking at the size of the opening where you insert the disk. You might need to refer to the reference manual for your computer to find out whether the drive can use high-density disks. For example, if you have a high-density 3½-inch disk drive, you should purchase and use high-density 3½-inch disks.

Floppy Disk Drives

Does a floppy disk drive give me fast access to my data?

The storage device that records and retrieves data on a floppy disk is a **floppy disk drive**. Refer to Figure 3-16 to find out how the rotation of the disk, combined with the lateral movement of the read-write head, allows the drive mechanism to access any sector of the disk.

The read-write head can read or write data from any sector of the disk, in any order. This ability to move to any sector is referred to as **random access** or **direct access**. Random access is a handy feature of disk-based storage that provides quick access to files anywhere on a disk. Even with random access, however, a floppy disk drive is not a particularly speedy device. It takes about 0.5 seconds for the drive to spin the disk up to speed and then move the read-write head to a particular sector.

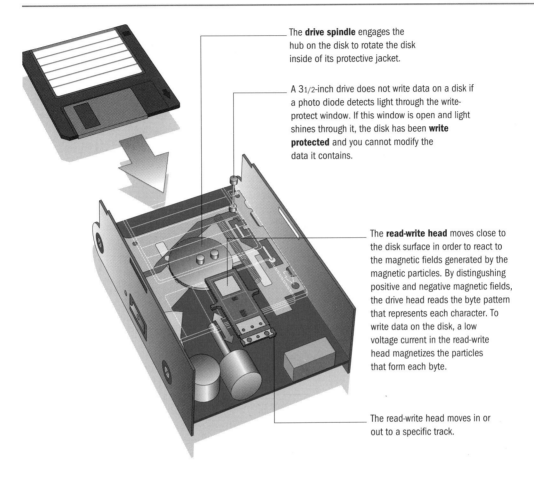

The **drive spindle** engages the hub on the disk to rotate the disk inside of its protective jacket.

A 3 1/2-inch drive does not write data on a disk if a photo diode detects light through the write-protect window. If this window is open and light shines through it, the disk has been **write protected** and you cannot modify the data it contains.

The **read-write head** moves close to the disk surface in order to react to the magnetic fields generated by the magnetic particles. By distingushing positive and negative magnetic fields, the drive head reads the byte pattern that represents each character. To write data on the disk, a low voltage current in the read-write head magnetizes the particles that form each byte.

The read-write head moves in or out to a specific track.

Figure 3-16
How a 3½-inch floppy disk drive works

Uses for Floppy Disk Storage

For what kinds of projects are floppy disks the best kind of storage technology?

Today, floppy disk storage is used for three purposes: distribution, sharing data, and backup.

The most prevalent use of floppy disks is for software distribution. When you purchase software, the package usually includes floppy disks containing programs and data files. However, floppy disks are used less frequently for distribution than they were in the past. Large applications and multimedia are frequently shipped on CD-ROM instead.

The second use for floppy disks is to share data with other computer users. For example, if you want to give a copy of a report to several colleagues, you can copy the report to several floppy disks. Today, instead of floppy disks, many computer users use computer networks or electronic mail to share data.

Another use for floppy disks is to make duplicate copies of your data files in case something happens to the originals, a process known as **backup**. The role of floppy disk storage for backup is being taken over, to some extent, by tape storage.

In the university setting, floppy disks are also used to hold student data. If you have your own computer, you would store most of your data on the hard disk. In a student lab, because you don't have your own computer and you never know which computer you will be assigned, you need to carry your data with you on a floppy disk.

In the past, floppy disks were the primary storage medium for microcomputer systems, but today hard disk storage has taken over that role.

Whether you use floppy disks or other storage media, making a backup of your data is important. Make sure you make regular backups of your data.

Hard Disk Storage

How can a hard disk be the same size as a floppy, but store so much more data?

Hard disk storage provides faster access to files than a floppy disk and is the preferred type of storage for most computer systems. A **hard disk platter** is a flat, rigid disk made of aluminum or glass and coated with a magnetic oxide. A **hard disk** is one or more platters and their associated read-write heads. You will frequently see the terms *hard disk* and *hard disk drive* used interchangeably. You might also hear the term *fixed disk* used to refer to hard disks.

Microcomputer hard disk platters are typically 3½ inches in diameter—the same size as the circular mylar disk in a floppy. However, the storage capacity of a hard disk far exceeds that of a floppy disk. Also, the access time of a hard disk is significantly faster than a floppy disk's. Hard disk storage capacities of 850 MB and access speeds of 11 ms (.0011 seconds) are not uncommon. Figure 3-17 explains how is it possible to pack so much data on a hard disk and access it so quickly.

Figure 3-17
How a hard disk drive works

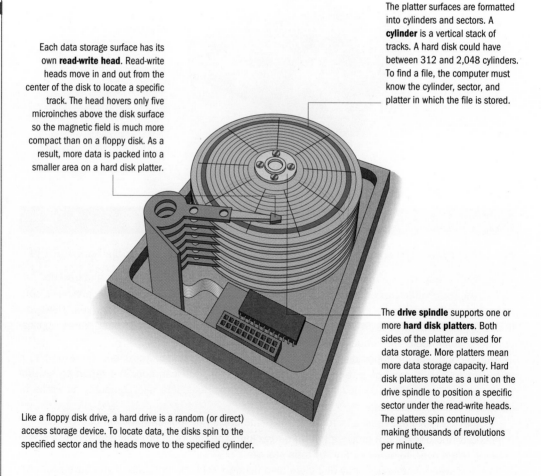

Each data storage surface has its own **read-write head**. Read-write heads move in and out from the center of the disk to locate a specific track. The head hovers only five microinches above the disk surface so the magnetic field is much more compact than on a floppy disk. As a result, more data is packed into a smaller area on a hard disk platter.

The platter surfaces are formatted into cylinders and sectors. A **cylinder** is a vertical stack of tracks. A hard disk could have between 312 and 2,048 cylinders. To find a file, the computer must know the cylinder, sector, and platter in which the file is stored.

Like a floppy disk drive, a hard drive is a random (or direct) access storage device. To locate data, the disks spin to the specified sector and the heads move to the specified cylinder.

The **drive spindle** supports one or more **hard disk platters**. Both sides of the platter are used for data storage. More platters mean more data storage capacity. Hard disk platters rotate as a unit on the drive spindle to position a specific sector under the read-write heads. The platters spin continuously making thousands of revolutions per minute.

Like floppy disks, hard disks provide random access to files by positioning the read-write head over the sector that contains the requested data. Unlike floppy disks, which begin to rotate only when you request data, hard disks are continually in motion, so there is no delay as the disk spins up to speed. As a result, hard disk access is faster than floppy disk access. You can ask your computer operating system to tell you the capacity of your hard disk and how much of the capacity is currently used for data. To do this in DOS, you can type CHKDSK at the C:\> prompt. In Windows 3.1, you can look at the status bar at the bottom of the File Manager window to find your hard disk's capacity. In Windows 95 you can select your hard disk drive icon under My Computer to view a graph of disk capacity and utilization. Figure 3-18 on this page and the next shows you how to find out your disk capacity and utilization under DOS, Windows 3.1, and Windows 95.

It is important to keep track of how much space is available on your disk, so you don't inadvertently fill it up. In Project 2 you can find out how much space is available on your computer's hard disk.

▶ **Figure 3-18**
Hard disk capacity and utilization

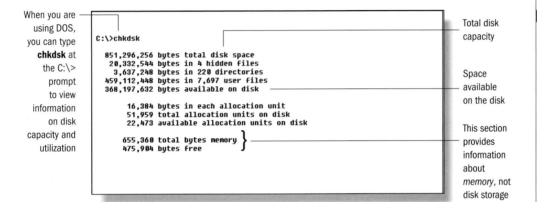

When you are using DOS, you can type **chkdsk** at the C:\> prompt to view information on disk capacity and utilization

```
C:\>chkdsk

    851,296,256 bytes total disk space
     20,332,544 bytes in 4 hidden files
      3,637,248 bytes in 220 directories
    459,112,448 bytes in 7,697 user files
    368,197,632 bytes available on disk

         16,384 bytes in each allocation unit
         51,959 total allocation units on disk
         22,473 available allocation units on disk

        655,360 total bytes memory
        475,904 bytes free
```

Total disk capacity

Space available on the disk

This section provides information about *memory*, not disk storage

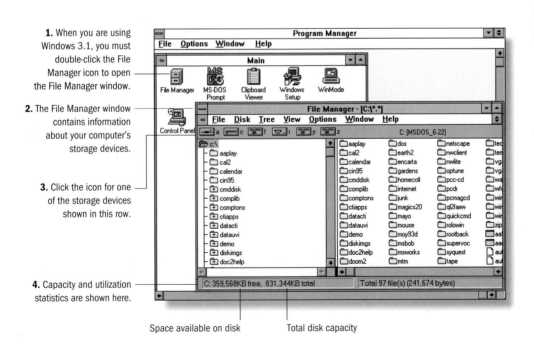

1. When you are using Windows 3.1, you must double-click the File Manager icon to open the File Manager window.

2. The File Manager window contains information about your computer's storage devices.

3. Click the icon for one of the storage devices shown in this row.

4. Capacity and utilization statistics are shown here.

Space available on disk   Total disk capacity

Figure 3-18
Hard disk capacity
and utilization
(continued)

1. When you are using Windows 95, you must double-click the **My Computer** icon to open the My Computer window.

2. In the My Computer window, click the storage device icon for which you want information.

3. Click **File**, then click **Properties** to display the properties of the storage device.

4. The properties are summarized in the Properties window.

Space available on disk

Total disk capacity

Graph shows the percentage of disk capacity used.

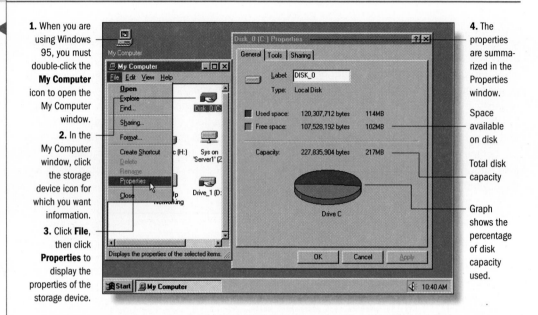

The read-write heads in a hard disk hover a microscopic distance above the disk surface. If a read-write head runs into a dust particle or some other contaminant on the disk, it might cause what is called a **head crash**. A head crash damages some of the data on the disk. To help eliminate contaminants from contacting the platters and causing head crashes, a hard disk is sealed in its case. A head crash can also be triggered by jarring the hard disk while it is in use. Although hard disks have become considerably more rugged in recent years, you should still handle and transport them with care.

Figure 3-19
How a removable
hard disk works

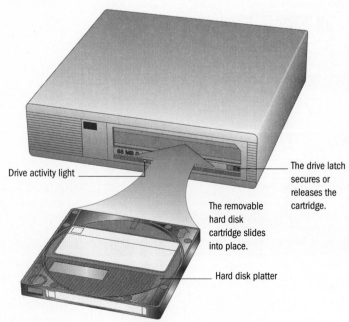

Drive activity light

The drive latch secures or releases the cartridge.

The removable hard disk cartridge slides into place.

Hard disk platter

Some hard disks are removable. **Removable hard disks** or hard disk cartridges, such as the one pictured in Figure 3-19, contain platters and read-write heads that can be inserted and removed from the drive much like a floppy disk. Removable hard disks increase the potential storage capacity of your computer system, although the data is available on only one disk at a time. Removable hard disks also provide security for your data by allowing you to remove the hard disk cartridge and store it separately from the computer.

Mainframe users refer to disk storage as DASD (pronounced "daz-dee"). **DASD** stands for direct access storage device. As a direct, or random, access device, DASD can directly access data, much like a microcomputer hard disk drive. The DASD at most mainframe installations is either disk packs—high-capacity fixed disks—or a redundant array of inexpensive disks (RAID).

Many mainframe installations still use removable disk packs, although they are a fairly old technology. A **disk pack** contains from 6 to 20 hard disks. Each disk is a little larger than 10 inches. The entire pack can be removed and replaced with another pack. Disk packs are gradually being replaced by high-capacity fixed disk drives. **High-capacity fixed disk drive** technology is similar to a microcomputer hard disk with its platters and read-write heads, but the storage capacity of a high-capacity fixed disk drive is measured in gigabytes (billions of bytes), rather than megabytes (millions of bytes). Each high-capacity fixed disk drive is housed in a cabinet. A mainframe computer system might include as many as 100 fixed disk drive cabinets.

RAID, another type of hard disk storage, is found in an increasing number of mainframe and microcomputer installations. RAID stands for redundant array of inexpensive disks. A **RAID** storage device contains many disk platters, provides redundancy, and achieves faster data access than conventional hard disks. The **redundancy** feature of RAID technology protects data from media failures by recording data on more than one disk platter.

To further increase the speed of data access, your computer might use a disk cache. A **disk cache** (pronounced "cash"), illustrated in Figure 3-20, is a special area of computer memory into which the computer transfers the data you are likely to need from disk storage.

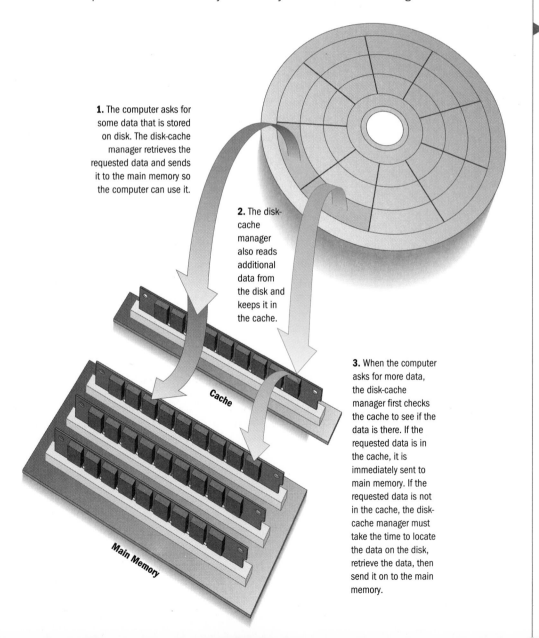

▶ **Figure 3-20**
How disk caching works

1. The computer asks for some data that is stored on disk. The disk-cache manager retrieves the requested data and sends it to the main memory so the computer can use it.

2. The disk-cache manager also reads additional data from the disk and keeps it in the cache.

Cache

Main Memory

3. When the computer asks for more data, the disk-cache manager first checks the cache to see if the data is there. If the requested data is in the cache, it is immediately sent to main memory. If the requested data is not in the cache, the disk-cache manager must take the time to locate the data on the disk, retrieve the data, then send it on to the main memory.

To understand cache, think of the disk as a supermarket. When you go to the supermarket, you have a shopping list. You need a package of chicken for dinner tonight, but you buy two packages of chicken and put one in the freezer. The freezer is like the cache—it stores something until you need it, and you don't have to go all the way to the store again to get it.

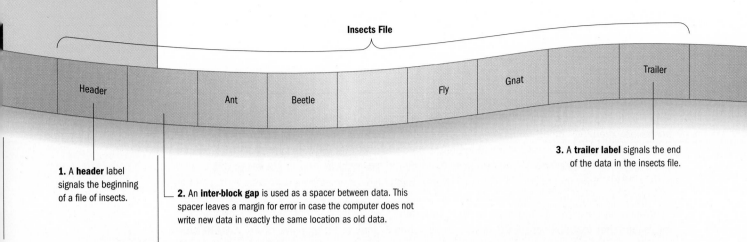

Insects File

| Header | | | Ant | Beetle | | Fly | Gnat | | Trailer | |

1. A **header** label signals the beginning of a file of insects.

2. An **inter-block gap** is used as a spacer between data. This spacer leaves a margin for error in case the computer does not write new data in exactly the same location as old data.

3. A **trailer label** signals the end of the data in the insects file.

Figure 3-21
Sequential file access on magnetic tape

How does a disk cache help speed things up? Suppose your computer retrieves the data from a particular sector of your disk. There is a high probability that the next data you need will be from an adjacent sector—the remainder of a program file, for example, or the next section of a data file. The computer reads the data from nearby sectors and stores it in the cache. If the data you need next is already in the cache, the computer doesn't need to wait while the mechanical parts of the drive locate and read the data from the disk.

Tape Storage

Do they still use those big tape drives on computers that you see in old movies?

In the 1960s, magnetic tape was the most popular form of mainframe computer storage. When IBM introduced its first microcomputer in 1981, the legacy of tape storage continued in the form of a cassette tape drive, similar to those used for audio recording and playback.

Using tape as a primary storage device instead of a hard disk would be slow and inconvenient because tape requires sequential, rather than random, access. With **sequential access**, data is stored and read as a sequence of bytes along the length of the tape. To find a file stored on a microcomputer tape storage device, you advance the tape to the approximate location of the file, then wait for the computer to slowly read each byte until it finds the beginning of the file. Study the sequential access diagram in Figure 3-21 to learn how computers store data on tape.

Microcomputer users quickly abandoned tape storage for the convenience and speed of random access disk drives. Recently, however, tape storage for microcomputers has experienced a revival—not as a principal storage device, but for making backup copies of the data stored on hard disks. As you have learned in this chapter, the data on magnetic storage can be easily destroyed, erased, or otherwise lost. Protecting the data on the hard disk is of particular concern to users because it contains so much data—data that would be difficult and time-consuming to reconstruct. Therefore, it is a good idea to have a copy of the data tucked safely away as a backup.

A **tape backup** is a copy of the data on a hard disk, stored on magnetic tape, and used to restore lost data. A tape backup is relatively inexpensive and can rescue you from the overwhelming task of trying to reconstruct lost data. If you lose the data on your hard disk, you can copy the data from the tape backup back to the hard disk. Typically, you do not use the data directly from the tape backup because the sequential access is too slow to be practical.

Make sure you understand the difference between sequential access and random access. It is the key to the popularity of disk storage technology and the limitation of tape storage technology.

Although tape storage devices are useful for data backup, many computer users still back up their data to floppy disks.

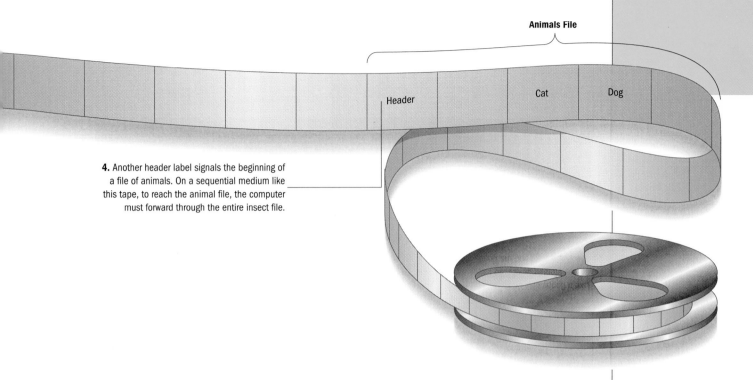

Animals File

Header   Cat   Dog

4. Another header label signals the beginning of a file of animals. On a sequential medium like this tape, to reach the animal file, the computer must forward through the entire insect file.

The most popular type of tape drive for microcomputers uses tape cartridges, but there are different tape specifications and cartridge sizes. The specifications for tape storage include tape length and width. When you purchase tapes, check the tape drive manual to make sure the tapes you purchase are the correct type for your tape drive. Figure 3-22 illustrates the basic concepts of tape storage.

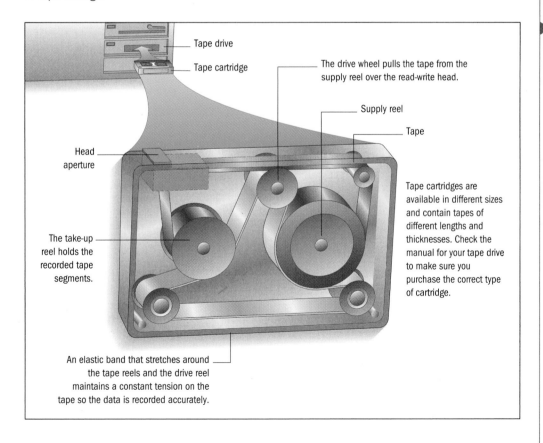

Figure 3-22
Cartridge tape storage

Tape drive

Tape cartridge

The drive wheel pulls the tape from the supply reel over the read-write head.

Supply reel

Tape

Head aperture

Tape cartridges are available in different sizes and contain tapes of different lengths and thicknesses. Check the manual for your tape drive to make sure you purchase the correct type of cartridge.

The take-up reel holds the recorded tape segments.

An elastic band that stretches around the tape reels and the drive reel maintains a constant tension on the tape so the data is recorded accurately.

CD-ROM Storage

If CD-ROMs are read only, doesn't that limit their use?

CD-ROMs are based on the same technology as the audio CDs you buy at your favorite music store. Their technology is derived from the compact disc digital-audio recording system. CD-ROM (pronounced "cee dee rom") stands for Compact Disc Read Only Memory. A computer CD-ROM disk, like its audio counterpart, contains data that has been stamped on the disk surface as a series of pits. To read the data on a CD-ROM, an optical read head distinguishes the patterns of pits that represent bytes. Figure 3-23 shows how you load a CD into the CD-ROM drive.

A CD-ROM drive supplements, rather than replaces, a hard disk drive because a CD-ROM is a read-only device.

Figure 3-23
CD-ROM storage

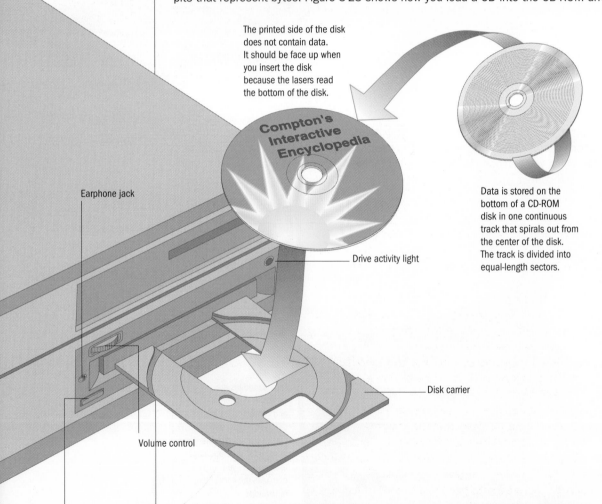

The printed side of the disk does not contain data. It should be face up when you insert the disk because the lasers read the bottom of the disk.

Data is stored on the bottom of a CD-ROM disk in one continuous track that spirals out from the center of the disk. The track is divided into equal-length sectors.

Earphone jack

Drive activity light

Disk carrier

Volume control

Push-button slides disk carrier in or out.

CD-ROMs provide tremendous storage capacity. A single CD-ROM disk holds up to 680 megabytes, equivalent to more than 300,000 pages of text, and is quite durable. The surface of the disk is coated with a clear plastic, making the data permanent and unalterable.

CD-ROM disks are limited by the fact that they are *read only*. **Read only** means that the computer can retrieve data from a CD-ROM but cannot save any new data on it. In this respect, CD-ROM technology differs from hard disk storage, on which you can write, erase, and read data. A read-only CD-ROM drive does not generally serve as the sole storage device for a microcomputer.

A CD-ROM disk is relatively inexpensive to manufacture, making it an ideal way for software publishers to distribute large programs and data files. CD-ROM is the media of choice for delivery of multimedia applications because it provides the large storage capacity necessary for sound, video, and graphics files.

A recent technological development is the creation of CDs on which you can write data. **CD-R** (compact disc-recordable) technology allows the computer to record data on a CD-R disk using a special CD-R recording device. Disks that have been produced with the CD-R device can be used on a regular CD-ROM drive, like the one you might have on your computer. As with regular CD-ROMs the data on the disk cannot be erased or modified. An earlier device called a WORM drive also stored data on CDs using optical technology. The CDs, however, could not be used in regular CD-ROM drives, so their use did not become widespread.

CD-R is a useful technology for archiving data. **Archiving** refers to the process of moving data off a primary storage device when that data is not frequently accessed. For example, a business might archive its accounting data for previous years or a hospital might archive billing records once the accounts are paid. What's the difference between an archive and a backup? Archived data does not generally change, but the data you back up might change frequently.

Physical File Storage

Do I need to know exactly where each file is stored on a disk?

Although a disk is formatted into tracks and sectors that provide physical storage locations for data, files are actually stored in clusters. A **cluster** is a group of sectors; it is the smallest storage unit the computer can access. The number of sectors that form a cluster depends on the type of computer. IBM-compatible microcomputers form a cluster from two sectors. Each cluster is numbered and the operating system maintains a list of which sectors correspond to each cluster.

When the computer stores a file on a random-access storage medium, the operating system records the cluster number that contains the beginning of the file in a file allocation table (FAT). The **FAT** is an operating system file that maintains a list of files and their physical location on the disk. The FAT is such a crucial file that if it is damaged by a head crash or other disaster, you generally lose access to all the data stored on your disk. This is yet another reason to have a backup of the data on your hard drive.

When you want to store a file, the operating system looks at the FAT to see which clusters are empty. The operating system then puts the data for the file in empty clusters. The cluster numbers are recorded in the FAT. The name of the new file and the number of the first cluster that contains the file data are recorded in the directory.

A file that does not fit into a single cluster will spill over into the next adjacent or *contiguous* cluster unless that cluster already contains data. If the next cluster is full, the operating system stores the file in a nonadjacent cluster and sets up instructions called *pointers*. These "point" to each piece of the file, as shown in Figure 3-24 on the following page.

When you want to retrieve a file, the operating system looks through the directory for the filename and the number of the first cluster that contains the file data. The FAT tells the computer which clusters contain the remaining data for the file. The operating system moves the read-write head to the cluster that contains the beginning of the file and reads it. If the file is stored in more than one cluster, the read-write head must move to the next cluster to read more of the file. It takes longer to access a file stored in nonadjacent clusters than one stored in adjacent clusters because the disk or head must move farther to find the next section of the file.

To differentiate between physical and logical file storage, remember that physical file storage refers to the way data is electronically stored on the storage medium. Logical file storage refers to the metaphor you use to visualize the organization of your files.

Lab

Defragmentation and Disk Operations

Figure 3-24
How the FAT works

1. The directory is a file maintained by the operating system that contains a list of files on the disk and the number of the cluster that contains the start of the file. The directory and FAT work together to keep track of the files on a disk.

2. The directory contains the filenames and the cluster number that contains the beginning of the file. Here the directory shows that a file called **Jordan.Wks** begins in cluster 7.

Directory	
Filename	**Starting Cluster**
Bio.Txt	**3**
Jordan.Wks	**7**
Pick.Wps	**9**

3. The file allocation table (FAT) is a file maintained by the operating system to keep track of the physical location of files on a disk.

4. Each cluster is listed in the FAT, along with a number that indicates the status of the cluster. If status is "1," the cluster is reserved for technical files. If status is "0," the cluster is empty, so new data can be stored there. If the status is "999," the cluster contains the end of a file. Other status numbers indicate the sector that holds more data for a file.

5. Looking at the FAT entry for cluster 7, you see that the **Jordan.Wks** file continues in cluster 8.

6. The FAT entry for cluster 8, shows that the **Jordan.Wks** file continues in the cluster 10. The file is stored in **non-contiguous** clusters 7, 8, and 10.

7. The FAT entry for cluster 10 shows that this is the end of the **Jordan.Wks** file.

Fat		
Cluster	Status	Comment
1	1	Reserved for operating system
2	1	Reserved for operating system
3	4	First cluster of Bio.Txt. Points to cluster 8 which holds more data for Bio.Txt.
4	999	Last cluster of Bio.Txt
5	0	Empty
6	0	Empty
7	8	First cluster for Jordan.Wks. Points to cluster 8 which holds more data for the Jordan.Wks file.
8	10	Points to cluster 10 which holds more data for the Jordan.Wks file.
9	999	First and last cluster containing Pick.Wps
10	999	Last cluster of Jordan.Wks

As you use random-access storage, files tend to become **fragmented**, that is, each file is stored in many nonadjacent clusters. Drive performance generally declines as the drive works harder to locate the clusters that contain the parts of a file. To regain peak performance, you can use a **defragmentation utility** to rearrange the files on a disk so that they are stored in adjacent clusters. Study Figure 3-25, which explains more about fragmentation and defragmentation.

Figure 3-25
Defragmenting
a disk

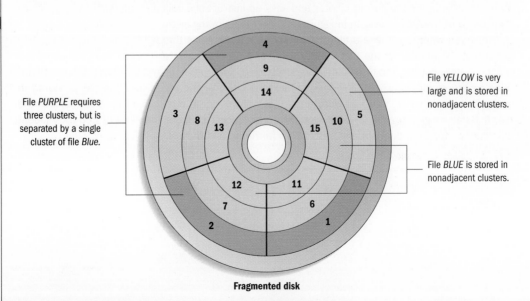

File *PURPLE* requires three clusters, but is separated by a single cluster of file *Blue*.

File *YELLOW* is very large and is stored in nonadjacent clusters.

File *BLUE* is stored in nonadjacent clusters.

Fragmented disk

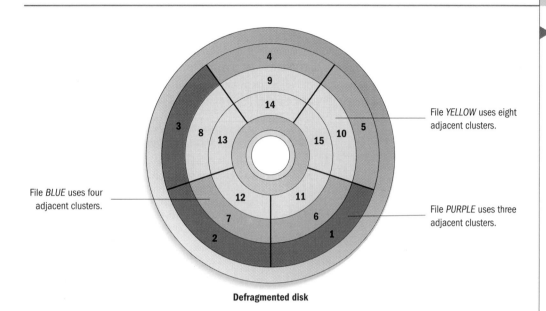

File *YELLOW* uses eight adjacent clusters.

File *BLUE* uses four adjacent clusters.

File *PURPLE* uses three adjacent clusters.

Defragmented disk

Figure 3-25
Defragmenting a disk
(continued)

When you erase a file, the operating system changes the status of the appropriate clusters in the FAT. For example, if a file is stored in clusters 1, 2, 5, and 7 and you erase it, the operating system changes the status for those four clusters to "empty." The data is not physically removed or erased from those clusters. Instead, the old data remains in the clusters until a new file is stored there. This rather interesting situation means that if you inadvertently erase a file, you might be able to get it back using the operating system's undelete utility. Of course, you can only undelete a file if you haven't recorded something new over it, so undelete works only if you discover and correct mistakes immediately. Not all operating systems provide an undelete utility. To find out if one is available, you can consult the reference manual for your operating system.

Quick Check

1 Storage capacity is measured in _____, and access time is measured in _____.

2 A magnet can disrupt data on _____ storage, but _____ storage technology is more durable.

3 The formatting process creates a series of concentric _____ and triangle-shaped _____ on the disk.

4 The computer can move directly to any file on a(n) _____ access device, but must start at the beginning and read through all the data on a(n) _____ access device.

5 When software is sold, it is typically distributed on either _____ or _____ media.

6 The primary storage device on a microcomputer is _____.

7 The _____ keeps track of the physical location of files on a disk.

8 True or False: Data files that are entered by the user, changed often, or shared with other users are generally stored on optical media.

User **Focus:**
3.3

Using Files

Lab

Using Files

Figure 3-26
File operations
for a typical
word processing
session

N ow that you have learned about logical and physical file storage, let's apply what you've learned to how you typically use files when you work with application software. Using word processing software to produce a document illustrates the way you use files on a computer, so let's look at the file operations for a typical word processing session. Examine Figure 3-26 to get an overview of the file activities of a typical word processing session.

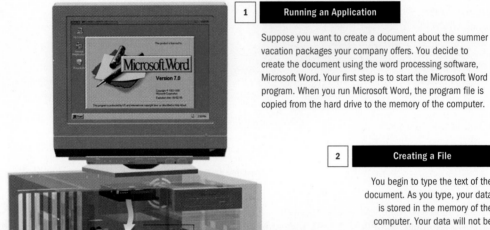

1   Running an Application

Suppose you want to create a document about the summer vacation packages your company offers. You decide to create the document using the word processing software, Microsoft Word. Your first step is to start the Microsoft Word program. When you run Microsoft Word, the program file is copied from the hard drive to the memory of the computer.

2   Creating a File

You begin to type the text of the document. As you type, your data is stored in the memory of the computer. Your data will not be stored on disk until you initiate the Save command.

Word.Exe is
loaded into
memory from
hard disk

Your data is stored in
memory while you type

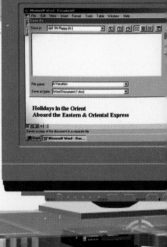

3   Saving a Data File

When you create a file and save it on disk for the first time, the application or the operating system prompts you to name the file so you can later retrieve it by name. You know from earlier in this chapter that the name you give to a file must follow the naming convention for the operating system. You name the file **A:Vacation.Doc.** By typing A: you direct the computer to save the file on the floppy disk in drive A: The computer looks for empty clusters on the disk where it can store the file. The computer then adds the filename to the directory, along with the number of the cluster that contains the beginning of the file. Once you have saved your file, you can exit the Word program or work on another document.

When you save your revisions they overwrite the old contents of **Vacation.Doc** on the disk.

The changes you make to **Vacation.Doc** the document are stored in memory

Word.Exe is loaded into memory

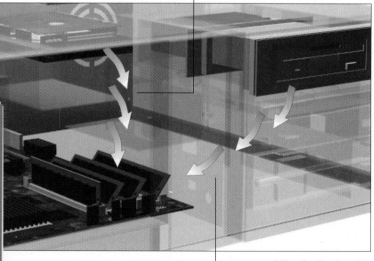

A:Vacation.Doc is copied from disk into memory

A:Vacation.Doc is copied from memory to the floppy disk

---

4 | **Revising a Data File**

When you see the **Vacation.Doc** file on the screen, you can make modifications to it. Each character that you type and each change that you make is stored temporarily in the main memory of the computer, but not on the disk. The main memory retains data only as long as the computer power is on. So to store your data on a more permanent basis, you must tell the computer to copy the data from the memory of the computer to the disk.

The **Vacation.Doc** file is already on the disk, however, so when you are done with the modifications you have two options. Option one is to store the revised version in place of the old version. Option two is to create a new file for your revision and give it a different name, such as **Holiday**.

If you decide to go with option one—store the revised version in place of the old version—the operating system copies your revised data from the computer memory to the same clusters that contained the old file. You do not have to take a separate step to delete the old file—the operating system automatically records the new file over it.

If you decide to go with option two—create a new file for the revision—the application prompts you for a filename. Your revisions will be stored under the new filename. The original file, **Vacation.Doc**, will still remain on the disk in its unrevised form.

5 | **Retrieving a Data File**

Now suppose that a few days later, you decide that you want to revise **Vacation.Doc**. You need to start Microsoft Word. Once the Word program is running, you can retrieve the **Vacation.Doc** file from the disk on which it is stored.

When you wat to use a data file that already exists on disk storage, you must tell the application to open the file. In Microsoft Word you either type the name of the file, **A:Vacation.Doc**, or select the filename from a list of files stored on the disk. The application communicates the filename to the operating system. The operating system looks at the directory and FAT to find which clusters contain the file, then moves the read-write head to the appropriate disk location to read the file. The electronics on the disk drive transfer the file data into the main memory of the computer where your application software can manipulate it. Once the operating system has retrieved the file, the word processing software displays it on the screen.

Lab

**DOS Directories
and File Management**

Figure 3-27
Using
Windows 3.1
to copy a file

Copying Files

Can I copy a file from the hard disk to my floppy disk and vice versa?

You can copy a file from one storage medium to another. When you copy a file, the original file remains intact. You'll find that copying files is a task you will do frequently. Making copies of important files as backup, copying files from your hard disk to a floppy disk to share with a friend, or transferring files you receive on a floppy disk to your hard disk are only a few of the tasks that require you to know how to copy files.

Suppose you want to copy the **Vacation.Doc** file from a floppy disk to your hard disk. The operating system is responsible for maintaining the list of files on your disk, so you usually use the operating system to copy files. With a graphical operating system such as Microsoft Windows, you can drag the icon that represents **Vacation.Doc** from its place in the directory of drive A: to the icon that represents drive C:, as shown in Figure 3-27.

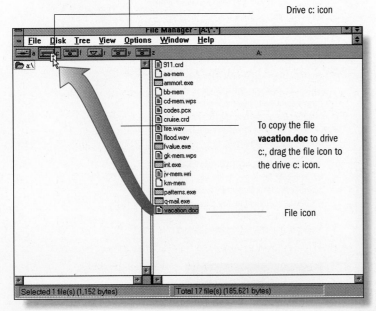

Drive c: icon

To copy the file **vacation.doc** to drive c:, drag the file icon to the drive c: icon.

File icon

With the DOS operating system, you use the Copy command to copy a file. Let's assume that the disk containing **Vacation.Doc** is in drive A: and your hard disk drive is drive C:. The DOS command to copy **Vacation.Doc** from drive A: to a subdirectory called Plans on drive C: is:

COPY A:Vacation.Doc C:\Plans\Vacation.Doc

Deleting Files

What if I delete a file that I still need?

Eliminating files that you no longer need opens space for new files. If you want to eliminate a file that you have saved on disk, you **delete** or **erase** the file. As you know, when you delete a file, the operating system does not physically erase the cluster that contains the data belonging to that file. Instead, it changes the entries in the FAT to indicate that the clusters are available for storing other files. As additional files are stored on the disk, the sectors that formerly contained the deleted file are gradually overwritten.

To delete the file **Vacation.Doc** from the disk in drive A: using DOS, you type: DEL A:Vacation.Doc. To delete a file using Windows 3.1, you highlight the file in the File Manager window, then press the Delete key. Using Windows 95 you delete a file by pressing the Delete key to delete the icon that represents the file.

If you accidentally erase a file, you should stop using the computer immediately. Do not store anything else on the drive that contains the erased file until you have successfully used an undelete utility program to restore the file.

End Note Having access to many files stored on hard disks or CD-ROMs is a valuable advantage of today's computer technology. To use files effectively, you should know how to interact with the computer's filing system: how to name, save, retrieve, copy, and erase files. You should now understand how storage devices, the operating system, and application software interact to help you maintain a filing system for your data.

Review

1. Answer the questions in italics below each heading in this chapter, using your own words.

2. List the three most *practical* things you learned from this chapter. Why do you think they are the most practical?

3. List each of the boldface terms used in this chapter, then use your own words to write a short definition of each term. If you would like clarification of one or more terms, refer to a computer dictionary or a computer science encyclopedia such as those listed in the Resources section of Chapter 1. You can also refer to the Glossary/Index on page 3-42.

4. Copy the following chart on paper. Place an X in the Data Files column if the feature applies to data files. Place an X in the Executable Files column if the feature applies to executable files. If a feature applies to both, put an X in both columns.

Feature	Data Files	Executable Files
Created by you, the user		
Created by programmers		
Use an application to view it		
Supplied with software		
Has an .EXE or .COM extension		
Referred to as a program or application		

5. Indicate which filenames in the following list are invalid under the operating system used in your school's computer lab. Which filenaming convention does each nonvalid filename violate?

Wp.Exe	Ppr	Win.Exe
Autoexec.Bat	Results*.Wks	Monthly.Wk1
Report#1.Txt	Smith&Smith.Doc	Sep/94.Wri
Aaia map.Doc	Ocean.Tif	Mn43-44.Dbf

6. Examine the directory listing in Figure 3-28 and answer the following questions:

Figure 3-28

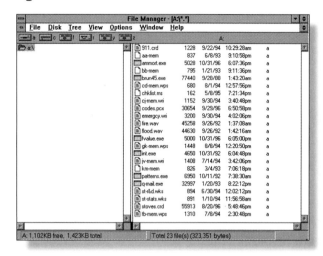

a. What is the size of the file **Stoves.Crd**?

b. On what date was **911.Crd** last modified?

c. How many program files are on the disk?

d. Approximately how many megabytes of storage are available on the disk?

e. What application was used to create **Cj-mem.Wri**?

f. How many of these files are data files?

g. What is the largest file on the disk?

h. Does **Codes.Pcx** contain text or graphics?

i. What type of data does the file **Fire.Wav** contain?

j. How many of the files appear to be memos?

k. How would you use a wildcard to get a directory of all the files with .Wri extensions?

l. How many files match the specification S*.*?

m. How many files match the specification *.*?

7. Suppose you have a disk with the following files:

Minutes.Doc	Report.Doc	Budget.Xls
Jacsmemo.Doc	Report1.Doc	Shipjan.Xls
Shipfeb.Xls	Shipmar.Xlx	Shipapr.Xls
Minutes.Txt	Roger.Txt	Roadmap.Bmp

If you could specify all the files with a .Doc extension by *.Doc. How would you specify the following files?

a. All the files with .Xls extensions

b. All the files that contain minutes

c. All the files that begin with "Ship"

d. All the files on the disk

e. All the files that begin with the letter "R"

8. Suppose you need to retrieve a file from Sarah's computer. She tells you that the file is stored as

Projects

C:\Data\Monthend.Doc.

   a. What is the filename?

   b. What is the file extension?

   c. On which drive is the file stored?

   d. In which directory is the file stored?

   e. What type of file is it likely to be?

   f. Will you need a specific software program to retrieve and view the file?

9. On each of the following three lines, indicate the relative position of floppy disk, hard disk ,tape, and CD-ROM storage by placing these storage types along the line. The first one is completed for you.

   a. Access time (slowest to fastest):

Tape   CD-ROM   Floppy disk   Hard disk
slow ─────────────────────────────────→ fast

   b. Capacity (smallest to largest):

small ─────────────────────────────────→ large

   c. Reliability (least reliable to most reliable):

easy to lose data ─────────→ data is very secure

10. How would you explain the difference between physical storage and logical storage to someone who is not "computer literate?" Can you think of noncomputer analogies in which the way we think about something (logical view) is different from the way it really is (physical view)?

11. Suppose you need to defragment the files manually on the disk shown in Figure 3-29. Using the disk on the right, show how the files are arranged after you complete the defragmentation. Use colored pencils or different patterns to show each file clearly.

Figure 3-29 ◄

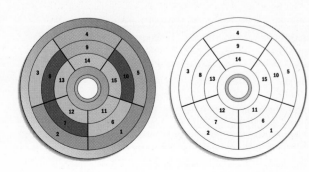

1. File Extensions Many software applications use a specific file extension for data files created with that application. Determine the extensions used by five applications on your own computer or a lab computer. Run each software application and attempt to retrieve a file. If the software application uses a specific file extension, you will usually see the extension indicated in a box on the screen. For example, you might see *.Doc if you are using Microsoft Word for Windows.

For each of the five programs you select:

   a. Specify the program name.

   b. Sketch a picture of the program icon (if you are using Windows) or indicate the executable filename (if you are using DOS).

   c. Indicate the filename extension the program uses. If the program does not use a specific filename extension, indicate that this is the case.

2. Storage Devices You Use You should be aware of the storage devices on your computer so that you use the best device for each task. You will need to take a hands-on look at your computer at home or a computer in your school lab to answer the following questions:

   a. Where is this computer located?

   b. What is the hard disk capacity? (Hint: Refer to Figure 3-18.)

   c. What is the hard disk drive letter?

   d. What is the floppy disk size?

   e. What is the floppy disk capacity?

   f. What is the floppy disk drive letter?

   g. Is there a tape storage device?

   h. Is there a CD-ROM drive?

   i. Which storage device do you usually use for the data files you create?

   j. Which storage device holds most of the applications software that you use?

   k. Which storage device would you use for backups?

3. Calculating Storage Requirements How much storage space would be needed to store this textbook? To calculate approximately how many bytes of storage space this text (not including pictures) requires:

   a. Count the number of lines on a typical page.

   b. Count the number of characters (including blanks) in the longest line of text on the page.

   c. Multiply the number of lines by the number of characters in the longest line to calculate the number of characters (bytes) per page.

   d. Multiply this figure by the number of pages in the book.

e. What do you estimate is the computer storage space required for this text?

4. Calculating Hard Disk Capacity Most manufacturers list the storage capacity of their hard disk drives on the drive itself or in the user manual. The manufacturer calculates storage capacity in bytes using the formula:

capacity = cylinders × surfaces × sectors × 512

The 512 in the formula is the number of bytes stored in each sector of each cylinder. Suppose you have a hard disk with 615 cylinders, 4 surfaces (two platters), and 17 sectors. What is the capacity in bytes of this disk?

5. Shopping for Storage Use a recent computer magazine or an Internet site such as Computer Express at *http://www.cexpress.com* to fill in the following "shopping list:"

Item	Brand	Merchant	Price
Package of 10 3½-inch floppy disks			
High-density 3½-inch floppy disk drive			
850 MB 10 ms hard disk drive			
Tape drive			
Quad-speed CD-ROM			

6. What's in That File? Earlier, you learned to distinguish between executable, data, and source files. In this project, you will look at the contents of each file type. When you view an executable file, you should see meaningless symbols. When you view a data file, you should be able to read the data applications. When you view a source file, you should be able to read the commands it contains. The Type command lets you view the contents of a file without changing it. You can use the Type command to look at the **Autoexec.Bat** source file, the **Command.Com** executable file, and the **Country.Txt** data file.

If you are using DOS, make sure you are at the C:\> prompt. If you are using Windows 3.1, double-click the MS-DOS prompt icon in the Main window. If you are using Windows 95, click the Start button, select Programs, then select MS-DOS prompt. Do each of the following steps, and write down the first line you see on the screen:

a. Type the following command (including "type"), then press the Enter key:
type c:\autoexec.bat I more

b. Type the following command, then press the Enter key:**type c:\command.com**

c. Type the following command, then press the Enter key: **type c:\dos\country.txt I more**

7. Troubleshooting a Storage Problem Read the following scenario and determine what went wrong, then write a paragraph describing what you would do to correct the problem. Your instructor will indicate if you should do this project individually or discuss it in a small group.

Toni's 80 MB hard disk contained about 75 MB of files on February 18. On that day, she made a tape backup of the entire disk. On February 19, Toni moved to a company office one block away. The company maintenance staff moved the computer, along with Toni's paper files, in the late afternoon. The people on the maintenance crew left the computer on the desk in the new office.

On February 20, Toni set up the computer and turned it on. Everything seemed fine. She used the computer to write a few memos using WordPerfect for Windows. On February 21, Toni tried to open a data file containing the names and addresses of her clients. The computer displayed a message—something about an error on drive C:. Toni turned off her computer and then turned it back on, hoping the error would go away, but the computer wouldn't let her access any data on the hard disk.

8. CD-Mania What's the difference between the CDs that contain your favorite music album and the CD-ROMs you use in a computer? You might be surprised to learn that some computer CD-ROM drives can play your music CDs. In fact, there are several CD formats, including CD-DA, CD-I, CD-ROM, PhotoCD, and CD-R. For this project, use your library and Internet resources to write a paper describing these CD formats. The length of your paper will depend on the scope of the project: a three-page paper is suitable for a short project, a term paper might require 10-15 pages. Be sure you include a bibliography.

Your paper can deal with CDs from the technical perspective or from the applied perspective. If you take the technical perspective, you should look for answers to questions such as, but not limited to:

a. What are the capacity and storage format for each type of CD?

b. Why did these specifications originate?

c. What are the advantages and disadvantages of each?

If you take the applied perspective, you should try to find the answers to questions such as, but not limited to:

   a. What are the primary uses for each type of CD?

   b. What are the advantages and disadvantages of each?

   c. How do the costs of each format compare?

9. Data Storage in Organizations Organizations take different approaches to data storage, depending on the volume of their data, the value of their data, and the need for data security. The purpose of this Project is to interview the person responsible for maintaining the data for an organization and discover the answers to the following questions:

   a. What is the position title of the person responsible for this organization's data storage?

   b. What preparation did this individual have to qualify for this position?

   c. What are this individual's job responsibilities?

   d. How does this individual keep up with trends that affect data storage?

   e. What type of data does the organization store?

   f. What percent of this data is stored on a computer system?

   g. What types of storage devices are used in this organization?

   h. What is the capacity of each storage device?

   i. What happens when the storage devices are full?

   j. What problems are associated with maintaining the data for this organization?

This project works well if the class is divided into teams and each team interviews a person from a different organization. Each team can then present a 15-minute report to the rest of the class, along with a two- to three-page written report of its findings.

10. The Future of Computer Storage Ten years ago, the idea of 500 MB of storage on a personal computer seemed incredible. But technology turned that dream into reality. What storage technologies might we use in the future? Will optical storage cubes the size of a nine-volt battery hold gigabytes of data? Will *smart* credit cards hold all our financial data? Will magneto-optical devices combine the flexibility of magnetic media with the permanence of optical media? Will data be stored as holograms?

Use recent computer magazines and journals to research trends and projections for computer storage technology.

You might want to do a survey and write a paragraph or two on each new technology, or you might want to take an in-depth look at a technology that you find interesting.

The paper you write as the result of your research can be as short as 3 pages or as long as 25 pages, depending on the scope of the project specified by your instructor.

Resources

- **IBM's Internet Web site** This Web site contains information on micro, mini, and mainframe computer storage. Look at the section on product information and select Storage from the list of product categories. Access this site at *http://www.ibm.com.*

- **The Internet Yahoo Directory** This directory is a list of Internet sites with information on CD-ROM and hard disk drives. Access this site at *http://yahoo.com/ Computers/Hardware/Peripherals.*

- **Rosch, W.** *The Winn L. Rosch Hardware Bible.* 3rd ed. Indianapolis: Sams Publishing, 1994. This book is one of the definitive references on microcomputer hardware. The emphasis is on technical details, but most of the explanations are clearly written for users who don't necessarily have a degree in electrical engineering or computer science. Chapters 21 through 25 cover microcomputer storage technology, including specifications for CD formats. This is a good source of information for Project 8.

- *Understanding Computers: Memory and Storage.* Alexandria, VA: Time-Life Books, 1987. Time-Life Books has produced a lavishly illustrated series of books on computers that provide substantial detail in an easy-to-understand format. One of the books, Memory and Storage, contains an excellent section on storage devices—how they were developed and how they work.

Lab Assignments

DOS Directories and File Management

DOS is an operating system used on millions of computers. Even if your computer has a graphical user interface, such as Microsoft Windows, understanding DOS commands helps you grasp the basic concepts of computer file management. In this Lab, you learn how to use basic DOS commands.

1. Click the Steps button to learn basic DOS commands. As you proceed through the Steps, answer all of the Quick Check questions that appear. After you complete the Steps, you will see a Quick Check Summary Report. Follow the instructions on the screen to print this report.

2. Go through the Steps for this Lab once again. This time, create a mini DOS manual by listing each DOS command and its function. For each command, you should also provide a sample of a valid command, for example:

DIR   Provides a listing of all the files on a disk

Example: DIR A:

3. Click the Explore button and make a new disk. (You can copy over the disk you used for Steps.) Do each of the following tasks and record the command you used:

a. Display the directory for drive A:.

b. Display only those files on drive A: that begin with the letter "T."

c. Erase all the files that have names beginning with "New."

d. Create a directory called PAPERS.

e. Move all the files with .DOC extensions into the PAPERS directory.

f. Rename OPUS27.MID to SONG.MID.

g. Delete all the files with names that start with "Budget."

4. In Explore, make a new disk. (You can copy over the disk you used for earlier Lab activities.) Do each of the following tasks, then give your disk to your instructor. Don't forget to put your name on the disk label.

a. Make two subdirectories on your disk: PICS and BUDGETS.

b. Move all the files with .BMP extensions into the PICS directory.

c. Move all the files with .WKS extensions into the BUDGETS directory.

d. Delete all the files except README.TXT from the root directory. (Do not delete the files from PICS or BUDGETS.)

e. Rename the file README.TXT to READ.ME.

5. Use the TYPE command to view the contents of the START.BAT file. Describe the file contents. Use the TYPE command to view the contents of OPUS27.MID. Describe what you see? Explain the different results you obtained when you used the TYPE command with START.BAT and OPUS27.MID.

Windows Directories, Folders, and Files

Graphical user interfaces such as MacOS, Windows 3.1, and Windows 95 use a filing system metaphor for file management. In this Lab, you will learn the basic concepts of these file system metaphors. With this background, you will find it easy to understand how to manage files with graphical user interfaces.

1. Click the Steps button to learn how to manipulate directories, folders and files. As you proceed through the Steps, answer all of the Quick Check questions that appear. After you complete the Steps, you will see a Quick Check Summary Report. Follow the instructions on the screen to print this report.

2. Click the Explore button. Make sure drive a: is the default drive. Double-click the a:\ folder to display the folder contents, then answer the following questions:

a. How many files are in the root directory of drive a:?

b. Are the files on drive a: data files or program files? How can you tell?

c. Does the root directory of drive a: contain any subdirectories? How can you tell?

3. Make sure you are in Explore. Change to drive c: as the default drive. Double-click the c:\ folder to display its contents, then answer the following questions:

a. How many data files are in the root directory of drive c:?

b. How many program files are in the root directory of drive c:?

c. Does the root directory of drive c: contain any subdirectories? How can you tell?

d. How many files are in the dos folder?

e. Complete the diagram in Figure 3-30 to show the arrangement of folders on drive c:. Do not include files.

▶ **Figure 3-30**

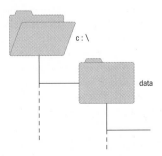

4. Open and close folders, and change drives as necessary to locate the following files. After you find the file, write out its file specification:

a. config.sys, b.win.ini, c.toolkit.wks, d.meeting.doc

e. newlogo3.bmp, f.todo.doc

Defragmentation and Disk Operations

 In this Lab you will format a simulated disk, save files, delete files, undelete files to see how the computer updates the FAT. You will also find out how the files on your disk become fragmented and what a defragmentation utility does to reorganize the clusters on your disk.

1. Click the Steps button to learn how the computer updates the FAT when you format a disk and save, delete, and undelete files. As you proceed through the Steps, answer all of the Quick Check questions that appear. After you complete the Steps, you will see a Quick Check Summary Report. Follow the instructions on the screen to print this report.

2. Click the Explore button. Click the Format button to format the simulated disk. Try to save files 1, 2, 3, 4, and 6. Do they all fit on the disk?

3. In Explore, format the simulated disk. Try to save all the files on the disk. What happens?

4. In Explore, format the simulated disk. Save FILE-3, FILE-4, and FILE-6. Next, delete FILE-6. Now, save FILE-5. Try to undelete FILE-6. What happens and why?

5. In Explore, format the simulated disk. Save and erase files until the files become fragmented. Draw a picture of the disk to show the fragmented files. Indicate which files are in each cluster by using color, crosshatching, or labels. List which files in your drawing are fragmented. Finally, defragment the disk and draw a new picture showing the unfragmented files.

Using Files

 In this Lab you manipulate a simulated computer to view what happens in memory and on disk when you create, save, open, revise, and delete files. Understanding what goes on "inside the box" will help you quickly grasp how to perform basic file operations with most application software.

1. Click the Steps button to learn how to use the simulated computer to view the contents of memory and disk

when you perform basic file operations. As you proceed through the Steps, answer all of the Quick Check questions that appear. After you complete the Steps, you will see a Quick Check Summary Report. Follow the instructions on the screen to print this report.

2. Click the Explore button and use the simulated computer to perform the following tasks.

a. Create a document containing your name and the city in which you were born. Save this document as NAME.

b. Create another document containing two of your favorite foods. Save this document as FOODS.

c. Create another file containing your two favorite classes. Call this file CLASSES.

d. Open the FOOD file and add another one of your favorite foods. Save this file without changing its name.

e. Open the NAME file. Change this document so it contains your name and the name of your school. Save this as a new document called SCHOOL.

f. Write down how many files are on the simulated disk and the exact contents of each file.

3. In Explore, use the simulated computer to perform the following tasks.

a. Create a file called MUSIC that contains the name of your favorite CD.

b. Create another document that contains eight numbers and call this file LOTTERY.

c. You didn't win the lottery this week. Revise the contents of the LOTTERY file, but save the revision as LOTTERY2.

d. Revise the MUSIC file so it also contains the name of your favorite musician or composer, and save this file as MUSIC2.

e. Delete the MUSIC file.

f. Write down how many files are on the simulated disk and the exact contents of each file.

Quick Check

Answers

3.1

1. data, information

2. drive letter, subdirectory, subdirectory, filename, filename extension

3. exe, com

4. Most Windows software automatically adds a specific extension to each file created with it.

5. logical

6. root

7. source

3.2

1. kilobytes (megabytes or gigabytes also acceptable), milliseconds

2. magnetic, optical

3. tracks, sectors

4. random, sequential

5. floppy disk, CD-ROM

6. hard disk drive

7. FAT (File Allocation Table)

8. false

Glossary/Index

Computer Architecture

Readers of the April 1985 issue of *Scientific American* were somewhat surprised by an article about a group of archaeologists who had discovered an ancient computer constructed from ropes and pulleys. The article explained that "archaeologists have discovered the rotting remnants of an ingenious arrangement of ropes and pulleys thought to be the first working digital computer ever constructed." The article continued to describe in detail how the people of an ancient culture, known as the Apraphulians, built complex devices of ropes and pulleys, housed these devices in huge black wooden boxes, and used them to perform complex mathematical computations. Some of the devices were so colossal that elephants were harnessed to pull the enormous ropes through the pulley system.

A computer constructed of ropes and pulleys? As you might have guessed, this was an April Fools' article. And yet, such a device, if it were constructed, could accurately be called a digital computer. That you could build a computer out of ropes and pulleys reinforces the notion that a computer is, in many respects, a very simple device.

In this chapter, we'll take a more detailed look inside the case of a modern computer system. The basic concepts you learn in this chapter apply to micro, mini, and mainframe computers.

Once you understand how a computer works, you will have more success troubleshooting problems you encounter in the lab, at work, or at home. You'll learn how, when, and why you should expand your computer system. You'll be better equipped to understand much of the jargon you read in computer ads and hear in conversations with computer professionals.

CHAPTER**PREVIEW**

In previous chapters you focused on how computers and software help you accomplish tasks. Now it is time to look under the hood and tackle some technical concepts about how computers store and process data. Can you apply these technical concepts? Of course! You'll find that the concepts you learn in this chapter will help you when you set up a new computer. You can also use the information to identify the source of hardware problems when your computer does not seem to work. When you have completed this chapter you should be able to:

- Identify the components that are on the main circuit board of a microcomputer

- Explain how RAM, virtual memory, CMOS, and ROM differ

- Explain how the CPU performs the instructions contained in a computer program

- List the factors that affect CPU performance

- Describe how the data bus and expansion bus work

- List the components necessary to connect a peripheral device to a computer and describe each component's role

- Trace the boot process of your computer system

LABS

Binary Numbers

CPU Simulator

Troubleshooting

Digital Electronics

Computer architecture refers to the design and construction of a computer system. The architecture of any computer can be broadly classified by considering two characteristics: what the computer uses for power and how the computer physically represents, processes, stores, and moves data. Most modern computers are electronic devices, that is, they are powered by electricity. Also, a modern computer uses electrical signals and circuits to represent, process, and move data.

Inside the System Unit

Figure 4-1
Inside the system unit

Today, most integrated circuits are manufactured on a chip of silicon crystal. Silicon Valley in California is so named because many of the computer companies located there either produce or use silicon chips in their products.

What does the inside of a computer look like?

If you have never looked inside a computer, you might stop reading for a moment and try to visualize the inside of a computer's system unit. Did you picture a maze of wires and other electronic gizmos? Many people do. But you might be surprised to find that the inside of a computer looks pretty simple. We took the cover off the microcomputer in Figure 4-1 to show you what's inside.

Most of the components inside a computer are integrated circuits, commonly called *chips* or *microchips*. An **integrated circuit** is a thin slice of crystal packed with microscopic circuit elements such as wires, transistors, capacitors, and resistors. A single integrated circuit less than a quarter-inch square could contain more than 100,000 microscopic circuit elements. The completed circuit is packaged in a ceramic carrier that provides connection pins, as shown in Figure 4-2.

Inside the system unit, integrated circuits are housed on a circuit board called the **main board** or **motherboard**. The main board is connected to peripheral devices that collect input and produce output. Use Figure 4-3 as a "map" to the electronic components you will learn about in this chapter.

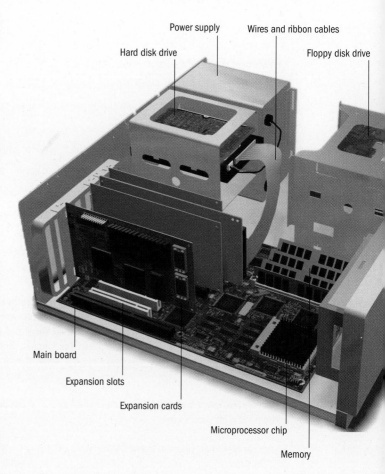

Power supply

Wires and ribbon cables

Hard disk drive

Floppy disk drive

Main board

Expansion slots

Expansion cards

Microprocessor chip

Memory

Fine wires connect the chip to metal leads called *pins*.

A plastic or ceramic case protects the chip.

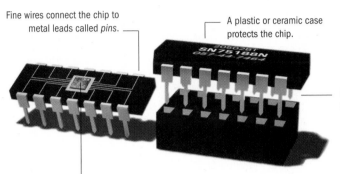

Metal pins plug into a socket on a circuit board.

The silicon chip is less than .25" square. The chip contains thousands of microscopic electronic components such as transistors, resistors, and capacitors.

Figure 4-2
An integrated circuit

If you are interested in how the computer industry might have developed without the invention of the integrated circuit, complete Project 3 at the end of this chapter.

ROM chips contain the programs that start the computer, run system diagnostics, and control low-level input and output activities.

RAM temporarily holds data that is waiting to be processed.

A **bus** transports data between components on the main board.

A battery powered **real-time clock** chip keeps the current date and time.

Figure 4-3
Microcomputer main board

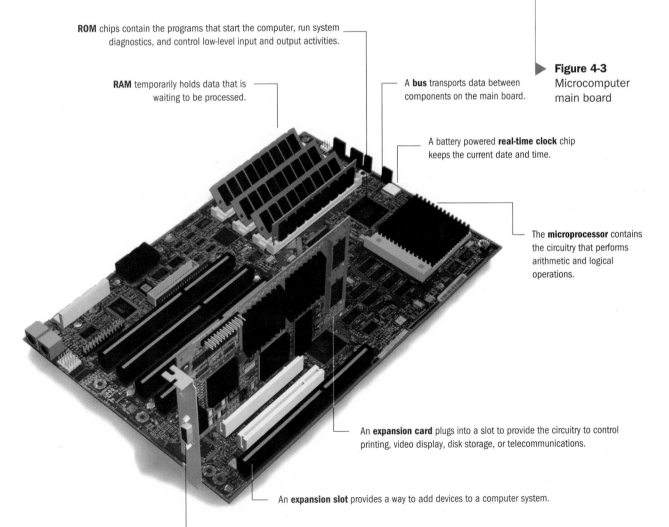

The **microprocessor** contains the circuitry that performs arithmetic and logical operations.

An **expansion card** plugs into a slot to provide the circuitry to control printing, video display, disk storage, or telecommunications.

An **expansion slot** provides a way to add devices to a computer system.

A **port** provides a plug for a cable that leads to a device, such as a printer, monitor, disk drive, or modem.

Digital Data Representation

But if a computer is just a bunch of electrical circuits, how can it manipulate numbers and letters?

Data representation refers to the form in which information is conceived, manipulated, and recorded. When you want to add a column of numbers or sort a list of names, you represent the numbers and names by writing symbols such as 2, G, a, and 8. A computer is an electronic device, so it doesn't write down the data it works with. A computer somehow needs to use electrical signals to represent data. How does a computer do this?

The way a computer represents data depends on whether the computer is a digital or an analog device. A **digital device** works with discrete, that is, distinct or separate numbers or digits, such as 0 and 1. An **analog device** operates on continuously varying data. For example, a digital watch displays the time 12:20 for an entire minute before switching to 12:21—the 0 changes to a 1 without intermediate steps. An analog watch, on the other hand, positions its hands to show you that it is 12:01, but then moves the minute hand very slowly through the space between the minute marks. Think about what's different about the analog and digital versions of the devices shown in Figure 4-4.

Figure 4-4
Examples of
analog and
digital devices

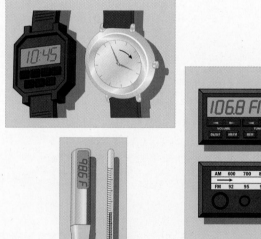

In an analog computer, the number 5 might be represented by .05 volts, the number 6 might be represented by .06 volts, and so on. An analog computer could add 5 + 5 by combining .05 volts and .05 volts. The resulting .10 volts would represent 10, the sum of 5 + 5.

In a digital computer, each number or letter is represented by a series of electrical signals. Think about the way Morse code uses dashes and dots to represent letters. In a similar way, digital computers represent numbers, letters, and symbols with a code that uses a series of 0s (zeros) and 1s.

A digital computer represents the number 5 with the code 00000101. The letter A could be represented with the code 01000001. Why 0s and 1s? A digital computer is an electronic device, and you know that electricity can be on or off. If you equate the on state with 1 and the off state with 0, you can grasp the basic principle of how a digital computer works. Data that is represented by a series of 1s and 0s can easily be moved or stored electronically as a series of "ons" and "offs."

Each 1 or 0 that represents data is referred to as a **bit**. Most computer coding schemes use eight bits to represent each number, letter, or symbol. A series of eight bits is called a **byte**. Study Figure 4-5 to make sure you understand how the term *byte* is related to the terms *bits* and *characters*.

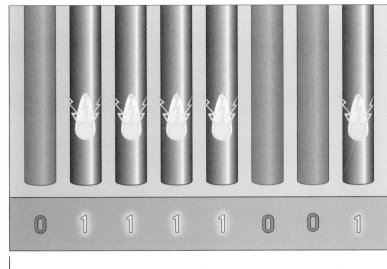

The smallest unit of information on a computer is a **bit**. A bit can be a 0 or a 1. The electronic circuits in a computer carry one bit as a pulse of electiricity through a circuit.

A collection of eight bits is called a **byte**. This byte is composed of eight bits: 01111001

A byte represents one **character**—a letter, numeral, or punctuation symbol. This byte, 01111001, represents a lowercase Y.

A digital computer uses the electronic equivalent of 1s and 0s to represent data.

▶ **Figure 4-5**
Bits, bytes, and characters

Lab

Binary Numbers

Data Representation Codes

Do all digital computers use the same code to represent data?

Digital computers use many different coding schemes to represent data. The coding scheme the computer uses depends on whether the data is numeric data or character data.

Numeric data consists of numbers that represent quantities and that might be used in arithmetic operations. For example, your annual income is numeric data. You use it in arithmetic operations every April when you calculate your income taxes.

Character data is composed of letters, symbols, and numerals that will not be used in arithmetic operations. Examples of character data include your name, hair color, and Social Security number. Are you surprised that your Social Security *number* is considered character data? Because you are not going to use your Social Security number in arithmetic operations it is considered character data.

Digital computers represent numeric data using the **binary number system**, or base two. In the binary number system, there are only two digits: 0 and 1. The numeral 2 cannot be used in the binary number system, so instead of writing "2," you would write "10." The first eight

Your phone number is considered character data because you don't manipulate it arithmetically.

numbers in the binary number system are 1, 10, 11, 100, 101, 110, 111, 1000. If you need to review binary numbers, study Figure 4-6.

Figure 4-6
Binary numbers

Decimal		Binary			
Place	Place	Place	Place	Place	Place
10	**1**	**8**	**4**	**2**	**1**
	0				0
	1				1
	2			1	0
	3			1	1
	4		1	0	0
	5		1	0	1
	6		1	1	0
	7		1	1	1
	8	1	0	0	0
	9	1	0	0	1
1	0	1	0	1	0

1. In the decimal number system, there are ten digits: 0, 1, 2, 3, 4, 5, 6, 7, 8, 9. When we put one of these digits in the column for the 1's place, it represents a different number than when we put it in the column for the 10's place. For example, the digit 1 in the 1's column is worth 1, ...but the digit 1 in the 10's column is worth 10. As you know, after you use the digit 9, you must "carry" a one to the next column and use a zero as a placeholder to represent the number 10.

2. The columns or "places" for the binary number system are 1s, 2s, 4s, 8s, and so on. To find out the value of the next place, you double the value of the previous place. The next place to the left would be 16s.

3. In the binary number system there are only two digits: 0 and 1. When you are counting in binary, you run out of digits when you get to the number 2. To represent "2" in binary, you must move the digit 1 left into the next column and use a zero for a place holder. In binary, the number 10 (pronounced "one zero") means "2".

4. Suppose you want to convert the binary number 11001 into its decimal equivalent.

$$? \quad ? \quad 11001 \quad ? \quad ? \quad ?$$

5. You can set up a conversion table like this one, using the the place values for the binary number system. Because the binary number 11001 has five places, our conversion table also needs five places: 16, 8, 4, 2, and 1.

16	8	4	2	1
1	1	0	0	1

$$16 + 8 \qquad + 1 = 25$$

6. Next, add the place values for any column that contains the digit 1. The sum is the decimal equivalent of the binary number. Here you see that binary 11001 is equivalent to the decimal number 25.

Digital computers use the binary number system to represent numeric data, but use either the ASCII or EBCDIC code to represent character data.

Digital computers typically represent character data using either the ASCII or EBCDIC codes. ASCII is the data representation code used on most microcomputers, on many minicomputers, and on some mainframe computers. **ASCII** stands for American Standard Code for Information Interchange and is pronounced "ASK ee." The ASCII code for an uppercase "A" is 01000001. Look at Figure 4-7 and notice that the ASCII code is used to represent symbols and numerals as well as uppercase and lowercase letters.

SYMBOL	ASCII	EBCDIC	SYMBOL	ASCII	EBCDIC	SYMBOL	ASCII	EBCDIC
(space)	0100000	01000000	?	0111111	01101111	^	1011110	
!	0100001	01011010	@	1000000	01111100	_	1011111	
"	0100010	01111111	A	1000001	11000001	a	1100001	10000001
#	0100011	01111011	B	1000010	11000010	b	1100010	10000010
$	0100100	01011011	C	1000011	11000011	c	1100011	10000011
%	0100101	01101100	D	1000100	11000100	d	1100000	10000100
&	0100110	01010000	E	1000101	11000101	e	1100101	10000101
'	0100111	01111101	F	1000110	11000110	f	1100110	10000110
(	0101000	01001101	G	1000111	11000111	g	1100111	10000111
)	0101001	01011101	H	1001000	11001000	h	1101100	10001000
*	0101010	01011100	I	1001001	11001001	i	1101001	10001001
+	0101011	01001110	J	1001010	11010001	j	1101010	10010001
,	0101100	01101011	K	1001011	11010010	k	1101011	10010010
−	0101101	01100000	L	1001100	11010011	l	1101000	10010011
.	0101110	01001011	M	1001101	11010100	m	1101101	10010100
/	0101111	01100001	N	1001110	11010101	n	1101110	10010101
0	0110000	11110000	O	1001111	11010110	o	1111111	10010110
1	0110001	11110001	P	1010000	11010111	p	1110100	10010111
2	0110010	11110010	Q	1010001	11011000	q	1110001	10011000
3	0110011	11110011	R	1010010	11011001	r	1110010	10011001
4	0110100	11110100	S	1010011	11100010	s	1110011	10100010
5	0110101	11110101	T	1010100	11100011	t	1110100	10100011
6	0110110	11110110	U	1010101	11100100	u	1110101	10100100
7	0110111	11110111	V	1010110	11100101	v	1110110	10100101
8	0111000	11111000	W	1010111	11100110	w	1110111	10100110
9	0111001	11111001	X	1011000	11100111	x	1111000	10100111
:	0111010	01111010	Y	1011001	11101000	y	1111001	10101000
;	0111011	01011110	Z	1011010	11101001	z	1111010	10101001
<	0111100	01001100	[	1011011	01001010	{	1111011	
=	0111101	01111110	\	1011100		}	1111101	
>	0111110	01101110	]	1011101	01011010				

Figure 4-7
ASCII and
EBCDIC codes

IBM-brand mainframe computers often use the EBCDIC code. **EBCDIC** stands for extended binary-coded decimal interchange code (pronounced "EB seh dick"). Figure 4-7 shows the EBCDIC codes in addition to the ASCII codes. See if you can spot some of the differences between the ASCII and EBCDIC coding schemes.

Data Transport

What happens to the data in a computer?

You now know that data exists in the computer as a series of electronic signals. These signals often must travel from one chip to another, so that the computer can process or store them.

Typically, data travels from one location to another within the computer on an electronic pathway or circuit called a **data bus**. The data bus is a series of electronic circuits that connect the various electrical elements on the main board. The bus contains data lines and address lines. **Data lines** carry the signals that represent data. **Address lines** carry the location of the data to help the computer find the data that it needs to process.

The term *bus* fairly accurately describes its function. Picture a school bus that goes to a neighborhood and picks up a load of children, drops them off at school, then goes to the next neighborhood on its route to pick up a second busload. After school, the bus transports loads of children home. A computer bus works in a similar way.

A computer data bus "picks up" a load of bits from one of the components on the main board, then transfers these bits to another main board component. After dropping off this load of bits, the bus collects another load, as shown in Figure 4-8.

Figure 4-8 ◀
How a data
bus works

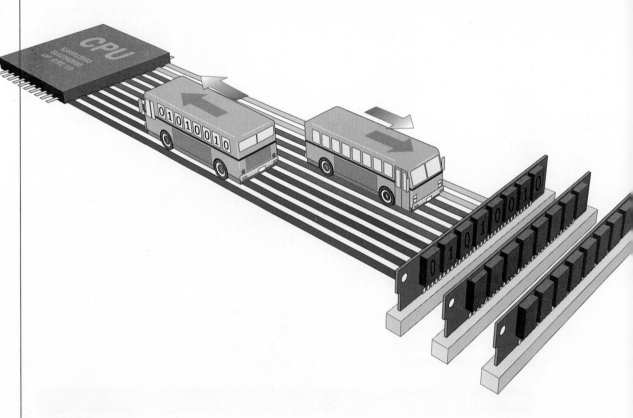

Quick Check

1 A(n) _____ is a collection of microscopic circuit elements such as wires, transistors, capacitors, and resistors packed onto a very small square of silicon.

2 The smallest unit of information in a computer is a(n) _____.

3 A series of eight bits is referred to as a(n) _____.

4 A computer uses the _____ or _____ codes to represent character data.

5 The _____ number system represents numeric data as a series of 0s and 1s.

6 A(n) _____ is an electronic pathway that links the chips on the main board of a computer.

Memory

So far in this chapter you have learned that digital computers represent data using electronic signals. You know that the data bus transports these electronic signals from one place to another inside the computer. Now you will find out where the computer puts data when it is not being transported from one place to another.

Memory is electronic circuitry that holds data and program instructions. Memory is sometimes called *primary storage*, but this term is easily confused with disk storage. It is preferable to use the term *memory* to refer to the circuitry that has a direct link to the processor and to use the term *storage* to refer to media, such as disks, that are not directly linked to the processor.

There are four major types of memory: random access memory, virtual memory, CMOS memory, and read-only memory. Each type of memory is characterized by the kind of data it contains and the technology it uses to hold the data.

Usually, RAM addresses are numbered using the binary number system. In this chapter, however, we use addresses such as M1, M2, and M3 to help you more easily grasp the basic concepts of RAM technology.

Random Access Memory

How does RAM work?

Random access memory, or **RAM**, is an area in the computer system unit that temporarily holds data before and after it is processed. For example, when you enter a document, the characters you type usually are not processed right away. They are held in RAM until you tell your software to carry out a process such as printing.

In RAM, microscopic electronic parts called **capacitors** hold the electronic signals for the ASCII, EBCDIC, or binary code that represents data. A charged capacitor represents an "on" bit. A discharged capacitor represents an "off" bit.

You can visualize the capacitors arranged in banks of eight. Each bank of capacitors holds eight bits, or one byte of data. A **RAM address** on each bank helps the computer locate the data contained in the bank, as shown in Figure 4-9.

In some respects, RAM is like a chalkboard. You can use a chalkboard to write mathematical formulas, erase them, and then write an outline for a report. In a similar way, RAM can hold numbers and formulas when you use a spreadsheet, then hold the text of your English essay when you use a word processor. The contents of RAM can change just by changing the charge of the capacitors. Because its contents can be changed, RAM is a reusable resource.

Unlike hard disk or floppy disk storage, most RAM is *volatile*. In other words, if the computer is turned off or the power goes out, all data stored in RAM instantly and permanently disappears. When someone unhappily says, "I have lost all my data!" it often means that the person was entering data for a document or worksheet, and the power went out before the data was saved on disk.

▶ **Figure 4-9**
How RAM works

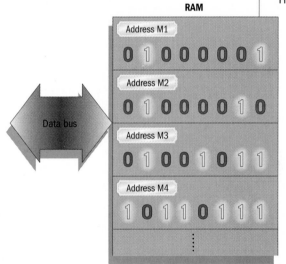

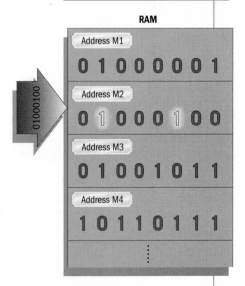

RAM Functions

In the context of RAM, volatile means that data is lost if the power goes out.

Why is RAM so important?

The contents of RAM are necessary for the computer to process any data. The central processing unit receives instructions from RAM, uses the data in RAM for processing, and keeps the results of processing temporarily in RAM until they are needed again or are stored on disk.

RAM stores user data, operating system instructions, and program instructions. As you have already learned, RAM holds data. When you type a document, each character you type is held in RAM until you save the document on a disk.

Every time you turn on your computer, it copies a set of operating system instructions from disk into RAM. These instructions, which help control basic computer functions, remain in RAM until you turn the computer off.

The computer keeps programs, data, and parts of the operating system in RAM.

RAM also holds program instructions. When you use a word processing program, the computer copies the instructions that turn your computer into a word processor from the disk into RAM.

RAM Capacity

How much RAM does my computer need?

The storage capacity of RAM is measured in megabytes. Today's microcomputers typically have between 4 and 32 megabytes of RAM, which means they can hold between 4 and 32 million bytes of data.

The amount of RAM your computer needs depends on the software you use. The amount of RAM required to run a software package is usually specified on the outside of the software box. What if the software you want to use requires more RAM than your computer has? You can purchase additional RAM to expand the memory capacity of your computer up to the limit set by the computer manufacturer.

When you purchase additional RAM, you must make sure it is the correct type, configuration, and speed for your computer system. The technical reference manual for your computer should contain the information you need to purchase the right type of RAM. Figure 4-10 explains the types of RAM that are available for microcomputers.

Figure 4-10 ◄
Microcomputer
RAM types

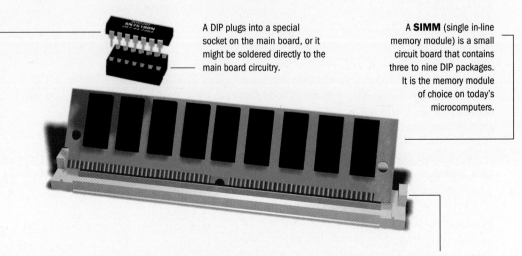

A typical **DIP** (dual in-line pin) memory module stores 256 kilobits of data. Note, that's kilobits, not kilobytes. Although RAM is measured in megabytes, the capacity of the memory modules that make up RAM is measured in bits. DIPs are not used for main memory in most of today's computer systems, but they were popular in the first generation of microcomputers.

A DIP plugs into a special socket on the main board, or it might be soldered directly to the main board circuitry.

A **SIMM** (single in-line memory module) is a small circuit board that contains three to nine DIP packages. It is the memory module of choice on today's microcomputers.

The edge of the SIMM circuit board plugs into a special SIMM slot in the main board.

Virtual Memory

What if I run out of RAM?

Suppose you use a word processing program that requires 4 MB of RAM and a spreadsheet program that requires 2 MB of RAM. You might suspect that you would run out of RAM if you tried to run both programs at the same time. However, you need only 4 MB to run both programs. How can this be so?

With today's operating systems, you won't run out of RAM because the computer uses space on your computer's hard disk as an extension of RAM. A computer's ability to use disk storage to simulate RAM is called **virtual memory**. Figure 4-11 explains how virtual memory works.

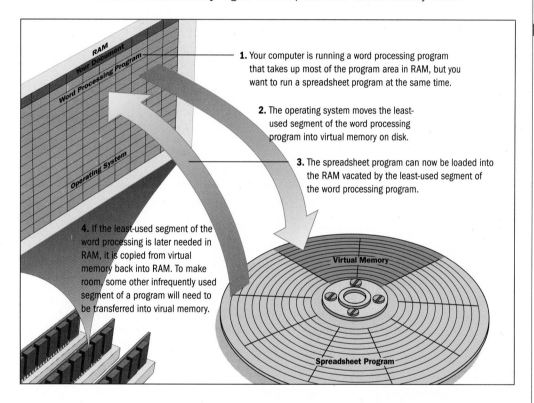

1. Your computer is running a word processing program that takes up most of the program area in RAM, but you want to run a spreadsheet program at the same time.

2. The operating system moves the least-used segment of the word processing program into virtual memory on disk.

3. The spreadsheet program can now be loaded into the RAM vacated by the least-used segment of the word processing program.

4. If the least-used segment of the word processing is later needed in RAM, it is copied from virtual memory back into RAM. To make room, some other infrequently used segment of a program will need to be transferred into virtual memory.

Virtual Memory

Spreadsheet Program

Figure 4-11
How virtual memory works

The term virtual *is associated with many computer technologies. In the context of computing,* virtual *usually means simulated.*

Normally disks do not lose data when the power goes off. Data in virtual memory is not erased from the disk if the power fails, but the computer can no longer access it, even after the power is restored.

Virtual memory allows computers without enough real memory to run large programs, manipulate large data files, and run more than one program at a time. One disadvantage of virtual memory is reduced performance. It takes longer to retrieve data from virtual memory than from RAM because the disk is a mechanical device. Another disadvantage is that any data in virtual memory becomes inaccessible if the power goes off.

Read-only Memory

If a computer has RAM, why does it need ROM?

Read-only memory, or **ROM**, is a set of chips containing instructions that help a computer prepare for processing tasks. The instructions in ROM are permanent, and the only way to change them is to remove the ROM chips from the main board and replace them with another set. You might wonder why the computer includes chips with programs permanently stored in them. Why not use the more adaptable RAM?

You'll find out more about the role ROM plays in the boot process later in Section 4.5.

The answer to this question is that when you turn on your computer, the central processing unit receives electrical power and is ready to begin executing instructions. But because the computer was just turned on, RAM is empty—it doesn't contain any instructions for the central processing unit to execute. This is when ROM plays its part. ROM contains a small set of instructions that tell the computer how to access the disk drives and look for the operating system. When you turn on your computer, the central processing unit performs a series of steps by following the instructions stored in ROM. This series of steps is called the *boot process*.

CMOS Memory

If the boot instructions are permanent, does that mean I can't change any hardware on my computer system?

CMOS memory is more permanent than RAM, but less permanent than ROM.

The computer is not ready to process data until it has copied certain operating system files from the hard disk into RAM. But, the computer can only find data on the hard disk if it has some information about how the hard disk is formatted. The computer must know the number of tracks and sectors and the size of each sector, or it cannot know where to look for the operating system files.

If information about the hard disk was permanently stored in ROM, you would never be able to replace your hard disk drive with a larger one. The computer could not access the new hard disk using information about the old disk. Therefore, a computer must have some semipermanent way of keeping boot data, such as the number of hard disk drive tracks and sectors. For this, a computer needs a type of memory more permanent than RAM, but less permanent than ROM.

CMOS memory (complementary metal oxide semiconductor, pronounced "SEE moss") holds data, but requires very little power to retain its contents. Because of its low power requirements, a CMOS chip can be powered by battery. CMOS uses battery power to retain vital data about your computer system configuration, even when your computer is turned off.

To remember the difference between memory types, remember:
- *RAM is temporary.*
- *Virtual memory is disk-based.*
- *ROM is permanent.*
- *CMOS is battery powered.*

When your system configuration changes, the data in the CMOS memory must be updated. To change the CMOS data, you usually run a CMOS configuration, or setup, program. The reference manual for your computer indicates how to start the setup program. Some operating systems have special utilities that help you update the CMOS settings. For example, the **plug-and-play** feature of the Windows 95 operating system helps you update CMOS if you install a new hard drive.

Quick Check

1. _____ is electronic circuitry that holds data and programs.

2. Having a steady power source is important for a computer because RAM is _____.

3. RAM is measured in _____.

4. In RAM, microscopic electronic parts called _____ hold the electrical signals that represent data.

5. Most of today's microcomputers use _____ instead of DIP memory modules.

6. If your computer does not have enough RAM to run several programs at once, your computer operating system might simulate RAM with disk-based _____ memory.

7. The series of instructions that a computer performs when it is first turned on are permanently stored in _____.

8. System configuration information, such as the number of the hard disk tracks and sectors, is stored in battery-backed _____ memory.

Central Processing Unit

So far in this chapter you have learned that digital computers represent data using a series of electrical signals. You know that data can be transported over the data bus or held in memory. But a computer does more than transport and store data. A computer is supposed to process data—perform arithmetic, sort lists, format documents, and so on. The computer processes data in the central processing unit (CPU). In this section of the chapter you will learn how the central processing unit works.

The **central processing unit** is the circuitry in a computer that executes instructions to process data. The central processing unit retrieves instructions and data from RAM, processes those instructions, then places the results back into RAM so they can be displayed or stored. Figure 4-12 will help you visualize the flow of data and instructions through the processor.

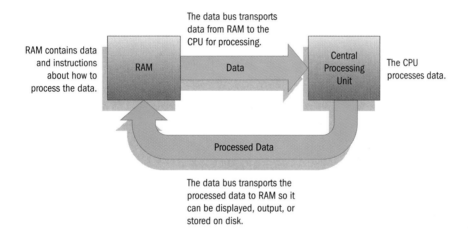

The data bus transports data from RAM to the CPU for processing.

RAM contains data and instructions about how to process the data.

RAM — Data — Central Processing Unit

The CPU processes data.

Processed Data

The data bus transports the processed data to RAM so it can be displayed, output, or stored on disk.

Figure 4-12
The data bus transports data and instructions between RAM and the CPU

Central Processing Unit Architecture

What does the CPU look like?

The central processing unit consists of one or more integrated circuits. The central processing unit of a mainframe computer usually contains several integrated circuits. In a microcomputer the central processing unit is a single integrated circuit called a **microprocessor**. Figure 4-13 shows a microprocessor similar to the one that is probably in the computer you use.

A microprocessor is not the same as a microcomputer. A microprocessor is the CPU chip found on the main board of a microcomputer.

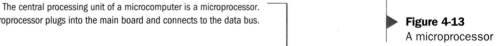

The central processing unit of a microcomputer is a microprocessor. The microprocessor plugs into the main board and connects to the data bus.

Figure 4-13
A microprocessor

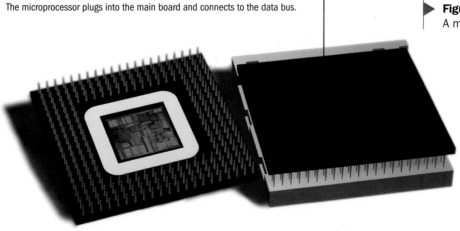

The central processing unit has two main parts: the arithmetic logic unit and the control unit. Each of these units perform specific tasks to process data.

The **arithmetic logic unit (ALU)** performs arithmetic operations such as addition and subtraction. It also performs logical operations such as comparing two numbers to see if they are the same. The ALU uses **registers** to hold the data that is being processed. In the ALU the result of an arithmetic or logical operation is held temporarily in the **accumulator**, as shown in Figure 4-14.

Figure 4-14
How the ALU works

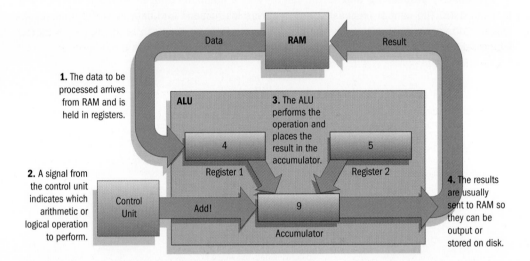

How does the ALU get its data, and how does it know which arithmetic or logical operation it must perform? The **control unit** directs and coordinates processing. It retrieves each instruction in sequence from RAM and places it in a special **instruction register**. The control unit then interprets the instruction to find out what needs to be done. According to its interpretation, the control unit sends signals to the data bus to fetch data from RAM, and to the arithmetic logic unit to perform a process, as shown in Figure 4-15.

Figure 4-15
How the control unit works

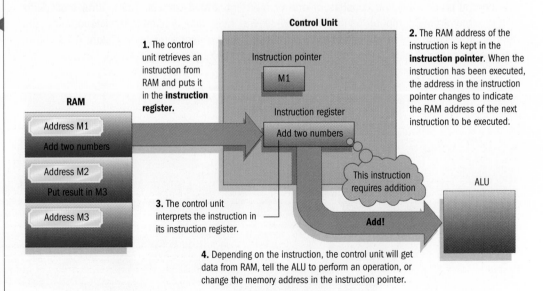

Instructions

What specifies the steps that the CPU must perform to accomplish a task?

A computer accomplishes a complex task by performing a series of very simple steps, referred to as instructions. An **instruction** tells the computer to perform a specific arithmetic, logical, or control operation.

An instruction has two parts: the op code and the operands. An **op code**, which is short for operation code, is a command word for an operation such as add, compare, or jump. The **operands** for an instruction specify the data or the address of the data for the operation. Let's look at an example of an instruction:

op code ⟶ **JMP M1** ⟵ **operand**

In the instruction JMP M1, the op code is JMP and the operand is M1. The op code JMP means *jump* or go to a different instruction. The operand M1 is the RAM address of the instruction to which the computer is supposed to go. The instruction JMP M1 has only one operand, but some other instructions have more than one operand. For example, the instruction to add the contents of register 1 and register 2 has two operands:

op code ⟶ **ADD REG1 REG2** ⟵ **second operand**
↑
first operand

The list of instructions that a central processing unit performs is known as its **instruction set**. Every task a computer performs must be described in terms of the limited list of instructions in the instruction set. As you look at the list of instructions in Figure 4-16, consider that the computer must use a set of instructions such as this for all the tasks it helps you perform—from word processing to database management.

> An instruction tells the computer how to perform a single operation. Many instructions are required to accomplish a task such as adding a column of numbers.

▶ **Figure 4-16**
A simple microcomputer instruction set

Op Code	Operation	Example
INP	Input the given value into the specified memory address	INP 7 M1
CLA	Clear the accumulator to 0	CLA
MAM	Move the value from the accumulator to the specified memory location	MAM M1
MMR	Move the value from the specified memory location to the specified register	MMR M1 REG1
MRA	Move the value from the specified register to the accumulator	MRA REG1
MAR	Move the value from the accumulator to the specified register	MAR REG1
ADD	Add the values in two registers, place result in accumulator	ADD REG1 REG2
SUB	Subtract the value in the second register from the value in the first register, place the result in the accumulator	SUB REG1 REG2
MUL	Multiply the values in two registers, place the result in the accumulator	MUL REG1 REG2
DIV	Divide the value in the first register by the value in the second register, place the result in the accumulator	DIV REG1 REG2
INC	Increment the value in the register by 1	INC REG1
DEC	Decrement the value in the register by 1	DEC REG1
CMP	Compare the values in two registers; values are equal, place 1 in the accumulator, otherwise place 0 in the accumulator	CMP REG1 REG2
JMP	Jump to the instruction at the specified memory address	JMP P2
JPZ	Jump to the instruction at the specified address if the accumulator holds a 0	JPZ P3
JPN	Jump to the instruction at the specified address if the accumulator does not hold a 0	JPN P2
HLT	Halt program execution	HLT

Figure 4-17 ◀
Instruction cycle

Figure 4-18 ◀
Processing an
instruction

Instruction Cycle

How does a computer process instructions?

The term **instruction cycle** refers to the process in which a computer executes a single instruction. The instruction cycle is repeated each time the computer executes an instruction. The steps in this cycle are summarized in Figure 4-17.

You have all the pieces you need to understand the details of the instruction cycle. You know how the ALU performs arithmetic and logical operations and how the control unit retrieves data from RAM and tells the ALU which operation to perform. Figure 4-18 shows how the ALU, control unit, and RAM work together to process instructions.

1. The instruction pointer indicates the memory location that holds the first instruction (M1).

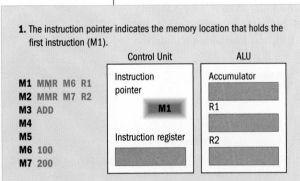

2. The computer fetches the instruction and puts it into the instruction register.

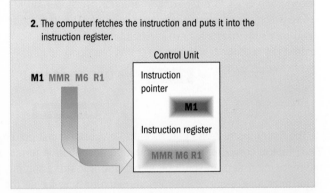

3. The computer executes the instructions in the instruction register; it moves the contents of M6 into register 1 of the ALU.

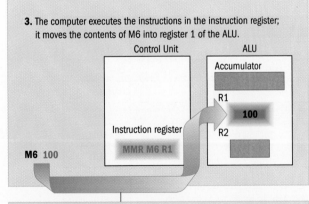

4. The instruction pointer changes to point to the memory location that holds the next instruction.

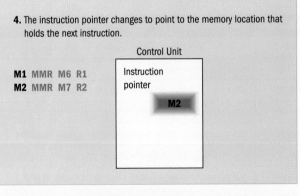

5. The computer fetches the instruction and puts it into the instruction register.

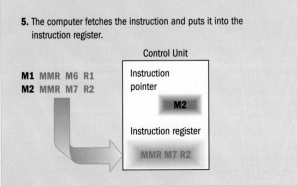

6. The computer executes the instructions; it moves the contents of M7 into register 2 of the ALU.

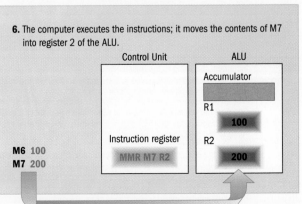

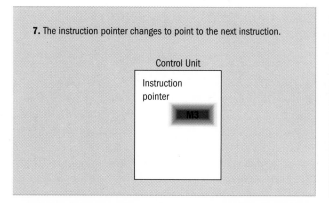

7. The instruction pointer changes to point to the next instruction.

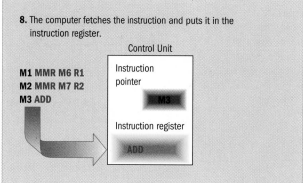

8. The computer fetches the instruction and puts it in the instruction register.

9. The computer executes the instruction. The result is put in the accumulator.

Study Figure 4-18 carefully so you understand the instruction execution cycle. You can test your understanding by answering Questions 8 and 9 in the Chapter Review.

CPU Performance

How does the architecture of a computer contribute to its performance?

All CPUs are not created equal; some process data faster than others. CPU speed is influenced by several factors including clock rate, word size, cache, and instruction set size. Specifications for these factors allow you to compare different CPUs.

Before you learn more about the factors that affect CPU performance, you should understand that a computer system with a high-performance CPU might not necessarily provide great overall performance. You know the old saying that a chain is only as strong as it weakest link. A computer system might also have weak links. Even with a high-performance processor, a computer system with a slow hard disk, no disk cache, and a small amount of RAM is likely to be slow at tasks such as starting programs, loading data files, printing, and scrolling through long documents.

Lab

CPU Simulator

Most microcomputers keep track of the date and time using a CMOS chip that runs on battery power.

Clock Rate

Do all computer clocks have to operate at the same rate to keep the right time and date?

A computer contains a **system clock** that emits pulses to establish the timing for all system operations. The system clock is not the same as a "real-time clock" that keeps track of the time of day. The system clock operates at a speed quite different from that of a clock that keeps track of minutes and seconds.

The system clock sets the speed for data transport and instruction execution. To understand how this works, visualize a team of oarsmen on a Viking ship. The ship's coxswain beats on a drum to coordinate the rowers. A computer's system clock and a ship's coxswain accomplish essentially the same task—they set the pace of activity. Boom! A stream of bits takes off from RAM and heads to the CPU. Boom! The control unit reads an instruction. Boom! The ALU adds two numbers together.

The clock rate of a computer is measured in MHz, millions of instructions per second.

The clock rate set by the system clock determines the speed at which the computer can execute an instruction and, therefore, limits the number of instructions the computer can complete within a specific amount of time. The time to complete an instruction cycle is measured in megahertz (MHz), or millions of cycles per second.

Although some instructions require multiple cycles to complete, you can think of processor speed as the number of instructions the processor can execute in one second. For example, the 4.77 MHz microprocessor in the very first model of the IBM PC executed 4.77 million instructions per second. Today, microprocessor speeds exceed 100 million instructions per second. If all other specifications are identical, higher megahertz ratings mean faster processing.

Word Size

Which is faster, an 8-bit processor or a 64-bit processor?

Word size refers to the number of bits the central processing unit can manipulate at one time. Word size is based on the size of the registers in the CPU and the number of data lines in the bus. For example, a CPU with an 8-bit word size is referred to as an 8-bit processor; it has 8 bit registers and manipulates 8 bits at a time.

Word size is measured in bits, not bytes.

Computers with a large word size can process more data in each instruction cycle than computers with a small word size. Processing more data in each cycle contributes to increased performance. For example, the first microcomputers used 8-bit microprocessors, but today's faster computers use 32-bit or 64-bit microprocessors.

Cache

Disk cache speeds up access to data on disk; is there a similar process that speeds access to data from RAM?

Disk cache, explained in Chapter 3, and RAM cache are not the same. Disk cache works between the disk and memory. RAM cache works with data between RAM and the central processing unit.

Another factor that affects CPU performance is cache. **Cache,** sometimes called **RAM cache** or **cache memory**, is special high-speed memory that gives the CPU more rapid access to data. A high-speed CPU can execute an instruction so quickly that it often waits for data to be delivered from RAM; this slows processing. The cache ensures that data is immediately available whenever the central processing unit requests it.

As you begin a task, the computer anticipates what data the central processing unit is likely to need and loads or *caches* this data into the cache area. Then, when an instruction calls for data, the central processing unit first checks to see if the required data is in the cache. If the required data is there, the central processing unit takes the data from the cache instead of fetching it from RAM, which takes longer. All other factors being equal, more cache means faster processing.

Instruction Set Complexity

What's the difference between CISC and RISC?

As programmers developed various instruction sets for computers, they tended to add more and more complex instructions that took up many bytes in memory and required several clock cycles for execution. A computer based on a central processing unit with a complex instruction set came to be known as a **complex instruction set computer**, or **CISC**.

In 1975 John Cocke, an IBM research scientist, discovered that most of the work done by a microprocessor requires only a small subset of the available instruction set. Further research showed that only 20% of the instructions of a CISC machine do about 80% of the work. Cocke's research resulted in the development of microprocessors with streamlined instruction sets, called RISC machines.

The microprocessor of a **reduced instruction set computer**, or **RISC**, has a limited set of instructions that it can perform very quickly. In theory, therefore, a RISC machine should be faster than a CISC machine for most processing tasks. Some computer scientists believe, however, that a balance or hybrid of CISC and RISC technologies produce the most efficient and flexible computers.

Pipelining and Parallel Processing

Can a CPU increase its performance by executing more than one instruction at a time?

Computers with a single processor execute instructions "serially," that is, one instruction at a time. Usually, the processor must complete all four steps in the instruction cycle before it begins to execute the next instruction. However, with a technology called **pipelining**, the processor begins executing an instruction before it completes the previous instruction. Pipelining speeds up processing in computers with a single processor; it is also implemented on computers with multiple processors.

A computer that has more than one processor can execute multiple instructions at the same time. This method of executing instructions is called **parallel processing**. Parallel processing increases the amount of processing a computer can accomplish in a specific amount of time.

You learned about John von Neumann in Chapter 1. The type of computers he defined in his 1945 paper are referred to as von Neumann machines.

To take advantage of parallel processing, however, requires special software. Computers that are capable of parallel processing are called parallel computers or non-von Neumann machines. Figure 4-19 explains the concept of parallel processing.

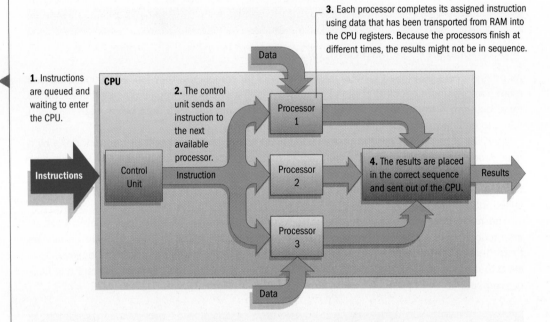

Figure 4-19
How parallel processing works

3. Each processor completes its assigned instruction using data that has been transported from RAM into the CPU registers. Because the processors finish at different times, the results might not be in sequence.

1. Instructions are queued and waiting to enter the CPU.

2. The control unit sends an instruction to the next available processor.

4. The results are placed in the correct sequence and sent out of the CPU.

Instructions

CPU

Control Unit

Instruction

Processor 1

Processor 2

Processor 3

Data

Data

Results

To get a clearer picture of serial, pipelining, and parallel processing techniques, consider an analogy—baking pizzas. Serial processing is like a pizzeria with only one oven that can bake only one pizza at a time. Just as this oven bakes only one pizza at a time, a serial processor processes only one instruction at a time.

Pipelining is similar to a pizza conveyor belt. A pizza starts moving along the conveyor belt, but before it reaches the end of the belt, another pizza starts moving along the belt. Likewise, a pipelining computer starts processing an instruction; but before it completes the instruction, it begins processing another instruction.

Finally, parallel processing is similar to a pizzeria with many ovens. Just as these ovens can bake more than one pizza at a time, a parallel processor can execute more than one instruction at a time.

Quick Check

1. A microcomputer uses a(n) _____ chip as its CPU.

2. The _____ in the CPU performs arithmetic and logical operations such as adding or comparing two numbers.

3. The _____ in the CPU directs and coordinates the operation of the entire computer system.

4. A computer instruction has two parts: the _____ and the _____.

5. What are the four steps in the instruction cycle?

6. What factors affect the speed of a CPU?

I/O

When you purchase a computer, you can be fairly certain that before its useful life is over, you will want to add equipment to expand its capabilities. If you understand computer I/O, you will see how it is possible to expand a computer system.

I/O, pronounced "eye-oh," is computer jargon for input/output. I/O refers to collecting data for the microprocessor to manipulate and transporting results to display, print, and storage devices. I/O between the central processing unit and peripheral devices often involves a long path that moves data over the expansion bus, slots, cards, ports, and cables. Figure 4-20 is an overview of the I/O architecture described in the rest of this section.

▶ **Figure 4-20**
I/O architecture

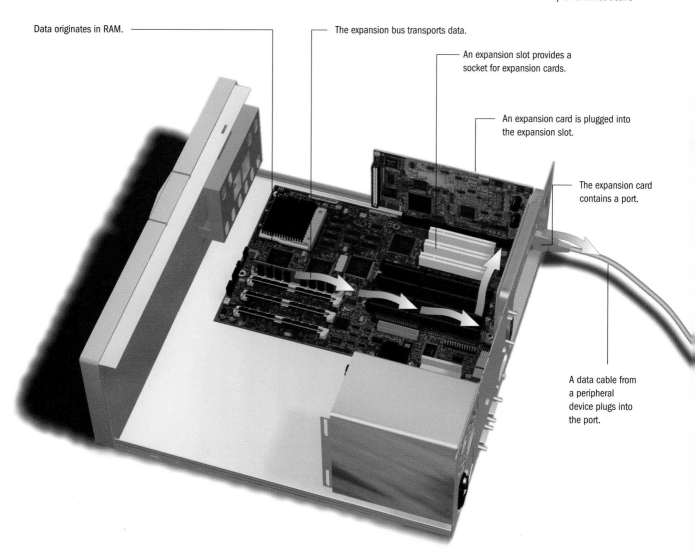

Data originates in RAM.

The expansion bus transports data.

An expansion slot provides a socket for expansion cards.

An expansion card is plugged into the expansion slot.

The expansion card contains a port.

A data cable from a peripheral device plugs into the port.

Expansion Bus

What's the difference between the expansion bus and the data bus?

You already learned that a data bus transports data between RAM and the CPU. The data bus also extends to other parts of the computer. The segment of the data bus that transports data between RAM and peripheral devices is called the **expansion bus**.

The expansion bus is an extension of the data bus.

Expansion Slots

How do I use expansion slots?

On the main board, the expansion bus terminates at an expansion slot. An **expansion slot** is a socket into which you can plug a small circuit board called an expansion card. The expansion slots on mainframes, minicomputers, and microcomputers provide a way to connect a large variety of peripheral devices.

Most microcomputers have four to eight expansion slots, but some of these slots usually contain expansion cards when you purchase the computer. The number of empty slots in your computer dictates its expandability.

Suppose that a few months after you purchase your computer, you decide you want to add sound capability. To find out if you have adequate expansion capability, turn your computer off, unplug it, then open the system unit case. Some computers contain more than one type of expansion slot, so the slots in your computer might appear to be different sizes. If you have an empty expansion slot, you can insert an expansion card, as shown in Figure 4-21.

Figure 4-21
Inserting an expansion card into a slot

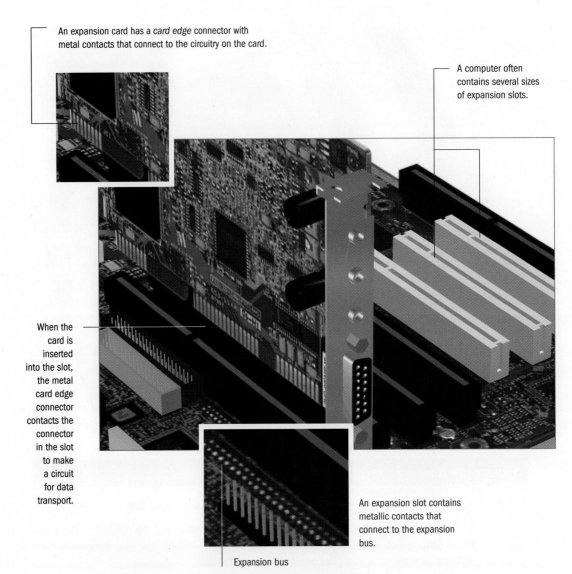

An expansion card has a *card edge* connector with metal contacts that connect to the circuitry on the card.

A computer often contains several sizes of expansion slots.

When the card is inserted into the slot, the metal card edge connector contacts the connector in the slot to make a circuit for data transport.

An expansion slot contains metallic contacts that connect to the expansion bus.

Expansion bus

Expansion Cards

What kinds of expansion cards are available?

An **expansion card**, also referred to as an **expansion board** or a **controller card**, is a circuit board that plugs into an expansion slot. An expansion card provides the I/O circuitry for peripheral devices and sometimes contains an expansion device. For example, if you want to add sound capability, you would purchase and install an expansion card called a sound card. The sound card contains the circuitry to convert digital signals from your computer to sounds that play through speakers. Once you have inserted the sound card into an expansion slot, you can connect speakers or headphones. Microcomputer users can select from a wide variety of expansion cards, such as those shown in Figure 4-22.

A **graphics card** connects your monitor and computer.

▶ **Figure 4-22**
Expansion cards

A **network card** connects your computer to the other computers on a local area network.

A **modem card** connects your computer to the telephone system so you can transport data from one computer to another.

A port is not the same as a slot. A port is located on the outside of the system unit, whereas a slot is located inside the unit.

Expansion Ports

How do I connect a peripheral device to an expansion card?

To connect a peripheral device to an expansion card, you plug a cable from the peripheral device into the expansion port on the expansion card. An **expansion port** is a location that passes data in and out of a computer or peripheral device. An expansion port is often housed on an expansion card in a way that it is accessible through a hole in the back of the computer system unit. A port might also be connected directly to the main board, instead of to an expansion card.

To many computer users, the back of a computer is a confusing array of unlabeled ports, connectors, and cables. Study Figure 4-23 to become familiar with the shapes of the most frequently used expansion ports.

Figure 4-23 ◀
Microcomputer
expansion ports

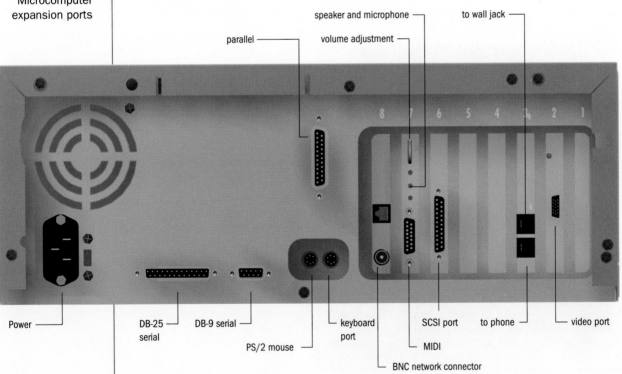

A **parallel port** provides a connection for transmitting data eight bits at a time over a cable with eight separate data lines. Because all eight bits travel at the same time, parallel transmission is relatively fast. Parallel transmission is typically used to send data to a printer.

In a microcomputer the parallel port is either built into the main board or mounted on an expansion card. The cable that connects two parallel ports contains 25 wires. Eight of these wires carry data and the remaining wires carry control signals that help maintain orderly transmission and reception.

Because the wires that carry data run parallel to each other for the full length of the cable, the signals in the cables tend to interfere with each other over long distances. Parallel cables can provide reliable connections for relatively short distances—from 10 to 50 feet, depending on how well the cable is shielded from electrical interference.

A **SCSI port** provides a connection for one or more peripheral devices. SCSI (pronounced "scuzzy") stands for small computer system interface. Unlike a parallel port, to which you can connect only one device, you can connect many devices to a single SCSI port by connecting one device to another in a chain. SCSI ports are particularly popular on Macintosh computers for attaching hard disk drives, CD-ROMs, and scanners.

A **serial port**, sometimes referred to as an **RS-232C port**, provides a connection for transmitting data one bit at a time. A serial port connects your computer to a device such as a modem, which requires two-way data transmission, or to a device such as a mouse, which requires one-way data transmission. A serial cable contains one data line and an assortment of control lines.

Because a serial cable requires fewer data lines, it is less susceptible to interference than a parallel cable. This makes serial connections more suitable than parallel connections for devices that are located greater distances from the computer.

A **MIDI port** is a special type of serial interface for connecting a computer to music synthesizers and musical instruments. MIDI (pronounced "middy") stands for musical instrument digital interface. Most of the keyboards used by rock musicians have a MIDI port so they can be connected to a computer to record, manipulate, and play back music.

Quick Check

1. A(n) _____ is an electronic path that transports data between RAM and expansion slots.

2. A(n) _____ is a small circuit board that plugs into an expansion slot.

3. An expansion _____ is located inside the system, whereas an expansion _____ is located on the exterior of the system unit.

4. Four types of expansion ports are _____, _____, _____ and _____.

User **Focus:**

4.5

The Boot Process

Lab

Troubleshooting

Now that you have an understanding about how I/O, RAM, ROM, and the CPU operate, you're ready to learn how they all work together to prepare a computer for accepting commands each time you turn it on.

The sequence of events that occurs between the time you turn on a computer and the time it is ready for you to issue commands is referred to as the **boot process**. Micro, mini, and mainframe computers all require a boot process. In this section of the chapter you'll learn about the microcomputer boot process because that is the type of computer you are most likely to use.

You'll find out what happens during each step of the boot process for a typical IBM-compatible computer and what you should do when the boot process doesn't proceed smoothly. Of course, even when you know how to troubleshoot computer problems, you should always follow the guidelines provided by your school or employer when you encounter equipment problems.

An Overview

If the computer memory is blank when I turn it on, how does it know how to start up?

As you learned earlier, one of the most important components of a computer—RAM—is volatile, so it cannot hold any data when the power is off. It also cannot hold the operating system instructions when the power is off. Therefore, the computer cannot use RAM to "remember" many basic functions, such as how to deal with input and communicate output to the external world. A computer needs some way to get operating system files into RAM. That's one of the main objectives of the boot process. In general, the boot process follows these six steps:

Figure 4-24
Power up

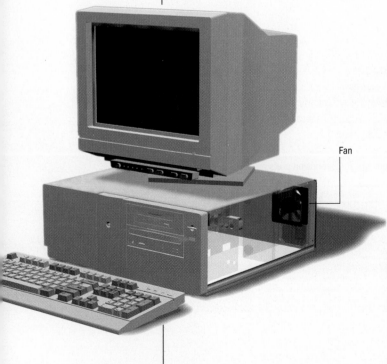

Fan

1. **Power Up**—When you turn on the power switch, the power light is illuminated, and power is distributed to the internal fan and main board.

2. **Start Boot Program**—The microprocessor begins to execute the instructions stored in ROM.

3. **Power-On Self-Test**—The computer performs diagnostic tests of crucial system components.

4. **Load Operating System**—The operating system is copied from a disk to RAM.

5. **Check Configuration and Customization**—The microprocessor reads configuration data and executes any customized start-up routines specified by the user.

6. **Ready for Commands and Data**—The computer is ready for you to enter commands and data.

Power Up

What's the first thing that happens when I turn the power on?

The first stage in the boot process is the power-up stage. The fan in the power supply begins to spin, and the power light on the case of the computer comes on, as shown in Figure 4-24.

If you turn on the computer and the power light does not come on, the system is not getting power. You can do several things to fix this problem. First, you can check the power cord at the back of the computer to make sure it is firmly plugged into the wall and into the system unit. If the plugs are in place, test the wall outlet by plugging in another electrical device, such as a lamp. If the wall outlet is supplying power, the power cord is plugged in, and the power light still does not come on, then the computer's power supply might have failed. If you encounter this problem, you need to contact a technical support person for assistance.

Start Boot Program

What happens if the ROM is malfunctioning?

When you turn on the computer, the microprocessor begins to execute the boot program stored in ROM, as shown in Figure 4-25.

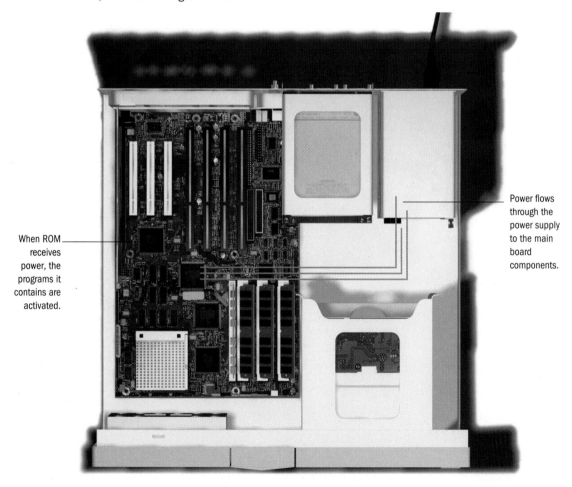

► **Figure 4-25**
ROM boot program
activated

When ROM receives power, the programs it contains are activated.

Power flows through the power supply to the main board components.

If the ROM chips, RAM modules, or microprocessor are malfunctioning, the microprocessor is unable to run the boot program and the computer stops or "hangs." You know you have a problem at this stage of the boot process if the power light is on and you can hear the fan, but there is no message on the screen and nothing else happens. This problem requires the assistance of a technical support person.

Power-On Self-Test

Can the computer check to determine if all its components are functioning correctly?

The next step in the boot process is the **power-on self-test (POST)**, which diagnoses problems in the computer, as shown in Figure 4-26.

The POST first checks the graphics card that connects your monitor to the computer. If the graphics card is working, a message such as "Video BIOS ver 2.1 1995" appears on the screen. Many computers beep several times if the graphics card fails the test. The number of beeps depends on the ROM used in your computer. If your computer beeps and does not display the graphics card message, the graphics card is probably malfunctioning. You should contact a technical support person to have the graphics card checked.

If the graphics card passes the diagnostic test, the computer next tests RAM by placing data in each memory location, then retrieving that data to see if it is correct. The computer displays the amount of memory tested. If any errors are encountered during the RAM test, the POST stops and displays a message that indicates a RAM problem.

The POST then checks the keyboard. On most computers you can see the keyboard indicator lights flash when the keyboard test is in progress. If the keyboard is not correctly attached or if a key is stuck, the computer beeps and displays a keyboard error message. If a keyboard error occurs, you should turn the computer off and make sure that nothing is holding down a key on the keyboard. Next, unplug the keyboard and carefully plug it back into the computer. Finally, turn on the computer again to repeat the boot process. If the problem recurs, you might need to have your keyboard repaired or replaced.

The final step in the POST is the drive test. If you watch the hard disk drive and floppy disk drives during this test, you will see the drive activity lights flash on for a moment, and you will hear the drives spin. The drive test should only take a second or two to complete. If the computer

Figure 4-26
Power-on self-test

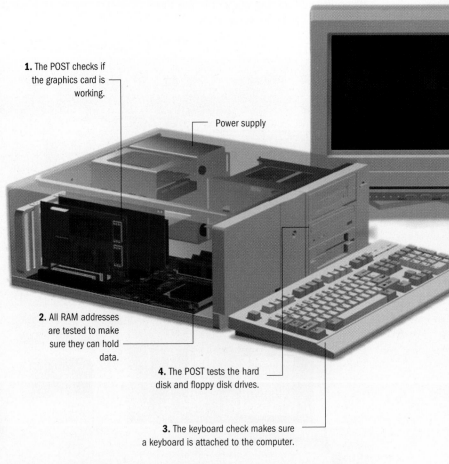

1. The POST checks if the graphics card is working.

Power supply

2. All RAM addresses are tested to make sure they can hold data.

4. The POST tests the hard disk and floppy disk drives.

3. The keyboard check makes sure a keyboard is attached to the computer.

pauses on this test, there might be a problem with one of the drives, and you should consult a technical support person.

Load Operating System

How does the computer find the operating system to load it into RAM?

After successfully completing the POST, the computer continues to follow the instructions in ROM to load the operating system, as shown in Figure 4-27.

Figure 4-27
Loading the operating system

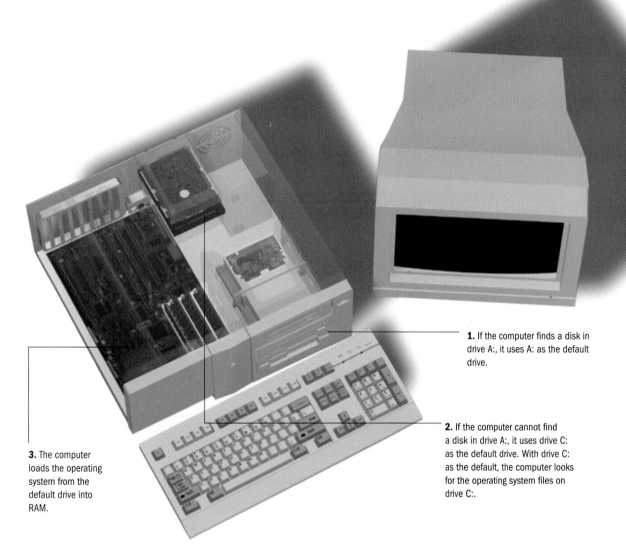

1. If the computer finds a disk in drive A:, it uses A: as the default drive.

2. If the computer cannot find a disk in drive A:, it uses drive C: as the default drive. With drive C: as the default, the computer looks for the operating system files on drive C:.

3. The computer loads the operating system from the default drive into RAM.

The computer first checks drive A: to see if it contains a disk. If there is a disk in this drive, drive A: becomes the **default drive**. The computer uses the default drive for the rest of the computing session unless you specify a different one.

If there is no disk in drive A: but the computer has a drive C:, the computer uses drive C: as the default drive. If your computer has a hard disk, you generally want drive C: to be the default drive, so it is best not to put disks in any of the floppy disk drives until the boot process is complete. Otherwise, the computer recognizes the floppy disk drive as the default.

Next, the computer tries to locate and load operating system files from the default drive. First, the computer looks for two operating system files: **Io.Sys** and **Msdos.Sys**. If these files do not exist on the disk, the boot process stops and displays a message such as "Non-system disk or disk error" or "Cannot load a file." If you see one of these messages, there is probably a disk in drive A: that should not be there—remember that you want your computer to use drive C: as the default. Remove the disk from drive A: so your computer looks at the hard drive for the operating system files.

The microprocessor next attempts to load another operating system file, **Command.Com**. Two problems could occur at this stage of the boot process, and both problems have the same error message—"Bad or missing command interpreter." First problem: the file **Command.Com** might be missing because someone inadvertently erased it. Second problem: your disk might contain the wrong version of **Command.Com** because someone inadvertently copied a different version onto the computer.

If you encounter either problem, you should turn off the computer and make sure drive A: is empty, then turn the computer on again. If the "Bad or missing command interpreter" message appears when you turn the computer on again, you should turn the computer off, then find a bootable floppy disk. A **bootable floppy disk**, such as the one that came with the computer, contains operating system files. Put this floppy disk in drive A: and turn on the computer again. Even if you are successful using a floppy disk to boot your system, you need to correct the **Command.Com** problem on your hard disk. A technical support person or experienced user can help you do this.

Check Configuration and Customization

Does the computer get all its configuration data from CMOS?

Early in the boot process, the computer checks CMOS to determine the amount of installed RAM and the types of available disk drives. Often, however, more configuration data is needed for the computer to properly access all available devices. In the next stage of the boot process, the computer searches the root directory of the boot disk for configuration files, as shown in Figure 4-28.

Figure 4-28
Load configuration data

The computer searches the hard disk for files such as **Config.Sys** and **Autoexec.Bat.**

Config.sys Autoexec.bat

Configuration files are copied into RAM, then executed.

The computer also searches the default drive for customized startup instructions. On some computers these instructions are stored in a file called **Autoexec.Bat** or a Windows startup group, which you can modify to customize your computing environment. For example, you might customize the startup instructions so your To-do list document appears every time you start your computer.

Ready for Commands and Data

How do I know when the computer has finished booting?

The boot process is complete when the computer is ready to accept your commands. Usually the computer displays the operating system main screen or prompt at the end of the boot process. If you are using Windows, you will see the Windows desktop. If you are using DOS, you will see the operating system prompt shown in Figure 4-29.

When the computer displays the operating system prompt, you can enter commands and launch programs.

▶ **Figure 4-29**
The boot process
is complete

End Note   Today's computers are digital electronic devices that accomplish complex tasks by performing a fairly limited set of instructions at breakneck speed. Understanding how a computer manipulates data coded as 1s and 0s should help dispel some of the mystery about what goes on "under the hood" of a microcomputer. Also, you can apply this understanding to troubleshooting your way past computer equipment problems.

Troubleshooting is not difficult if you follow a logical procedure and think creatively. When you have a problem with a computer, first try to make a specific statement that describes the problem. Saying "It's broken!" is not very useful. A more specific description might be something like, "I turned my computer on, but the monitor is blank."

Try to make some hypotheses, or guesses, about the cause of the problem. Be creative—try to think of at least three potential causes. For the monitor problem you might hypothesize that the monitor isn't getting power, that it is not getting a video signal, or that it has somehow "burned out."

Ask yourself which of these potential causes would have the simplest solution. Start with the simple solution first—the monitor might not be getting power because it's not turned on or because the power cable isn't plugged in. These are the things you check first. Of course, you should follow the repair policies of your school or place of employment by not trying to fix equipment that must be repaired by a qualified service agent. And remember the golden rule of troubleshooting: Try at least three things before you call for help.

Review

1. Below each heading in this chapter, there is a question. Look back through this chapter and answer each of these questions using your own words.

2. Make a list of the boldface terms in this chapter, and use your own words to define each term.

3. Place an X in the following table to indicate which characteristics apply to each type of memory.

	RAM	Virtual Memory	ROM	CMOS
Holds user data such as documents				
Holds program instructions such as word processor				
Holds boot program				
Holds configuration data for hard disk type				
Temporary				
Permanent				
Battery powered				
Disk-based				

4. Label the microcomputer components shown in a through g.

a.

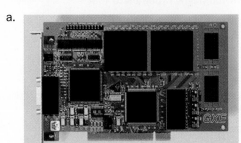

b.

c.

d.

e.

f.

g.

5. Use Figure 4-7 to write out the ASCII code for the following phrase: **Power Up!**

6. Create a conceptual diagram like the one in Figure 4-9 to show how the phrase **Power Up!** is stored in RAM.

7. Imagine you are a teacher. Write a one- or two-page script explaining the instruction cycle to your class, and design at least three visual aids you would use as illustrations.

8. In Figure 4-30, after the processor executes the three instructions in RAM, what are the final values in Register 1, Register 2, and the accumulator? (Hint: Refer to Figure 4-16.)

▶ **Figure 4-30**

Program			
P1	MMR	M1	REG1
P2	MMR	M2	REG2
P3	ADD	REG1	REG2
P4	MAM	M3	
P5	HLT		
Data			
M1	5		
M2	3		
M3	0		

CONTROL UNIT	
INSTRUCTION POINTER	P1
INSTRUCTION REGISTER	

ALU	
ACCUMULATOR	
REG1	
REG2	

9. What are the values in Register 1, Register 2, and the accumulator when the computer has completed the instructions in the RAM of Figure 4-31?

Figure 4-31

Program			
P1	MMR	M1	REG1
P2	MMR	M2	REG2
P3	INC	REG1	
P4	DEC	REG2	
P5	MUL	REG1	REG2
P6	MAM	M3	
P7	HLT		
Data			
M1	7		
M2	4		
M3	0		

CONTROL UNIT	
INSTRUCTION POINTER	P1
INSTRUCTION REGISTER	

ALU	
ACCUMULATOR	
REG1	
REG2	

10. Suppose you are using the Microsoft Word for DOS word processor, and you are creating a document called **Report1.Doc**. Describe the contents of RAM.

11. Compare the specifications for Computer 1 and Computer 2 below. Is 100 MHz better than 75 MHz? Is a 32-bit word size better than a 64-bit word size? Circle the best performance rating in each category.

Performance Factor	Computer 1	Computer 2
Clock Rate	100 MHz	75 MHz
Word Size	32 bits	64 bits
Cache	256 K	32 K
Instruction Set	CISC	RISC
Pipelining	Yes	No
Parallel Processing	No	Yes

12. Use your own words to write a one-paragraph description of pipelining.

13. Label each of the I/O components illustrated in Figure 4-32.

Figure 4-32

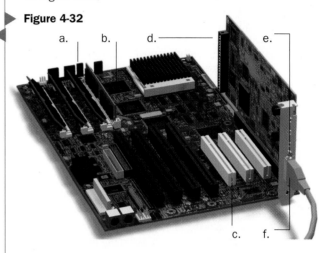

14. Think about the concepts in the first four sections of this chapter: Digital Electronics, Memory, Central Processing Unit, and I/O. Using these concepts, put together your own description of how a computer processes data. You can use a narrative description and/or sketches.

Projects

1. The Araphulians' Computer Read the article about the Araphulian computer in the April 19, 1988 issue of *Scientific American*, entitled "An Ancient Rope-and-Pulley Computer is Unearthed in the Jungle of Araphulia," then answer the following questions:

    a. The Araphulians did not use electricity. How then did they represent 0s and 1s?

    b. What did the Araphulian's *inverter box* accomplish?

    c. The archaeologists excavating the Araphulian site found a large overgrown field where several thousand rotting flip-flop boxes were buried. What part of the computer was at this site?

    d. Redraw the flip-flop diagram from the article and label it to show how it worked.

2. Looking From the Inside Out After disconnecting the power cable, carefully open the case of a computer system unit. Draw a sketch and label each of the components you see inside. Try to locate and label all the components shown in Figure 4-1.

3. The History of the IC Computers would not be available to individuals today if not for the invention of the integrated circuit. Just four months apart in 1959, Jack Kilby and Robert Noyce independently created working models of the circuit that was to transform the computer industry. Jack Kilby worked at Texas Instruments, and you can find reproductions of his original research notes on the Web site *http://www.ti.com/corp/docs/history/firstic.htm*. Robert Noyce developed the integrated circuit while CEO of Fairchild Semiconductor, but he left Fairchild to form Intel.

Use your library and Internet resources to research the impact of the integrated circuit on the computer industry, then do one of the following:

a. Write a two- to three-page paper summarizing how the integrated circuit was used in the first five years after it was invented.

b. Write two one-page biographical sketches; one of Jack Kilby and one of Robert Noyce.

c. Create a diagram of the "family tree" of computer technologies that resulted from the development of the integrated circuit.

d. Based on the facts you have gathered about the development of the computer industry, write a two- to three-page paper describing the computer industry today if the integrated circuit had not been invented.

4. Scanning a Computer Ad for Key Terms Photocopy a full-page computer ad from a current issue of a computer magazine, such as *Computer Shopper*. On the copy of the ad use a colored pen and circle any of the key terms that were presented in this chapter. Make sure you watch for abbreviations; they are frequently used in computer ads. On a separate sheet of paper, or using a word processor, make a list of each term you circled and write a definition of each.

5. Researching and Writing about RAM Suppose you are a computer industry analyst preparing an article on computer memory for a popular computer magazine. Gather as much information as you can about RAM, including current pricing, the amount of RAM that comes installed in a typical computer, tips for adding RAM to computers, and so forth. If you have Internet access, you might find useful information at sites such as *http://www.micron.com*. Use a word processor to write a one- to two-page article that would help your magazine's readers understand all about RAM.

6. Researching and Writing about RISC Write a one- to two-page paper about RISC technology. You might want to explore the history of the concept beginning with John Cocke's research. You can also look at the use of RISC processors for the type of powerful workstations typically used for engineering and CAD applications. You might also research Apple's new PowerPC computer that uses the PowerPC RISC chip. If you have Internet access check IBM's site: *http://www.ibm.com*.

7. Expansion Ports Look in computer magazines to find advertisements for three peripheral devices that connect to a computer using different ports or buses. For example, you might find a modem that connects to the serial port. Photocopy each of these three ads. For each device circle on the photocopy the device's brand name, model name and/or number, and the port or bus it uses. Also make sure you provide your instructor with the name and publication date of the magazine and the page number on which you found the information.

8. Interview with a Computer User Complete the following steps to interview one of your friends who has a computer, and write a report that describes how your friend could expand his or her computer system.

a. Find out as many technical details as you can about your friend's computer, including the type of computer, the type and speed of the microprocessor, the amount of memory, the configuration of disk drives, the capacity of the disk drives, the resolution of the monitor, and so on.

b. Find out how your friend might want to expand his or her computer system either now or sometime in the future. For example, your friend might want to add a printer, a sound card, CD-ROM drive, memory, or a monitor.

c. Look through computer magazines to find a solution for at least one of your friend's expansion plans. What you would recommend as a solution? If money was no object would your recommendation change? Why or why not? And what would your new recommendation be?

d. Write a two-page report describing your friend's computer and his or her expansion needs. Then describe the solution(s) you found.

9. Observing the Boot Process Using Section 4.5 as your guide, make a detailed list of each step in the boot process. Take your list into the computer lab and boot one of the computers. As the computer boots, read your list to make sure it is correct. For which steps in the boot process can you see or hear something actually happening?

Resources

INTERNET OPTIONAL

10. Can a Computer Make Errors?

In 1994 Intel released the Pentium microprocessor. Within a matter of weeks, rumors began to circulate that the Pentium chip had a bug that caused errors in some calculations. As the rumors spread, corporate computer users became nervous about the numbers that appeared on spreadsheets calculated on computers with the Pentium processor. How can a computer make such mistakes? Are computers with Pentium processors destined for the dumpster? Is there any way users can save the money they have invested in their Pentium computers?

Suppose you own a computer store that sold many computers with the flawed Pentium microprocessor. Your customers are calling you to get the straight facts. Use your library and Internet resources to gather as much reliable information as you can about the Pentium flaw. Use this information to write a one-page information sheet for your customers. You might find the following resources useful:

- Intel's Internet site: *http://www.intel.com*

- "The Truth Behind the Pentium Bug" *Byte*, March 1995.

11. Troubleshooting Scenarios—What Would You Do?

Your instructor might want you to do this project individually or in a small group. For each of the following scenarios, indicate what might be wrong.

a. You turn on the computer's power switch and nothing happens—no lights, no beep, nothing. What's the most likely problem?

b. You turn on your computer and the computer completes the POST test. You see the light on drive A: and you hear the drive power up, but you get a message on the screen that says "Cannot load file." Explain what caused this message to appear and explain exactly what you should do to complete the boot process.

c. You are using a word processor to write an essay for your English composition course. You have completed eight pages, and you have periodically saved the document. Suddenly, you notice that when you press a key nothing happens. You try the mouse, but it no longer moves the pointer on the screen. What should you do next?

d. You turn on your computer, see the power light, and hear the fan. Then, the computer begins to beep repeatedly. What would you suspect is the problem?

- **Advanced Micro Devices, Inc. Web site**, *http://www.amd.com* AMD is one of the industry leaders in microprocessor research and production. At its Web site you'll find information on current and future microprocessor technology.

- **Dewdney, A. K.** "Computer Recreations: An ancient rope-and-pulley computer is unearthed in the jungle of Apraphul." *Scientific American*, April 1985, pp. 118–121. What begins as an April Fools' joke turns out to be an excellent explanation of the basic circuitry in a digital computer.

- **Foster, C.** *Computer Architecture.* New York: Van Nostrand Reinhold, 1970. If you want to learn more about computer architecture, this is one of the classics. Be warned, it's not easy reading.

- **Intel web site**, *http://www.intel.com* Intel is the world leader in microprocessor development and production. At its Web site you'll find information about the newest microprocessors. Intel has devoted substantial research efforts into parallel processing, and you can find information on this topic at the Intel site.

- **Kidder, T.** *The Soul of a New Machine.* Boston: Little, Brown, 1981. Kidder writes insightfully about the heady days when the computer industry was venturing into brave new worlds. This book describes a team of researchers who are consumed by a project to build the best computer.

- **Micron, Inc. Web site**, *http://www.micron.com* Micron, Inc. manufactures memory, main boards, and computer systems. Its Internet site contains useful information on memory technology.

- **Motorola Web site**, *http://www.motorola.com* Apple Computer introduced RISC architecture in its PowerPC products in 1994. The PowerPC microprocessor is manufactured by Motorola. At the Motorola Web site, you can find more information on RISC architecture.

- **Rosch, W. L.** *The Winn L. Rosch Hardware Bible*, 3rd ed. New York: Prentice Hall, 1994. Voted as one of the 20 all-time best microcomputer books by *Computer Magazine*, this 1,097-page book is packed with facts about personal computers.

- **Shurkin, J.** *Engines of the Mind: A History of the Computer.* New York: W. W. Norton & Company, 1984. This book is a lively account of the pioneers of the computer industry. It focuses on people and personalities, rather than on machines, and gives the reader a human perspective on the nature of creativity and invention.

■ **Texas Instruments Web site**, *http://www.ti.com* Jack Kilby, an employee of Texas Instruments, was one of the pioneers in the invention of the integrated circuit. Texas Instruments' Web site contains some historical information on integrated circuits as well as information about current developments in memory and processor technology.

■ **White, R.** *How Computers Work*. Emeryville, CA: Ziff-Davis Press, 1993. This book might be called the illustrated guide to how computers work because it contains so many great diagrams. If you are interested in what happens inside the system unit, this is the place to begin.

■ **Wyant, G. and Hammerstrom, T.** *How Microprocessors Work*. Emeryville, CA: Ziff-Davis Press, 1994. If you want to understand microprocessors in more detail, you can pick up this book at most bookstores. Full-page diagrams help to explain technical concepts clearly.

Lab Assignments

Binary Numbers

Computers process and store numbers using the binary number system. Understanding binary numbers helps you recognize how digital computers work by simply turning electricity on and off. In this Lab, you learn about the binary number system and you learn how to convert numbers from binary to decimal and from decimal to binary.

1. Click the Steps button to learn about the binary number system. As you proceed through the Steps, answer all of the Quick Check questions that appear. After you complete the Steps, you will see a Quick Check Summary Report. Follow the instructions on the screen to print this report.

2. Click the Explore button, then click the Conversions button. Practice converting binary numbers into decimal numbers. For example, what is the decimal equivalent of 00010011? Calculate the decimal value on paper. To check your answer, enter the decimal number in the decimal box, and then click the binary boxes to show the 1s and 0s for the number you are converting. Click the Check It button to see if your conversion is correct.

Convert the following binary numbers into decimals:

  a. 00000101

  b. 00010111

  c. 01010101

  d. 10010010

  e. 11111110

3. In Explore, click the Conversions button. Practice converting decimal numbers into binary numbers. For example, what is the binary equivalent of 82? Do the conversion on paper. To check your answer, enter the decimal number in the decimal box, and then click the binary boxes to show the 1s and 0s of its binary equivalent. Click the Check It button to see if your conversion is correct.

Convert the following decimal numbers to binary numbers:

  a. 77

  b. 25

  c. 92

  d. 117

  e. 214

4. In Explore, click the Binary Number Quiz button. The quiz provides you ten numbers to convert. Make each conversion and type your answer in the box. Click the Check Answer button to see if you are correct. When you have completed all ten quiz questions, follow the instructions on the screen to print your quiz results.

CPU Simulator

In a computer central processing unit (CPU), the arithmetic logic unit (ALU) performs instructions orchestrated by the control unit. Processing proceeds at a lightning pace, but each instruction accomplishes only a small step in the entire process. In this Lab you work with an animated CPU simulation to learn how computers execute assembly language programs. In the Explore section of the Lab, you have an opportunity to interpret programs, find program errors, and write your own short assembly language programs.

1. Click the Steps button to learn how to work the simulated CPU. As you proceed through the Steps, answer all of the Quick Check questions that appear. After you complete the Steps, you will see a Quick Check Summary Report. Follow the instructions on the screen to print this report.

2. Click the Explore button. Use the File menu to open a program called **add.cpu**. Use the Fetch Instruction and Execute Instruction buttons to step through the program. Then answer the following questions:

    a. How many instructions does this program contain?

    b. Where is the instruction pointer after the program is loaded but before it executes?

    c. What does the INP 3 M1 instruction accomplish?

    d. What does the MMR M1 REG1 instruction accomplish?

    e. Which memory location holds the instruction that adds the two numbers in REG1 and REG2?

    f. What is in the accumulator when the program execution is complete?

    g. Which memory address holds the sum of the two numbers when program execution is completed?

3. In Explore, use the File menu to open a program called **count5.cpu**. Use the Fetch Instruction and Execute Instruction buttons to step through the program. Then answer the following questions:

    a. What are the two input values for this program?

    b. What happens to the value in REG1 as the program executes?

    c. What happens when the program executes the JPZ P5 instruction?

    d. What are the final values in the accumulator and registers when program execution is complete?

4. In Explore, click File, then click New to make sure the CPU is empty. Write a program that follows these steps to add 8 and 6:

    a. Input 8 into memory address M3.

    b. Input 6 into memory address M5.

    c. Move the number in M3 to Register 1.

    d. Move the number in M5 to Register 2.

    e. Add the numbers in the registers.

    f. Move the value in the accumulator to memory address M1.

    g. Tell the program to halt.

Test your program to make sure it produces the answer 14 in address M1. When you are sure your program works, use the File menu to print your program.

5. In Explore, use the File menu to open a program called **Bad1.cpu**. This program is supposed to multiply two numbers together and put the result in memory location M3. However, the program contains an error.

    a. Which memory location holds the incorrect instruction?

    b. What instruction will make this program produce the correct result?

6. In Explore, use the CPU simulator to write a program to calculate the volume, in cubic feet, of the inside of a refrigerator. The answer should appear in the accumulator at the end of the program. The inside dimensions of the refrigerator are 5 feet, by 3 feet, by 2 feet. Make sure you test your program, then print it.

Troubleshooting

 Computers sometimes malfunction, so it is useful to have some skill at diagnosing, if not fixing, some of the hardware problems you might encounter. In the Troubleshooting Lab, you use a simulated computer that has trouble booting. You learn to make and test hypotheses that help you diagnose the cause of boot problems.

1. Click the Steps button to learn how to make and test hypotheses about hardware malfunctions during the boot process. As you proceed through the Steps, answer all of the Quick Check questions that appear. After you complete the Steps, you will see a Quick Check Summary Report. Follow the instructions on the screen to print this report.

2. Click the Explore button. Use the File menu to load **System11.trb**. Click the Boot Computer button and watch what happens on the simulated computer (in this case, actually, what does not happen!). Make your hypothesis about why this computer does not boot. Use the Check menu to check the state of various cables and switches. When you think you know the cause of the problem, select it from the Diagnosis list. If you correctly diagnosed the problem, write it down. If your diagnosis was not correct, form another hypothesis and check it, until you have correctly diagnosed the problem.

3. Sometimes problems that appear very similar, result from different causes. In Explore, use the File menu to load **System03.trb**, then diagnose the problem. Do the same for **System06.trb**. Describe the problems with these two systems. Then describe the similarities and differences in their symptoms.

4. In Explore, use the File menu to load System02 and System08. Both systems produce keyboard errors, but these errors have different causes. Describe what caused the problem in System02, and what caused the problem in System08. Once you have diagnosed these problems, what can you do about them?

5. In Explore, use the File menu to load Systems 04, 05, 07, 09, and 14. These systems produce similar symptoms on boot up. However, these systems have different problems. Diagnose the problem with each of these systems and indicate the key factor (the symptom or what you checked) that led to your diagnosis.

Quick Check

Answers

4.1

1. integrated circuit

2. bit

3. byte

4. ASCII, EBCDIC

5. binary

6. bus (or data bus)

4.2

1. Random access memory (RAM)

2. volatile

3. megabytes

4. capacitors

5. SIMM

6. virtual

7. ROM

8. CMOS

4.3

1. microprocessor

2. ALU

3. Control unit

4. opcode, operand

5. fetch, interpret, execute, increment instruction pointer

6. clock rate, word size, cache, instruction set

4.4

1. expansion bus

2. expansion card

3. slot, port

4. parallel, SCSI, serial, MIDI

Glossary/Index

The Computer

CHAPTER**PREVIEW**

When you have completed this chapter, you should be able to:

▦ Read a computer ad and understand how the technical specifications affect price and performance

▦ Explain why there are so many models of computers at so many different prices

▦ Research reliable information about computer products

▦ Determine which products are of good quality and value

▦ Take a systematic approach to shopping for a computer

▦ Explain how buying hardware is different from buying software

Marketplace

It is one of those dreary afternoons when the rain fogs up the windows. Your friend Matt is sprawled on the floor, tearing Post-it™ notes into tiny pieces of confetti.

"Hey, what's up?" you ask.

"I'm depressed or frustrated or something," he complains. "I finally have enough money to buy a computer, but now I also have one big headache!"

"What do you mean?"

"See all these magazines! See all these ads! How's a person supposed to know what to buy? The more I look, the more confused I get!" He opens the latest issue of *Computer Shopper*—all 800 pages of it—and you see that he has marked at least 30 ads with Post-it notes!

"Look," he says, "here's a computer with a Pentium processor...$1,995. Here's another one from a different company...$2,295."

"There's got to be some difference between them." You try to help.

Matt frowns. "Yeah. That's the trouble. This one for $1,995 has 8 megs of RAM, but the $2,295 computer has 16 megs."

"Well, that accounts for the price difference, right?" It seems simple to you.

But it is not so simple to Matt. "Hah!" he exclaims. "The cheaper computer has a 15-inch monitor, but the more expensive computer only has a 14-inch monitor." His eyes glaze over, and his voice becomes high-pitched. "And look. Here I can get one with 16 megs and all kinds of software for $2,395."

"Well, that sounds good." You try to encourage him.

"Yeah, but have you ever heard of this company?" he asks, pointing to the ad. "What if they go out of business right after I buy a computer from them? What am I going to do?"...

Sometime in the not-too-distant future you are likely to participate in a computer purchase decision—if not for your own computer, then one for your friend, your parents' small business, your employer, or your children. Buying the right computer and keeping within your budget are challenges.

The purpose of this chapter is to help you learn about computers and software from the consumer's perspective and to help you discover what you need to know to be a smart computer shopper. In Chapter 4 you learned how computers work. You know the purpose of computer components such as the processor, RAM, bus, expansion cards, and disk drives. In Chapter 5 you will learn about different options and models of these components and how they affect the pricing and performance of today's microcomputers.

5.1

Consumer's Guide to Desktop Computer Systems

Lab

Buying a Computer

Figure 5-1 ◄
MicroPlus
computer ad

uppose you decide to buy a computer. You'll probably look at computer ads to get an idea of features and prices. Most computer ads list technical **specifications** describing the computer's components, capabilities, and special features. Do you need to understand the technical specifications to make an intelligent purchase decision? The answer is definitely "yes!" Suppose, for example, that you consider buying the MicroPlus computer advertised in Figure 5-1. It costs $2,295. Would it be a good "deal"?

Sections 5.1 and 5.2 will help you understand the most frequently used terminology that you might encounter in computer ads. You can learn additional terms and practice comparison shopping in the Buying a Computer Lab.

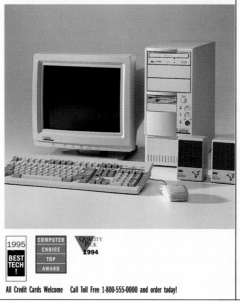

MicroPlus HomePC's

MicroPlus award-winning computers offer strong performance at a reasonable price. Simply the fastest Windows machines you can buy. MicroPlus computers feature superior engineering, starting with a genuine Intel processor and a motherboard designed specifically to take advantage of the latest technological advancements. Of course, you are covered by our one-year on-site parts and labor warranty.*

*ON-SITE SERVICE AVAILABLE FOR HARDWARE ONLY AND MAY NOT BE AVAILABLE IN CERTAIN REMOTE AREAS. SHIPPING AND HANDLING EXTRA. ALL RETURNS WILL BE EXCHANGED FOR LIKE PRODUCT ONLY. ALL RETURNS MUST BE IN ORIGINAL BOX WITH ALL MATERIALS. CALL FOR AN RMA NUMBER. DEFECTIVE PRODUCTS WILL BE REPAIRED AT MICROPLUS DISCRETION. THE COST FOR RETURNED MERCHANDISE IS NOT INCLUDED WITH ANY MONEY-BACK GUARANTEE. PRICES AND AVAILABILITY SUBJECT TO CHANGE WITHOUT NOTICE.

- Intel Pentium-133 with 256 K cache
- 8 MB RAM expandable to 128 MB
- 528 MB 11 MS Local bus enhanced EIDE hard drive with 120 K cache
- 4X CD-ROM Drive
- 3 1/2-inch 1.44 MB floppy drive
- 16-bit Sound Blaster®-compatable sound card and Koss® speakers
- 64-bit PCI local bus SVGA color graphics card with 1 MB DRAM
- 15-inch 1024 x 768 non-interlaced SVGA color monitor, .28 dot pitch
- Six-bay tower case
- Mouse
- MS-DOS 6.2, Windows 95
- Three PCI & four ISA slots
- Two high-speed serial ports and one parallel port
- 14.4 bps fax/modem with software

1995 **BEST TECH!** | COMPUTER CHOICE TOP AWARD | QUALITY PICK **1994**

All Credit Cards Welcome   Call Toll Free 1-800-555-0000 and order today!

You can't tell if the Micro Plus computer is a good deal unless you can compare its specifications to those of computers from other vendors. Let's take a closer look at what the specifications mean in terms of price and performance.

Comparing Microprocessors

Which microprocessor is best for my computing needs?

The microprocessor is the core component in a computer and is featured prominently in product descriptions. Computer ads typically indicate the type of microprocessor and its speed. Most of today's microcomputers are designed around a microprocessor from one of three product families: x86, 68000-series, or PowerPC.

In 1981 the original IBM PC used the Intel 8088 microprocessor, a slightly modified version of the 8086 model. The descendants of the 8086 microprocessors are often referred to as the **x86** family of microprocessors. Today's IBM-compatible computers still contain processors in the x86 **family**. Most of these processors are manufactured by Intel, but a few companies, such as Cyrix and AMD, have produced what are called "work-alike" processors. Computers with work-alike processors are generally less expensive than an equivalent model with an Intel processor. How can you tell what brand of processor a computer contains? Look for the "Intel Inside" logo in computer ads.

The **68000-series** microprocessors are manufactured by Motorola and used by Apple in its Macintosh Classic, SE, Quadra, and Performa computers. The instruction set for the 68000-series is different from that for the x86 family, which is why software written for x86 IBM-compatible computers does not work on 68000-based computers.

The **PowerPC** microprocessor implements RISC architecture to provide relatively fast performance at a low cost. The PowerPC chip is used by both Apple and IBM in their PowerPC computers. Although the PowerPC chip cannot directly execute the x86 or 68000 instruction set, PowerPC computers with an emulator can run software designed for IBM-compatible or Macintosh 68000-series computers. An **emulator** is software or hardware that enables one device to behave as if it were another.

The MicroPlus computer in the ad is a 133 MHz Pentium. The genealogy tree in Figure 5-2 will help you compare the specifications of this microprocessor to 68000-series and PowerPC microprocessors.

Recall from Chapter 4 that microprocessor speed is measured in megahertz (MHz), and higher MHz ratings mean a faster processor. A Pentium 133 MHz processor, therefore, is faster than a Pentium 75 MHz processor.

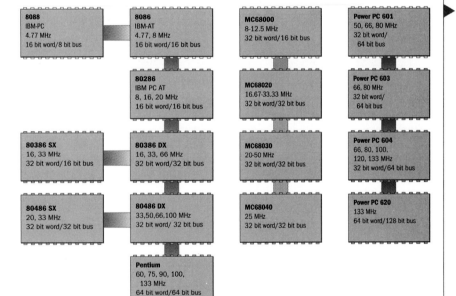

Figure 5-2
Microprocessor families

The microprocessor, to a great extent, determines the software titles you will be able to use. If you want to run Windows software, select a computer with an x86 microprocessor. If you want to use software designed for Macintosh computers, select a computer with a 68000-series or PowerPC microprocessor.

The Cost and Benefits of RAM Cache

Does a RAM cache affect the price of a computer?

A RAM cache is very important for optimum performance of computers with high-speed processors because the CPU can process data faster than it can retrieve it from the regular RAM area. A computer with an 80486 microprocessor should have at least 128 K of RAM cache; Pentium systems should have at least 256 K. Cache memory chips add to the cost of a computer system—a 256 K cache adds about $100.

In Chapter 4 you learned that a RAM cache speeds up processing by placing data in a special high-speed memory area.

RAM: Requirements and Cost

How much RAM is enough?

The amount of RAM a computer needs depends on the operating system and applications software you plan to use. It is theoretically possible to run Windows 3.1 in as little as 2 MB of RAM. Most Windows 3.1 applications, however, require at least 4 MB and perform even better with 8 MB or more. Windows 95 requires at least 4 MB of RAM, but performs better with 8 to 16 MB.

RAM costs about $50 per megabyte, so a 16 MB computer costs significantly more than an 8 MB system. Although some computer systems have 4 MB of RAM, 8 MB is the recommended minimum for the computing needs of today's typical computer user.

It is possible to add RAM after you purchase a computer system. For example, the MicroPlus computer includes 8 MB of RAM, but additional memory modules can be added up to a maximum of 128 MB. Before you purchase additional RAM, you must check the computer manual to find out the type of memory modules your computer uses and what memory configurations are possible.

Recall from Chapter 4 that most of today's computers use SIMM modules for RAM. To expand the RAM capacity of these computers, you would purchase additional SIMMs and install them in empty SIMM sockets.

Floppy Disk Drives: How Many?

Do I need more than one floppy disk drive?

Most microcomputers today are configured with a single 3½-inch high-density floppy disk drive. Older computers often were configured with a 5¼-inch disk drive in addition to a 3½-inch drive. These two disk drive sizes were useful during the transition from the earlier 5¼-inch disks to the newer 3½-inch disks. Today, most software is shipped on 3½-inch disks or on CD-ROMs, so a 5¼-inch drive is unnecessary.

A popular misconception is that a computer needs two disk drives to copy the contents of one disk to another, but this is not the case. Both Windows and DOS allow you to make a copy of an entire disk by reading data from the original disk into memory, then inserting the destination disk and copying the data from memory to the destination disk. One 3½-inch floppy disk drive should be sufficient for your computing needs.

Recall that a high-density disk drive stores up to 1.44 MB on a high-density floppy disk.

CD-ROM Drive: Worth the Cost?

Do I need a CD-ROM drive?

A CD-ROM drive is a worthwhile investment that lets you use multimedia, game, educational, and reference applications that are available only on CD-ROM disks.

Most microcomputers are configured with a double-speed (2×), quad-speed (4×), or six-speed (6×) CD-ROM drive. A faster CD-ROM drive will deliver data at a faster rate and provide better performance, especially with multimedia applications. You should purchase the fastest CD-ROM drive that you can afford.

If you plan to use multimedia software, you should be aware of current MPC standards. **MPC standards** specify the recommended computer configuration for running current multimedia software. These standards change about every two years. The chart in Figure 5-3 shows you the current MPC standard, MPC3, as well as earlier versions.

	MPC1	MPC2	MPC3
Date introduced	March 1991	May 1993	June 1995
Processor	16 MHz 386X	25 MHz 486SX	75 MHz Pentium
RAM	2 MB	4 MB	8 MB
Hard drive capacity	30 MB	160 MB	540 MB
CD-ROM drive speed	single-speed	double-speed	quad-speed
Sound board	8-bit	16-bit	16-bit
System software	Windows 3.0	Windows 3.0	Windows 3.1 or 3.11

▶ **Figure 5-3**
MPC standards

Try not to confuse memory and storage. Memory is on the main board; storage is handled by the disk drive.

Hard Drive Specifications

Why do computer ads include specifications on the hard drive bus and controller?

The factors that influence hard drive performance and price include storage capacity, controller type, cache capacity, and bus speed. Figure 5-4 provides an overview of these factors.

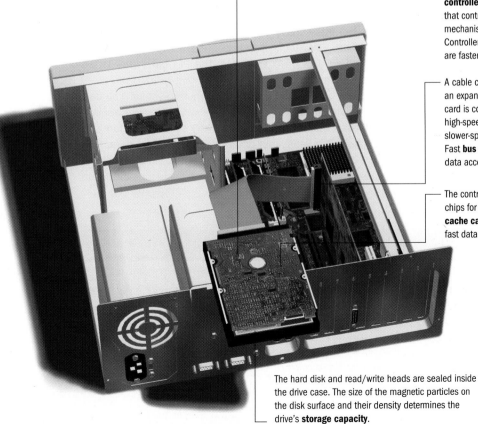

The hard disk circuit board, called a **controller**, contains the electronics that control the mechanical drive mechanism and data transfer. Controllers such as EIDE and SCSI are faster than IDE, MFM, or RLL.

A cable connects the controller to an expansion card. The expansion card is connected to a special high-speed local bus or the slower-speed expansion bus. Fast **bus speed** means faster data access

The controller often contains the chips for a disk cache. A large **cache capacity** contributes to fast data access times.

The hard disk and read/write heads are sealed inside the drive case. The size of the magnetic particles on the disk surface and their density determines the drive's **storage capacity**.

▶ **Figure 5-4**
Hard drive storage overview

As explained in Chapter 3, the access time of a hard disk drive is measured in milliseconds. A drive with a 13 ms access time is slightly slower than a drive with a 10 ms access time.

The more storage space you have, the better, so when comparing computer systems, the hard drive capacity is a significant factor. Most computers today are shipped with at least 500 MB hard disk drives.

Computer ads usually specify hard disk access time as an indication of drive performance. Access times of 9 to 13 ms are typical for today's microcomputer hard drives.

The two most popular types of hard drives are EIDE and SCSI. A drive mechanism includes a circuit board called a **controller** that positions the disk and read-write heads to locate data. Disk drives are categorized according to the type of controller they have. An **EIDE** (Enhanced Integrated Device Electronics) drive features high storage capacity and fast data transfer. **SCSI** drives provide a slight performance advantage over EIDE drives and are recommended for high-performance microcomputer systems and minicomputers.

In addition to drive capacity, access time, and type, most ads provide information about disk cache capacity and bus type. Disk cache, such as the 120 K cache in the MicroPlus computer, is an advantage because it will speed up system performance. A local bus, such as the one featured in the MicroPlus ad, increases data transport speed by providing a separate high-speed bus to carry data between storage devices and RAM.

Chapter 3 explained that a disk cache speeds up access to data by temporarily placing data where it can be accessed more quickly than from the drive. The cache area can be on the circuit board in the disk drive, on the controller card, or in RAM.

Microcomputer Bus and Slot Types

Why do I need to pay attention to the bus type?

Computer ads generally specify the type of expansion bus the computer uses to transport data. The capacity of the expansion bus is determined by its speed and the number of bits that can be transported during each clock cycle. Bus speed is measured in megahertz, as is the microprocessor. A 33 MHz bus is faster than a 4.77 MHz bus, for example.

In some computers, the expansion bus is supplemented by special-purpose high-speed buses. The **VESA Local Bus** and the **PCI Local Bus** provide high-speed 32-bit or 64-bit paths that transfer data to display and storage devices. The local bus specified in the MicroPlus ad increases data transfer rates between the hard disk drive and RAM. The PCI Local Bus in the MicroPlus ad speeds up data transfer from RAM to the display.

In a computer system with a high-speed local bus, the amount of data carried on the regular expansion bus is reduced, but it continues to carry data for slower devices such as the printer and mouse.

A local bus is built into the main board and adds to the cost of a computer system. You cannot add a local bus to a computer unless you replace the main board. If your computer applications require extensive data access or graphics displays, you should make sure the system you purchase includes the appropriate local buses. The initial cost of including a local bus is far less than the cost of replacing your computer's main board if you later discover you need additional data transfer speed. Figure 5-5 summarizes the important features about microcomputer data buses.

Figure 5-5 ◄
Microcomputer data bus summary

Bus Name	Number of Bits	Speed
XT Bus	8 bits	4.77 MHz
ISA Bus	16 bits	8 MHz
EISA Bus	32 bits	6–8.33 MHz
Micro Channel Bus	16 or 32 bits	10 MHz
VESA Local Bus	32 bits	33–66 MHz
PCI Local Bus	32 or 64 bits	33–66 MHz

Many computers provide one to three local bus slots for video adapter cards and hard disk controller cards. The MicroPlus computer has three high-speed PCI slots and four slower ISA slots. This sounds like a reasonable amount of room for expansion, but be careful. Some of these slots might be used by the devices shipped with the computer. When you are considering a particular computer, it is a good idea to ask how many of the expansion slots are *free*, that is, available for devices that you might want to install later.

Selecting a System Unit Case

What are bays, and why are they important?

The system unit case holds the main board and provides openings, called **bays**, for mounting disk, CD-ROM, and tape drives. Some bays are external, and some are internal.

An **external bay** provides an opening for installing a device that you need to access from the outside of the case. For example, you would install a floppy disk drive in an external bay because you need to insert and remove the floppy disks. An **internal bay** provides a mounting bracket for devices that do not need to be accessible from outside the system unit case. Hard disk drives typically use internal bays because you don't need to access them while using the computer.

A system unit with many bays provides greater expansion capability. Notice in Figure 5-1 that the MicroPlus computer tower case has six bays. From the picture in the ad, it appears that there are four external bays, so two of the bays must be internal. The hard disk drive occupies one internal bay, while the floppy disk drive and CD-ROM each occupy one external bay. That leaves one internal bay and two external bays for expansion—probably adequate for most home and business uses.

Video Adapters and Monitors

What is the relationship between the video adapter and the monitor?

You learned in Chapter 1 that many of today's graphical user interfaces require high-resolution graphics. As a consumer, your goal is to buy the best display that fits your budget. The quality of a computer display depends on two interrelated factors: the specifications of the monitor and the features of the video display adapter.

Monitor specifications include screen size, maximum resolution, and dot pitch. **Screen size** is the measurement in inches from one corner of the screen diagonally across to the opposite corner. Most computer systems are packaged with a 14-inch or 15-inch screen. You might want to consider paying an additional $300 to $500 for a 17-inch monitor if you have a vision problem or if you like to work with more than one program at the same time. With a 17-inch monitor you can use 1024×768 resolution to fit more windows on the screen, and the text will still be reasonably large.

Dot pitch is a measure of image clarity; a smaller dot pitch means a crisper image. Technically, dot pitch is the distance in millimeters between like-colored pixels. A .28 dot pitch is typical for today's monitors.

The specifications for a monitor include its **maximum resolution**, typically 1024×768. It is important to realize that the maximum resolution you can use is determined by both the video adapter and the monitor. If your video adapter supports 1280×1024 resolution, but your monitor supports only 1024×768, the maximum resolution you can use will be 1024×768.

Many older high-resolution monitors displayed an undesirable strobe-light effect called **flicker** at resolutions higher than 640×480. Most monitors sold today are non-interlaced. A **non-interlaced** (often abbreviated in ads as NI) monitor provides an image with less flicker at higher resolutions than an interlaced monitor. Figure 5-6 explains the difference between interlaced and non-interlaced monitor technology.

Figure 5-6
Producing an image

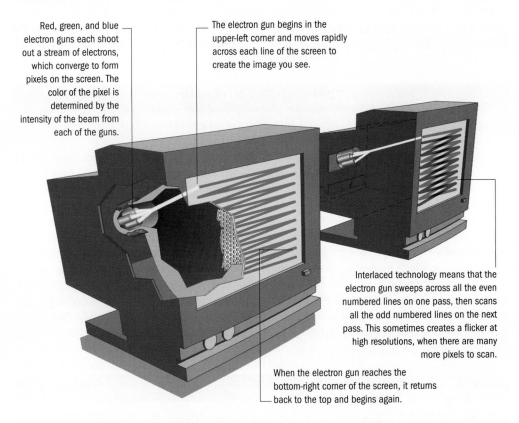

Red, green, and blue electron guns each shoot out a stream of electrons, which converge to form pixels on the screen. The color of the pixel is determined by the intensity of the beam from each of the guns.

The electron gun begins in the upper-left corner and moves rapidly across each line of the screen to create the image you see.

Interlaced technology means that the electron gun sweeps across all the even numbered lines on one pass, then scans all the odd numbered lines on the next pass. This sometimes creates a flicker at high resolutions, when there are many more pixels to scan.

When the electron gun reaches the bottom-right corner of the screen, it returns back to the top and begins again.

A video adapter is required for your computer to display any kind of text, graphics, or animations. It is not only for watching video segments on your computer screen.

Imagine the impact millions of computers have on electricity usage. Computer companies have responded to the concerns of environmentalists by designing **energy star compliant** monitors and computer systems. These systems use less energy by switching to a low-power stand-by mode after a specified period of inactivity. You can help save energy and reduce pollution by looking for the EPA pollution prevention logo on energy-saving products. Some people believe that radiation from monitors might have long-term health effects. Low-radiation monitors are advertised as meeting MPR-II and TCO standards for reduced radiation emission.

A **video display adapter**, also called a **video card** or graphics card, is an expansion card that provides a data pathway from the main board to the monitor. Most video display adapters use special graphics chips to boost performance. These **accelerated video adapters** can greatly increase the speed at which images are displayed. An accelerated video adapter connected to a fast VESA or PCI local bus can move data between the microprocessor and the video adapter as fast as the microprocessor can process it. Your computer will perform better, especially for graphical user interfaces, if it has an accelerated video adapter connected to a VESA or PCI bus.

Display resolution depends on the video display adapter that connects the monitor to the computer. Today, most computers have a **super VGA** (SVGA) video adapter that supports resolutions of 640×480, 800×600, and 1024×768. Older computers with VGA, not super VGA, video adapters do not support 800×600 or 1024×768 resolutions.

The amount of memory on the video adapter limits the number of colors that can be displayed at each resolution. Video adapter memory capacity is an important consideration if you are using multimedia software with photographic-quality images. To display photographic-quality images at 640×480 resolution, a video adapter should have at least 1 MB of memory. If you plan to display such images at 800×600 or 1024×768 resolutions, the video adapter should have 2 to 4 MB of memory.

Why Buy a Sound Card?

Should I spend extra money for a sound card?

If you want to run games or multimedia software, you should purchase a computer system that includes a sound card. A basic sound card adds less than $100 to the price of a computer system. A 16-bit sound card costs slightly more, but it provides higher quality sound output than an 8-bit sound card.

Most games and many multimedia applications require a Sound Blaster-compatible sound card. The original Sound Blaster card was manufactured by Creative Labs. Many software manufacturers designed their software to use these cards. Now, so called "Sound Blaster-compatible" cards from other manufacturers also work with this software and are popular with consumers.

Selecting a Modem

Does a fax/modem turn my computer into a fax machine?

Many computer systems include a modem that transmits to and receives data from other computers over telephone lines. The speed of transmission is usually expressed as baud rate or as bits per second. The **baud rate** is the number of signal changes that occurs in one second during data transmission. **Bits per second**, abbreviated bps, is the number of data bits transmitted by the modem in one second. When comparing computer system specifications, you just need to remember that faster modem speeds mean faster data transmission. A 14,400 or 28,800 bps modem is typical for today's computer systems.

A **fax/modem** is a modem that includes fax capability. This means that it can send a document that is in the memory of your computer to any standard fax machine—where the document is printed on paper. Modems with fax capability can also receive fax transmissions from standard fax machines or other fax/modems. You can view the received fax on your monitor or print it on your computer printer.

A modem requires communication software that helps you enter the settings required to establish communications with a variety of different computers. When you buy a computer system that includes a modem, the computer vendor has probably installed the communications software needed to operate the modem. But it's a good idea to check to be sure that the software is included in the system price.

A fax/modem does not provide a way for you to feed a piece of paper through your computer, so the documents you fax must be in electronic form, not on paper.

The Value of Bundled Software

What software is typically included when I purchase a computer system?

The price of most computers includes the operating system, so if you purchase an IBM-compatible computer, you can expect that the latest version of DOS and Windows will be installed on the hard drive by the vendor or manufacturer. Many computer vendors also include applications software such as a word processing package or personal finance manager. Multimedia computer systems usually include several CD-ROMs, such as encyclopedias, fact books, and games.

All other factors being equal, a system with bundled software will cost only slightly more than a system without bundled software. So bundling is often a good value even if not all of the software meets your needs. The slight increase in the price of a computer system with bundled software is generally less than you would pay if you bought the software separately.

Figure 5-7 ◀
Printers

Dot matrix printers create letters and graphics by striking an inked ribbon with a column of small wires called *pins*. By activating some wires in the column, but not activating others, the printer creates patterns for letters and numbers. The more pins in the column, the better the print quality. Therefore, a 24-pin dot-matrix printer is capable of better quality output than a 9-pin printer. Dot matrix printers create color printouts using a ribbon with bands of colored ink. Color printouts from a dot matrix printer tend to look faded and of low quality.

Dot matrix printer operating costs are low. Replacement ribbon cartridges are usually less than $20. The cost of dot-matrix printing is less than $.01 per page.

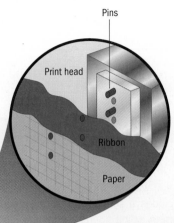

Pins

Print head

Ribbon

Paper

A 9-pin print head creates an uppercase letter using a 5 X 7 matrix. The two lower pins of the print head are used for letters that go below the line, such as g, y, and q.

Ribbon
Print head

Dot Matrix printer

Characteristics	
✓	Low price
✓	Noisy
✓	Inexpensive to operate
✓	Low-to medium-quality output
✓	Can print multipart forms
✓	Slow
✓	Low-cost, low-quality color
✓	Durable

9-pin print sample

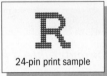

24-pin print sample

The print quality of a 24-pin dot matrix printer, sometimes referred to as *near letter quality*, is much smoother and easier to read.

Ink-jet printers produce characters and graphics by spraying ink onto paper. The print head is a matrix of fine spray nozzles. Patterns are formed by activating selected nozzles. An ink-jet printer typically forms a character in a 20 X 20 matrix, producing a high-quality printout.

Color ink-jet printers cost a little more, but produce much higher-quality output than color dot-matrix printers. Using special paper, some color ink-jet printers can produce vivid, high-quality, color printouts. The other option for color output, a color laser printer, is far beyond the budget of most home or small business users. Ink-jet printers are inexpensive to operate, requiring only a new ink cartridge or ink refill. Estimated cost per page is about $.01.

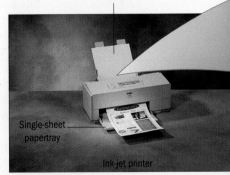

Paper output here

Single-sheet papertray

Ink-jet printer

Choosing the Right Printer

What kind of printer should I buy?

Recall that in Chapter 1 you learned about the three categories of printers: dot matrix, ink-jet, and laser.

Occasionally a computer vendor offers a *hardware bundle* that includes a computer, printer, and software. More often, however, printers are sold separately so consumers can choose the quality, features, and price they want. Ink-jet and personal laser printers are most popular with today's consumers because they provide high-quality print on plain paper.

If you want color printouts, color ink-jet printers offer the best price-performance value because of the high price of color laser printers and the poor quality of color dot matrix printers. Figure 5-7 is a guide to the types and features of printers.

Laser printers use the same technology as duplicating machines. A laser charges particles on a drum. Then, a powdery black ink called *toner* onto paper. In the past, the price of laser printers limited their use to businesses and large organizations. Laser printer prices have decreased, however, making them affordable for individuals.

Color laser printers work by reprinting each page for each primary color. For each reprint, the paper must be precisely positioned so each color is printed in exactly the right spot. This dramatically increases the complexity of the print mechanism and the amount of time required to print each page. Like color photocopies, color laser printers are relatively uncommon due to their high price.

Operating costs of laser printers include replacement toner cartridges and print drums. The estimated cost of laser printing is about $.05 per page.

A laser charges a pattern of particles on a drum which picks up a powdery black sustance called toner. The toner is transferred onto paper that rolls

Laser

Drum

Single-sheet paper feed tray

Toner   Paper

Laser printer

Laser print sample

R

Now that you have completed the section on desktop computers, see how well you can interpret the specifications in the MicroPlus ad by answering Question 3 in the Chapter Review.

Characteristics	
✓	Moderate to high price
✓	High-quality output
✓	More expensive to operate
✓	Cannot print multipart forms
✓	Fast
✓	Quiet
✓	Expensive, high-quality color
✓	Durable

Print head nozzles

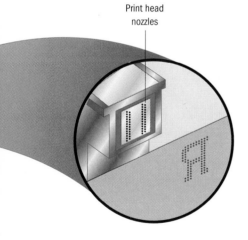

Characteristics	
✓	Moderate price
✓	High-quality output
✓	Inexpensive to operate
✓	Cannot print multipart forms
✓	Slow
✓	Quiet
✓	Low-cost, low-quality color
✓	Durable

R

Ink-jet print sample

Quick Check

1. The three families of microprocessors are _____, _____, and _____.

2. The amount of RAM you need in your computer depends on _____ and _____.

3. The two most popular types of hard drive are _____ and _____.

4. VESA and PCI are types of _____.

5. High resolution and small _____ are two characteristics of a monitor with a clear image.

6. If you want to display photographic-quality images at 640 × 480 resolution, you need a video adapter with at least _____ of video memory.

7. Modem speeds of 14,400 or 28,800 _____ are typical for today's computer systems.

8. The best value for color printing is a(n) _____ printer.

5.2

Consumer's Guide to Notebook Computers

When shopping for a notebook computer, you'll notice that many of the technical specifications are the same as for desktop computers—processor type and speed, amount of RAM, hard disk capacity, and bundled software. The purpose of this section is to point out additional considerations you need to make when comparing and evaluating notebook computers like the one advertised in Figure 5-8.

Figure 5-8
MicroNote
computer ad

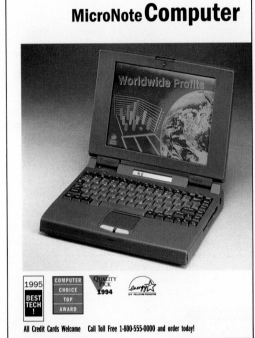

MicroNote Computer

For dependable computing on the go, the MicroNote can't be beat. As powerful as a desktop computer, with built in sound capabilities and active matrix display, this notebook is designed to meet your most exacting computer needs.

- 80486DX4-100 MHz
- 8 MB RAM max 32 MB
- 3½-inch 1.44 MB floppy drive
- 520 MB hard drive
- 9.5 inch active matrix VGA display
- Local bus video with 1 MB video RAM
- External VGA and keyboard port
- PCMCIA type III slot
- One parallel and one serial port
- Touch Pad
- 16-bit stereo Sound-Blaster®-compatible sound
- Advanced power managment
- NiMH battery with hot swap
- 5.7 lbs.

*ON-SITE SERVICE AVAILABLE FOR HARDWARE ONLY AND MAY NOT BE AVAILABLE IN CERTAIN REMOTE AREAS. SHIPPING AND HANDLING EXTRA. ALL RETURNS WILL BE EXCHANGED FOR LIKE PRODUCT ONLY. ALL RETURNS MUST BE IN ORIGINAL BOX WITH ALL MATERIALS. CALL FOR AN RMA NUMBER. DEFECTIVE PRODUCTS WILL BE REPAIRED AT MICROPLUS DISCRETION. THE COST FOR RETURNED MERCHANDISE IS NOT INCLUDED WITH ANY MONEY-BACK GUARANTEE. PRICES AND AVAILABILITY SUBJECT TO CHANGE WITHOUT NOTICE.

1995 BEST TECH ! | COMPUTER CHOICE TOP AWARD | QUALITY PICK 1994 | energy

All Credit Cards Welcome   Call Toll Free 1-800-555-0000 and order today!

The Advantage of PCMCIA Cards

There doesn't seem to be much room in a notebook computer case—how do I add expansion cards?

A **PCMCIA slot** (Personal Computer Memory Card International Association) is a special type of expansion slot developed for notebook computers, which do not have space in the case for full-size expansion slots and cards. A PCMCIA slot is a small, external slot into which you can insert a PCMCIA card.

PCMCIA cards, also called **PC cards**, are credit-card-sized circuit boards that incorporate an expansion card and a device. So, for example, some PCMCIA cards contain a modem, others contain memory expansion, and others contain a hard disk drive. You can plug in and remove PCMCIA devices without turning the computer off, unlike traditional expansion cards. In this way you can switch from one PCMCIA device to another without disrupting your work, as shown in Figure 5-9.

PCMCIA slots are categorized by size. Type I slots accept only the thinnest PCMCIA cards such as memory expansion cards. Type II slots accept most of the popular PCMCIA cards—those that contain modems, sound cards, and network cards. Type III slots accept the thickest PCMCIA cards, which contain devices such as hard disk drives. Many notebooks provide a multipurpose PCMCIA slot that will accept two Type I cards, two Type II cards, or one Type III card.

PCMCIA cards

 Figure 5-9
Using PCMCIA
cards

PCMCIA card
inserted into
PCMCIA slot of a
notebook computer.

Phone jack on PCMCIA
modem card.

Comparing Notebook Displays

Is it true that the screen image on a notebook computer is not as good as the image on a desktop computer?

Notebook computers do not use monitors because they are big and heavy, and they require too much electrical power to run on batteries. Instead, notebooks have a flat panel liquid crystal display. A **liquid crystal display (LCD)** uses a technically sophisticated method of passing light through a thin layer of liquid crystal cells to produce an image. The resulting flat panel screen is lightweight and compact.

Notebook LCDs are either passive or active matrix. A **passive matrix screen** relies on timing to make sure the liquid crystal cells are illuminated. As a result, the process of updating the screen image does not always keep up with moving images, and the display can appear blurred. Passive matrix displays are available in monochrome and color versions. A computer with a monochrome passive matrix screen costs several hundred dollars less than a computer with a color passive matrix screen.

An **active matrix screen** updates more rapidly and provides image quality similar to that of a monitor. Active matrix screens are essential for a crisp display of animations and video. However, active matrix screens are difficult to manufacture—approximately 80% are rejected due to defects—and add significantly to the price of a notebook computer.

Most notebook computers have a VGA or SVGA port for an external monitor. The advantage of an external monitor is the high-quality display. The disadvantage is that you need to disconnect the external monitor when you transport the computer.

Multimedia Notebooks: Pros and Cons

Can I use a notebook computer for multimedia computing?

Notebook computer manufacturers have found it difficult to pack a CD-ROM drive and sound card into a small notebook case, but they have been making progress. Notebooks with built-in CD-ROM drives and sound cards are available, even though they are slightly heavier and more expensive than their non-multimedia counterparts.

You can use a docking station as an alternative to built-in multimedia components. A **docking station** is essentially an additional expansion bus into which you plug your notebook computer. The notebook provides the processor and RAM. The docking station provides expansion slots for cards that would not fit into the notebook case. It allows you to purchase inexpensive expansion cards and peripherals designed for desktops, instead of the more expensive devices designed specifically for notebooks. You sacrifice portability—you probably won't carry your docking station and external CD-ROM drive with you—but you gain the use of low-cost, powerful desktop peripherals. Figure 5-10 illustrates how a docking station works.

Figure 5-10
Notebook docking station

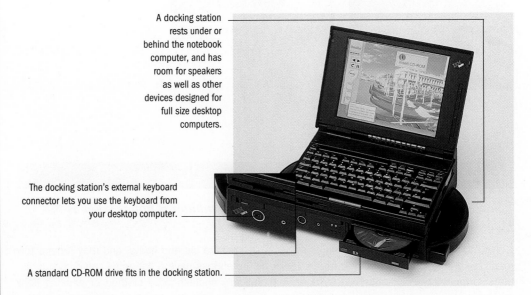

A docking station rests under or behind the notebook computer, and has room for speakers as well as other devices designed for full size desktop computers.

The docking station's external keyboard connector lets you use the keyboard from your desktop computer.

A standard CD-ROM drive fits in the docking station.

If you don't need multimedia capabilities, a port replicator makes it more convenient to connect and disconnect your notebook computer from devices such as an external monitor, mouse, and keyboard. A **port replicator** is an inexpensive device that connects to a notebook computer by a bus connector plug; it contains a duplicate of the notebook computer's ports. Port replicators do not include expansion slots and typically cannot be used to add a sound card or CD-ROM drive to your notebook computer.

Why would you want a port replicator? Suppose that when you use your notebook computer at home you plug in an external monitor, a full-size keyboard, and a printer. Every time you want to travel with your notebook, you must unplug each of these devices, then plug them in again when you return home. It is more convenient to plug the external devices into a port replicator, then plug the port replicator into the bus connector of the notebook. In this way, you only have one plug to connect, instead of many, as Figure 5-11 shows.

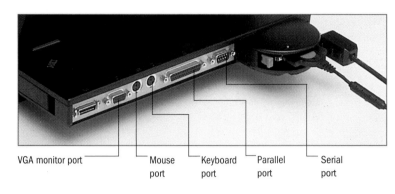

VGA monitor port   Mouse port   Keyboard port   Parallel port   Serial port

A typical notebook computer has many ports. Plugging and unplugging devices can be inconvenient if you are frequently traveling with the computer.

A port replicator plugs into a notebook computer using a special connector port and contains ports for external devices. When you want to take the computer traveling, you can leave the external devices plugged into the port replicator and unplug the port replicator from the computer.

Figure 5-11
Notebook port replicator

Which Notebook Pointing Device Is for You?

Isn't it clumsy to use a mouse with a notebook computer?

Although a mouse is the standard pointing device used with desktop computers, a mouse can be inconvenient to carry and use while traveling. Most notebook computers include an alternative pointing device. The three most popular options—built-in track ball, track point, and touch pad— are explained in Figure 5-12.

Figure 5-12
Notebook pointing devices

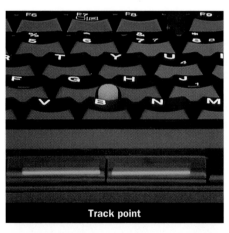

Track point

A track point is a small eraser-like device embedded among the typing keys. To control the on-screen pointer, you push the track point up, left, right, or down. Buttons for clicking and double-clicking are located in front of the spacebar.

Track ball

A track ball is like an upside-down mouse. By rolling the ball with your fingers, you control the on-screen pointer. Buttons for clicking are often located above or to the side of the track ball.

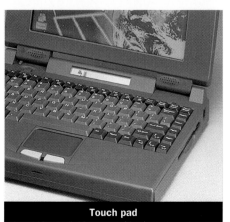

Touch pad

A touch pad is a touch-sensitive device. By dragging your finger over the surface, you control the on-screen pointer. Two buttons equivalent to mouse buttons are located in front of the touch pad.

Considerations for Notebook Power Sources

How long will a notebook computer run on batteries?

Most notebook computers operate on power from either rechargeable batteries or a wall outlet. Because notebooks are designed for portability, the computing time provided by batteries is important. For example, an executive who frequently travels to Asia might want at least eight hours of computing time during the 14-hour flight.

The length of time a notebook computer can operate from battery power depends on many factors. Fast processors, active matrix LCDs, and additional peripheral devices demand significant power from notebook computer batteries. Notebook manufacturers attempt to reduce power consumption by building power-saving features into their computers. These features automatically switch off the hard disk drive, LCD display, or even the processor if you do not interact with the computer after a short period of time. These devices are reactivated when you press a key or move the mouse.

On battery power, notebook computers typically provide two to four hours of operating time before the batteries need to be recharged. Most notebook computers use one of three types of batteries: Nicad (nickel cadmium), NiMH (nickel-metal hydride), or Lithium ion. Nicad batteries typically store less power than NiMH or Lithium ion batteries of equivalent size and weight. Therefore, Nicad batteries provide the shortest operating times. Most ads for notebook computers indicate the battery type and estimated computing times. Consumers need to be aware that many ads indicate maximum operating times. An ad that proclaims "Runs *up* to six hours!" might mean that the battery can supply six hours of operating time with no additional devices attached and with minimal use of the hard disk drive. Under typical working conditions the computer may run for significantly less than six hours on a charge.

The easiest way to extend the operating time of your computer is to purchase extra batteries. When the first battery wears down, you can swap in a new battery and get back to work. Some notebook computers allow you to insert several batteries at the same time; as soon as one is discharged, the notebook switches to the next. Switching batteries while the computer is on is called a **hot swap**.

Most notebook computers require an external AC adapter to plug into a wall outlet or recharge the batteries. This adapter—about the size and weight of a small brick—can add significantly to the traveling weight of the notebook. Some notebook computers have eliminated the external adapter and require only a power cable to plug into a wall outlet. It is a good idea to use AC power whenever possible, such as when you use your notebook at home. Using AC power saves your batteries for when AC power is not available.

Now that you have completed the section on notebook computers, see how well you can interpret the specifications in the MicroNote ad by answering Question 4 in the Chapter Review.

Quick Check

1 In a notebook computer, a(n) _____ slot provides an expansion port for credit-card-sized circuit boards and devices.

2 A(n) _____ matrix LCD display is required for acceptable display of animation and video on notebook computers.

3 A(n) _____ provides an additional expansion bus to which a notebook computer can be connected.

4 A(n) _____ makes it more convenient to connect and disconnect peripheral devices from a notebook computer.

5 The three pointing devices used with notebook computers as alternatives to a mouse are _____, _____, and _____.

6 A battery-powered notebook computer is using a(n) _____ feature if the screen goes blank when you don't type anything for a while.

Product Life Cycles

The computer industry is dynamic. Expensive new models eagerly awaited by consumers and highly touted by industry analysts appear all too soon in discount catalogs. You just master the features of one word processor version when a new version appears. Product advertisements and announcements, like the one in Figure 5-13, frequently appear in national magazines and newspapers, as well as in computer industry publications.

NEW YORK TIMES, JULY 31, 1995 (FRONT PAGE)

Microsoft's Mobilization

Now Taking Reservations

Windows 95

James Dawson for The New York Times

Software Hype and Hopes

It is not a lunar landing or the cure for a disease. It is simply an improved version of a computer's operating system — like a more efficient transmission for a car. But 100 million personal computers use the Microsoft Corporation's software. And on Aug. 24, when Microsoft begins selling a new version of Windows, a multibillion-dollar economy will be set in motion. Besides deciding whether to buy the $100 Windows 95 software itself, consumers and corporations will need to consider whether to spend hundreds of dollars more on hardware and software that takes advantage of it — or thousands more to buy whole new machines. Meanwhile, the Justice Department is still considering whether to try to prevent Microsoft from including access to its new on-line service in Windows 95.

Coverage begins on page D1.

This glitzy roll-out of Microsoft Windows 95 included full-page ads in national newspapers, television ads, and product rallies.

Initially announced for delivery in 1994, Microsoft releases its system on August 24, 1995. Microsoft chairman Bill Gates promotes his company's upcoming product.

Can the savvy consumer take advantage of the dynamics of the computer industry? To some extent, the answer is yes. Consumers who understand the computer industry are more likely to make wise purchasing decisions and avoid costly mistakes.

Hardware Product Life Cycle

Does the computer industry introduce new models annually like the automotive industry?

Automobile manufacturers introduce new models every year. The new models incorporate new and improved features and, therefore, give customers an incentive to buy. Computer manufacturers also introduce new models—and for the same reasons as their counterparts in the automotive industry. But the computer industry is not on an annual cycle; the computer marketplace seems rather chaotic with new product announcements and pre-announcements, ship dates, and availability dates all occurring at irregular intervals.

In the computer industry, the life cycle of a new computer model typically includes product development, product announcement, introduction, maintenance, and retirement. Let's look at the aspects of the hardware product life cycle that affect purchasing decisions.

Product Announcement

I saw a great product announcement, but no one has it in stock. Why?

A **product announcement** declares a company's intention of introducing a new product. Products are announced at trade shows and press conferences.

Ideas for new products are everywhere; users express their needs for improved features, engineers produce more efficient designs, scholars publish new theories, and competitors announce new products. Periodically, hardware manufacturers evaluate ideas for new products and decide which new products could most increase profits. As part of the evaluation process, a manufacturer considers how many people might be interested in buying the product, the costs required to produce the product, the time it will take to bring the product to market, and the product's effect on the competition.

Although sometimes a product announcement means that a new product is now on store shelves, this is not always the case. Often a product announcement is a "trial balloon," designed to assess customer interest and to see what countermoves the competition might make. Therefore, a product announcement often means, "We're thinking of making this product; what would happen if we did?" Manufacturers also use product announcements as a way to prevent consumers from buying competitors' products. These announcements mean, "We've got a hot new product coming out soon...wait for it...don't buy from the competition!"

As a consumer, you should be wary of making purchasing decisions based on product announcements. A product announcement can precede the actual product by several years. Sometimes, products are announced but are never made or marketed. These products are referred to as **vaporware**.

Product Introduction, Maintenance, and Retirement

Why are products so expensive when they are first introduced?

When a hardware product is first introduced, the hardware manufacturer usually establishes a suggested list price slightly higher than the previous generation of its products. Initial supplies of the product are generally low while manufacturing capacity increases to meet demand; consumers who want the scarce product must pay a higher price.

Figure 5-14
Pentium prices

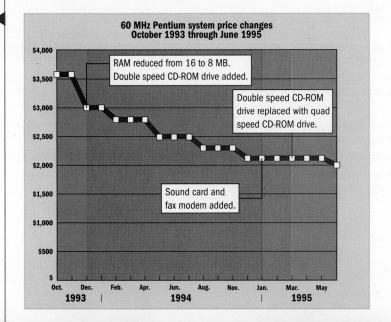

As supply and demand for the product reach an equilibrium, the price of the product decreases slightly. Usually the price decrease is due to discounting by dealers, rather than a change in the manufacturer's list price. Manufacturers tend to maintain a slightly high list price; this practice gives their dealers room to give customer discounts. In Figure 5-14, you can see that the price of computers using the Pentium processor dropped significantly during the first year after their introduction.

▶ **Figure 5-15**
Microcomputer product line

ZEOS® Can Ship Today!

Our most popular packages can be shipped the day you call.* Guaranteed!

It's true. With our special *Computers Now!* program, many of our award-winning and most popular packages can be shipped the day you call.

It's As Easy As:

1 Choose the ZEOS system package you want. (A sampling of our *Computers Now!* packages is shown at right.)

2 For same-day shipping, call ZEOS today at 800-554-5220 before 1 p.m. Central Time, Monday-Friday.

3 Upon credit approval, we'll ship your system *the same day you order!*

Our Guarantee:

If we accept your order for immediate shipment and fail to ship your system under the conditions outlined, we will ship it *at our expense* as soon as it is ready.*

Need A Bigger Monitor?

We can upgrade your *Computers Now!* desktop or vertical system with a larger monitor—and still ship it the same day you order!*

Pantera™
486DX2-66	**$1595**
Pentium-60	**$1845**
Pentium-75	**$1945**

Package #2:
- 8MB RAM
- 850MB local bus EIDE hard drive
- 4X CD-ROM drive, 3.5" 1.44MB FDD
- Diamond Stealth 64-bit PCI local bus graphics card with 1MB DRAM
- 14" SVGA color monitor
- 6-bay desktop case
- MS-DOS, Windows for Workgroups, Microsoft® Mouse
- MS Works Multimedia CD

Pentium-75	**$2145**
Pentium-90	**$2245**

Discovery™ MM:
The above system modified to include:
- 528MB local bus EIDE hard drive
- Sound Blaster™ 16 sound card, stereo speakers
- 14,400 bps send/receive fax modem

Pantera™
Pentium-75	**$2545**
Pentium-90	**$2745**
Pentium-100	**$2895**
Pentium-120	**$3145**

Hottest:
- 16MB EDO RAM, 256K synchronous SRAM cache
- 1GB local bus EIDE hard drive
- 4X CD-ROM drive, 3.5" 1.44MB FDD
- Diamond Stealth 64 Video PCI local bus graphics card with 2MB VRAM
- 15" SVGA color monitor
- 6-bay desktop case (Pentium-75) 10-bay vertical case (Pentium 90, 100 & 120)
- MS-DOS, Windows for Workgroups, Microsoft Mouse
- MS Office Pro & Bookshelf® CD

Pantera™
Pentium-75	**$2995**
Pentium-90	**$3095**
Pentium-133	**$3745**

Best MM:
- 16MB EDO RAM, 256K synchronous SRAM cache
- 850MB local bus EIDE hard drive
- 4X CD-ROM drive, 3.5" 1.44MB FDD
- Sound Blaster® 16 sound card, stereo speakers
- Diamond Stealth 64 Video PCI local bus graphics card with 2MB VRAM
- 17" SVGA color monitor
- 10-bay vertical case
- MS-DOS, Windows for Workgroups, Microsoft Mouse
- MS Office Pro & Bookshelf® CD

Pentium-100	**$3795**
Pentium-120	**$4045**
Pentium-133	**$4295**

Best MM Supreme:
The above system modified to include:
- 24MB EDO RAM
- 1.2GB local bus EIDE hard drive
- High-power speakers w/ subwoofer

Ambra™
486DX2-66	**$1345**

Package #2:
- 8MB RAM, 128K SRAM cache
- 528MB hard drive
- 3.5" 1.44MB floppy drive
- VESA local bus SVGA color video
- 14" SVGA color monitor
- 4-bay desktop case
- MS DOS, Windows for Workgroups, Microsoft Mouse
- MS Works

Meridian™ 400C
DX4-100	**$2995**

Package #3:
- 8MB RAM
- 350MB IDE hard drive
- External 3.5" 1.44MB floppy drive
- 14.4 PCMCIA fax/modem
- 7.9" dual-scan color VGA display
- Custom leather carrying case
- Extra battery
- MS-DOS, Windows for Workgroups
- MS Works
- 7.8" to 10.2" x 1.7"; 4.1 lbs.

For active matrix display, add **$700**.

Meridian™ 850C
Pentium-75	**$3795**

Package #2:
- 16MB RAM, 256K SRAM cache
- 810MB IDE hard drive
- Internal 3.5" 1.44MB floppy drive
- Integrated 16-bit stereo sound
- 10.3" dual-scan color SVGA display
- Custom nylon carrying case
- Extra battery
- MS-DOS, Windows for Workgroups
- MS Office Pro
- 8.9" to 11.7" x 2.1"; 6.8 lbs.

For active matrix display, add **$800**.

*Orders must be for Computers Now! configurations, we've listed just a sampling here. Since we continuously update this list of configurations, please call to confirm your system is on the list. This offer is good only as long as these pre-built systems remain in stock. Other ZEOS systems and custom configurations may take slightly longer—about a week. All orders are subject to credit approval. Monitor upgrades available on all desktop Computers Now! packages. Orders must be received by 1 p.m. Central Time, M-F.

Purchase orders are subject to approval. Business leasing programs available. All prices, specifications and availability are subject to change without notice; call to confirm these and warranty details. Prices do not include shipping. All products and company names are trademarks or registered trademarks of their respective holders. Intel Inside and Pentium Processor Logos are trademarks of Intel Corporation. ZEOS is a registered trademark; Computers Now! is a registered servicemark; Z-Card is a servicemark; Pantera, Ambra and ZEOS Meridian are trademarks of Micron Electronics, Inc. ©1995 MEI. ZEOS, 1301 Industrial Blvd., Minneapolis, MN 55413 USA. Micron Electronics, Inc. is a publicly traded company (NASDAQ symbol: MUEI). NOW-PCM-9509A

800-554-5220
24 Hours a Day • 365 Days a Year

Fax Orders: 800-362-1205 or 612-362-1205. Phone Orders: Outside U.S. and Canada: 612-362-1212, Government: 800-245-2449, ZEOS Information Systems, Inc. GSA #GS00K94AGS5176. Purchase Orders, MasterCard, VISA, Am Ex, Discover, Z-Card, COD and leasing programs.

Circle 219 on reader service card

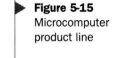

When a new product becomes available, it is usually added to the manufacturer's current product line, as shown in Figure 5-15. The prices of the older products, such as the 486DX2-66, are reduced to keep them attractive to buyers. Gradually, the oldest products are discontinued as demand for them declines.

New products offer the latest features and usually sell for a premium price. Older products don't include the latest features and must be sold at a discounted price. Very old products are usually available at super-low, close-out prices. For the consumer, this means that the latest generation of products is the most expensive, while products from a previous generation are less expensive and might offer good performance for the price.

Figure 5-16
Price performance
curve

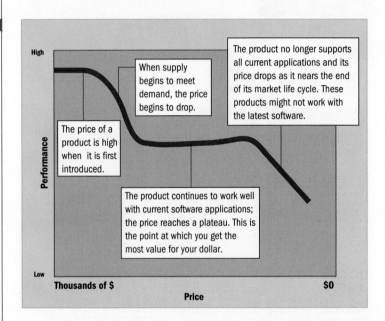

The price and performance of the computers in a typical microcomputer product line can be illustrated by a curve, as shown in Figure 5-16. The products in the middle of a typical microcomputer product line—those that are 8 to 18 months old—tend to offer the best performance for the price.

Software Product Life Cycle

What's the difference between a version and a revision?

Companies that produce computer software are referred to as **software publishers**. Software, like hardware, begins with an idea that is then shaped by a design team and marketing experts. Product announcements are information-gathering tools for software publishers, just as they are for hardware manufacturers, and the software industry also has its share of vaporware. The software life cycle, however, is somewhat different from the hardware life cycle.

A new software product can be an entirely new product, a new **version** (also called a **release**) with significant enhancements, or a **revision** designed to add minor enhancements and eliminate bugs found in the current version. Before you buy software, you should be familiar with the difference between versions and revisions, as illustrated by Figure 5-17.

New software products are usually released with a major advertising campaign. New versions of an existing product also are often released with much fanfare as companies tout the latest features and advantages that the new version has over competitors' products. New versions of

Software publishers typically are not also hardware manufacturers. Most of the software written for IBM-compatible computers is produced by software publishers other than IBM.

software are often offered at discounted prices to owners of the older versions to encourage them to update to the new version and to discourage them from switching to a competing product.

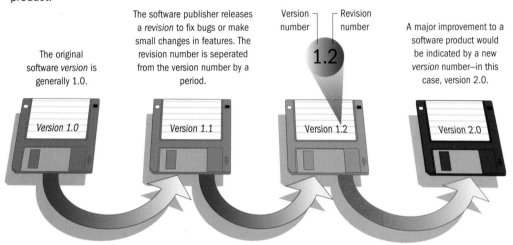

The original software *version* is generally 1.0.

The software publisher releases a *revision* to fix bugs or make small changes in features. The revision number is seperated from the version number by a period.

Version number ⎤ ⎡ Revision number

1.2

A major improvement to a software product would be indicated by a new *version* number—in this case, version 2.0.

Version 1.0 Version 1.1 Version 1.2 Version 2.0

Figure 5-17
Software versions and revisions

Revisions are often made available to current owners of the software at little or no cost. However, revisions are often released with little publicity because software companies can't afford to have every owner of the product request the new revision. This is especially true for revisions that fix bugs that are infrequently encountered by users. Sometimes customers don't know a revision is available until they call the publisher's technical support line with a problem. If the problem has been fixed in the latest revision, the technical support person informs the customer of the existence of the revision and arranges for the customer to receive it.

Alpha and Beta Testing

Why does software have bugs?

Once a software publisher begins serious development of a new software product or a new version of a current product, programming teams code the program according to the design specifications. The program code is tested by programmers and software testers employed by the publisher, a process known as **alpha testing**.

Modern programs are so large, however, that it is virtually impossible to test every logical branch of the program or to find out how the program interacts with the many programs and hardware devices that might be found on the computer systems of typical users. Therefore, the publisher sends the software to selected users for testing under realistic conditions. This phase of testing is referred to as **beta testing**. Software in this phase is called a **beta version**. The users who test the software are referred to as **beta testers**.

Beta testers use the beta version and report any problems to the publisher, who then tries to fix the problems before publishing the final version of the software. Beta testers usually do not get paid for their work, but they might receive a complimentary copy of the finished product.

Sometimes a software product undergoes several rounds of beta testing before it is ready for market. Generally, even after extensive alpha and beta testing, the software still contains some bugs that will be corrected in subsequent revisions and versions.

Introductory Offers

Do those ads really mean that I can upgrade my brand x word processor to the latest version of brand y for only $99?

When a new software product first becomes available, it often appears on the market at a special introductory price to entice customers. Several software products that now carry a list price of $495 were introduced at a special $99 price.

Another type of introductory offer might be called "switch and save." The way this works is that customers can switch to a new software product for a special price—often $129—if they own a competitor's product. Microsoft ran an aggressive switch-and-save campaign in 1992, hoping to convince WordPerfect users to switch to Microsoft Word for Windows. Microsoft ran full-page ads with the headline, "No wonder WordPerfect users prefer Word for Windows. It has 'easy' written all over it." The ads offered Word for Windows at a special $129 price to people with current licenses for competing word processing software, such as WordPerfect, MultiMate, WordStar, and DisplayWrite.

Software Product Line

Should I upgrade whenever the software publisher offers a new version?

Soon after a new version of a product is released, the software publisher usually stops selling earlier versions. For example, WordPerfect Corporation discontinued version 4.2 of its word processing software soon after it released version 5.0. When a new product is released for a different operating system or computer type, however, other versions of the software are still maintained in the product line. For example, WordPerfect was first produced for IBM-compatible computers. A short time later, a new product, WordPerfect for the Macintosh, was produced. Both products remained in the product line.

When a publisher offers a new version of the software you are using, it is usually a good idea to upgrade, but you can wait for several months until the initial rush for technical support on the new product decreases. If you don't upgrade, you might find that the software publisher offers minimal technical support for older versions of the program. Also, if you let several versions go by without upgrading, you might have to purchase the software at full price when you do decide to upgrade.

Although you might purchase computer hardware that is not the latest model, you should purchase only the most current software version. The cost of a new version is usually comparable to that of the previous version, but you get more features.

Quick Check

1. What are the five phases in the life cycle of a computer hardware product?

2. Many companies use a(n) _____ as a "trial balloon" to assess customer interest and see how the competition will respond.

3. Products that are announced, but never shipped are called _____.

4. The _____ is the point in the price-performance curve at which a typical home user might buy computer hardware.

5. A new _____ of a software product features significant enhancements, whereas a _____ of a software product eliminates bugs and adds only a few enhancements.

6. A software publisher sends a(n) _____ version of a product to selected customers so they can test the product under realistic conditions.

The Computer Industry: Tiers, Channels, and the Press

The **computer industry** consists of the corporations and individuals that supply goods and services to people and organizations that use computers. The computer industry is in a continual state of change as new products appear and old products are discontinued; as corporations form, merge, and die; as corporate leadership shifts; as consumers' buying habits evolve; and as prices steadily continue to decrease. You will be a better informed consumer if you understand the tiered structure of computer companies, the five market channels from which you can purchase hardware and software, and the types of publications encompassed by the computer press.

Market Tiers

What accounts for price differences for computers with the same specifications from different vendors?

Since 1981, hundreds of companies have produced IBM PC clones and other personal computers. Industry analysts often refer to three tiers or categories of microcomputer companies, although not all analysts agree on which companies belong in each tier.

The top tier consists of large companies that have been in the computer business for more than ten years and have an identifiable percentage of total computer sales—companies such as IBM, Apple, Compaq, Digital, Toshiba, Epson, AT&T, and Hewlett-Packard. The second tier includes newer companies with high sales volume, but with somewhat less financial resources than companies in the first tier. Most analysts place companies such as Gateway and Dell in the second tier. The third tier consists of smaller startup companies that sell primarily through mail order.

Computer prices vary by tier. Computers from the top-tier vendors generally are more expensive than computers offered by second- or third-tier vendors. For example, a computer with specifications similar to the MicroPlus computer featured in the ad at the beginning of this chapter might cost $2,699 from a first-tier vendor, $2,199 from a second-tier vendor, and $1,999 from a third-tier vendor.

Why do these prices vary by tier? Because first-tier companies often have higher overhead costs, management is often paid higher salaries, and substantial financial resources are devoted to research and development. The first-tier companies are responsible for many of the innovations that have made computers faster, more powerful, and more convenient. Also, many consumers believe that computers sold by first-tier companies are better quality and are a safe purchasing decision. They believe there is less risk that computers from first-tier companies will quickly become obsolete or that the vendor will go out of business.

Computers from second-tier companies are generally less expensive than those from the first tier, although the quality can be just as good. Most IBM-compatible computers are constructed from off-the-shelf circuit boards, cables, cases, and chips. This means that the components in the computers sold by second-tier companies are often the same as those in computers sold by the first tier. The quality of the off-the-shelf parts, however, is not uniform; it is difficult for the consumer to determine the quality of parts.

Second-tier companies often maintain their low prices by keeping the price of their corporate operations low. These companies have a limited research and development budget. Also, they try to maintain a relatively small work force by contracting with another company to provide repair and warranty work.

Computers from third-tier companies often appear to be much less expensive than those in other tiers. Sometimes this reflects the low overhead costs of a small company, but other times it reflects poor-quality components. A consumer who is knowledgeable about the market and has technical expertise can often get a bargain on a good-quality computer from a third-tier company. But some consumers think it's risky to purchase computers from third-tier companies. Third-tier companies are smaller and perhaps more likely to go out of business, leaving their customers without technical support.

Marketing Channels

Is it safe to buy a computer by mail?

Computer hardware and software are sold by marketing outlets or "channels," as shown in Figure 5-18.

Figure 5-18 ◄
Marketing channels

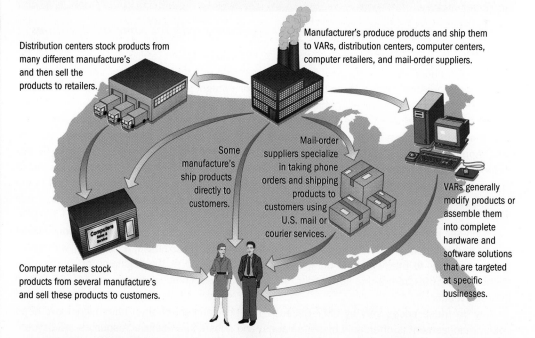

Distribution centers stock products from many different manufacture's and then sell the products to retailers.

Manufacturer's produce products and ship them to VARs, distribution centers, computer centers, computer retailers, and mail-order suppliers.

Some manufacture's ship products directly to customers.

Mail-order suppliers specialize in taking phone orders and shipping products to customers using U.S. mail or courier services.

VARs generally modify products or assemble them into complete hardware and software solutions that are targeted at specific businesses.

Computer retailers stock products from several manufacture's and sell these products to customers.

A **computer retail store** purchases computer products from a manufacturer or distribution center and then sells the products to consumers. Computer retail stores are either small local shops or nationwide chains that specialize in the sale of microcomputer software and hardware. The employees at computer retail stores are often knowledgeable about a variety of computer products and can help you select a hardware or software product to fit your needs. Many computer retail stores also offer classes and training sessions, answer questions, provide technical support, and repair hardware products.

Computer retail stores can be a fairly expensive channel for hardware and software. Their prices reflect the cost of purchasing merchandise from a distributor, maintaining a retail storefront, and hiring technically qualified staff. A computer retail store is often the best source of supply for buyers who are likely to need assistance after the sale, such as beginning computer users or those with complex computer systems such as networks.

Mail-order suppliers take orders by mail or telephone and ship the product directly to consumers. Mail-order suppliers generally offer low prices but provide limited service and support. A mail-order supplier is often the best source of products for buyers who are unlikely to need support or who can troubleshoot problems with the help of a technical support person on the telephone. Experienced computer users who can install components, set up their software, and do their own troubleshooting are often happy with mail-order suppliers. Inexperienced computer users might not be satisfied with the support and assistance they receive from mail-order suppliers.

Value-added resellers (VARs) combine commercially available products with special hardware or software to create a computer system designed to meet the needs of a specific industry. Although VARs charge for their expertise, they are often the only source for a system that really meets the needs of a specific industry. For example, if you own a video rental store and want to automate your store, the best type of vendor might be a VAR. The VAR can offer you a complete hardware and software package that is tailored to the video rental business. This means that you do not need to piece together a computer, scanner, printer, and software components for a computer system to keep track of video rentals. VARs are often the most expensive channel for hardware and software, but their expertise can be crucial in making sure that the hardware and software work correctly in a specific environment.

Manufacturer direct refers to hardware manufacturers that sell their products directly to consumers using a sales force or mail order. The sales force usually targets large corporate or educational customers where large volume sales can cover costs and commissions. Manufacturers also use mail order to distribute directly to individual consumers. Manufacturers can sell their products directly to consumers for a lower price than when they sell them through retailers, but they cannot generally offer the same level of support and assistance as a local retailer. In an effort to improve customer support, some manufacturers have established customer support lines and provide repair services at the customer's place of business.

The Computer Press

Where can I get reliable information in order to make computer purchases?

Computer publications provide information on computers, computing, and the computer industry. The type of computer publication you need depends on the kind of information you are trying to obtain.

Computer Magazines contain articles and advertisements for the latest computer products. One of the earliest computer magazines, *Byte*, began publication in August 1975 and still remains one of the most widely read sources of computer information. The success of *Byte* might be attributed to its wide coverage of computers and computing topics. Many magazines that featured only a single type of computer, such as the Apple II, had staying power only as long as the computer maintained good sales. There are exceptions, however, magazines for specific computers, such as *MacWorld*, have a healthy subscription list.

Computer magazines generally target users of both personal and business computers. Articles often focus on product evaluations, product comparisons, and practical tips for installing hardware and using software. These magazines are full of product advertisements, which are useful if you want to keep informed about the latest products available for your computer. You can find computer magazines on virtually any newsstand and at your public library.

Computer Industry Trade Journals have a different focus than computer magazines because they target computer professionals, rather than consumers. Computer trade journals, such as *InfoWorld* and *Computer Reseller News*, focus on company profiles, product announcements, and sales techniques. Often free subscriptions to trade journals are given to corporate decision makers because advertisers want them to be aware of their products. Trade journals are not always available on newsstands, and subscriptions are not always available to the general public.

Computing Journals offer an academic perspective on computers and computing issues. Such journals focus on research in computing, with articles on such topics as the most efficient sorting technique to use in a database management system, the implication of copyright law for educational institutions, or the prevalence of spreadsheet use by executives in Fortune 500 companies. Academic journals rarely advertise hardware and software products because it might appear that advertisers could influence the content of articles.

An article in a computing journal is usually "refereed," which means that it is evaluated by a committee of experts who determine if the article is original and based on sound research

Project 12 at the end of this chapter guides you to some of these sites to discover what kinds of information you can expect to find at Internet World Wide Web sites.

techniques. The best place to find computing journals is in a university library. Some of the most respected journals in the computing field include *Communications of the ACM* (Association for Computing Machinery), *Communications of the IEEE* (Institute of Electrical and Electronics Engineers), *SIAM* (Society of Industrial and Applied Mathematics) *Journal on Computing*, and *Journal of Information Science*.

Internet Sites are an excellent source of information about the computer industry and computer products. Several computer magazines and trade journals maintain Internet sites with articles from back issues. Current issues are also available from some sites for a fee.

Many computer companies have Internet sites where consumers can access up-to-date information about products and services. Here you can usually find product specifications, product announcements, sales literature, technical support forums, and pricing information.

Figure 5-19
Industry analysts

MARKETING

Windows 95 Buzz Will C

By DON CLARK
Staff Reporter of THE WALL STREET JOURNAL

Companies don't usually rush to buy ads in another company's infomercial, and the Rolling Stones don't usually sell rights to their songs for television ads.

But then, none of the old rules seem to apply to the selling of Windows 95.

Microsoft Corp. has already caused a marketing frenzy in the computer world during the long delayed introduction of the new computer operating system, which will make its debut next Thursday. Now, it is orchestrating a buzz that is reaching far beyond the tech world, involving a wide range of business partners — including the Stones, whose "Start Me Up" will be a sort of Windows 95 theme song, anchoring TV ads set to start airing Thursday evening.

Microsoft is believed to be spending about $200 million of its own money marketing and advertising Windows 95. But marketing experts say the product is getting 10 times that amount in free publicity from other companies' ads and the effects of a tidal wave of news coverage. Even the Doonesbury comic strip is featuring the new system this week.

"Microsoft has been in the news almost on a daily basis," said Rajiv Lal, a professor of marketing at Stanford University business school. "It's an amazing thing for a company that was perceived as being nerdy."

The latest uproar followed leaks to London newspapers that the Stones had agreed to let Microsoft use "Start Me Up" in Windows 95 TV spots. In one 60-second commercial, the song, from the Stones' 1981 album "Tattoo You," will be heard throughout. A button labeled start is a key new feature for navigating through the software and a consistent theme in Microsoft's print and broadcast advertising.

It is the first time Stones songwriters

DOONESBURY copyright 1995 G.B. Trudeau. Re

they own the copyright, except i tising related to the group's ow The Stones have had other cor ventures, though, including a Stones Visa and MasterCard i October 1994 by the Chevy Chase Chevy Chase, Md.

British press reports said Mr set a price of $12 million for the song, but one person familiar matter put the true figure at clo million, an amount that would a record in the field. Microsoft comment on the price. "You can get what you want, but if you're you get what you need," said Al music licensing expert and reti president of Time Warner's Warn pell Music unit.

People familiar with one of dows 95 commercials said that with a view of the Windows 95 s and Mr. Jagger's voice singing Up." Viewers then see a fast MTV-like assemblage of images which feature people using Micro ucts, among them kids, students workers, and executives.

Microsoft hasn't broken down keting expenditures for Windows has projected that advertising for all of its products will tot $200 million in the year ending 1996, up from $100 million the prio

Industry Analysts

Who's got the inside scoop on computer companies and products?

The computer industry has many **industry analysts** who monitor industry trends, evaluate industry events, and make predictions about what the trends seem to indicate. Computer industry analysts range from professional financial analysts, who report on the computer industry for the *Wall Street Journal* and *Forbes* magazine, to the "rumor-central" analysts, who spark up the back pages of trade journals and computer magazines with the latest gossip about new products.

If you want to invest in a computer corporation's stock, the financial analysts might offer some good insights. If you want to invest in a personal computer, the rumor-central columns are the place to get the scoop about product shortages, hardware glitches, software bugs, and impending customer service problems. Figure 5-19 contains an example of a *Wall Street Journal* market analysis for the rollout of Windows 95.

You can get better acquainted with the views of industry analysts by doing Project 6 at the end of this chapter.

Quick Check

1. Computer vendors are often categorized into three _____ based on market share and financial resources.

2. List the four marketing channels in the computer industry.

3. A(n) _____ is a computer publication designed for computer professionals, rather than the general consumer.

4. A(n) _____ sells complete computer solutions for a specific industry such as video stores or medical offices.

5. Articles in _____ journals are usually accurate because they are refereed by a committee of experts before being published.

User Focus:

Computer **Shopping Strategies**

If you are like most consumers in pursuit of a good computer value, you will talk to sales people, read computer magazines, look through computer catalogs, and chat with your friends who own computers. Here are some shopping strategies that should help you purchase a computer that meets your needs within a budget you can afford.

Determine Your Needs and Budget

Where do I start?

Start by setting a budget and stick to it! Computer vendors have very carefully priced the computers in their model line so that you will be tempted to spend "just a few hundred dollars more" to get a model with more features. The trouble is that if you decide to spend that few hundred dollars, you will be tempted to spend just a little more to get even more features.

Once you have established a budget, consider how you plan to use the computer. A computer can be a valuable tool for completing your college degree, it can be a useful educational tool for your children, and it can increase your competitive edge in your career. Consider these factors before you begin shopping for a computer:

Notebook or desktop? If you plan to carry your computer with you, a notebook computer is the optimal choice. However, a notebook costs more than a similarly configured desktop, so you will pay for portability or give up features.

Multimedia? If you want to use multimedia applications, you should buy a system with a CD-ROM drive and sound card. Multimedia notebooks can be pricey, but a docking bay might allow you to add multimedia capabilities and still stay within your budget.

Compatibility? Most computers sold today are IBM compatible. However, you should consider a Macintosh computer if most of the computers in your school are Macintoshes, if the computer is for your children who are using Macintosh computers in school, or if Macintosh is the major computer used in your career field.

Printer? Remember that you must include the cost of a printer in your budget. Unless you need to print multipart forms, you should not buy a dot matrix printer. A black-and-white ink jet printer is in the same price range, but it uses single-sheet paper and produces better print quality. Inexpensive laser printers, referred to as "personal laser printers," cost $100 to $300 more than a black-and-white ink-jet printer. Also consider a printer's operational cost. If you are on a very limited budget, it is easier to replace a $15 ink cartridge than a $100 toner cartridge.

Collect the Facts

What information do I need?

Before you make a decision, shop around to collect information on pricing, features, and support. Although you might be tempted to buy the computer with the lowest price and best features, don't forget to consider the warranty and the quality of the support you are likely to get from the vendor. The checklist in Figure 5-20 will help you gather facts about pricing, features, and support.

▶ **Figure 5-20**
Comparison data sheet

Computer Purchase Data Sheet

Computer brand, model, and manufacturer: _____

Processor type: _____

Processor speed: _____ MHz

RAM capacity: _____ megabytes

Type of bus: ❏ EISA ❏ ISA ❏ MicroChannel ❏ Local Bus ❏ PCI

Number and size of floppy disk drives: _____

Capacity of hard drive: _____ megabytes

Speed of CD ROM drive: _____ ms

Capacity and speed of tape drive: _____

Amount of cache memory: _____ kilobytes

Monitor screen size: _____ inches

Monitor resolution: _____ by _____

Type of video adaptor: ❏ VGA ❏ SVGA

Amount of video memory: _____ megabytes

Number of parallel ports: _____

Number of serial ports: _____

Number of SCSI ports: _____

Number of expansion slots: _____

Operating system: _____

Mouse included: ❏ Yes ❏ No

Sound card and speakers included: ❏ Yes ❏ No

Value of bundled application software: $ _____

Does it have good expansion capabilities? ❏ Yes ❏ No

Does it have an upgrade path for new technologies, such as new processors? ❏ Yes ❏ No

Does the vendor have a support team in place that will meet my needs? ❏ Yes ❏ No

Are technical support hours sufficient? ❏ Yes ❏ No

Is it inexpensive to get support? ❏ Yes ❏ No

Can I contact technical support personnel without being put on extended time? ❏ Yes ❏ No

Are technical support people knowlegeable? ❏ Yes ❏ No

Can I get my computer fixed in an acceptable time period? ❏ Yes ❏ No

Are the costs and procedures for fixing the computer acceptable? ❏ Yes ❏ No

What is the warranty period? _____ years

Does the warranty cover parts and labor? ❏ Yes ❏ No

Are other users satisfied with this computer? ❏ Yes ❏ No

Is the manufacturer a well-financed and stable company? ❏ Yes ❏ No

Are the computer parts and components standard? ❏ Yes ❏ No

Price: _____

Evaluate the Facts

How do I make the decision?

After you have collected the facts, your decision might be obvious. In an ideal situation, a local vendor with a reputation for excellent support is selling a computer with features and price comparable to those sold by many reputable mail-order vendors. In the real world, however, your local vendor's price might be higher, and then your decision is not so clear. You might want to make a decision support matrix like the one shown in Figure 5-21.

Figure 5-21
Decision support
worksheet

1. List at least two possible options. This worksheet is designed to help you choose between Computer #1 and Computer #2.

2. List the factors that are important criteria for making your selection.

3. Assign a "weighting factor" to each criterion using a scale of 1 to 10.

4. After you reasearch the options, assign a raw score for each factor.

5. Add a formula in the spreadsheet to multiply the raw score by the weighting factor to produce a weighted score.

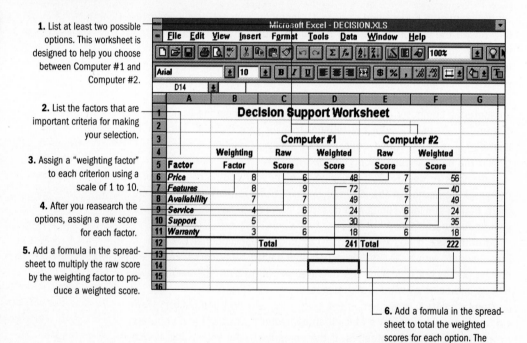

6. Add a formula in the spreadsheet to total the weighted scores for each option. The option that has the hightst total is the best system for you to purchase.

Project 11 at the end of this chapter helps you work with a decision support worksheet like the one in Figure 5-21.

End Note
One strategy for buying a computer is to decide how much you want to spend and then buy whatever computer a major manufacturer offers at that price. You probably won't get a great deal. You might not even get a computer that really meets your needs. But you will have a computer. If you would like to be a more effective consumer in today's computer marketplace, you must understand the terminology in computer ads; and use magazines, journals, and the Internet to keep up-to-date on the latest computer models. In many respects it is part of keeping up with current events. By browsing through an occasional computer magazine and by paying attention to computer-related events in the news, you can keep fairly up-to-date.

Review

1. Make a list of the key points you need to remember about buying a desktop computer.

2. Make a list of the additional factors you must consider when buying a notebook computer.

3. Demonstrate your understanding of the terminology and issues involved in purchasing a computer by answering the following questions about the computer ad in Figure 5-1.

    a. The microprocessor in the MicroPlus computer would be categorized in which microprocessor family?

    b. The software that you could run with the MicroPlus computer would not generally be compatible with which other types of computers?

    c. Is the amount of RAM cache in the MicroPlus computer adequate considering the type of processor in the computer?

    d. Does the MicroPlus computer have enough RAM to run Windows 95?

    e. About how much would it cost to upgrade the MicroPlus computer to 32 MB of memory?

    f. Why does the MicroPlus computer come with only one floppy disk drive?

    g. How fast is the CD-ROM drive?

    h. What is the advantage of the local bus used by the hard drive?

    i. How many types of buses does the MicroPlus computer include?

    j. Can you add a second internal hard disk drive to the MicroPlus computer? Why or why not?

    k. Would you be able to display photographic-quality images at 1024×768 resolution? Why or why not?

    l. Would you be able to run multimedia software on the MicroPlus computer? Why or why not?

    m. What bundled software, if any, is included with the MicroPlus computer?

    n. If you purchase the MicroPlus computer and a week after you receive it, the monitor stops working, what is the MicroPlus company policy on repairs?

4. Demonstrate your understanding of the MicroNote computer ad in Figure 5-8 by answering the following questions:

    a. Who manufactures the processor for the MicroNote computer?

    b. How would you expand the MicroNote computer to include a modem?

    c. Can you disconnect the monitor from your desktop computer and connect it to the MicroNote?

    d. Is the display on the MicroNote suitable for multimedia applications?

    e. Can the MicroNote computer use Macintosh software? Why or why not?

    f. What options would you have if you wanted to connect a CD-ROM drive to the MicroNote?

    g. Can you switch batteries while the MicroNote computer is on?

    h. Can you display photographic quality images at 1024×768? Why or why not?

    i. Which two of the equipment options do you think would be most important for your computing needs if you owned the MicroNote computer?

5. For each of the following computer components, indicate the unit of measurement used to describe the component's capacity:

microprocessor speed	microprocessor word size
hard disk capacity	disk drive access time
floppy disk capacity	CD-ROM drive speed
RAM capacity	video memory
disk cache capacity	bus speed
bus capacity	screen resolution
image clarity	modem speed

6. Draw a diagram to illustrate the life cycle of a computer hardware product.

7. Describe the characteristics of each of the three market tiers in the computer industry.

8. List the advantages and disadvantages of purchasing a computer from each computer industry market channel.

9. Describe the differences among computer magazines, trade journals, and computing journals.

10. Your parents are thinking of buying a computer. Because you are taking a computer course, they turn to you for advice. The first thing you tell them is to decide how much they want to spend. Think about everything you have learned in this chapter—especially the tips in the User Focus section. Based on what you have learned, compose a letter to your parents giving them advice about buying a computer.

Projects

1. The *Computer Shopper* Experience The story about Matt at the beginning of this chapter is fairly realistic. Many people purchase mail-order computers, and the *Computer Shopper* is the most popular source of information for mail-order prices. Suppose you decide to buy a computer, and you decide your budget is $2,000. You don't need to buy a printer because your friend is giving you a useable, but older printer. Look through the ads in a recent issue of the *Computer Shopper* to find the best computer that fits your computing needs and your budget. Write the list of features, the price, and the vendor for the computer, as well as the month and page of the issue. Then explain why you think this computer is the best one for the money.

2. Product Announcements Find a product announcement in a computer magazine. How would you classify this announcement? Is it a trial balloon, an anticipated ship date, or a product release? How can you tell? Was it written by a vendor or by a reporter?

3. Today's Microprocessors Microprocessor technology changes rapidly. New models arrive every couple of years, and the clock speed for a particular model seem to increase every few months. As you learned in this chapter, computers that contain state-of-the-art microprocessors are usually priced at a premium. Because the latest microprocessors are so expensive, the most popular computers—those that are purchased by the most people—tend to contain a previous model microprocessor. When you are in the market for a computer, it is useful to be able to differentiate between the state-of-the art microprocessors and previous models.

Browse through several computer magazines to determine which microprocessor is most popular and which microprocessor is currently state-of-the-art. Write a brief description of your findings. Include the following information:

   a. The clock speed, processor model name or number, and word size for the most popular microprocessor.

   b. The clock speed, processor model name or number, and word size for the state-of-the-art microprocessor.

   c. A brief explanation of what factors helped you determine that these particular microprocessors are the most popular and the most state-of-the-art.

   d. A bibliography of your sources.

4. Comparison Shopping Comparison shopping is a good strategy for finding the best deal in a computer system. Use the hardware checklist in Figure 5-20 to gather comparative information about two computer systems. You can gather the information from a computer magazine, the Internet, or from a local computer retail store. Be sure you exercise courtesy, especially if you visit a small retail store. Let the salesperson know that you are working on a class project, and recognize that the sales person's priority is shoppers who intend to actually buy a computer. Your instructor might suggest that you and one or two other students do this project as a small group.

5. Computer Industry Although the computer industry is less than half a century old, it has more than its share of good luck and hard luck stories. The history of each computer company has contributed in some way to the current state of the computer industry. Select a well-known company in the computer industry such as IBM, Digital, Microsoft, Apple, Compaq, Hewlett-Packard, Cray Research, or Toshiba. Use library and/or Internet resources to research the history of the company and trace the events that led to the company's current status in the computer industry. Write a report that summarizes your research. Follow your instructor's requirements for the length of your report.

6. The Latest "Scoop" Different industry analysts tend to give their readers the scoop on many of the same "hot topics." It's fascinating to see how the rumors spread and how analysts see events from different perspectives. Read at least 10 industry analysts' columns from several computer magazines published in the same month and year. Although 10 columns might sound like a lot, they are not long and many are fairly entertaining. Summarize what you read by indicating the topics that were "hot" that month and how the analysts agreed or disagreed.

7. Your Dollar Buys a Lot More Today You have probably heard that computer technology changes at an amazing speed. Today, your money buys much more computing power than it did in 1990. How much more? Look through the computer ads in back issues of computer magazines for June 1990, June 1993, and June 1995. Create a chart that shows the changes in the specifications for computers for a price of $2,000. Be sure you compare the processor type, processor speed, RAM capacity, hard disk drive capacity, screen resolution, and bus type.

8. Product Comparison Reviews Many computer magazines feature extensive product comparison reviews in which several hardware or software products are evaluated and compared. For example, a magazine might feature a comparison and evaluation of seven word processing software packages or eight notebook computers.

Suppose you are working for an organization and your job is to select hardware and software products.

    a. Describe the organization for which you work, then specify which type of product (notebook computers, word processing software, group scheduler, and so on) you are looking for and why.

    b. Explain the important factors that will influence your decision such as budget or special features that your organization requires from the product.

    c. Find and read an appropriate comparative review in a recent computer magazine.

    d. Based on the comparative review, which product would you recommend? Why?

9. Careers in Computer Sales Computer industry careers related to computer and software sales include retail sales representative, retail store manager, technical support line representative, customer service representative, and phone sales representative. Select one of these careers. Use interviews, if possible, or library resources to determine what educational background is required, the entry level pay scale, the maximum salary, and the job description.

10. Your Compatibility Needs When you purchase a computer, it is likely you will want to maintain compatibility with the type of computers used in your field. For example, if most elementary schools use Apple computers and your field is elementary education, you might have a strong reason for purchasing an Apple computer instead of an IBM compatible. For this project, research the type of computers most typically used in your field or major. Keep a lookout for hard data, such as the number of Apple II computers still in use in schools. Write a one-to two-page report describing your findings; conclude with the computer you would purchase today to prepare for your career of the future. Your instructor might suggest that you do this project in a small group with other students who have similar career goals.

11. Using a Decision Support Spreadsheet for Buying a Computer A decision support spreadsheet like the one in Figure 5-21 helps you prioritize your computing needs and compare the value of several computers based on these priorities. For this Project, do the following:

    a. Create a spreadsheet like the one shown in Figure 5-21.

    b. Modify the factors listed in column A to reflect your computing needs.

    c. Modify the weighting factors in column B to reflect their importance to you.

    d. Gather information about two different computer systems that you might consider purchasing.

    e. Give each computer a raw score for each factor. For example, if Computer #1 has all the features you seek, enter a 10 in cell B7. If Computer #2 only has half the features you want, enter a 5 in cell E7.

    f. Notice which computer has the highest total score. This should be the best computer for your needs.

    g. Somewhere on the spreadsheet include a short description of each computer, including its brand name, price, and model.

    h. Print out your spreadsheet. Be sure to include your name.

12. Computer Companies on the Internet Many hardware and software companies maintain Internet sites. A major purpose of these sites is to distribute information to potential and existing customers. Access the Web page for one of the following companies, then answer questions a through d:
http://www.microsoft.com
http://www.ibm.com
http://www.intel.com
http://www.apple.com

    a. How would you characterize the information at this site? Is it primarily sales, technical, and/or company background?

    b. Give an example of information at this site that would help you decide whether you wanted to buy a particular product.

    c. Would you be able to use this site to contact a company representative? If so, how would you do this?

    d. Even if you weren't thinking of purchasing a product from this company, describe in detail something at the site you found to be interesting.

Resources

- *Computer Shopper. The* magazine for people who buy computers by mail order. Each issue is packed full of computer ads from vendors in all marketing tiers. Hidden between the ads, you'll actually find articles with helpful hints and product evaluations.

- Freiberger, P. and M. Swaine. *Fire in the Valley: The Making of the Personal Computer.* Berkeley: Osborne/McGraw Hill, 1984. This book provides energetic coverage of the development of the micro-computer from the first microprocessor through the Altair, CP/M, IMSAI, Microsoft, Apple, and the IBM PC. The authors include many photos and anecdotes about the colorful figures who played prominent roles in the early days of the microcomputer industry.

- Rodgers, W. *THINK: Biography of the Watsons and IBM.* New York: Stein and Day, 1969. Rodgers wrote an unauthorized but lively account of IBM and its leaders. Published in 1969, this book ends before the advent of the microcomputer and is, therefore, an account of the "glory days" of mainframe computing.

- Rogers, E. and J. Larson. *Silicon Valley Fever: Growth of High-Technology Culture.* New York: Basic Books, 1982. Rogers, a professor of International Communi-cation at Stanford University, and Larson, a Silicon Valley research scientist, teamed up to create a very readable account of the impact of technology on the businesses and people of Silicon Valley. The legends are all here: the multimillion-dollar companies that started in a garage, the teenagers who became corpo-rate magnates, the most successful public stock offer-ing in history, and the spreadsheet empire that went from rags to riches and back to rags.

- *http://www.awa.com* Downtown anywhere is a World Wide Web site with many of the amenities of a cyber-space city: museums, travel, sports, education, and, of course, shopping! This is an excellent site for checking out current computer pricing.

- *http://www.cexpress.com* Computer Express bills itself as "Your Online Superstore." It is a great place to browse for computer hardware and software. You can even download demos of many software products.

- *http://www.internet.net* This is the Internet site for the Internet Shopping Network. Here you will find several stores selling computer hardware and software, so it is a good place to look if you're interested in current computer pricing and features.

Lab Assignments

Buying a Computer

 When buying from a mail-order or Internet computer vendor, consumers don't have an opportunity to take various computer models for a "test drive." They make a computer purchase decision based solely on a list of specifica-tions. Thus, it is essential to understand the specifica-tions in computer ads. In this Lab, you will find out how to use a Shopping Glossary to interpret the specifications.

1. Click the Steps button to learn how to use the Shop-ping Glossary. As you proceed through the Steps, answer all of the Quick Check questions that appear. After you complete the Steps, you will see a Quick Check Summary Report. Follow the instructions on the screen to print this report.

2. Click the Explore button and read the ad for the VectorMicro VP5-120 Computer system. Use the Shopping Glossary to define the following terms:

    a. Write-back cache, b. EIDE, c. DRAM

    d. Baud, e. Wavetable , f. EDO memory

3. In Explore, read the ads for the ZeePlus Multimedia Value Pak and the ZeePlus Multimedia Pro computers. The two systems differ substantially in price—$1,129 for the Multimedia Value Pak and $1,599 for the Multimedia Pro computer. If you purchase the more expensive sys-tem, what additional features do you get?

4. In Explore, read the ad for the ZeePlus Multimedia Pro Computer and the and Nevada Tech Systems P5/120 Multimedia Computer. If you get a system configured with 8 MB RAM, 850 MB hard disk, and a Pentium 120 MHz processor, what is the price difference between these two systems? What factors might account for this price difference?

5. In Explore, read the ads to find a notebook computer that's priced within $100 of the VP5/120 desktop com-puter. Make a list of the features the desktop computer has, that the notebook computer does not have. Which one would you buy? Why?

6. Photocopy a computer ad from a recent issue of a computer magazine. On a separate sheet of paper, write each specification (for example, Intel Pentium processor). For each specification, define each term (for example, Intel is a microprocessor manufacturer, Pentium is a type of microprocessor in the x86 family). Write out all acronyms (for example, RAM means random access memory). If you have difficulty with some of the terms and acronyms, click the Explore button and use the Shopping Glossary.

Quick Check

Answers

5.1

1. x86, 68000-series, PowerPC

2. the operating system and application software you intend to use

3. EIDE, SCSI

4. local buses

5. dot pitch

6. 1 MB

7. bps

8. inkjet

5.2

1. PCMCIA

2. active

3. docking station

4. port replicator

5. track point, touch pad, track ball

6. power saving

5.3

1. product development, product announcement, introduction, maintenance, retirement

2. product announcement

3. vaporware

4. plateau

5. version, revision

6. beta

5.4

1. tiers

2. computer retail store, mail-order suppliers, value-added resellers, manufacturer direct

3. trade journal

4. value-added reseller

5. computing journals

Glossary/Index

C

cache capacity High-speed memory capacity used to give the CPU more rapid access to data, 5-7

computer industry The corporations and individuals that supply goods and services to the people and organizations that use computers, 5-26, 5-26–5-29

computer retail store A local retail business that purchases computer products from a manufacturer or distribution center and then sells the products to customers, 5-27

controller A hard disk circuit board containing the electronics that control the mechanical drive mechanism and data transfer, 5-7, 5-27

D

docking station An additional expansion bus into which you plug a notebook computer that allows you to use inexpensive expansion cards and peripherals designed for desktop systems, 5-16

dot matrix printer A printer that creates letters and graphics by striking an inked ribbon with pins, 5-12, 5-30

Local Area Networks and E-mail

Local Area Networks
and **E-mail**

In the decade between 1976 and 1986 the microcomputer industry boomed. Microcomputer companies made record profits. *Time* magazine named the microcomputer "Man of the Year." Yet, while mainframe users enjoyed the connectivity provided by electronic mail and shared files, microcomputer users were generally isolated on their standalone computers. Communication between microcomputers was jokingly referred to as "the sneaker net"—meaning that to transfer a file from one computer to another, you put the file on a floppy disk, then walked with the disk to another computer. White Reeboks were popular corporate footwear at the time.

The idea that microcomputer users could benefit by connecting their computers into a network became feasible about 10 years ago with the introduction of reliable, reasonably priced software and hardware designed for microcomputer networks. The availability of this hardware and software ushered in a new era of computing, which increasingly provides ways for people to collaborate, communicate, and interact.

The purpose of this chapter is to help you understand the type of local area computer networks you would typically find in a college, university, or business. This chapter emphasizes the user perspective, beginning with a tour of network resources, then presenting practical information on network hardware and software including network applications such as groupware and electronic mail.

CHAPTER**PREVIEW**

In this chapter you will learn how computer networks and electronic mail work. The concepts you learn are useful for effectively using microcomputer networks, such as those in your school labs or in a business where you work. You'll learn how to select a secure password and how to log into a network. You'll also learn how to share files with other users, and you'll pick up some tips for using electronic mail. When you have completed this chapter you should be able to:

- Describe the resources you would find on a typical local area network

- Explain how using a computer on a network is different from using a standalone computer

- List the advantages of using a local area network

- Explain the difference between sharing files on a network and using groupware

- Describe how processing differs on networks that use dedicated file servers, peer-to-peer capability, client-server architecture, and host-based time-sharing

- Describe the types of software you can use on a local area network

- Explain how software licenses for networks differ from those for standalone computers

- Explain how a network uses store-and-forward technology for e-mail

LAB

E-mail

6.1 Local Area Networks

Most users and technical support people refer to local area networks simply as "networks."

A **computer network** is a collection of computers and other devices that communicate to share data, hardware, and software. A network that is located within a relatively limited area such as a building or campus is referred to as a **local area network** or **LAN**. A network that covers a large geographical area is referred to as a **wide area network** or **WAN**. In this chapter you will learn about local area networks.

Local area networks are found in most medium-sized and large businesses, government offices, and educational institutions. Worldwide an estimated 25 million computers are connected to local area networks.

Not all LANs are the same. Different types of networks provide different services, use different technology, and require users to follow different procedures. The information in this chapter describes how a majority of microcomputer networks work. However, any specific network you use might work differently and require different user procedures. Don't hesitate to ask questions when you use an unfamiliar network.

Network Resources

What's the advantage of a computer network?

A computer that is not connected to a network is referred to as a **standalone computer**. When you physically connect your computer to a local area network, using a cable or other communications channel, your computer becomes a **workstation** on the network and you become a "network user."

Your workstation has all its usual resources, referred to as **local resources**, such as your hard drive, software, data, and printer. You also have access to **network resources**, which typically include application software, storage space for data files, and printers other than those with your local workstation.

On a network, application software and storage space for data files are typically provided by a network server. A **network server** is a computer connected to the network that "serves," or distributes, resources to network users. A **network printer** provides output capabilities to all the network users. Each device on a network, including workstations, servers, and printers, is referred to as a **node**. Locate the workstations, network server, and other network resources in Figure 6-1.

Figure 6-1
Local and network resources

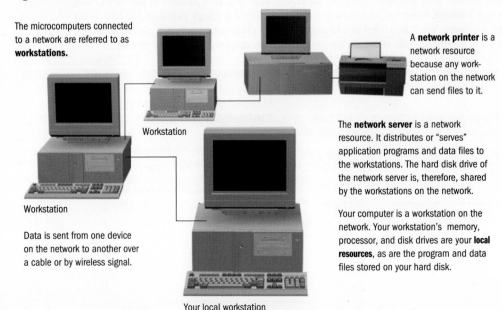

The microcomputers connected to a network are referred to as **workstations.**

Workstation

Workstation

Data is sent from one device on the network to another over a cable or by wireless signal.

Your local workstation

A **network printer** is a network resource because any workstation on the network can send files to it.

The **network server** is a network resource. It distributes or "serves" application programs and data files to the workstations. The hard disk drive of the network server is, therefore, shared by the workstations on the network.

Your computer is a workstation on the network. Your workstation's memory, processor, and disk drives are your **local resources**, as are the program and data files stored on your hard disk.

The main advantage of a computer network is that all the users can share resources, instead of users each maintaining their own. For example, a LAN permits many users to share a single printer. Most organizations with LANs are able to reduce the total number of printers needed, reduce printer maintenance costs, and use the money saved to buy higher quality printers.

The Login Process

Do I have to do anything special to access network resources?

Even if your computer is physically connected to a network, you cannot use network resources until you log into the network. When you log in, you formally identify yourself to the network as a user.

During the login you are prompted to enter your user ID and password. Your **user ID**, sometimes referred to as your **user name**, is a unique set of letters and numbers. Your **password**, a special set of symbols known only to you and the network administrator, gives you security clearance to use network resources. Your user ID and password are the basis for your user account. A **user account** provides access to network resources and accumulates information about your network use by tracking when you log in and log out.

On most networks, users can select their own passwords. If you have this option, you should select a secure password so other people cannot log in as you and access your files. Your password should be unique, yet something you can remember. How do you select a secure password? Refer to the chart in Figure 6-2 for some password do's and don'ts.

Do	Don't
• Select a password that is at least five characters long.	• Select a password that is a word that can be found in the dictionary.
• Try to use numbers as well as letters in your password.	• Use your name, nickname, Social Security number, birth date, or name of a close relative.
• Select a password you can remember.	• Write your password where it is easy to find—under the keyboard is the first place a password thief will look.
• Consider making a password by combining two or more words.	
• Consider making a password by using the first letters of the words in a poem or phrase.	
• Change your password periodically.	

A network administrator, also called a network supervisor, is the person responsible for maintaining a network. One of the network administrator's jobs is to create your account and provide you with a user ID and starter password. You can find out more about network-related careers in Projects 4 and 5 at the end of this chapter.

▶ **Figure 6-2**
Password do's and don'ts

Entering a valid user ID and password is the beginning of the **login process**. As the login process continues, your workstation is connected to network drives, allowing you to use programs and data files stored on a server. The login process also connects your workstation to network resources such as a network printer. The next two sections explain how this works.

Drive Mapping

How does my computer access data files and application software from a network server?

Your workstation gains access to the file server and its hard drive when the server hard drive is *mapped* to a drive letter. **Mapping** is network terminology for assigning a drive letter to a network server disk drive. For example, on a typical workstation with a floppy drive A: and a hard drive C:, the login process maps the server hard drive as drive F:.

Once a drive letter has been mapped, you can access data files and application software from that drive just as you would from your local hard disk drive. Drive mappings vary from one network to another, depending on the needs of the organization and its users. One organization might map the server drive as F:, while another organization might map the server drive as J:. In other organizations, multiple drives on more than one server might be mapped as F:, I:, J:, and Z:. As a network user, you will find it useful to know the drive mapping so you can more easily find programs and files. Figure 6-3 shows the drive mapping available to a workstation in a network with a single server.

Figure 6-3
A typical workstation drive map

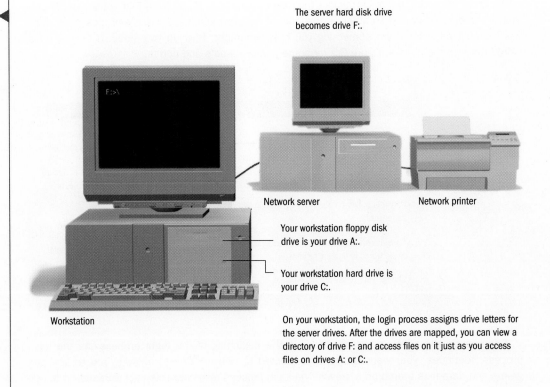

The server hard disk drive becomes drive F:.

Network server

Network printer

Your workstation floppy disk drive is your drive A:.

Your workstation hard drive is your drive C:.

Workstation

On your workstation, the login process assigns drive letters for the server drives. After the drives are mapped, you can view a directory of drive F: and access files on it just as you access files on drives A: or C:.

Using Programs on a Network

When I start a program supplied by a network server, is it the same as starting a program on a standalone computer?

You should remember from Chapter 4 that when you launch a program on a standalone computer, it is copied from your hard disk into RAM. Suppose you want to use a word processing program that is stored on the hard disk of a network server. Will the program be loaded into the memory of the server or into the memory of your workstation?

When you start a program that is stored on a server, the program is copied to the RAM of your workstation. Once the program is in memory, it runs just as if you had started it from your workstation hard disk drive. Figure 6-4 shows how this works.

You might wonder if more than one user on a network can simultaneously use the same program. One advantage of a network is that with proper licensing many users can access a program at the same time. This is called **sharing** a program. For example, while Lotus 1-2-3 is running on your workstation, other users can start the same program. The network server sends a copy of Lotus 1-2-3 to the RAM of each user's workstation.

Sharing programs is effective for several reasons. First, less disk storage space is required because the program is stored only once on the server, instead of being stored on the hard disks of multiple standalone computers. Second, when a new version of the software is released, it is easier to update one copy of the program on the server than to update many copies stored on standalone computers. Third, purchasing a software license for a network can be less expensive than purchasing single-user licenses for each workstation on the network.

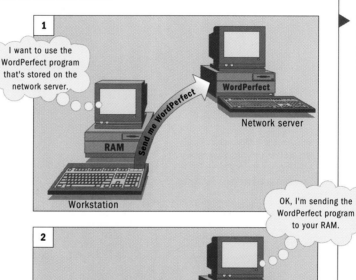

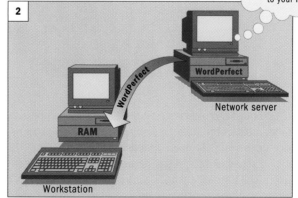

▶ **Figure 6-4**
Starting a program that is stored on the file server

If several users try to start a program at the same time, does it take longer than when only a single user starts the program? To find out, do Project 2 at the end of this chapter.

For security reasons, the network administrator might limit your access to open, change, or store files on network drives, folders, or files.

Using Data Files on a Network

Is there any advantage to storing data files on the server instead of my local hard disk?

Suppose that while connected to a network, you create a document using a word processing program. You can store the document either on your local hard disk or on the server hard disk. If you store the file on your local hard disk, you can access the file only from your workstation. However, if you store the file on the hard disk of the server, you, or any other user, can access the file from any workstation on the network, as shown in Figure 6-5.

Figure 6-5
Network file access

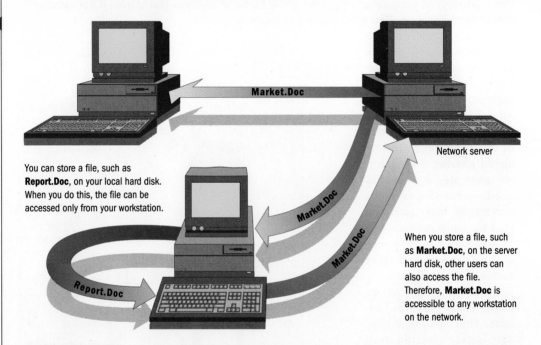

You can store a file, such as **Report.Doc**, on your local hard disk. When you do this, the file can be accessed only from your workstation.

Network server

When you store a file, such as **Market.Doc**, on the server hard disk, other users can also access the file. Therefore, **Market.Doc** is accessible to any workstation on the network.

Make sure you understand that more than one person can typically access a program file from the server, but typically only one person at a time can access a particular data file.

Although a *program file* on the file server can be accessed by more than one user at the same time, most of the *data files* on a network server can be opened by only one user at a time. When one user has a file open, it is **locked** to other users. File locking is a sensible precaution against losing valuable data. If the network allowed two users to open and edit the same data file, both users could make changes to the file; but one user's changes might contradict the other user's changes. Whose changes would be incorporated in the final version of the file?

Suppose two users were allowed to make changes to the same file at the same time. Each user would open a copy of the original file and make changes to it. The first user to finish making changes would save the file on the server. So far so good—the first user has replaced the original version of the file with an edited version. Remember, however, that the second user has been making revisions to the *original* file, but she has no idea of the first user's revisions. When the second user saves her revised version of the file, the changes made by the first user are overwritten by the second user's version, as shown in Figure 6-6.

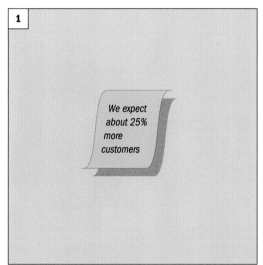

The original document is not well written and the percentage is wrong. Sam and Gracie both decide to fix it.

▶ **Figure 6-6**
Why networks lock files

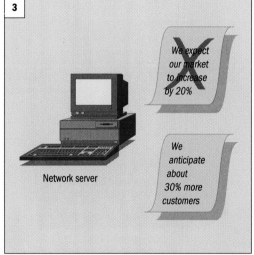

Network server

Sam stores the edited document on the server, but when Gracie stores her version of the document on the server, it overwrites Sam's version, erasing all of his work.

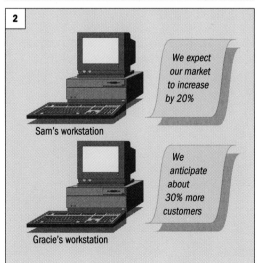

Sam's workstation

Gracie's workstation

If Sam and Gracie were allowed to open the document at the sametime, they could edit the document in two different ways.

If you have a local printer in addition to a network printer, you can typically select the printer you want to use.

Using a Network Printer

How does my word processing software know it is supposed to send documents to the network printer instead of to my local printer?

Most application software sends files you want to print to the printer that is connected to your computer's parallel port. But network workstations often do not have local printers. Instead, they need to access a network printer. Figure 6-7 shows how data sent to your workstation's parallel port is **captured** and **redirected** to the network printer.

Figure 6-7
Capturing your
workstation
printer port

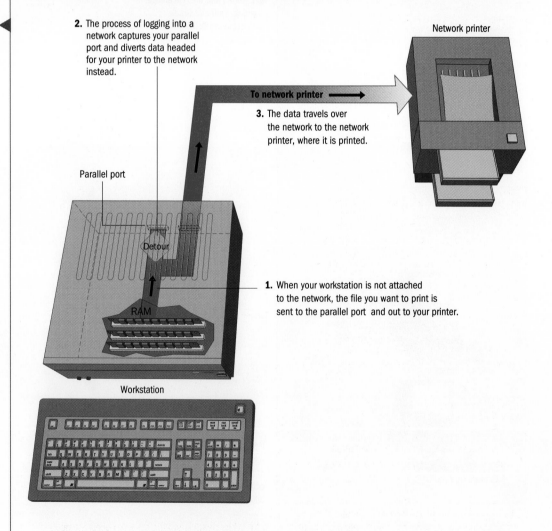

2. The process of logging into a network captures your parallel port and diverts data headed for your printer to the network instead.

Network printer

To network printer ⟶

3. The data travels over the network to the network printer, where it is printed.

Parallel port

Detour

RAM

1. When your workstation is not attached to the network, the file you want to print is sent to the parallel port and out to your printer.

Workstation

What happens if a network printer receives more than one file to print? Most networks would not allow two files to travel simultaneously over the network. However, it is possible that before the printer has completed one printout, other files arrive to be printed. Files sent to a network printer are placed in a **print queue**. A print queue is a special holding area on a network server where files are stored until they are printed. When more than one user sends a file to the print queue, the files are added to the print queue and printed in the order in which they are received.

Figure 6-8 shows what happens when one user sends a document to the printer before another user's printout is completed.

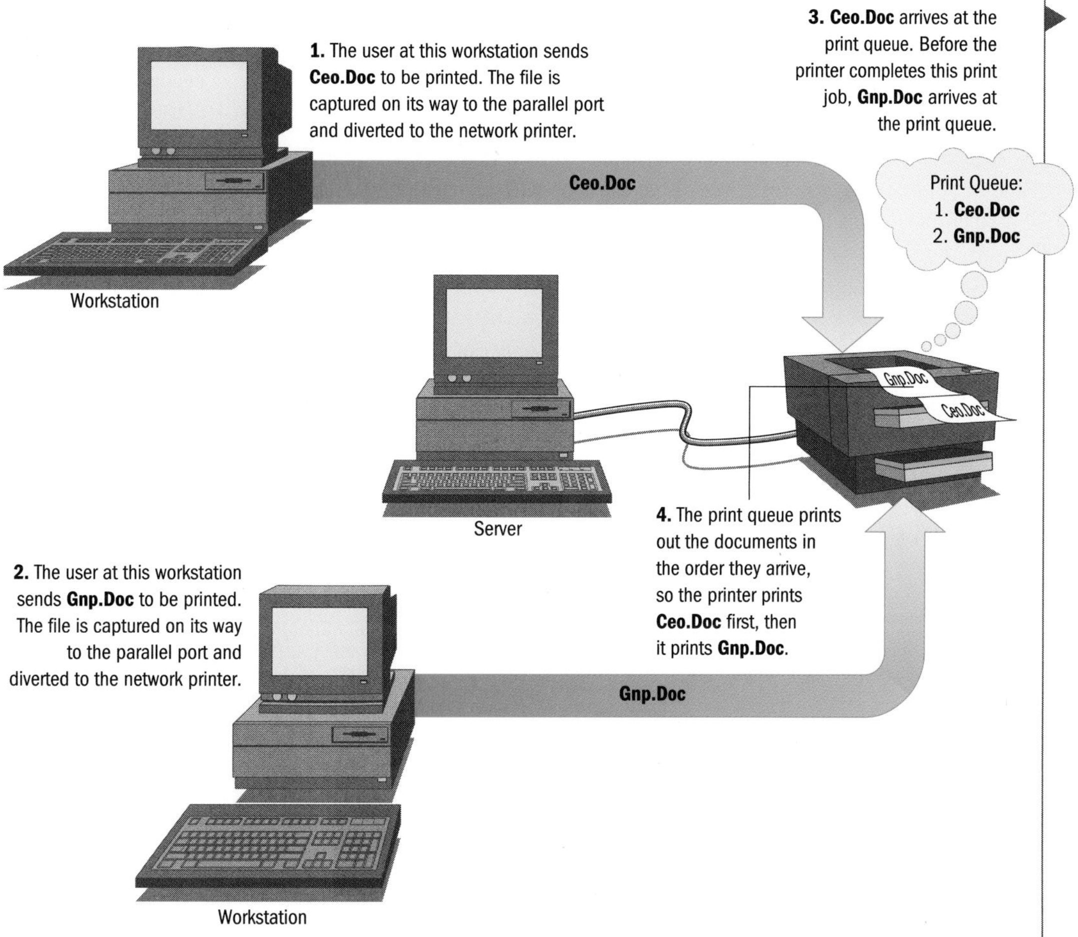

3. Ceo.Doc arrives at the print queue. Before the printer completes this print job, **Gnp.Doc** arrives at the print queue.

1. The user at this workstation sends **Ceo.Doc** to be printed. The file is captured on its way to the parallel port and diverted to the network printer.

Ceo.Doc

Print Queue:
1. **Ceo.Doc**
2. **Gnp.Doc**

Workstation

Server

Gnp.Doc

Ceo.Doc

4. The print queue prints out the documents in the order they arrive, so the printer prints **Ceo.Doc** first, then it prints **Gnp.Doc**.

2. The user at this workstation sends **Gnp.Doc** to be printed. The file is captured on its way to the parallel port and diverted to the network printer.

Gnp.Doc

Workstation

Figure 6-8
The network print queue

Quick Check

1 A network _____ is a computer connected to a network that distributes files to network users.

2 _____ is network terminology for assigning a drive letter to a file server disk drive.

3 A(n) _____ provides access to network resources and accumulates information about your use of the network.

4 Assuming proper licensing, while Jenny uses a spreadsheet program from the file server, Atkin can also use this spreadsheet program at the same time. True or False?

5 While Sandi is editing a word processing document called **Budget.Doc**, Karl can also edit this document at the same time. True or False?

6 When a network printer is assigned to your workstation, any data sent to the workstation's parallel port is _____ and _____ to the network printer.

6.2

Network Hardware

In the previous section, you looked at local area network resources and learned about the advantages of computer networks. Now let's look at network hardware.

Network Interface Cards and Cables

What establishes the physical connection for the computers in a network?

A network interface card is the key hardware component for connecting a computer to a local area network. A **network interface card** or **NIC** (pronounced "nick") is a small circuit board designed to plug into an expansion slot on a computer main board. Each workstation on a network must have a NIC. The network interface card sends data from your workstation out over the network and collects incoming data for your workstation.

Different types of networks use different types of network interface cards. If you want to add a computer to a network, you need to know the network type so you can purchase the appropriate NIC. Popular network types include **Ethernet**, **Token Ring**, **ARCnet**, **FDDI**, and **ATM**.

Most network interface cards contain a cable connector into which you plug the cable that connects workstations, network servers, and other devices. On the back of your computer, you might see one of the cable connectors like those shown in Figure 6-9.

Figure 6-9 ◀
A network interface card and cable connectors

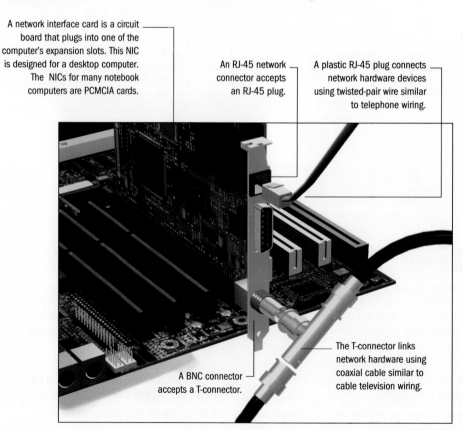

A network interface card is a circuit board that plugs into one of the computer's expansion slots. This NIC is designed for a desktop computer. The NICs for many notebook computers are PCMCIA cards.

An RJ-45 network connector accepts an RJ-45 plug.

A plastic RJ-45 plug connects network hardware devices using twisted-pair wire similar to telephone wiring.

The T-connector links network hardware using coaxial cable similar to cable television wiring.

A BNC connector accepts a T-connector.

Instead of using cables, some **wireless networks** use radio or infrared signals to transmit data from one network device to another. The network interface cards on a wireless network contain the transmitting devices necessary to send data to other devices on the local area network. Wireless networks are handy in environments where wiring is difficult to install.

Network Servers

When I use a network, is my data processed locally or on the network server?

You have already learned the general functions of a network server. However, there are different kinds of network servers. They are explained in this section. When you use a standalone computer, all your data is processed by your computer's microprocessor. The device that processes your data when you are connected to a network depends on the type of servers included on your network.

A **dedicated file server** is devoted only to the task of delivering programs and data files to workstations. As you can see in Figure 6-10, a dedicated file server does not process data or run programs for the workstations. Instead, programs run using the memory and processor of the workstation.

A key feature of a network with a dedicated file server is that the server stores files and data, but the workstations process the data.

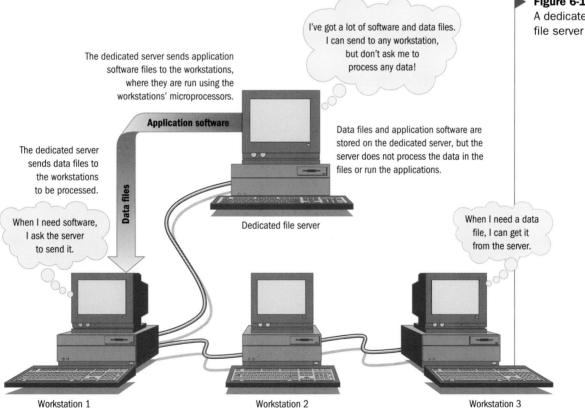

Figure 6-10
A dedicated file server

A typical local area network uses a microcomputer as a file server. However, a minicomputer or a mainframe computer can also be a file server.

In some cases, a network computer performs a dual role as both file server and workstation. This is referred to as a **non-dedicated server** or **peer-to-peer** capability.

"Dedicated file server" does not mean a network has only one server. Many networks have more than one dedicated file server.

When you use a non-dedicated server, your computer functions like a normal workstation, but other workstations can access programs and data files from the hard disk of your computer, as shown in Figure 6-11.

Figure 6-11 ◄
A non-dedicated file server

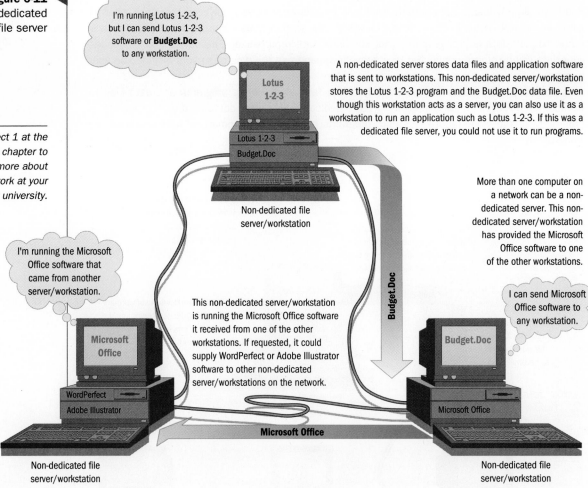

I'm running Lotus 1-2-3, but I can send Lotus 1-2-3 software or **Budget.Doc** to any workstation.

A non-dedicated server stores data files and application software that is sent to workstations. This non-dedicated server/workstation stores the Lotus 1-2-3 program and the Budget.Doc data file. Even though this workstation acts as a server, you can also use it as a workstation to run an application such as Lotus 1-2-3. If this was a dedicated file server, you could not use it to run programs.

Lotus 1-2-3

Lotus 1-2-3
Budget.Doc

Non-dedicated file server/workstation

More than one computer on a network can be a non-dedicated server. This non-dedicated server/workstation has provided the Microsoft Office software to one of the other workstations.

I'm running the Microsoft Office software that came from another server/workstation.

This non-dedicated server/workstation is running the Microsoft Office software it received from one of the other workstations. If requested, it could supply WordPerfect or Adobe Illustrator software to other non-dedicated server/workstations on the network.

I can send Microsoft Office software to any workstation.

Microsoft Office

WordPerfect
Adobe Illustrator

Budget.Doc

Microsoft Office

Microsoft Office

Non-dedicated file server/workstation

Non-dedicated file server/workstation

Do Project 1 at the end of this chapter to find out more about the network at your college or university.

A key feature of a peer-to-peer network is that workstations also perform the role of server by storing and distributing data and programs.

A **print server** stores files in a print queue and sends each queued file to the network printer. A **print job** is a file that has been sent to the printer. Print jobs are processed locally on workstations that have a local printer, but a print server controls the print jobs on a network server. A print server can be the same computer as the file server, or it can be another micro, mini, or mainframe computer connected to the network.

An **application server** is a computer that runs application software and forwards the results of processing to workstations as requested. An application server makes it possible to use the processing power of both the server and the workstation. Also referred to as **client-server architecture**, use of an application server splits processing between the workstation *client* and the

Client-server architecture is becoming increasingly popular in corporations. Project 3 at the end of this chapter helps you find more information on this topic.

network *server*. Suppose you want to search for a particular record in a 50,000-record database stored on a network server. Study Figure 6-12 to see how client-server architecture makes use of the processing capacity of both the workstation and server.

A key feature of a client-server network is that the data sent by the server can be processed, not just viewed, by the workstations.

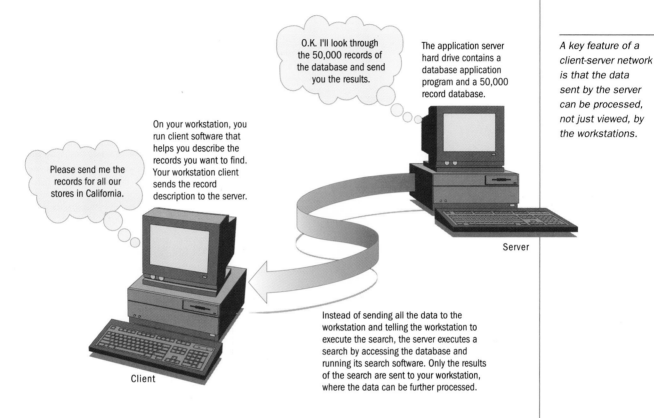

O.K. I'll look through the 50,000 records of the database and send you the results.

The application server hard drive contains a database application program and a 50,000 record database.

On your workstation, you run client software that helps you describe the records you want to find. Your workstation client sends the record description to the server.

Please send me the records for all our stores in California.

Server

Instead of sending all the data to the workstation and telling the workstation to execute the search, the server executes a search by accessing the database and running its search software. Only the results of the search are sent to your workstation, where the data can be further processed.

Client

Some networks include a **host computer**, usually a minicomputer or a mainframe with attached terminals. When you use a host computer from a terminal, all the processing takes place on the host. Your **terminal** has a keyboard and a screen, but it does not have a local storage device, and it does little or no processing on its own.

Connecting terminals to a host computer provided relatively low-cost computer access before powerful microcomputer networks became available. For economic reasons, many organizations have not yet moved important data and programs from mainframe hosts to microcomputers. Can you use a microcomputer to access the data stored on a mainframe host computer?

You can access a host computer from a microcomputer workstation by using terminal emulation software. **Terminal emulation software** makes a microcomputer appear to the host as a terminal. While the terminal emulation software is active, your microcomputer does very little local processing, as you can see in Figure 6-13 on the following page.

Although a system containing a host computer and terminals fits our general definition of a *network*, it is more customary to call it a **time-sharing system**. Because terminals can do little or no processing of their own, every terminal must wait for the host to process its request. The terminals essentially *share* the host's processor by being allocated a fraction of a second of processing time.

A key feature of networks with a mainframe host is that all the processing takes place on the host, not on workstations or terminals.

Now that you have looked at different server models—dedicated server, non-dedicated server, print server, application server, and host—you should be able to see that the device that processes your data depends on the type of server or servers connected to your local area network.

Figure 6-13 ◄
Mainframe host

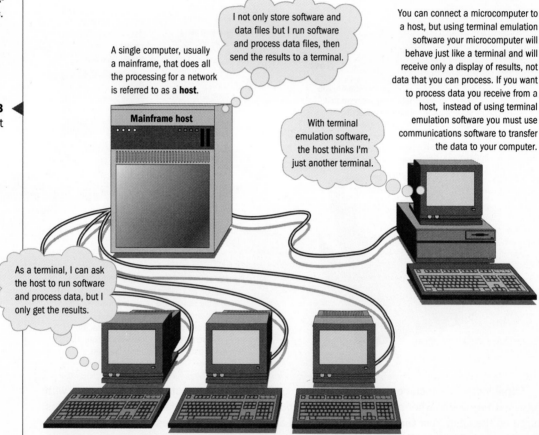

The host accepts commands from terminals and sends back a display of results. Because the terminals do not have processing power of their own, they cannot further process the results they receive. For example, if your terminal receives a list of 50 people sorted by address, you could not sort the list by last name on your terminal. You would have to ask the host to sort the list and send you the new results.

Quick Check

Make sure you can explain the difference between a dedicated file server, peer-to-peer (non-dedicated server), client-server (application server), and host (time-sharing system).

1 The circuit board that connects a computer to a local area network is called a(n) _____ .

2 If a network computer functions both as a file server and as a workstation, it is referred to as a(n) _____ .

3 A(n) _____ is devoted to the task of delivering program and data files to workstations.

4 Client-server architecture takes advantage of the processing capabilities of both the workstations and the server. True or false?

5 On some networks, a(n) _____ computer processes data, then outputs the results on the screen of a terminal.

Software for Networks

The software on a local area network typically includes specialized network software as well as many of the same applications you might use on a standalone computer.

Network Operating System

Does a network require any special software?

A network requires **network software** or a **network operating system** to control the flow of data, maintain security, and keep track of user accounts.

Network operating systems such as **Novell NetWare**, **Banyan Vines**, and **Lantastic** are software packages designed exclusively to control network data flow. Network software is sometimes included as a component of popular computer operating systems such as Windows for Workgroups, Windows 95, UNIX, and OS/2.

A network operating system usually has two components: server software and client software. **Network server software** is installed on a file server and controls file access from the server hard drive, manages the print queue, and tracks user data such as IDs and passwords. **Network client software** is installed on the local hard drive of each workstation and is essentially a device driver for the network interface card. When your computer boots up, the network client software is activated and establishes the connection between your workstation and other devices on the network.

Windows 3.1 does not include network software. Therefore, if your school uses the Windows 3.1 operating system, your school network also requires a network operating system such as Novell NetWare.

Standalone Applications

Do I need to buy a special version of my favorite application software to use it on a network?

Most applications designed for standalone computers can be installed on a network server, which sends them to individual workstations as requested. Most of your favorite word processing, spreadsheet, graphics, and presentation software will work on a network just as they do on a standalone computer.

Some applications that you use on a standalone computer have built-in features for networking that appear only when the software is installed on a network. For example, when your word processing software is installed on a network, it might show you a dialog box that lets you send files to another person on the network.

As you learned in Section 6.1, a network can supply an application to more than one person at a time by copying the program into the memory of the workstations. This capability applies to most standalone software. Therefore, software designed for standalone computers can usually be used on a network by more than one user at a time. However, most applications designed for standalone computers do not allow more than one person at a time to work on the same *data file.*

In Chapter 2 you learned that a device driver is software that enables a computer to use a specific device. You can go back to Chapter 2, Section 2 to review device drivers.

Groupware

Is there a way for two or more people to work together on the same data file?

When local area networks were first introduced, the concept of sharing files was limited to a sequential process in which one user at a time could work on a document. However, this process did not support many of the organizational activities that require collaboration and communication among employees. For example, in most organizations, people exchange information using memos, phone conversations, and face-to-face meetings. Employees collect, organize, and share information, which must be stored in a centralized repository. Documents and forms flow through

Groupware encompasses a wide variety of software designed to enhance workgroup activities. For in-depth coverage of groupware, refer to the book Groupware, Workflow, and Workgroup Computing, cited in the Resources list at the end of this chapter.

Figure 6-14
Groupware

organizations, picking up required signatures and approvals. Employees contribute sections of text that are compiled into a single report.

A **workgroup** is basically two or more people who work on the same project. Recent advances in workgroup technology have provided ways for local area networks to help workgroups become more efficient by coordinating group work and sharing information. Groupware is an important aspect of workgroup technology.

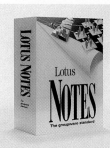

Groupware software such as Collabra Share and Lotus Notes help work groups collaborate on projects.

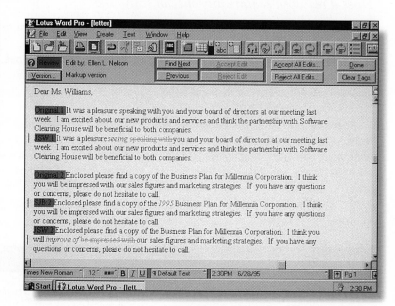

Group editing features are used when more than one person revises a document. Each person's revisions are separately marked to show who made each change. A document can be open by more than one person at a time, however, users will not be able to see each other's edits until their work is saved.

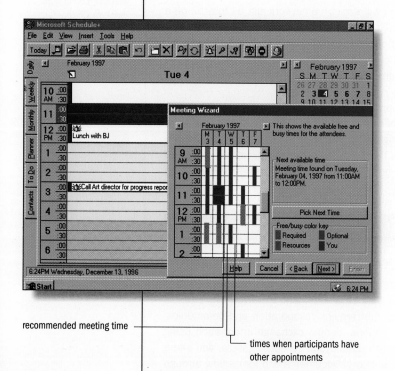

Group scheduling programs generally simplify the process of scheduling meetings. You just select the people that need to attend the meeting, and the group scheduling program finds a date and time when everyone can attend. The meeting appears as a tentative appointment on each person's individual schedule. Each user can then confirm the meeting or send a reply indicating that he or she cannot attend.

recommended meeting time

times when participants have other appointments

Groupware is application software that supports collaborative work, usually on a local area network. As you read the description of the groupware applications in Figure 6-14 consider how you might apply them for school projects or in your career.

Figure 6-14
Groupware
continued

Document routing, also referred to as **workflow management**, electronically forwards a document to a series of people for approval. As soon as one person signs off on the document, it is forwarded to the next person in the routing list. Some systems make it easy to check the status of a document to find out who has signed off on the document and who is currently holding it.

Loan application form

Loan manager evaluated application

Evaluated

Bank board members approve

Approved

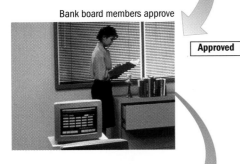

Branch manager processes loan

Processed

Desktop videoconferencing provides a live video image of each participant in a real-time conference. Videoconferencing requires special software on each participating workstation, as well as a small video camera and video input board. Most videoconferencing systems provide optimal image quality using networks or dedicated communication lines, although some systems allow limited videoconferencing using modems and telephone lines.

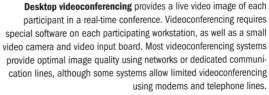

Software Licenses for Networks

Can an organization buy just one copy of a software package and put it on the network for every one to use?

You might want to review the Software Copyright section in Chapter 2 to see why it is illegal for more than one person to use a software package unless the software license specifically allows it.

It would be very inexpensive for an organization to purchase a single copy of a software package, then place it on the network for everyone to use. In an organization with 100 users, for example, word processing capability might cost $295 for a single copy, instead of $29,500 for 100 copies. However, using a single-user license for multiple users violates copyright law.

Most single-user software licenses allow only one person to use the software at a time. However, many software publishers also offer a **network license** that permits use by multiple people on a network. Typically, such a network license will cost more than a single-user license, but less than purchasing single-user licenses for all of the users. For example, a word processing software package that costs $295 for a single-user license might have a $5,000 network license that allows up to 100 people to use the software. Network licenses are available for most software packages by contacting the software publisher.

Quick Check

1 Novell NetWare would be classified as a(n) _____ system.

2 True or false? When run on a network, most application software designed for standalone computers allows only one person at a time to access the same data file.

3 If an organization is planning to use software on a network, it should purchase a(n) _____ so multiple users can legally use the software.

4 If you are a team leader and you want your team members to collaborate on a project using the network, you might try to find a(n) _____ product.

5 If you were the manager of a loan department in a bank, you might request _____ groupware so the network will automatically send loan applications to each member of your department for processing and approval.

User **Focus:**

Electronic Mail

Lab

E-mail

Electronic mail, or **e-mail**, is correspondence conducted between one or more users on a network. E-mail is a more efficient means of communication than ground or air mail. Rather than waiting for a piece of paper to be physically transported across the country, you can send an electronic version of a message directly to someone's electronic "mail box." E-mail also helps you avoid frustrating "telephone tag."

How E-mail Works

When I send an e-mail message does it go directly to the recipient's workstation? What if the recipient's workstation is not turned on?

An **e-mail message** is essentially a letter or memo sent electronically from one user to another. An **electronic mail system** is the hardware and software that collects and delivers e-mail messages. Typically, a local area network provides electronic mail services to its users. The software on the network server that controls the flow of e-mail is called **mail server software**. The software on a workstation that helps each user read, compose, send, and delete messages is called **mail client software**. Electronic mail systems are often classified as groupware because they facilitate communication among members of a workgroup.

E-mail messages are *stored* on a server. When you want to read this mail, the server *forwards* the messages to your workstation. Hence e-mail is called a **store-and-forward** technology. Because the server stores the messages, your workstation does not need to be on when someone sends you e-mail (Figure 6-15).

The Lotus Notes mail client software handles each user's personal mail box.

Icons and tools help you easily read mail, send mail and replies.

The Lotus Notes window shows you a list of arriving messages; the time they were sent, the sender's name and the subject of each message.

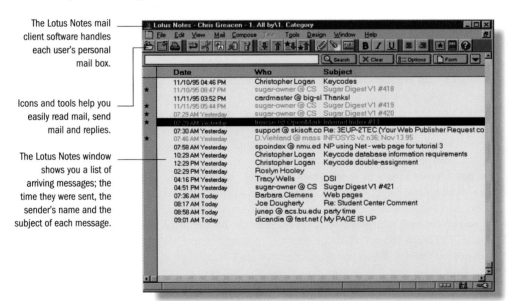

▶ **Figure 6-15**
Using e-mail

Your e-mail is transmitted through an electronic mail system and stored on a host or network server in an area you can think of as your **mailbox**. When you log into the electronic mail system and check your mail, the message is listed as new mail. You can choose to display and read the mail on your computer screen, print it, delete it, reply to it, forward it, or save it on disk.

Some e-mail systems allow you to send an **attachment**, which is a file such as a word processing document, worksheet, or graphic that travels through the e-mail system along with an electronic mail message. For example, suppose you receive e-mail from your department head about the proposed budget for next year. Your department head writes that there is a spreadsheet attachment called Budget containing the budget figures. To see the attachment after you read the e-mail message, your computer starts your spreadsheet program and opens the file Budget.

Some electronic mail systems offer features such as **priority mail**, which immediately alerts the recipient that an important e-mail message has arrived; **return receipt**, which sends a message back to you when a recipient receives your message; **carbon copy**, which sends a copy of the message to another user; and **group addressing**, which allows you to send a copy of an e-mail message to all members of a group at the same time.

What if you want to send e-mail to someone who is not connected to your computer network or host? Many e-mail systems are connected to other e-mail systems through electronic links called **gateways**. When you send an e-mail message to a user on another computer network, the message is transferred through the gateway to a larger e-mail system, which delivers the message to the recipient's network or host computer system.

Managing Your E-mail

I know how to write letters and memos—is there anything special I need to know about writing e-mail messages?

E-mail is not exactly the same as using the post office. With e-mail you can send messages right away—your letters don't sit around waiting for you to take them to the post office. You can send the same message to multiple people as easily as to a single person. It is easy to send replies automatically to messages you receive as well.

The advantages of e-mail can also create potential problems—for example, you might regret the contents of a message sent off in haste. Also, it's easy to accumulate an overwhelming number of messages in your mail box. Here are some tips to help you avoid e-mail problems:

Read your mail regularly. When you use electronic mail, your correspondents expect a quick response. You lose much of the advantage of e-mail if you check your mailbox only once every two weeks!

Delete messages after you read them. Your e-mail is stored, along with everyone else's, on a file server where storage space is valuable. Leaving old messages in your mailbox takes up space that could be used more productively.

You don't have to reply to every e-mail message. The purpose of some e-mail messages is to give you information. Don't reply unless you have a reason to respond, such as to answer a question. Sending a message to say "I got your message" just creates unnecessary mail traffic.

If you receive mail addressed to a group, it might be better to reply only to one person in the group. You might receive mail as a member of a mailing list; the same message will be sent to everyone on the list. If you use the automatic reply feature of your e-mail system, your message is likely to be sent to everyone on the list. Do this only if your reply is important for everyone to see.

Think before you send. It is easy to write a message in haste or in anger and send it off before you have time to think it through. If you're upset, write your message, but wait a day before you send it.

Don't write anything you want to remain confidential. Remember that with electronic mail forwarding messages is easy. Suppose you write something unflattering about Rob in an e-mail message to Julie. Julie can easily forward your message to Rob.

Don't get sloppy. Your e-mail is a reflection of you, your school, and your employer. Use a spellchecker if one is available; if not, proofread your message before you send it. Use standard grammar, punctuation, and capitalization. A message in all uppercase means you're shouting.

E-mail Privacy

Is my e-mail confidential?

You should be aware that your e-mail might be read by someone other than the recipient. Although the U.S. justice system has not yet made a clear ruling, current legal interpretations indicate that e-mail is not legally protected from snooping. You cannot assume that the e-mail you send is private. Therefore, you should not use e-mail to send any message that you want to keep confidential.

Why would an employer want to know the contents of employee e-mail? You might immediately jump to the conclusion that employers who read employee e-mail are snooping. This might be the case with some employers who, for example, want to discover what a union is planning. However, some employers read employee e-mail to discover if any illegal activities are taking place on the computer system. Many employers are genuinely concerned about such activities because they could, in some cases, be held responsible for the actions of their employees.

Also, the network administrator sometimes sees the contents of e-mail messages while performing system maintenance or when trying to recover from a system failure. Even if an employer does not intentionally read e-mail exchanges, technical difficulties might still expose the contents of e-mail messages to people other than the intended recipient.

End Note Local area networks have come a long way since the days of the sneaker net; they now provide connectivity for workgroups using groupware and for individuals exchanging e-mail. Although local area networks provide connectivity within a limited geographical area, electronic mail gateways provide connections between these small networks.

Review

1. Use your own words to answer the questions in italics below each heading in the chapter.

2. List each of the boldface terms used in this chapter, then use your own words to write a short definition.

3. List three reasons why sharing programs is effective for an organization.

4. Suppose Latisha Simms needs to select a password for herself. Rank the following, listing the most secure password first: XX32nsa (a totally random selection of letters and numbers), LASIMMS (for Latisha Alexandra Simms), RRRYBGDTS (the first letters of row, row, row your boat gently down the stream), SMMIS (Latisha's last name spelled backwards), Henry (Latisha's husband's name).

5. Create a sentence outline of Section 6.1 that highlights the main concepts network users need to know.

6. Explain the difference between sharing files on a network and using a groupware product on a network.

7. Fill in the following table to summarize the characteristics of different network servers:

	File Server	Print Server	Non-dedicated Server	Client-Server	Host
Are shared files stored locally?					
Are shared programs stored locally?					
Does some, all, or none of the processing take place on the server?					
Does some, all, or none of the processing take place on the terminals or workstations?					

8. Explain the purpose of network server software and network client software.

9. Describe four types of groupware.

10. Summarize the software licensing issues that pertain to local area networks.

11. Explain how store-and-forward technology applies to electronic mail systems.

Projects

1. Your School Network Research your school network to answer the following questions:

   a. What is the network operating system?

   b. What drives are mapped to a student workstation?

   c. Is the file server a micro, mini, or mainframe computer?

   d. Is the print server a different device than the file server?

2. Network Operating System Efficiency Network operating systems are designed to optimize the process of sending program and data files to workstations. This means that the amount of time it takes multiple users to open the same file should not be much longer than it takes a single user to open the file. How efficient is the file server in your lab? To find out, form a team of three to five class members and do a through d:

   a. Using a stopwatch or the second hand of your watch, record the number of seconds it takes a word processing software application to start on a workstation in your lab. For example, if your lab has WordPerfect for Windows, click the WordPerfect icon to highlight it, then start timing when you press the Enter key to launch the program. Stop timing when the word processor is ready for you to start typing.

   b. Exit the word processing application to get ready for the second part of the test.

   c. Position each member of your team at other workstations on the network. Each team member should click the word processing icon so it is highlighted. One of the team members should give a signal so all the team members press the Enter key at the same time. Each team member should record how long it takes before the word processing application is ready for typing.

   d. Record each team member's results. Prepare a one-page document in which you summarize your experiment and results. Be sure you explain exactly how you carried out the experiment—how many members were on your team, which lab you used, and which software you used. Also, present your conclusions about the efficiency of your network server.

3. Client-Server Architecture in Corporations Client-server architecture is becoming more and more popular in corporations. To find out more about client-server computing, use library and Internet resources to look for case studies and articles about corporations using client-server applications. Write a one-page or two-page description of an effective use of client-server computing. Be sure to include a list of references.

4. Networks in Action Make an appointment to interview the network supervisor in an organization or business related to your career field. To prepare for the interview, make a list of questions you will ask about how the network works and how it is used. Use the topics in this chapter to help organize your questions about network hardware, network software, applications software, and groupware. After the interview, write a two- to three-page summary of your findings. Include the name of the person you interviewed, the business or organization, and the date of the interview. In addition to the report summarizing your findings, submit a list of your questions.

5. Network Careers The companies that produce network operating systems encourage computer professionals to obtain professional certification to demonstrate their knowledge of networking. Such certification is often one of the qualifications listed in ads for network supervisor jobs. Novell offers certification as a CNE (Certified NetWare Engineer) or a CNA (Certified NetWare Administrator). Microsoft also offers a certification program for its Windows NT operating system. Write a one- to two-page paper that describes Microsoft's or Novell's certification process. Include the answers to the following questions: What is the process for certification? What is the cost? How would you prepare for the certification exam? What sort of jobs would you qualify for once you are certified?

INTERNET

OPTIONAL

6. E-mail Smileys E-mail has spawned a language of *emoticons*, or *smileys*, that are composed of keyboard characters. For example, the smiley ;-) looks like a person winking. You could use this smiley in an e-mail message to indicate that you are joking. Lists of smileys have been published on the Internet and in books, computer magazines, and newspapers. Find a list of smileys and select five that you would like to use. Make a list of your five smileys and describe what each means. Submit your list and indicate the source of your selection.

7. Anonymous E-mail? When you send e-mail, your user ID is automatically attached to your message. This return address indicates who sent the message (in case you forgot to include your name), lets your correspondents easily send you replies, and helps the mail system return messages that have incorrect addresses. Recently, some networks have offered a way to send anonymous e-mail. What are the pros and cons of anonymous mail? Under what circumstances would you want to send anonymous mail? Would you expect people to abuse this capability? Discuss this issue in a small group or research the issue individually. Write a one-page summary of your position on whether people should be allowed to send anonymous e-mail.

8. E-mail Ethics Assume that you are the network administrator at a small manufacturing company. While doing some maintenance work on the electronic mail system, you happen to view the contents of a mail message between two employees. The employees seem to be discussing a plan to steal equipment from the company. What would you do? Write a one-page essay explaining what you would do and describing the factors that affected your decision.

9. E-mail Practice Learn how to use the e-mail system available on your school network. Briefly describe how you do each of the following:

a. Compose and send a message.

b. Reply to a message you received.

c. Delete a message you received.

d. Forward a message you received to someone other than the person who sent the message.

e. Send a carbon copy of the message.

f. Send a message to a mailing list.

Resources

■ **Derfler, F. and L. Freed**. *How Networks Work.* Emeryville, CA: Ziff-Davis Press, 1993. This illustrated guide to networks is the place to begin if you want to learn more about networks.

■ **Feibel, W.** *Novell's Complete Encyclopedia of Networking.* San Jose: Novell Press, 1995. This is an excellent reference for definitions of technical terms. Although it is published by Novell, whose networking products are used world wide, the information is relevant to local and wide area networks of all types.

■ *http://www.microsoft.com* Microsoft Windows 95 and Windows NT operating systems contain network capabilities. Microsoft encourages computer developers and network administrators to become certified Microsoft network administrators. You can learn more about Microsoft's networks and certification programs at their Internet site.

■ *http://www.novell.com* Novell, Inc. publishes Novell NetWare, the most popular microcomputer network operating system. Novell's Internet site contains a copious amount of information about local area networks, network certification, and Novell products.

■ **Khoshafian, S. and M. Buckiewicz**. *Introduction to Groupware, Workflow, and Workgroup Computing.* New York: John Wiley & Sons, 1995. A complete, clearly written and well-documented book about groupware and its role in organizations. Especially useful are its conceptual illustrations, such as Figure 1.16, Time and Place Interactions.

■ **Sanderson, D.** *Smileys.* Sebastopol, CA: O'Reilly & Associates, 1993. A collection of more than 650 smileys and answers to your deepest questions, such as "Why are smileys sideways?" Tilt your head for some examples: =l:-) Abe Lincoln, :`-(crying, :-? smoking a pipe.

Lab Assignments

E-mail

E-mail that originates on a local area network with a mail gateway can travel all over the world. That's why it is so important to learn how to use it. In this Lab you use an e-mail simulator, so even if your school computers don't provide you with e-mail service, you will know the basics of reading, sending, and replying to electronic mail.

1. Click the Steps button to learn how to work with e-mail. As you proceed through the Steps, answer all of the Quick Check questions that appear. After you complete the Steps, you will see a Quick Check Summary Report. Follow the instructions on the screen to print this report.

2. Click the Explore button. Write a message to re@films.org. The subject of the message is "Picks and Pans." In the body of your message, describe a movie you have recently seen. Include the name of the move, briefly summarize the plot, and give it a thumbs up or a thumbs down. Print the message before you send it.

3. In Explore, look in your In Box for a message from jb@music.org. Read the message, then compose a reply indicating that you will attend. Carbon copy mciccone@music.org. Print your reply, including the text of JB's original message before you send it.

4. In Explore, look in your In Box for a message from leo@sports.org. Reply to the message by adding your rating to the text of the original message as follows:

Equipment:	Your Rating:
Rollerblades	2
Skis	3
Bicycle	1
Scuba gear	4
Snow mobile	5

Print your reply before you send it.

5. Go into the lab with a partner. You should each log into the E-mail Lab on different computers. In Explore, look at the Addresses list to find the user ID for your partner. You should each send a short e-mail message to your partner. Then you should check your mail for a message from your partner. Read the message and compose a reply. Print your reply before you send it. (Note: Unlike a full-featured mail system, the e-mail simulator does not save mail in mailboxes after you log off.)

Quick Check Answers

6.1

1. server
2. Mapping
3. account (or user account)
4. True
5. False
6. Captured, redirected

6.2

1. network interface card
2. non-dedicated server
3. file server
4. True
5. Host

6.3

1. network operating
2. True
3. network license
4. groupware
5. Document routing

ssary/Index

P

password A special set of symbols, known only to you and the network administrator, that gives you security clearance to use network resources, 6-5
    local area networks, 6-5
    selecting, 6-5

peer-to-peer capability, 6-13–6-14

peer-to-peer network A type of computer network in which the workstations act as both workstations and file servers, 6-13

printers, networks. *See* network printers

print job A file that has been sent to the printer, 6-14

print queue A special holding area on the file server where files are stored until they are printed, 6-10

print server A server that stores files in a print queue and sends each queued file to the network printer, 6-14

priority mail A feature in an e-mail system that immediately alerts the recipient that an e-mail message has arrived, 6-22

privacy, e-mail, 6-22, 6-23

programs
    local area networks. *See* network software
    standalone, on networks, 6-17

R

radio signals, local area network data transmission, 6-12

return receipt A feature in an e-mail system that tells the sender when a recipient receives a message, 6-22

redirected A process where data is captured by a workstation's parallel port and sent to the network printer, 6-10

resources
    local, 6-4
    network, 6-4

return receipt, 6-22

S

selecting passwords, 6-5

servers, 6-4
    application, 6-14
    file. *See* file servers
    mail, 6-21
    network. *See* network servers
    print servers, 6-14

server software, local area networks, 6-17

sharing A network's ability to give many users access to a program at the same time, 6-7
    programs, 6-7
    time, 6-15

software
    e-mail, 6-21
    local area networks. *See* network software
    terminal emulation, 6-15

software licenses
    local area networks, 6-7
    network, 6-7, 6-20
    single-user, 6-20

standalone computer A computer that is not connected to a network, 6-4

standalone programs, 6-17

store-and-forward The technology that stores e-mail messages on a server, then forwards the messages to a workstation, 6-21

T

terminal An input and output device for a host computer, 6-15

terminal emulation software Software that enables a microcomputer to act as a terminal and communicate with a host computer, 6-15

time-sharing system A system containing a host computer and terminals, 6-15

Token Ring A type of network, 6-12

UNIX, network software, 6-17

updates, local area networks, 6-8–6-9

uppercase letters, e-mail messages, 6-22

user account Based on your user ID and password, a mechanism for giving you access to network resources and accumulating information about your network use, 6-5

user ID A unique set of letters and numbers that identifies a particular user of a computer system, 6-5

user name A unique set of letters and numbers enabling you to access the network. Also called user ID, 6-5

W

wide area network (WAN) A network that covers a large geographical area, 6-5

Windows 3.1, network software, 6-17

Windows 95, network software, 6-17

Windows for Workgroups, network software, 6-17

wireless network A network that uses radio or infrared signals, instead of cables, to transmit data from one network device to another, 6-12

workgroup Two or more people who work on the same project, 6-18

workstation An individual computer when it is physically connected to a network, 6-4

CHAPTER SEVEN

The Internet and the

The data jack slipped smoothly into the socket just behind Kyle's ear. He flipped the switch on his computer. The power light blinked green, and the universe shifted.

Information Highway

He looked out over a computer-generated landscape of surrealistic terrain and fantastic buildings. Messages swirled and pulsed down massive conduits, creating data links between heavily guarded corporate computing centers. The World Health Organization cube spun lazily, tipped on one of its corners. Kyle considered it briefly. It is open to the public. Lots of free data. In the distance—the towers of the Library of Congress. More free data. Interesting, but not what Kyle was after today.

He turned his attention to the golden pyramid. He'd heard rumors on the street that this was the computing headquarters of a major drug cartel. Kyle studied it carefully. It was surrounded by a translucent security globe. Really tough to get at that data, but his job was on the line. The data was critical to the prosecutor's case.

This is a vision of **cyberspace**—a computer-generated mental image of a computer world. The term *cyberspace* was coined in 1984 by science fiction writer William Gibson. Today the term cyberspace has been popularized by journalists writing about worldwide information networks. No, you cannot plug your brain into a computer to prowl around in cyberspace. But your computer can provide you access to a digital "information highway" that winds through a landscape of useful and fascinating information, on topics as diverse as hip hop music and military academies. In this chapter you will discover the astonishing potential of the information highway.

CHAPTER**PREVIEW**

In this chapter you will learn how to use a computer to access information from commercial information services and the Internet. First, you will take an on-line tour to get a flavor of the tremendous variety of information available on the information highway. You will learn about the software that helps you navigate through the vast landscape of data along the information highway. You will learn how to subscribe to a commercial information service. And finally, you will learn how to connect your own computer to the Internet. When you have completed this chapter, you should be able to:

■ List examples of the information available on the information highway

■ Compare and contrast the information and services available on the Internet with those available on commercial information services

■ Describe how to subscribe to a commercial information service

■ Describe how Gopher, Usenet, Telnet, FTP, and the World Wide Web help you access information on the Internet

■ Explain the elements of an Internet address

■ Explain how Internet communications software such as SLIP and PPP are used to establish an Internet connection

■ Follow good "netiquette" when using on-line services

■ Discuss the elements of virtual reality that are currently available on-line

LAB

The Internet:
World Wide Web

7.1 | Touring the **Information Highway**

The term "on-line service" has two meanings. It can be a synonym for a commercial information service, or it can refer to services offered on-line, such as e-mail.

A WAN (wide area network) connects computers in widely scattered geographic locations, as opposed to a LAN, which connects computers in a building or small campus.

B efore you go on-line for a drive on the information highway, it's a good idea to get a general idea of what you are likely to find. Section 7.1 presents an overview of the information highway and a sample of what's available on it.

Information Highway Map

What is the information highway?

The **information highway** is a world-wide network of computers linked by telephone lines and satellites. The "towns" or **sites** on the information highway are computers of all descriptions—micros, minis, and mainframes. The "roads" that connect the computers are communications systems provided by common carriers such as AT&T, MCI, and the French telephone company, Minitel. The "cars" that travel along the information highway carry information of all kinds. This information, sometimes referred to as **on-line information**, includes reports, magazine articles, books, photographs, music, film clips, library card catalogs, advertisements, computer programs, stock market quotes, and U.S. government publications. The information highway also provides services, called **on-line services**, to help you find information and communicate with other people.

You can access the information on this highway using a microcomputer and a communications link such as a modem or network. The information highway includes a huge computer network called the Internet and an assortment of commercial information services that provide information for a fee.

The **Internet** is a collection of local, regional, and national computer networks that are linked together to exchange data and distribute processing tasks. These networks can communicate because they use the same networking language. The Internet is similar to a WAN because it covers a wide geographical area. However, each network on the Internet is independently administered, so the Internet lacks the cohesive structure of a single WAN.

To use the Internet, you must have an account on a network that is connected to the Internet, and your network administrator must approve your account for Internet use. If your school network is connected to the Internet, it is likely that you have access to the Internet from the computers in your lab.

A **commercial information service**, sometimes called an **on-line service**, provides access to computer-based information and services for a fee. To use a commercial information service, you subscribe to it, just like you do to a magazine or newspaper. Commercial information services range from small neighborhood bulletin boards that run on a single microcomputer, to large corporate enterprises using multiple mainframes to provide information to customers in the U.S., Europe, and Asia.

If someone were to draw a simplified diagram or "map" of the information highway it might look like Figure 7-1.

Figure 7-1 ◄ Commercial information services + the Internet = the information highway

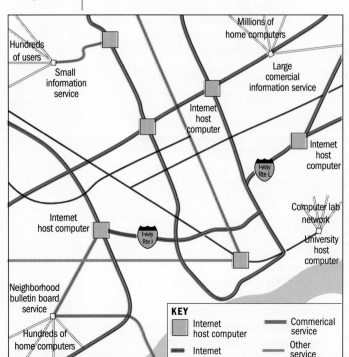

Trip Log

What's out there on the information highway?

To get an idea of what's on the information highway, you can follow this student's account of one day's on-line activities.

—**9 a.m.** I'm in the lab first thing this morning to check my e-mail. Today, I've got two messages. The first is from my Chemistry lab partner. She missed class yesterday. I send her a reply so she knows what the instructor assigned. The other message, signed "Dad," reminds me that Mom's birthday is coming up. Dad subscribed to a commercial information service when he found out that e-mail can travel virtually anywhere on the information highway—even between his commercial service and the network here at school.

—**9:05 a.m.** Got to shop for Mom's birthday present. With a couple of mouse clicks, I'm accessing an on-line shopping mall. The stores include Hammacher Schlemmer, Hilyard and Hilquist, Omaha Steaks, FTD Flowers, Global Plaza, Sharper Image, and Celestial Seasonings. I zap right over to the FTD Flowers store (Figure 7-2). My mom loves flowers, so I order a bouquet for her, using my newly acquired MasterCard. Mom should get them tomorrow.

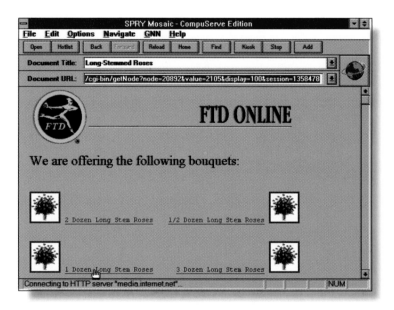

Figure 7-2
FTD flowers on-line store

—**9:10 a.m.** I access headline news to get a quick overview of current events and sports scores. Our rivals on the gridiron got trounced, so it looks like our team will make it to the semi finals.

—**9:30 a.m.** I want to see if anyone in the Bikes discussion group replied to my message about the best tires to use for riding in snow. A **discussion group** is an on-line forum for discussing issues with a group of people. I've participated in on-line discussion groups on basketball, skydiving, Star Trek, and fitness, to name a few.

Now I'm really into mountain bikes, and I get a lot of useful information from the Bikes discussion group. I entered my question about snow tires three days ago, so someone should have replied. Let's see.

My question seems to have opened the floodgates to a lengthy discussion of the dangers of riding in the snow. Well, some of us can't afford a car. O.K. Here's a message about tires. It looks like the tires I have are about the best for winter riding. Good. I don't have to invest in new tires.

—**10:00 a.m.** I log into another discussion group on elementary school education. It's my major and I think its a good idea to keep informed of innovations in my field. Most of the participants are university professors. I don't usually post any messages; I just *lurk*—that's the term for people who watch discussions, but don't participate. I might participate more when I feel more knowledgeable. I glance at the clock. I'm late for my 10:00 class. Time to log out. I'll come back later.

—**1:00 p.m.** My friend Coreen has a computer in her dorm room; but when she runs some multimedia software, Windows freezes up. She thinks something must be wrong with her CD-ROM drive. Most computer hardware manufacturers have technical support information on line, so we go to the lab and log in. We find information about Coreen's CD-ROM drive. It appears that the trouble she has with multimedia software is caused by her video driver software, not the CD-ROM.

We hop over to the on-line site for ATI, the manufacturer for Coreen's video card, and we think we've found a solution.

To fix the problem with Coreen's computer, she needs to install updated driver software for her video card. ATI allows us to legally download a copy of the software. **Download** means electronically transporting a file from a host computer to a local computer. We download the updated driver software from the manufacturer's site and store it on a floppy disk. Coreen can take the disk to her dorm room and install the updated driver on her computer.

While we're on-line, Coreen wants to get the newest dungeon levels for her Doom adventure game. Unfortunately this popular site is busy, so we decide to try another time.

—**1:15 p.m.** Coreen leaves, but I need some information for a paper I'm writing on alternative music. My first stop on-line is at the Library of Congress (Figure 7-3). I look through their card catalog but I can't read the books on-line. I jot down four references. After logging out of the Library of Congress, I connect to our campus library to see if we have these books. We have three of the four books. I can probably get the fourth book through interlibrary loan.

Figure 7-3
Accessing the Library of Congress card catalog

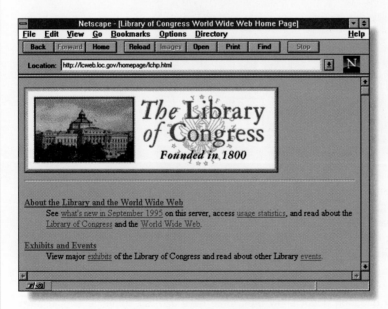

—**1:30 p.m.** I look for more on-line information on alternative music. My favorite index to information is at the "Yahoo" site. I log into Yahoo and quickly find a list of alternative music information, including the Indie List Digest, an on-line magazine called a *zine* (Figure 7-4). I browse through the zine and print out a few particularly interesting pages.

Figure 7-4
Using Yahoo to locate information on alternative music

I notice a new music video by my favorite hip hop group. I put on earphones so the sound track doesn't disturb other students in the lab. I watch the 30-second video clip. Pretty cool.

—**2:00 p.m.** I see it's 2:00. Science fiction author Ray Bradbury is hosting a chat session on another part of the "net." I tune in. In a **chat session** many people participate in an on-line discussion by typing in their comments. As soon as a participant presses the Enter key, his or her comment is displayed on the chat screen. Other participants can respond, and their responses will also immediately appear on the screen, creating a continuous dialog.

In this chat session, Ray Bradbury answers questions about how science fiction has changed in the last 20 years. Interesting stuff.

—**2:30 p.m.** Time flies when I'm on-line. I've got to log off so I can get those alternative music references from the library before my 3:00 class.

Quick Check

1 The term _____ was originally coined by science fiction writer William Gibson to refer to a computer-generated reality that people could experience by connecting their brain to a computer network.

2 The _____ is a collection of local, regional, and national computer networks that are linked together to exchange data and distribute processing tasks.

3 A(n) _____ charges its subscribers a fee to access information.

4 A(n) _____ is an on-line discussion in which participants post a question or comment, then log in later after other participants have had a chance to respond.

5 When you participate in a(n) _____, all the participants can view your comments as soon as you press the Enter key.

6 The process of transferring files containing text, graphics, music, or video clips from a remote computer to your computer is called _____.

7.2

Commercial Information Services

Figure 7-5
A basic model
of a commercial
information system

The concept of a commercial information service is relatively easy to grasp, so it's a good place to begin before tackling the complexities of the Internet. The first commercial information services provided access to information stored on a mainframe host computer. Using a modem, subscribers could dial into the service's mainframe using terminal emulation software. Once connected, subscribers could view data, run programs, and download files. An important characteristic of commercial information services is that even today they are based on a model in which many computers use terminal emulation software to access a remote host computer (Figure 7-5).

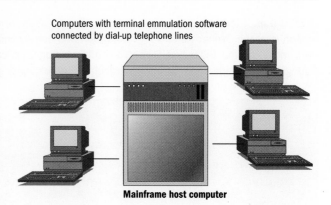

Computers with terminal emmulation software connected by dial-up telephone lines

Mainframe host computer

Commercial Service Providers

What are the major commercial information service providers?

Four of the largest commercial information services are America Online, CompuServe, Microsoft Network, and Prodigy. Each service has about two million subscribers. Study Figure 7-6 to get an idea of the services offered by the "Big Four" service providers.

Figure 7-6
The "Big Four"
service providers

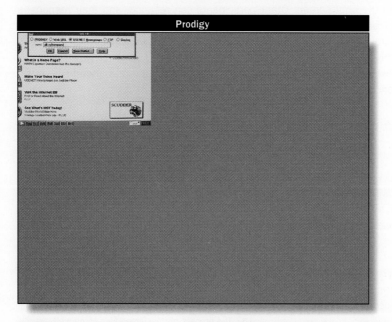

Prodigy. Established in 1990 as a joint venture between IBM and Sears Roebuck & Co., Prodigy is the most family-oriented of the "Big Four" on-line services. It rigorously maintains only G-rated material in all its data. Prodigy claims to have more female subscribers than other services. It pioneered a homework helper for school children and also offers an on-line version of Sesame Street where children can interact with Big Bird to learn their ABCs. For adults Prodigy provides the latest news stories, sports scores, movie reviews, and *Consumer Reports* articles. Prodigy also provides electronic mail, Eaasy Sabre travel reservations, Fodor's on-line travel guide, on-line shopping, current news, encyclopedia, financial information, and discussion groups. Links to many Internet services are also available. Prodigy has an easy-to-use graphical interface. A unique feature of Prodigy—and a feature that you might not like—is that advertisements pop up on your screen from time to time.

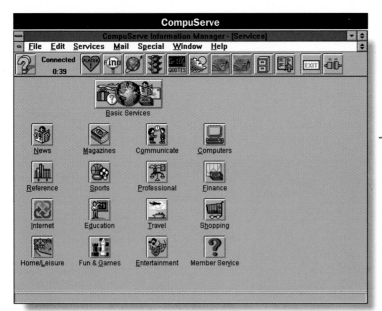

► **Figure 7-6**
The "Big Four"
service providers
(continued)

CompuServe. Established in 1979, CompuServe is the oldest of the services. It originally catered to business users, but now appeals to a very broad audience. For excellent news coverage, financial information, and computer technical support, CompuServe is one of the best information services. CompuServe electronic mail is easy to use, and its discussion groups cover almost every conceivable topic. For travelers, CompuServe services include Eaasy Sabre travel reservations, the Zagat restaurant Survey, and State Department travel briefings. Of interest to entrepreneurs are Standard and Poor's Company

Information, Business Demographics, Entrepreneurs' Small Business Forum, and Citibank's Global Report. For entertainment, you can read Roger Ebert's movie reviews, or select from over 18 single and multiplayer games. Shop on-line at Electronic Mall stores such as JCPenney, Land's End, Hammacher Schlemmer, and Barnes & Noble. Microsoft, IBM, Apple, Novell, and many other computer companies have active forums and technical support on CompuServe. You will find on-line versions of computer publications such as *Dr. Dobbs Journal, PC World, PC Week, and MacWeek.*

The CompuServe user interface reflects the legacy of command line user interfaces. The standard way to navigate CompuServe is to use menus and commands such as GO NEWS or GO WEATHER. The advantage of this user interface is that CompuServe can be accessed by virtually any type of computer with standard communication software. Special software from CompuServe is required only if you want to use Windows or Macintosh-style menus instead of non-graphical menus and GO commands.

America Online. Often abbreviated as AOL, America Online was established in 1985. AOL has a reputation as the flashiest of the commercial information services. It pioneered celebrity chat sessions—the rock band Depeche Mode went on-line to interact with fans. AOL also provides access to MTV Online and has excellent news coverage. On AOL you'll find the top news stories from the *New York Times*, the *Chicago Tribune*,

and *Time* Magazine. You'll also find automotive tips in the on-line version of *Car & Driver* magazine, computer product reviews from *PC World* magazine, transcripts of C-Span broadcasts, and articles from *Atlantic Monthly* magazine. AOL's Center Stage features a schedule of dates when you can chat on-line with celebrities including well-known actors, authors, musicians, entrepreneurs, and athletes. For the young crowd,

the Academic Assistance center provides elementary school students with a forum where their questions are answered by teachers, educators, and experts. *Comptons Encyclopedia* is on-line as a resource for school reports. For fun, AOL offers a photo tour of Walt Disney World, and kids' clubs for young astronomers, environmentalists, and Star Trek fans. AOL's graphical user interface makes navigation easy.

Figure 7-6
The "Big Four"
service providers
(continued)

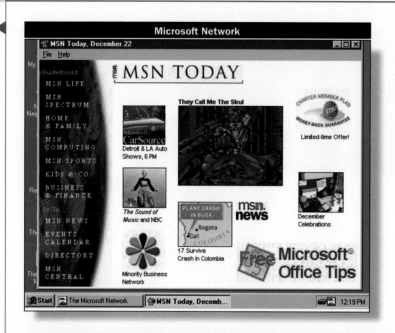

Microsoft Network. Founded in 1995, Microsoft Network (often abbreviated MSN) is the newest giant in the commercial information service industry. Industry watchers attribute its rapidly growing popularity to the fact that software for the Microsoft Network is included with Windows 95. MSN provides e-mail, discussion groups, chat rooms, games, download service, and access to the Internet. The core clientele of MSN is young professionals with a strong interest in computers and technology. Microsoft provides technical support for many of its software products and is expanding its technical offerings in an attempt to match CompuServe's excellent technical support services.

On-line Services

Why would I want to subscribe to a commercial information service?

The type and variety of services offered by a commercial information service depend on the size of the service, but generally include electronic mail, discussion groups, chat sessions, downloads, computer technical support, on-line shopping, reference information, government documents, educational opportunities, interactive games, and connections to other commercial information services, including the Internet.

If you have free access to the Internet provided by your school, you might not want to pay for a subscription to a commercial information service. However, many people do not have free Internet access, but would still like to send and receive e-mail, participate in on-line discussions, shop on-line, and have access to on-line information. For these people, a commercial information service might be the right choice.

Fees

Is it expensive to use a commercial information service?

Use Project 6 to gather current rate information since the rates charged by commercial information services change frequently.

It is easy to accumulate large bills for your on-line activities. Many subscribers lose track of time while they are in the middle of an on-line project and forget that the meter is running. Some commercial information services have fairly complex rate structures; so understanding these rates will help you stay within your budget.

Most commercial information services have a number of **basic services** included in a monthly flat fee. Monthly fees are typically about $10. Basic services usually include access to current news reports, games, discussion groups, on-line shopping, and electronic mail. Even if you do not use the service during a month, you are billed the monthly flat fee. Many services limit the number of hours per month covered by the flat fee. For example, you might be limited to five hours a month. Additional hours cost extra.

You might be charged additional fees, called **surcharges**, for premium services. A **premium service** is information that has been designated as more valuable by the commercial information service. More valuable often means that customers will pay extra for this service. For example, many business-related services such as airline reservations, up-to-the-minute stock reports, and legal searches are often premium services.

Premium service billing depends on what type of information you are accessing. You could be billed per item of information, per report, per search, or per hour. For example, on CompuServe you are billed 1.5 cents for each stock quote, $5 for a money market report, $9 for a database search, and $28 an hour for access to the Airline Guides Travel Service.

Connect time refers to the number of minutes your computer is connected to the service. Connect time charges vary depending on the time of day and the speed of your modem connection. For example, between 8:00 a.m. and 5:00 p.m. the connect time rate might be $10 per hour, while the rate after 5:00 p.m. is only $6. Slower modem speeds have lower connect time charges.

Subscribing to a Commercial Information Service

How do I subscribe?

Even if you currently have free Internet access, when you graduate you might want to subscribe to a commercial information service. Or, your parents might ask you to help them get on-line. Let's walk through the steps you would take to subscribe to a commercial information service.

1. Obtain a startup kit. To subscribe to a commercial information service, you should first request the service's startup kit for the operating system you use. The startup kit typically contains disks with the service's communication software, a user manual, and a temporary user ID and password, as shown in Figure 7-7.

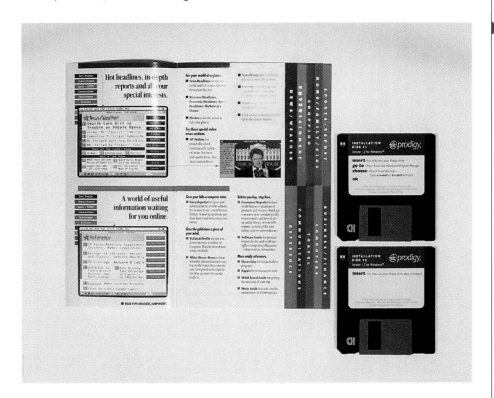

Figure 7-7
Prodigy
startup kit

You can request the startup kit by telephone, fax, or mail. Kits are also available at computer stores and packaged in computer magazines. Most kits are free and include some free access time on-line.

2. **Make sure your computer has a modem.** In addition to the startup kit, you will need a modem. The modem connects your computer to your telephone line, which is the communication link between your computer and the on-line service. A fast modem is an advantage for quickly navigating through on-line menus and downloading files.

3. **Install communications software provided in the startup kit.** When you receive the startup kit, you must install the communications software on your computer. Once installed, you can use the software to begin the subscription process.

4. **Select a local access number.** A **local access number** is a telephone number in your local area code that your modem can dial to connect with the on-line service. A list of these numbers is already programmed into the software provided with the startup kit. By entering your area code and city, you will be able to see a list of numbers to choose from. After you select a number, the software stores it so you can use it whenever you dial in.

5. **Dial in.** Follow the on-screen prompts to have your modem dial the local access number and connect to the on-line service.

6. **Log in.** You will be prompted for a user ID and password. A temporary user ID and password is supplied in the startup kit. You can change the password later to one that is more personalized.

7. **Provide information for your subscription.** The on-line subscription process usually continues with a request for your name and address. Enter the information as requested.

8. **Select a billing option.** If you want your monthly fees billed to your credit card, you must provide your card number. If you want to pay by check, you must supply your checking account number.

9. **Choose your unique user ID and password.** Most services allow you to select your own user ID and password. You should make a note of them and put the note in a secure place. Many people don't use their on-line service regularly and consequently forget their user ID and password. When you have selected a user ID and password, the subscription process is complete and you're on line.

Quick Check

1. Commercial information services are based on a model in which a number of _____ use terminal emulation software to access a(n) _____ computer.

2. What are the four largest commercial information services?

3. On most commercial information services, _____ include services such as electronic mail, current news, games, discussion groups, and on-line shopping.

4. _____ refers to the length of time your computer is attached to a commercial information service.

5. When deciding to subscribe to an information service, it is important to make sure it has a(n) _____ so you don't have to make long distance calls to connect.

The Internet

The history of the Internet begins in 1957 when the Soviet Union launched Sputnik, the first artificial satellite. In response to this display of Soviet technical expertise, the U.S. government resolved to improve its science and technical infrastructure. One of the resulting initiatives was the Advanced Research Projects Agency (ARPA), created by the Department of Defense. ARPA swung into action with a project to design a computer system that could survive nuclear attack. The plan was to construct a network of geographically dispersed computers that would continue to function even if one of the computers on the network was destroyed. In 1969 four computer networks were connected to each other and called ARPANET. Connecting two or more networks creates an **internetwork** or **internet**, so ARPANET was one of the first examples of an internet (with a lowercase i). Gradually, more and more networks were connected to the ARPANET, and it became known as the Internet (with an uppercase I). So, the Internet is essentially a network of networks, as shown in Figure 7-8.

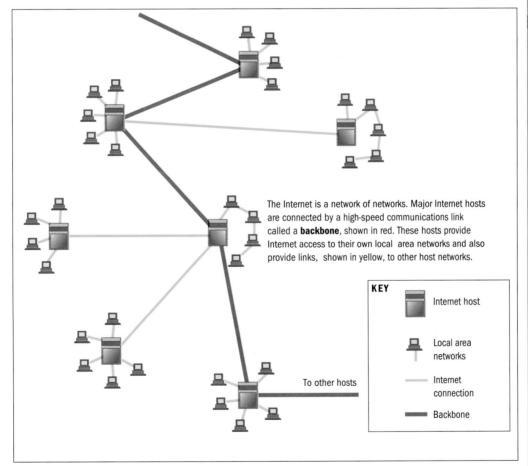

The Internet is a network of networks. Major Internet hosts are connected by a high-speed communications link called a **backbone**, shown in red. These hosts provide Internet access to their own local area networks and also provide links, shown in yellow, to other host networks.

To other hosts

KEY

▣	Internet host
💻	Local area networks
—	Internet connection
▬	Backbone

Figure 7-8
The Internet is a network of networks

Compare the structure of the Internet to the much simpler structure of a commercial information service illustrated in Figure 7-5.

Today, the Internet is the largest and most widely used network in the world, connecting over 20,000 computer networks, in more than 130 countries, with an estimated 30 million users.

Each of the networks included in the Internet is referred to as a **site**. The graph in Figure 7-9 shows the incredible increase in the number of Internet sites over the past 30 years.

Figure 7-9
Internet growth

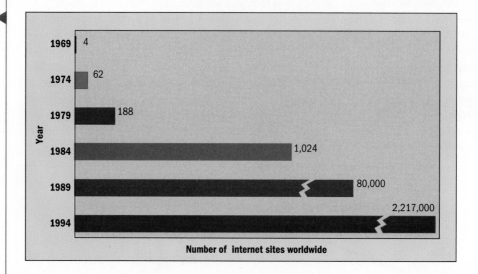

The Internet is unique in many ways—not just because of its incredible size. Although each of the smaller networks connected to the Internet is owned by an individual, a corporation, an educational institution, or a government agency, no one "owns" the Internet. This accounts for the chaotic organization of information on the Internet. On the Internet, no one screens the data, so it is easy to get "junk" along with quality information. Further, no one decides where information is stored on the Internet—you will rarely find all the data pertaining to a topic stored in one location.

With more than 2 milliion sites computers providing information on the Internet and no centralized directory of services, even experienced users have a hard time navigating through the seemingly endless miles of information. Is the information on the Internet worth the trouble it takes to find it? To answer this question let's look at what you can find on the Internet and show you some of the tools you can use to facilitate your search.

Internet Services and Access Software

What kind of information can I find on the Internet?

Imagine a commercial information service such as CompuServe, but a thousand times larger and without a main menu. That's the Internet. Many services provided by CompuServe, America Online, Microsoft Network, and Prodigy are also available on the Internet. Like commercial information services, the Internet offers electronic mail, discussion groups, government documents, computer technical support, on-line shopping, interactive entertainment, and downloadable software, music, graphics, and video clips. The Internet has more information than commercial information services. On the Internet there are *thousands* of discussion groups and *millions* of documents.

Compared to a commercial information service, the Internet requires a wider variety of software to access information. When you are a Prodigy subscriber, for example, you use only one type of software to access Prodigy's on-line services—the communications software supplied in Prodigy's startup kit lets you send mail, participate in discussion groups, read the news, download software, and so on. Using Internet services is not so simple. Many different software packages are available to help you access different types of information and services, such as writing e-mail, participating in discussion groups, looking for information, accessing library card catalogs, and so on.

The trend today is to use a single software package to access most Internet services. However, it is still handy to understand the different types of software available to access information and services. With this understanding you will be able to decide which software you need to access the information *you* want on the Internet.

On-line Activity	Service	Software Tool
Send electronic mail	E-mail	Lotus cc:Mail, Eudora, Pegasus, Microsoft Mail, and other mail client software
Find and view information on a wide variety of topics	World Wide Web	Web browser such as Netscape, Mosaic, Lynx, Winweb
Download files of text, graphics, music, animations, and videos	FTP	FTP software, Netscape, Mosaic, Gopher client software
Run programs on a remote host, play interactive games, use remote library card catalogs	Telnet	Telnet client software
Search for documents, databases, library card catalogs	Gopher	Gopher client software, Netscape, Mosaic
Participate in on-line discussion groups	Usenet	Newsreader software

Figure 7-10
Internet retrieval and communications software

In the rest of Section 7.3 you will learn about Internet information retrieval and communications software. Use Figure 7-10 as a guide.

Internet E-mail

Is Internet e-mail different than e-mail on a LAN?

Internet e-mail is essentially the same as e-mail on a LAN or commercial information service. Learning about Internet e-mail has two advantages. First, you learn how to send mail to virtually anyone who has an e-mail box anywhere in the world. Second, you get a better idea of how the Internet works.

To send mail over the Internet, you must have access to e-mail on a computer that is connected to the Internet. When you want to send mail over the Internet, you simply compose the message on your computer using your e-mail client software, address the message, and tell your e-mail system to send it. Each person with access to Internet e-mail has a unique Internet address. An Internet e-mail address looks something like this:

president@whitehouse.gov

The first part of the address, *president*, is the **user ID**—in this case the user ID of the President of the United States. The **@ sign** separates the user ID from the machine name. A **machine name** is the unique set of numbers and letters that identifies each computer connected to the Internet. In the example, the machine name is *whitehouse*, a computer in Washington D.C. that handles the White House Internet connection. A period separates the machine name from the domain name. The **domain name** groups the computers on the Internet into the following categories: com (commercial), edu (educational), gov (nonmilitary government), mil (military), org (other organizations), or net (network resources). In the address *president@whitehouse.gov*, the domain is *gov*, indicating that the *whitehouse* computer is maintained by a non-military agency of the government.

When you send e-mail, your local mail server software examines the machine name in the address of each message. Those messages addressed to users on the local machine are delivered by the local mail server. Messages addressed to users on other machines are sent out over the Internet.

A mail client is the software you use to compose and send e-mail. The messages you create with one mail client can be read by someone who uses a different mail client.

What happens to e-mail when it leaves your local network? How does the message travel from your local network to the recipient? The answers to these questions reveal how the Internet works.

Recall that the Internet is a collection of networks. With over 20,000 of these networks, it would be impossible for your school to have direct links to every network on the Internet. So, e-mail is rarely sent directly from your network to the recipient's network. Instead, an e-mail message is handed from one network to another until it reaches its destination. Figure 7-11 shows how the Internet routes e-mail from a student at the University of Alaska to a student at the University of the Virgin Islands.

Figure 7-11
Internet e-mail routes

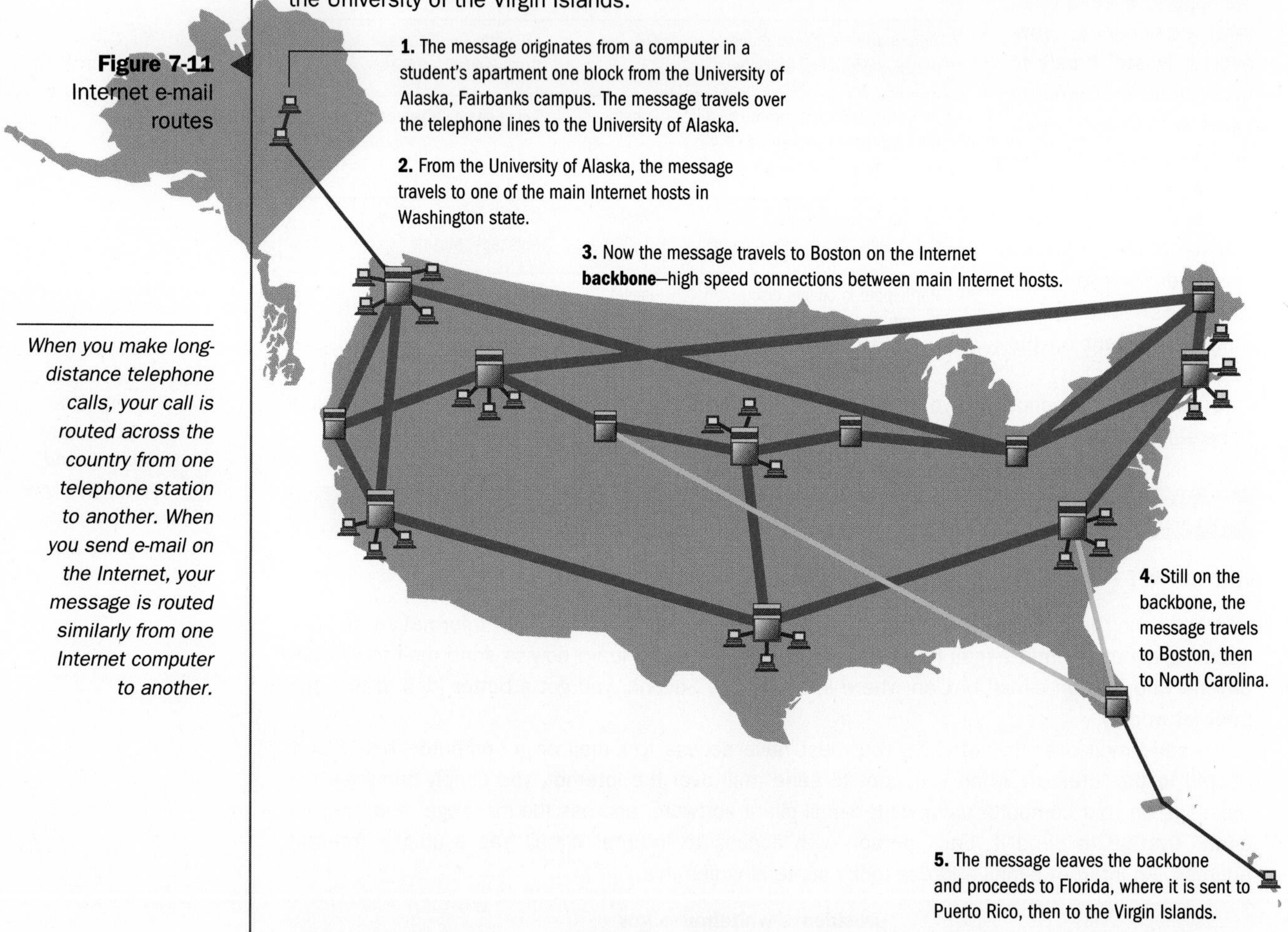

When you make long-distance telephone calls, your call is routed across the country from one telephone station to another. When you send e-mail on the Internet, your message is routed similarly from one Internet computer to another.

1. The message originates from a computer in a student's apartment one block from the University of Alaska, Fairbanks campus. The message travels over the telephone lines to the University of Alaska.

2. From the University of Alaska, the message travels to one of the main Internet hosts in Washington state.

3. Now the message travels to Boston on the Internet **backbone**—high speed connections between main Internet hosts.

4. Still on the backbone, the message travels to Boston, then to North Carolina.

5. The message leaves the backbone and proceeds to Florida, where it is sent to Puerto Rico, then to the Virgin Islands.

The World Wide Web

What's the easiest way to access information on the Internet?

Currently, some of the best organized and most accessible information on the Internet is available through a service called the **World Wide Web**, abbreviated WWW, but often referred to as "the Web." The information available on the World Wide Web covers almost every conceivable topic, and the information is often presented in multimedia format with graphics, music, or video clips. You can use the World Wide Web to take a tour of the Louvre Museum in Paris, view the Library of Congress African-American collections, read a Stephen King novella (complete with sound effects), check out the latest tunes on the Underground Music Archive, create a sports newsletter that will report on your favorite teams, purchase merchandise from the Worldwide Marketplace, and more.

The official description of the World Wide Web is a "wide-area hypermedia information retrieval initiative aiming to give universal access to a large universe of documents." The World Wide Web consists of pages, called **Web pages**, that contain information on a particular topic. In addition to topic information, a Web page might also include one or more links to other Web pages. **Links** are pointers to other Web pages that make it easy to follow a thread of related information, even if the pages are stored on computers located in different countries. Figure 7-12 shows a conceptual model of how the World Wide Web works.

If you want a quick review of hypertext and hypermedia, reread Section 2.4 in Chapter 2.

Figure 7-12
How the World Wide Web works

1. Honolulu Community College (HCC), maintains an exhibit containing images, video clips, narration, and text about dinosaurs. Each image, video and document is a separate **page**, stored as a file on the HCC computer. You can jump from one page to another at HCC. For example, you can begin at the introductory screen, called a **home page**.

2. From the home page, you can jump to a page about iguanadons.

3. From this page you can jump to a page that contains a movie.

4. HCC also has links to other web sites with dinosaur information. You can jump to one of these sites by clicking the underlined text.

Lab

The Internet: World Wide Web

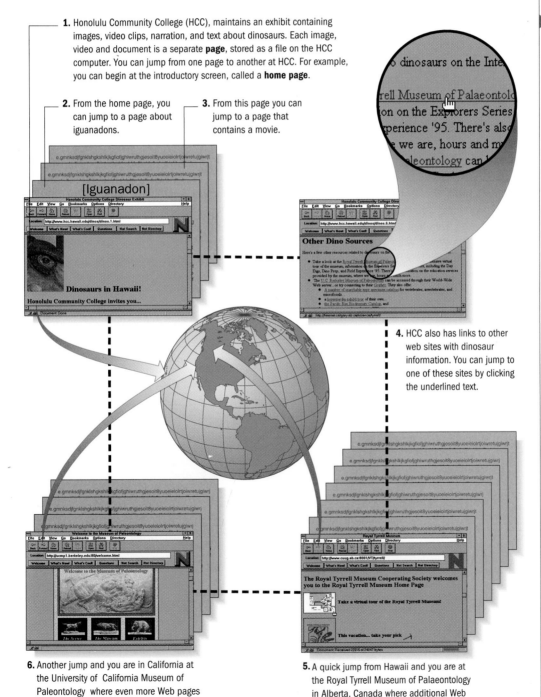

6. Another jump and you are in California at the University of California Museum of Paleontology where even more Web pages on dinosaurs are stored.

5. A quick jump from Hawaii and you are at the Royal Tyrrell Museum of Palaeontology in Alberta, Canada where additional Web pages on dinosaurs are stored.

At many schools students create their own Web pages, using an HTML editor. In Project 10 at the end of this chapter you will create your own Web page.

To offer World Wide Web service, an Internet site must set up Web server software and format its information into pages using a Hypertext Markup Language (HTML) editor. An **HTML editor** creates links between pages, displays links in boldface underlined text, and positions graphics.

Each Web page has a unique address called a **uniform resource locator (URL)**. To access a Web page, you must either follow a link or type a URL. You can find listings of Web page URLs in books, such as *Walking the World Wide Web*, and in Internet magazines, such as *Wired*. You can also access an on-line directory of Web pages using the URL *http://www.yahoo.com*.

A URL is similar to an e-mail address. For example, Honolulu Community College is the Web site for a dinosaur exhibit. The URL for this exhibit is:

http://www.hcc.hawaii.edu/dinos.1.html

And that's just a short URL! Let's look at each part of the URL to see what it means.

http:// Web pages are sent between sites using HyperText Transfer Protocol (HTTP). The *http://* at the beginning of the dinosaur URL indicates that this is a Web page. Whenever you see a long string of characters that begins with http://, you know it is referring to a Web page.

www.hcc.hawaii.edu Some elements of this URL might look familiar—*www.hcc.hawaii.edu* is the Internet address for the World Wide Web server at Honolulu Community College. Many Web server addresses begin with *www*. The *.edu* indicates this is a site maintained by an educational institution.

/dinos.1.html The last part of the URL, */dinos.1.html*, refers specifically to the dinosaur Web page. Honolulu Community College might have other Web pages, such as *dinos.2.html* and *dinos.3.html*. This last part of the URL differentiates among the pages at a particular site.

To access World Wide Web information, you need a computer with Internet access and software called a Web browser. A **Web browser** displays the text, graphics, and links for a Web page. It also helps you follow the links from one Web page to another. Popular Web browser software packages are Netscape, Mosaic, Lynx, and Cello. Figure 7-13 shows you how to use a Web browser to access information on the World Wide Web.

The Resources section at the end of this chapter contains more sources for WWW URLs.

Figure 7-13
Using the Netscape Web browser

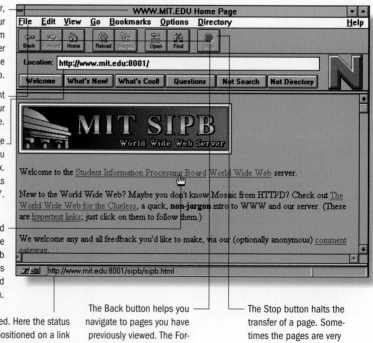

When you start the Web browser, it displays the home page of your Internet service provider. From this page you can jump to other Web pages anywhere on the World Wide Web.

You can use the File menu to print out pages or save them on your local hard disk drive.

If you know the URL of the page to which you want to jump, you can type the URL in this box. All World Wide Web URLs begin with **http://**.

You can jump to linked documents by clicking any of the underlined text. On most Web browsers, the pointer changes to a hand when it is positioned over a text or graphical link.

The status bar keeps you updated. Here the status bar shows that the pointer is positioned on a link to Student Information Processing located at **http://www.mit.edu.8001/sipb/sipb.html**. If you select this link, the status bar shows how long it will take for the page to be transmitted.

The Back button helps you navigate to pages you have previously viewed. The Forward button shows you the next page in the sequence.

The Stop button halts the transfer of a page. Sometimes the pages are very large, and you won't want to wait for them.

FTP

Can I download software and graphics files from the Internet?

Named after the yellow pages you use in the telephone book to find products and services, *The Internet Yellow Pages* is one of many published guides to find information on the Internet. Suppose you're interested in some new productivity software. *The Internet Yellow Pages* lists many Internet sites where you can obtain software, such as the Garbo Internet site, described as: "Software, software, software! This anonymous FTP site has gobs of software for DOS, Windows, Macs, and UNIX machines."

FTP (File Transfer Protocol) is a method for transferring files from one computer to another. The files can contain software, text, graphics, sound, animation, or video clips. Usually, the transfer takes place from a host computer to your microcomputer. If you want to download files from the Internet, you will generally use FTP software. **FTP software** connects your computer to a remote host computer called an **FTP server**. Your computer then essentially becomes a part of the FTP server's network.

Once your computer is connected to a remote host, you can look through the directory of files stored on the host. When you find the file you want, you can instruct the FTP software to transmit a copy of the file to your computer's hard disk. If the file you transferred contains software, you can install the software and run it on your computer. If the file you download contains data, you can edit that data using the appropriate type of word processing, graphics, or spreadsheet application software.

On most hosts, you must log in before you can access the files stored on its disks. But what if you don't have an account on the remote host? You can't expect to have an account on every Internet host, so you log in as an *anonymous* user. **Anonymous FTP** means that anyone without an account on a host computer can use FTP software to log in using the user ID "anonymous."

Not every Internet host accepts anonymous logins. You can find lists of those that do in *The Internet Yellow Pages* and similar Internet directories. Alternatively, you can find FTP sites using an on-line Internet service called Archie. **Archie** searches a special FTP database to find all the hosts that contain the file you need and that allow anonymous FTP.

For security reasons, an anonymous user is rarely given access to all the data on a remote host. Anonymous users are given access only to those files available for downloading. Figure 7-14 shows an FTP session in which a user downloads a to-do list manager from the Garbo FTP server.

What is the difference between the World Wide Web and FTP? You access the World Wide Web to read Web pages and follow links to related information. FTP helps you download data and program files onto your hard disk, which you can later view, run, or edit using your application software.

1. The FTP software connects to the host **garbo.uwasa.fi** at the University of Vaasa, Finland. The host is an anonymous FTP server, so you are allowed to log into the computer as an anonymous user.

Figure 7-14
A typical
FTP session
(continued on next page)

Figure 7-14
A typical FTP
session
(continued)

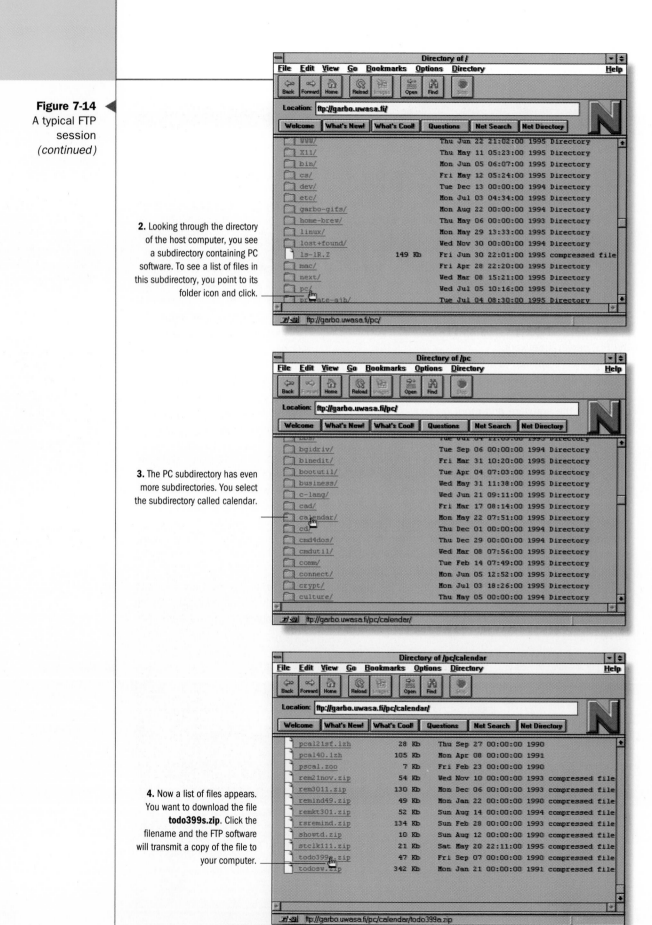

2. Looking through the directory of the host computer, you see a subdirectory containing PC software. To see a list of files in this subdirectory, you point to its folder icon and click.

3. The PC subdirectory has even more subdirectories. You select the subdirectory called calendar.

4. Now a list of files appears. You want to download the file **todo399s.zip**. Click the filename and the FTP software will transmit a copy of the file to your computer.

Telnet

Can I play interactive games with other Internet users?

Some Internet activities require you to run a program on a remote host. For example, you might want to run a program that lets you play backgammon with other players from around the country. Or, suppose you are visiting a friend at another school and you want to read the mail stored in your e-mail box on your own campus.

Telnet is an Internet service that establishes a connection between your computer and a remote host so you can use the processing power of a remote host to run software. You would need to run software on a remote host if the software was not written for the type of computer you have, if the software is too complex for your computer's processor, or if copyright restrictions prevent you from downloading the software.

To use Telnet, your computer must have Telnet software. When you use **Telnet software**, your computer is connected to the remote host and essentially becomes part of the host's network. Once the Telnet connection is established, you can use the resources of the host computer to send mail, run programs, copy files, create files, and so forth.

A popular entertainment on the Internet is MUDing. A **MUD (Multiple User Dimension)** is a computer-generated environment in which you talk to other participants, solve puzzles, and explore computer-generated objects around you. A MUD is text-based—the computer provides you with narrative descriptions of the environment. A **MOO (Multi-user Object-Oriented)** is similar to a MUD, but uses graphics. MUDs and MOOs are often called virtual reality because the computer generates a virtual environment—one that does not exist. Although current MUDs and MOOs, like the one in Figure 7-15, are mostly used for entertainment, they could also be used for activities such as virtual business meetings, virtual classrooms, and virtual town forums.

When you use Telnet, your computer acts as a terminal for the remote host. You might want to review the relationship between terminals and mini/mainframe hosts in Section 1.2 of Chapter 1.

If you want to learn more about virtual reality, MUDs, and MOOs, try Project 7 at the end of this chapter.

Figure 7-15
A MOO

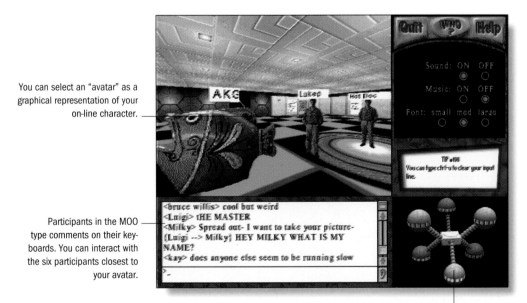

You can select an "avatar" as a graphical representation of your on-line character.

Participants in the MOO type comments on their keyboards. You can interact with the six participants closest to your avatar.

This map shows you different rooms you can explore. Your current location is the main room, indicated by the center box.

Gopher

What does a Gopher have to do with the Internet?

Gopher is a menu-driven Internet service that helps you locate information. The best analogy for Gopher is the directional signs used on roadways (see Figure 7-16).

Figure 7-16 ◄
The signs point
you in the right
direction

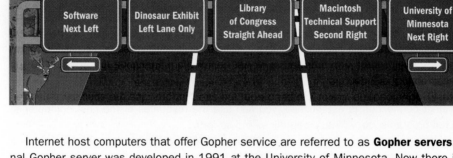

*How is Gopher differ-
ent from the World
Wide Web? Both
Gopher and WWW
help you locate infor-
mation by jumping
from one Internet site
to another. The World
Wide Web places the
links within docu-
ments. Gopher links
are not in the docu-
ments, but in the
menus that direct you
to the documents.*

Internet host computers that offer Gopher service are referred to as **Gopher servers**. The original Gopher server was developed in 1991 at the University of Minnesota. Now there is a world-wide network of linked Gopher servers, referred to as **Gopherspace**. Although it is a relatively new service on the Internet, Gopher will probably be replaced by the World Wide Web because the Web has a graphical user interface that is easier to use.

To use Gopher, you need Gopher software on your computer, and you need to connect to a Gopher server. Using Gopher is easy. The Gopher server shows you a menu of options, and you select the one you want. Many of the Gopher menu items are links to other Gopher sites.

As with Windows menus, Gopher menus use certain menu conventions to indicate what type of information a menu option points to. Figure 7-17 shows how these menu conventions appear in a typical Gopher session.

Figure 7-17 ◄
Menu conventions
in a typical Gopher
session

1. The Gopher client software connects you to the Gopher server you request—in this case the Gopher server at the University of Minnesota.

2. The Gopher menu displays a list of resources.

3. The folder icon in front of a menu option indicates that the option leads to another menu.

4. The binocular icon indicates that the menu option will lead to a screen that asks for search specifications, instead of scrolling through the menus. For example, you could search for "Africa."

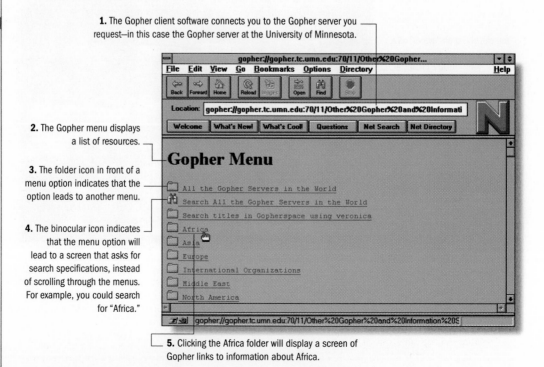

5. Clicking the Africa folder will display a screen of Gopher links to information about Africa.

6. A search for "Africa" results in a menu of Internet resources related to Africa. Each of the folders on this menu represents a different Gopher server. You can select one of the Gopher servers to see what information it contains.

7. Click this reference to see information from the ANC.

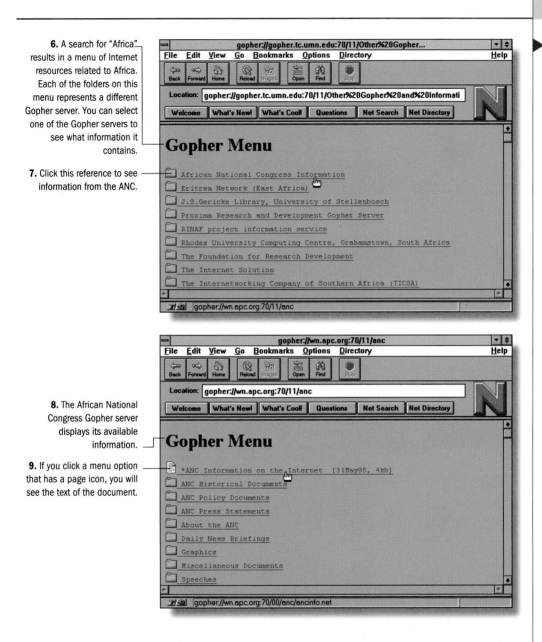

Figure 7-17
Menu conventions in a typical Gopher session *(continued)*

8. The African National Congress Gopher server displays its available information.

9. If you click a menu option that has a page icon, you will see the text of the document.

Usenet Newsgroups

Can the Internet help me if I don't have a lot of time to spend looking for information, but I want to keep current on certain topics?

Usenet is an Internet service that maintains thousands of discussion groups involving millions of people from all over the world. Each discussion group focuses on a particular topic such as music, business, computers, education, civil rights, and so on. Many of these groups foster scholarly discussion on topics, with postings contributed by reliable researchers and subject-area experts. Other discussion groups are more informal and the information posted might not be as reliable.

Usenet is often referred to as **the News** or **Netnews** because it was originally used as a sort of bulletin board for posting messages and news items. For the same reason, Usenet discussion groups are called **newsgroups** and user comments in the discussion are called **articles** or **postings**. Today, however, newsgroups carry little of what we think of as headline news. Instead, they carry conversations among the members of a group.

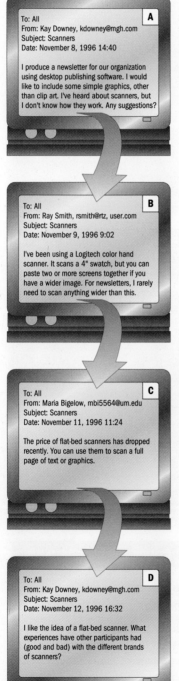

Figure 7-18
A Usenet thread

To: All
From: Kay Downey, kdowney@mgh.com
Subject: Scanners
Date: November 8, 1996 14:40

I produce a newsletter for our organization using desktop publishing software. I would like to include some simple graphics, other than clip art. I've heard about scanners, but I don't know how they work. Any suggestions?

A

Kay Downey initiates a discussion about scanners on November 8. Her question is added to the newsgroup transcript.

To: All
From: Ray Smith, rsmith@rtz, user.com
Subject: Scanners
Date: November 9, 1996 9:02

I've been using a Logitech color hand scanner. It scans a 4" swatch, but you can paste two or more screens together if you have a wider image. For newsletters, I rarely need to scan anything wider than this.

B

As other users log into the newsgroup, they read Kay's posting. They can post a reply at any time. Here, participants Smith and Bigelow post replies on November 9 and November 11.

To: All
From: Maria Bigelow, mbi5564@um.edu
Subject: Scanners
Date: November 11, 1996 11:24

The price of flat-bed scanners has dropped recently. You can use them to scan a full page of text or graphics.

C

To: All
From: Kay Downey, kdowney@mgh.com
Subject: Scanners
Date: November 12, 1996 16:32

I like the idea of a flat-bed scanner. What experiences have other participants had (good and bad) with the different brands of scanners?

D

On November 12, Kay logs into the newsgroup again and reads the transcripts for November 9, 10, 11. She sees the replies from Smith and Bigelow, then continues the thread by posting another question.

The chat session you read about at the beginning of this chapter is synchronous, *because all the participants were on-line at the same time. Discussion groups are* asynchronous *because the participants do not need to be on-line at the same time.*

Usenet conversations are **asynchronous**—they do not take place in real time. For example, suppose Shirley is a member of a marine biology discussion group. Her research on water quality in coral reefs has turned up some rather starting results, and she would like to know if other researchers have found anything similar. She posts her research results on Monday along with a request for comments and additional data. Over the next several days, other members of the group respond. Later in the week when Shirley checks the newsgroup, she reads these responses. The handy thing about Usenet is that you can tune in when you have time, read all the postings since you last logged in, and post your response.

Some discussion groups are moderated, others are not. A **discussion group moderator** screens contributions to the discussion. This might involve eliminating postings that were mistakenly sent to the discussion group, routing personal messages to individual subscribers, and ensuring that the context of postings do not violate the ethical or editorial code of the organization that provides the site for the discussion group.

Sometimes a newsgroup has several conversations going at the same time. The sequence of comments for a particular conversation is called a **thread**. Some threads continue for years. Others are very short. In Figure 7-18 you can read the transcript of a Usenet thread.

To read Usenet articles, you use newsreader software. **Newsreader software** keeps track of the newsgroups you use and provides the commands you use to read articles, follow threads, and post replies.

When you participate in newsgroups, you should be aware of some unwritten rules, referred to as **netiquette**—a term made from combining the words *net* and *etiquette*.

Put your best foot forward. When you post a message to a newsgroup, your message is a reflection of you and your organization. Try to use correct grammar and spelling.

Use conventions to avoid misunderstandings. When you post a message that contains sarcasm or a joke, some readers might misunderstand your point. Identify the jokes and sarcasm in your postings using smileys like :-) for jokes and ;-) for sarcasm. Don't capitalize your entire message—your on-line readers will interpret this as shouting.

Help readers follow the thread. When you respond to a posting, provide the context for your response by including a portion of the original message in your reply.

Be brief. Keep your postings short and to the point.

Avoid flames. A **flame** is a nasty or insulting message posted to an Internet newsgroup or commercial information service discussion. If you reply to a flame with another flame, you could find yourself in the middle of a "flame war." Most on-line pros consider flame wars a waste of time. You can avoid these wars by ignoring flames that come your way. Also, when you post messages, choose your words carefully so you don't inadvertently offend other participants.

Read before you ask. Before you post questions to a newsgroup, take the time to understand the current threads and to read transcripts of previous discussions. Newsgroup participants do not like to answer the same questions repeatedly.

Personal messages belong on e-mail. If you have a personal message for one member of a newsgroup, use e-mail instead of posting it to the entire newsgroup. The other participants will thank you when they don't have to read these personal messages.

Quick Check

1. When you connect two or more networks, you form a(n) _____.

2. The _____ is the largest and most widely used network in the world.

3. Identify each part of the Internet address **coco@canine.com**.

4. Which Internet service would you use to access the URL *http://physics7.berkeley.edu/home.html?*

5. If you want to find information by making selections from a series of menus, you would use the Internet service known as _____.

6. If you want to download a file from an Internet host, but you don't have an account on that host, you can use an Internet service called _____.

7. To run a program on a remote host, you can use the Internet service called _____.

8. A(n) _____ is a computer-generated virtual reality in which you can explore graphical objects and interact with other participants.

9. The set of unwritten rules of proper behavior on the Internet is called _____.

User Focus:

Connecting to the Internet

7.4

If your school has Internet access, your Academic Computing department has installed the hardware and software you need to access the Internet from your school lab, and possibly from your dorm room. But what if you want to access the Internet from your computer at home? To access the Internet from your home computer, you must set up the necessary computer equipment, locate an Internet service provider, install the appropriate software on your computer, then dial in.

Set Up Equipment

What special equipment do I need to access the Internet?

The basic equipment for setting up on-line communications is a computer, a modem, and a telephone line. The equipment you use does not change the activities you can do on-line, but it can affect the speed at which you can accomplish these activities.

IBM-compatible computers, Macintoshes, and PowerPCs can all connect to on-line services. A fast computer such as a 133 MHz Pentium speeds up some activities such as viewing graphics on-line. However, the overall speed of on-line activities is limited by the speed of the host computer, the speed of your modem, and the speed of your communications link.

The speed of your computer is only one factor that affects the speed at which you can send or receive data on-line.

A modem converts the data from your computer into signals that can travel over telephone lines. It also translates arriving signals into data that your computer can store, manipulate, and display. A fast modem speeds the process of sending and receiving data, so a 28.8K bps modem provides you with faster on-line response than a 14.4K bps modem. Faster modems are more expensive—you should buy the fastest modem you can afford.

The telephone line that you use for voice communications is suitable for on-line activities as well. Corporations sometimes use faster communications links such as ISDN or T1. Your telephone line, though not the speediest communications link, is certainly the least expensive.

When you are using your telephone line for on-line activities, you can't simultaneously use it for voice calls; while you are on-line, people who call you will get a busy signal. If you pick up the telephone receiver to make an outgoing call while you are on-line, your on-line connection will terminate.

Locate an Internet Access Provider

Who will provide me with an Internet connection, and how much will it cost?

An **Internet access provider** supplies you with a user account on a host computer that has access to the Internet. When you connect your personal computer to the host computer using a modem and the appropriate software, you gain access to the Internet. Your school might provide Internet access for students and faculty who want to use the Internet from off campus. An Internet connection provided by an educational institution is typically free. Many commercial information services such as CompuServe, Prodigy, Microsoft Network, and America Online provide Internet access. Expect to pay additional monthly or connect time fees for this service.

Internet connections are also offered by some telephone companies, cable TV companies, and independent telecommunications firms. These firms charge between $20 and $30 per month for Internet access. Unlike commercial information services, they usually do not maintain their own on-line information, discussion groups, or downloadable software.

Install Communications Software

Where do I get the communications software I need?

Your Internet access provider should supply you with **Internet communications software** that allows your computer to transmit and receive data using Internet communications protocol. A **communications protocol** is a set of rules that ensures the orderly and accurate transmission and reception of data. An analogy in human communication is that during a conversation only one person speaks at a time. Communications protocols help computers recognize when a message starts and stops. They standardize which part of the transmission is an address and which is the message. They also help a computer recognize when a transmission error has occurred, so the data can be retransmitted.

All computers connected to the Internet must use a communications protocol called **TCP/IP (Transmission Control Protocol/Internet Protocol)**. Standard TCP/IP software handles Internet communication between computers that are directly cabled to a network. **SLIP (Serial Line Internet Protocol)** and **PPP (Point to Point Protocol)** are versions of TCP/IP designed to handle Internet communications for a computer that connects to the Internet using a modem. When you want to access the Internet from a computer using a modem, you must use PPP, SLIP, or other similar communications software. This is the communications software you receive from your Internet access provider.

In the past, luck played an important role in establishing successful computer communications. Today, the communications software supplied by most Internet access providers is self-configuring; in other words, the first time you run the software, it examines your computer system and automatically selects the appropriate software settings. You have to deal with technical specifications only if your computer equipment, modem, or telephone line are not standard.

Install Browsers and Other Software

How do I get the other software I need to access information and services on the Internet?

In addition to Internet communications software, you must have software that helps you access Internet information and services such as e-mail, the World Wide Web, and FTP. You will probably want to start with e-mail client software and a Web browser. This software is typically supplied by your Internet access provider. You can add additional software as you need it.

Some text, graphical, sound, and video information on the Internet is stored in special file formats. This information can be viewed only if you use special software, referred to as a **viewer**. You can usually download the viewer you need from the site that provides the specially formatted text, graphical, sound, or video file.

To install an e-mail client, Web browser, or viewer, follow the instructions that accompany the software. If you obtained the software on disk, open a file called "readme" on the disk for instructions. If you downloaded the software, you should find installation instructions at the on-line site.

You can refresh your memory about Internet software by referring back to Figure 7-10.

Dial In

After my hardware is set up and my software is installed, how do I dial in to the Internet?

Most Internet communications software is represented by an icon on your computer's desktop or start screen. You start the software by clicking this icon, and it automatically establishes a connection to the Internet. Figure 7-19 shows what happens when you dial in.

Figure 7-19
Dialing into the Internet

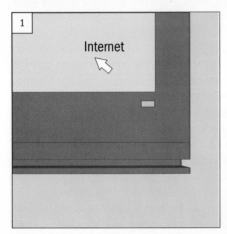

Click the Internet icon supplied by your Internet service provider.

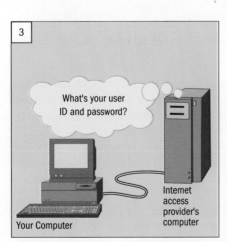

By clicking the Internet icon, you tell the computer to load your Internet communications client software. Your communications client will probably use SLIP or PPP to handle the TCP/IP protocols as your computer transmits and receives data through your modem.

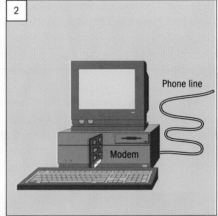

Your communications client dials into Internet service provider. Usually, your communication client has stored the telephone number, so you do not need to enter it each time you want to connect.

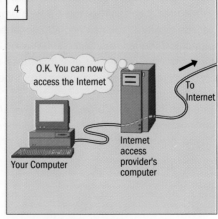

If your communications client has stored your user ID and password, it will automatically log you in. Some people prefer to enter their password manually for better security.

End Note

The information highway has received much publicity. Many people agree that such a vast information network has potential to improve the quality of our lives. It provides us with an opportunity to interact with people of diverse backgrounds, engage in life-long education, and enrich our knowledge of the global community.

Fifty years ago a new technology called television promised similar advantages. Today, many people believe that television has failed. They point to inane soap operas, an overabundance of graphic violence, the commercialization of gratuitous sex, and popularity of talk shows featuring bizarre human experiences.

Will the information highway also fail to fulfill its potential? The answer to this question is difficult to predict. The amount of information available on-line is growing. Much of this data is useful, but other information is of questionable value. On-line computer technical support helps thousands of people keep their computers operational, but who is helped by on-line instructions for manufacturing homemade bombs? Satellite photographs from NASA's on-line database contribute to our knowledge of the universe, but what is the contribution of graphical images of sexual exploitation? In many ways, the information highway is a reflection of the interests as well as the problems of our society. Its development is worth watching throughout your lifetime.

Review

1. Below each heading in this chapter, there is a question in italics. Look back through the chapter and answer each of these questions using your own words.

2. Think about the terms *information highway*, *cyberspace*, *Internet*, and *commercial information service*. Using your own words, write a definition of each. Make sure your definitions clearly explain the differences between these terms.

3. Make a list of the services offered by large commercial information services such as CompuServe.

4. List the steps for subscribing to a commercial information service.

5. Define the following terms:

    a. basic service

    b. premium service

    c. connect time

6. Define the following terms:

    a. internetwork

    b. download

    c. URL

    d. virtual reality

    e. TCP/IP

    f. communications protocol

    g. MUD

    h. MOO

7. Describe in your own words each of the following Internet services:

    a. e-mail

    b. Telnet

    c. FTP

    d. Gopher

    e. World Wide Web

    f. Usenet

8. Suppose you have access to the Internet. For each of the following situations, indicate which Internet service(s) you would use:

    a. You are having a problem with the CD-ROM drive on your Macintosh, and you want some help figuring out what might be wrong.

    b. You want to download a file of information about the Voyager spacecraft from seds.lpl.arizona.edu.

    c. You want to find an Internet site with information on international business.

    d. You want to correspond with your friend at Colorado State University.

    e. You want to try out a MUD called "Island."

    f. You want to join a discussion group on desktop publishing.

    g. You want to see what's at the Internet site *http://symbolicnet.mcs.kent.edu.*

    h. You are doing DNA research, and you want to use a DNA modeling program that runs on the University of Michigan Medical School computer.

    i. You want to take an on-line tour of the Treasures of the Czars exhibit, viewing graphics of the items in the exhibit and reading about their history.

9. Make a list of at least five differences between the Internet and commercial information services.

10. In an Internet address, such as **president@ whitehouse.gov**, the *gov* domain name specifies that the Internet site type is *government*. What are the other Internet domain names and their site types?

Projects

1. The Great Internet Hunt For several years Rick Gates hosted a monthly Internet scavenger hunt. The object of his hunt was to find information on the Internet. The hunt in this project is a little different from Gates' hunt. For this hunt, there are 10 questions. The questions are located at the CTI Web site, *http://www.vmedia.com/cti/concepts2/chap7np.html*. Go to this site and print out the questions. Each question carries a point value between 1 and 5. Answer as many questions as you can using the Internet or other resources. For your answer you must write down the location of the information on the Internet—the URL, FTP site, newsgroup name, and so on. You must also supply at least a one-page printout to verify that you actually visited the site.

2. Internet: Past, Present, Future
Use Internet or library resources to write a research paper about the Internet. In your paper be sure to answer, but do not limit yourself to, the following questions:

a. What are the key events in the development of the Internet? Include a time line of these key events.

b. What is the Internet's current status?

c. What changes are likely to take place in the future?

d. What ethical issues do you think are raised by the existence of the Internet?

3. Censored! Prodigy, which bills itself as a family information service, monitors the content of its services to remove X-rated and R-rated text and graphics. However, no such policing occurs at most other Internet services.

The Internet and commercial information services provide a growing forum for discussions on a wide range of topics. Recently, some on-line observers have begun to question the advisability of information exchanged over the Internet. Megabytes of Internet storage space are devoted to X-rated images. Several Usenet groups regularly discuss the details of making bombs and hollow point bullets. Other groups discuss methods of torture. In a well-publicized incident, a discussion group participant described in gory detail how he was going to murder a female college student.

Free speech laws protect the rights of Americans to express themselves, but should the Internet, which is supported with public taxes, provide a forum for such information and discussions? Senator James Exon does not think so and has sponsored Senate Bill 314: the Communications Decency Act, which would make it a federal crime to annoy, abuse, threaten, or harass anyone on-line. Further, it would be a crime to transmit anything "obscene, lewd, filthy, or indecent." Do you think this Act violates free speech?

For this project, research the issue of on-line censorship. Write a position paper arguing for or against censorship. Support your position with facts and examples. Be sure to include a bibliography. After you complete your research, your instructor might suggest that you discuss your ideas in a small group session.

4. Yellow Pages Printed Internet directories such as *The Internet Yellow Pages* help you find information on the Internet. Browse through an Internet directory, such as those listed in the Resources section of this chapter. Find an example of each of the following, and write down the site name, address, or URL:

a. A World Wide Web site that relates to your academic major or career plans.

b. An anonymous FTP site that contains something you would like to download.

c. A Usenet newsgroup that focuses on a topic related to one of your hobbies or leisure time interests.

If you have Internet access, collect a sample of information from each site using download capabilities or the Print menu. When you turn in your project include a cover page that describes why you selected each site and the value of the information you found.

5. No One Knows You're a Dog In a novel called *Ender's War*, two children are catapulted to national prominence because they have innovative ideas about how to solve critical social and economic issues. No one knows they are children, however, because they communicate their ideas on a public information service, which is the central political forum in their society. This brings up an interesting issue, humorously alluded to in the P. Steiner cartoon in Figure 7-20 on the next page.

Figure 7-20

"On the Internet, nobody knows you're a dog."

Discuss this issue in a small group. In your discussion address questions a through e.

a. Does a communication medium that depends on the written word, rather than on videos, reduce cultural, class, ethnic, and gender bias?

b. According to pollsters, in 1980 many Americans voted for Ronald Reagan because they didn't like his opponent's southern accent. Do you think the election would have been different if campaigning was carried out over the Internet?

c. There is evidence that the younger generation does not like to read and write. Do you think this generation needs a communications medium that is more like television?

d. Do you believe that on-line communications have the potential to reduce biases in our society?

e. Can anyone in your group relate an experience when on-line communication would have been preferable to face-to-face communication?

6. Compare Commercial Information Services The rates for commercial information services such as Compu-Serve, Prodigy, and America Online change frequently. Rather than provide you with outdated information in this chapter, this project will help you compare the rates and services of commercial information services. Select three of the following commercial information services: Compu-Serve, Prodigy, America Online, eWorld (for Macintosh users), Delphi, Microsoft Network, or ImagiNation. Use library resources or materials provided by your instructor to complete the following table for the three services you selected.

Criteria	Service 1	Service 2	Service 3
Need special communications software?			
Setup kit available for DOS?			
Setup kit available for Windows?			
Setup kit available for OS/2?			
Setup kit available for Mac OS?			
Basic monthly fee:			
How many free hours included in basic fee?			
Connect charge for additional hours at 1200 baud:			
Connect charge 2400 baud:			
Connect charge at 9600 baud:			
Connect charge at 14.4K baud:			
Surcharge for discussion groups (Y/N)?			
Database search surcharge (Y/N)?			
Prime time surcharge (Y/N)?			
Number of free e-mail messages included in basic service			
Fee for additional e-mail messages:			
Internet connection available?			
World Wide Web browser available?			

7. Virtual Reality: MUDs, MOOs, Goggles, and Doom Writer William Gibson envisioned a time when people would connect their brains directly to a computer to experience a virtual world in cyberspace. Technology and medical science have not found a way to make a direct connection between our brains and a computer, but today virtual reality takes other forms. On the Internet, MUDs and MOOs provide virtual environments for games, meetings, and socializing. On microcomputers, the multiplayer game Doom provides hours of virtual reality adventure. Using equipment, such as the stereo-optic goggles and sensor gloves shown in Figure 7-21, you can see and manipulate objects that do not exist.

Figure 7-21 ◄

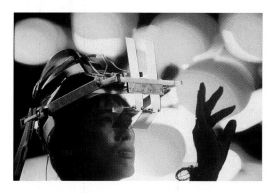

Use your library and Internet resources to learn more about virtual reality. You might also try some virtual reality experiences. If you have Internet access, participate in a MUD or MOO. Play a virtual reality computer game such as Doom or Myst. If available, try out virtual reality goggles.

Now suppose you are asked to produce a three-minute TV news segment on virtual reality. Based on the information you gathered from your library, the Internet, and your personal experiences, write the narrative and describe the images and video clips you would show.

8. Connecting Your Own Computer to the Internet
Suppose you have a computer at home or in your dorm room. You want to connect it to the Internet. To complete this project, answer the following questions:

    a. Does your school offer Internet connections to students who have their own computers? If so, how do you sign up for an account? What is the name of the Internet communications client? If you use your school's Internet connection, are all Internet services available? Which ones are and are not?

    b. If your school does not offer an Internet connection for students' home computers, which commercial service would you select? Explain why.

9. Good Netiquette Design a mini-poster of the rules of good netiquette. You can decide what audience your poster targets: children, high school students, college students, business people—you could even select a specific business. Try to use words and images that will appeal to your target audience.

10. Your Own Web Page Use an HTML editor to design your own Web page. Your instructor will provide you with instructions for locating your HTML editor and for submitting your home page either on disk or on your network.

Resources

- **Benedikt, M.** (ed.) *Cyberspace: First Steps*. Cambridge, MA: The MIT Press, 1993. Michael Benedikt is the editor of this collection of articles about cyberspace—its history, current status, and future potential. Looking at the authors' occupations gives you some idea about the direction of cyberspace research. Contributors include a science fiction writer, architects, computer interface experts, artists, sociologists, anthropologists, and computer engineers.

- **Gibson, W.** *Neuromancer*. New York: Ace books, 1984. Neuromancer is the science fiction novel that started a new genre of cyberspace sci-fi. Gibson paints a world in which Japanese influence has slowly enveloped Western pop culture, and in which the search for information—or even entertainment—means plugging your brain into a computer.

- **Hahn, H. and Stout, R.** *The Internet Yellow Pages*, second edition. Berkeley, CA: Osborne McGraw-Hill, 1995. Find it all here. A fun, but informative listing of thousands of Internet sites.

- **Hoffman, P.** *The Internet*. Foster City, CA IDG Books Worldwide, 1994. This is the companion book to public television's The "Internet Show." It is a great guide for beginners who want an overview of the Internet. Explanations are clear and nicely illustrated.

Internet sites with information about the Internet:

- A multimedia course on the history and status of the Internet at: *http://www.nlm.nih.gov/LECTURES.dir/ internet_course.dir/starting_page.html*

- A timeline and growth statistics for the Internet at: *http://tig.com/IBC/Timeline.html*

- Excerpts from talks and tutorials on the Internet at: *http://town.hall.org/university/index.html*

- Lots of Internet info at *http://www.internic.net*

- **Kent, P.** *The Complete Idiot's Guide to the Internet*, second edition. Indianapolis, IN: Alpha Books, 1994. Don't let the title insult you. This book covers some fairly technical material, but the explanations are well done. You'll hardly realize that you're learning anything, but you are—lots of information about connecting to the Internet, sending e-mail, participating in newsgroups, Telnetting, FTP-ing, and Web browsing.

- **Stoll, C.** *Silicon Snake Oil: Second Thoughts on the Information Highway*. New York: Doubleday, 1995. Stoll, a seasoned Internet user, takes a cautionary—some might say reactionary—view of the effect of the information highway on society. He contends that we often mistake information for knowledge and cautions that cyberspace is no substitute for experience in the real world. He also suggests that the ease of firing off your opinion to an on-line discussion fosters flames, rather than reasoned debate.

- **Turlington, S.** *Walking the World Wide Web*. Chapel Hill, NC: Ventana Press, 1995. A clearly-written book about the World Wide Web and the Mosaic Web browser. Also contains a terrific list of web sites. Ventana Press has its own web site: *http://www. vmedia.com*.

- **Wired** This is the magazine of choice among Internet aficionados. It's artsy, glitzy, and off-beat; but it has some high quality articles with non-conventional perspectives. Senior columnist Nicholas Negroponte is well known for his work at the MIT Media Lab. *Wired* has an Internet site at *http://wired.com*.

Lab Assignments

Quick Check

Answers

The Internet: World Wide Web

 One of the most popular services on the Internet is the World Wide Web. This Lab is a Web simulator that teaches you how to use Web browser software to find information. You can use this Lab whether or not your school provides you with Internet access.

1. Click the Steps button to learn how to use Web browser software. As you proceed through the Steps, answer all of the Quick Check questions that appear. After you complete the Steps, you will see a Quick Check Summary Report. Follow the instructions on the screen to print this report.

2. Click the Explore button on the Welcome screen. Use the Web browser to locate a weather map of the Carribean Virgin Islands. What is its URL?

3. A SCUBA diver named Wadson Lachouffe has been searching for the fabled treasure of Greybeard the pirate. A link from the Adventure Travel Web *www.atour.com* site leads to a Wadson's Web page called "Hidden Treasure." In Explore, locate the Hidden Treasure page and answer the following questions:

    a. What was the name of Greybeard's ship?

    b. What was Greybeard's favorite food?

    c. What does Wadson think happened to Greybeard's ship?

4. In the Steps, you found a graphic of Jupiter from the photo archives of the Jet Propulsion Laboratory. In the Explore section of the Lab, you can also find a graphic of Saturn. Suppose one of your friends wanted a picture of Saturn for an astronomy report. Make a list of the blue, underlined links your friend must click to find the Saturn graphic. Assume that your friend will begin at the Web Trainer home page.

5. Enter the URL *http://www.atour.com* to jump to the Adventure Travel Web site. Write a one-page description of this site. In your paper include a description of the information at the site, the number of pages the site contains, and a diagram of the links it contains.

6. Chris Thomson is a student at UVI and has his own Web pages. In Explore, look at the information Chris has included on his pages. Suppose you could create your own Web page. What would you include? Use word processing software to design your own Web pages. Make sure you indicate the graphics and links you would use.

7.1

1. cyberspace

2. Internet

3. commercial information service (or on-line service)

4. discussion group

5. chat session

6. downloading

7.2

1. computers, host (mainframe)

2. Prodigy, CompuServe, America Online, Microsoft Network

3. basic services

4. connect time

5. local access number

7.3

1. internet (or internetwork)

2. Internet

3. coco = user ID, @canine = machine name, com = domain name

4. World Wide Web

5. Gopher

6. Anonymous FTP

7. Telnet

8. MOO

9. netiquette

Glossary/Index

Data Security and Control

CHAPTER**PREVIEW**

In this chapter you learn about threats to the data stored on computer systems. With this information, you can begin to assess your risk of losing important data, becoming the target of computer vandalism, or being affected by inaccurate data. You will find out why data backup is one
of the most effective security measures for protecting your data. On a practical level, you will
learn how to disinfect disks that contain viruses, make backups, and design an effective backup
plan for your data. After you have completed this chapter you should be able to:

■ List some of the causes for lost or inaccurate
data

■ Describe how you can protect your computer
data from damage caused by power problems
and hardware failures

■ List at least five symptoms that might indicate
your computer is infected by a virus

■ Differentiate between the terms virus, Trojan
horse, worm, logic bomb, and time bomb

■ Describe techniques for avoiding, detecting,
and eradicating a computer virus

■ Explain why special computer crime laws are
necessary

■ Describe the process of risk management

■ List the advantages and disadvantages of
the most popular data security techniques

Data Security
and Control

According to legend, the war between the Trojans and the Greeks continued for more than nine years, until one of the Greek leaders conceived a brilliant plan. He ordered his men to create a huge wooden horse. When it was completed, a few Greek soldiers hid inside and the Greek army pretended to sail away. In the morning, the Trojans found a magnificent horse statue at the city gates. Believing that the horse was a gift, the Trojans pulled it into the city and spent the day celebrating what they thought was a great victory. Late that night, the Greek soldiers hidden inside the horse crept out and opened the city gates for the waiting Greek army.

What does the Trojan War have to do with computers? Like the city of Troy, modern computer users are under siege. They are battling computer criminals, pranksters, viruses, equipment failures, and human errors. There is even a modern software version of the Trojan horse that might erase your data after you unknowingly bring it into your computer system.

Today's computer users battle to avoid lost, stolen, and inaccurate data. **Lost data**, also referred to as **missing data**, is data that is inaccessible, usually because it was accidentally removed. **Stolen data** is not necessarily missing, but it has been accessed or copied without authorization. **Inaccurate data** is data that is not accurate because it was entered incorrectly, was deliberately or accidentally altered, or was not edited to reflect current facts.

This chapter begins by describing mistakes and equipment failures that inadvertently cause lost or inaccurate data. Next, the focus moves to intentional acts of vandalism and computer crime in which data is tampered with or stolen. The section on risk management explains the steps you can take to protect your data. This chapter concludes with an in-depth look at a most important computing activity—data backup.

LAB

Data Backup

What Can Go Wrong

The data on a computer system is important, but events occur that destroy data or make it inaccurate. For example, people make mistakes. Suppose you store your English Composition term paper on your home computer, but before you turn it in, you inadvertently erase it. Another example is hardware failure. The medical records that a doctor stores on the clinic's computer are important for the correct treatment of patients. What happens if the power goes off or the hard drive fails and no one can access the data? Disasters also occur. The client records that your medical insurance provider stores on its computer system ensure accurate and expedient reimbursement for your medical expenses. What if the insurance provider's computer system is destroyed by fire? The list of examples like these seems endless, but the point remains the same: Important data stored on computers is vulnerable to human error, power problems, hardware failure, and natural disasters.

Operator Error

What's the most likely cause of lost or inaccurate data?

Despite all the sensational press coverage of computer criminals and viruses, the most common cause of lost data is operator error. **Operator error** refers to a mistake made by a computer user. At one time or another, everyone who has used a computer has made a mistake. A few examples will illustrate that it is not an exclusive club.

- Working late at night the President's press secretary finished the final revisions for the next day's speech. Intending to make a copy of the speech as a backup, he mistakenly copied the old version of the speech over the new version.
- The head of the information systems department at a Fortune 500 firm was in a hurry to copy some files onto a floppy disk. Grabbing a disk without a label and thinking it was unformatted, she shoved it in the disk drive and started the formatting process. Unfortunately, the disk contained her only copy of a report that had been mailed from the Houston office.
- A clerk in the medical records office of a metropolitan hospital was embarrassed to learn that he had billed a patient for 555 aspirins instead of 5.

It might seem that nothing can prevent operator error. After all, mistakes do happen. However, the number of operator errors can be reduced if users pay attention to what they're doing and establish habits that help them avoid mistakes.

Many organizations have reduced the incidence of operator errors by using direct source input devices. A **direct source input device**, such as a bar code reader, collects data directly from a document or object, without human intervention. This reduces the possibility of input errors that occur because of such human mistakes as typing the wrong number.

Good user interface design can also reduce operator error. Computer software designers can help prevent mistakes by designing products that anticipate mistakes that users are likely to make and that help users avoid them. For example, Microsoft Windows 95 users can activate a feature that requests confirmation before the computer carries out any activity that might destroy data. Figure 8-1 shows a Windows 95 dialog box that asks for confirmation before a file is deleted.

1. The user selects the file Sales Summary. Pressing the Delete key initiates an operation that will, in effect, destroy the data in the selected file.

2. The Microsoft Windows 95 operating system displays a prompt asking the user to confirm the Delete. The file is deleted only if the user clicks the Yes button.

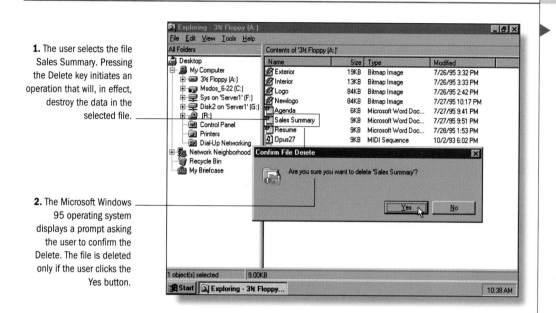

Figure 8-1
Confirmation dialog box helps reduce operator error

Although a power failure results in lost data from RAM, it is unlikely to cause data loss from disk because magnetic storage does not require power to maintain data.

Power Failures, Spikes, and Surges

If the power goes out, will I lose all my data?

A **power failure** is a complete loss of power to the computer system. Although you can lose power by accidentally bumping the computer on/off switch, a power failure is usually caused by something over which you have no control, such as a downed power line or a malfunction at the local power plant.

Data stored in RAM is lost if power is not continuously supplied to the computer system. Even a brief interruption in the power supply, noticeable only as a flicker of the room lights, can force your computer to reboot and lose all the data in RAM.

An uninterruptible power supply is the best protection against power problems. An **uninterruptible power supply**, or **UPS**, is a device containing a battery and other circuitry that provides a continuous supply of power. A UPS is designed to provide enough power to keep your computer working through momentary power interruptions and to give you time to save your files and exit your programs in the event of a longer power outage. A UPS for a microcomputer costs from $100 to $600,

Figure 8-2
An uninterruptible power supply

A UPS contains a battery that keeps your computer going for several minutes during a power failure. The battery does not supply indefinite power, so in the event of a power failure that lasts more than two or three minutes you should save your work and turn off your computer.

A light on the case lets you know that the UPS is charged and ready.

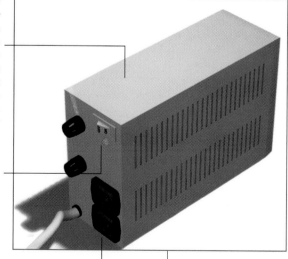

To connect a UPS, plug it into a wall outlet, then plug your computer and monitor cables into the outlets on the UPS.

depending on the power requirements of the computer and the features of the UPS. Most computer dealers can help you determine your computer's power requirements and recommend the appropriate size and features for a UPS that meets your needs. Figure 8-2 shows a typical UPS.

Two other common power problems are spikes and surges. Both of these can damage sensitive computer components. A **power spike** is an increase in power that lasts only a short time—

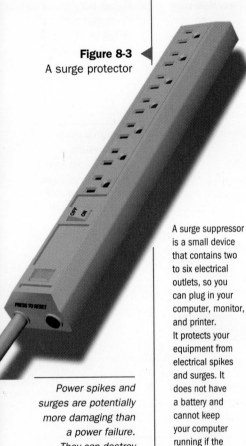

Figure 8-3
A surge protector

A surge suppressor is a small device that contains two to six electrical outlets, so you can plug in your computer, monitor, and printer. It protects your equipment from electrical spikes and surges. It does not have a battery and cannot keep your computer running if the power goes off.

Power spikes and surges are potentially more damaging than a power failure. They can destroy the circuitry that operates your hard disk drive, so you lose access to all the data it contains.

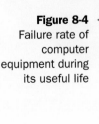

less than a millionth of a second. A **power surge** lasts a little longer—a few millionths of a second. Malfunctions in the local generating plant and the power distribution network can cause surges and spikes. Lightning can also cause a surge that damages computer equipment circuitry. Power surges and spikes are potentially more damaging than power failures. A surge or spike can damage your computer's main board and the circuit boards on your disk drives, putting your computer out of action until the boards are replaced.

Many experts recommend that you unplug your computer equipment, including your modem, during electrical storms. Unfortunately, there is not much you can do to increase the reliability of the local power system. However, the same UPS you use to provide a few minutes of power in the event of a power loss will also filter out power surges and spikes. As a low-cost alternative, you can plug your computer into an inexpensive **surge protector**. Just remember that a surge protector does not protect the data in RAM if the power fails. Figure 8-3 explains how a surge protector works.

Hardware Failure

How reliable are the components of my computer system?

The reliability of computer components is measured as **mean time between failures**, or **MTBF**. This measurement is somewhat misleading to most consumers. For example, you might read that your hard disk drive has an MTBF of 125,000 hours, which is about 14 years. Does this mean your hard drive will work for 125,000 hours before it fails? Unfortunately, the answer is no.

The MTBF is an estimate based on laboratory tests of a few sample components. The tests are conducted in a regulated laboratory environment where power problems, failure of other components, and regular wear and tear do not exist. A 125,000 hour MTBF means that, *on average*, a hard disk drive like yours is likely to function for 125,000 hours without failing. The fact remains, however, that your hard disk drive might work for only 10 hours before it fails. With this in mind, plan for hardware failtures, rather than hope they won't happen.

Much of the equipment that fails does so within the first hours or days of operation, but after that it can be expected to work fairly reliably until it nears the end of its useful life. The failure rate of computer components is illustrated by the graph in Figure 8-4.

Figure 8-4
Failure rate of computer equipment during its useful life

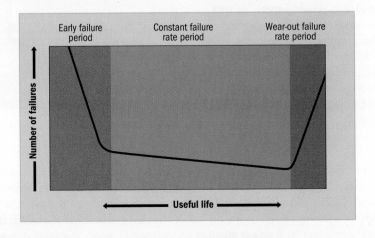

The effect of a hardware failure depends on the component that fails. Most hardware failures are simply an inconvenience. For example, if your monitor fails, you can obtain a replacement monitor, plug it in, and get back to work. On the other hand, a hard disk drive failure can be a disaster because you might lose all the data stored on the hard disk drive. The impact of a hard disk drive failure is considerably reduced if you have complete, up-to-date backups of the programs and data files on your hard disk.

Fires, Floods, and Other Disasters

Should I buy insurance for my computer?

Computers are not immune to unexpected damage from smoke, fire, water, and breakage. However, it is not practical to barricade your computer from every potential disaster. Many insurance policies provide coverage for computers. Under the terms of many standard household and business policies, a computer is treated like any other appliance. You should make sure, however, that your insurance policy covers the full cost of purchasing a new computer at current market prices.

Replacing your damaged computer equipment will not replace your data. Some insurance companies provide extra coverage for the data on your computer. This coverage would provide you a sum of money to cover the time it takes to reload your data on a replacement computer. However, being able to reload your data assumes that you have a backup of your data. Without a backup, much of your data cannot be reconstructed. For a business, the situation is even more critical. Customer accounts, inventory, daily transactions, and financial information are difficult, if not impossible, to reconstruct.

To summarize, a good insurance policy provides funds to replace computer equipment, but the only insurance for your data is an up-to-date backup tape or disk.

Quick Check

1 The most common cause of lost data is _____.

2 As a result of a power failure your computer will lose all the data stored in RAM and the hard drive. True or false?

3 A(n) _____ contains a battery that provides a continuous supply of power to your computer during a brief power failure.

4 A(n) _____ protects your computer from electrical spikes and surges, but it does not keep your computer operating if the power fails.

5 The circuitry on your computer circuit boards can be damaged by accidentally turning off your computer. True or false?

6 MTBF tells you how often an electronic device needs to be serviced. True or false?

7 The failure of which computer component is potentially the most disastrous?

8 The best insurance for your data is _____

Viruses, Vandalism, and Computer Crime

8.2

Data stored on micro, mini, or mainframe computers can be damaged, destroyed, or altered by vandalism. The vandals are called **hackers**, **crackers**, or **cyberpunks**. The programs these hackers create are colorfully referred to by various sources as *malware*, *pest programs*, *vandalware*, or *punkware*. More typically, these programs are referred to as *viruses*. What would you do if you saw the message in Figure 8-5 on your computer screen?

Figure 8-5
A virus alert: real or fake?

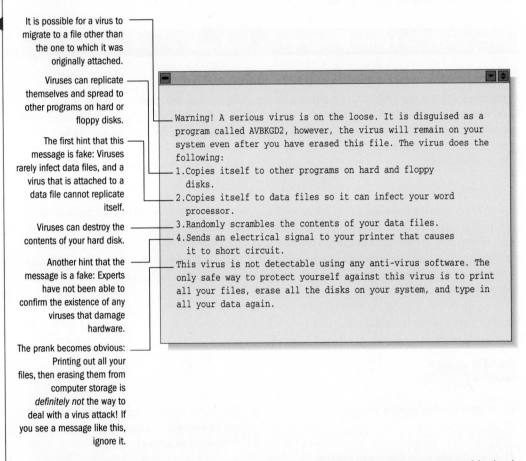

It is possible for a virus to migrate to a file other than the one to which it was originally attached.

Viruses can replicate themselves and spread to other programs on hard or floppy disks.

The first hint that this message is fake: Viruses rarely infect data files, and a virus that is attached to a data file cannot replicate itself.

Viruses can destroy the contents of your hard disk.

Another hint that the message is a fake: Experts have not been able to confirm the existence of any viruses that damage hardware.

The prank becomes obvious: Printing out all your files, then erasing them from computer storage is *definitely not* the way to deal with a virus attack! If you see a message like this, ignore it.

> Warning! A serious virus is on the loose. It is disguised as a program called AVBKGD2, however, the virus will remain on your system even after you have erased this file. The virus does the following:
> 1. Copies itself to other programs on hard and floppy disks.
> 2. Copies itself to data files so it can infect your word processor.
> 3. Randomly scrambles the contents of your data files.
> 4. Sends an electrical signal to your printer that causes it to short circuit.
> This virus is not detectable using any anti-virus software. The only safe way to protect yourself against this virus is to print all your files, erase all the disks on your system, and type in all your data again.

The term *virus* technically refers to only one type of trouble-making program created by hackers. Hackers also cause mischief with programs such as Trojan horses, time bombs, logic bombs, and worms. As you'll learn in this chapter, each of these programs behaves differently when attacking a computer system.

Viruses, Trojan horses, time bombs, logic bombs, and worms lurk on disks and computer bulletin boards waiting to destroy data and cause mischief to your computer system. Understanding how these programs work is the first line of defense against attacks and pranks.

Computer Viruses

Exactly what is a computer virus?

A **computer virus** is a program that attaches itself to a file and reproduces itself to spread from one file to another. A virus can destroy data, display an irritating message, or otherwise disrupt computer operations. The jargon that describes a computer virus sounds similar to medical jargon. Your computer is a "host," and it can become "infected" with a virus. A virus can reproduce itself and spread from one computer to another. You can "inoculate" your computer against many viruses. If your computer has not been inoculated and becomes infected, you can use anti-viral software to "disinfect" it.

A computer virus generally infects the executable files on your computer system, not the data files. When you run an infected program, your computer also runs the attached virus instructions to replicate or deliver its payload. The term **payload** refers to the ultimate mission of a virus. For example, the payload of the "Stoned" virus is the message, "Your PC is now stoned." Figure 8-6 illustrates how a computer virus spreads and delivers its payload.

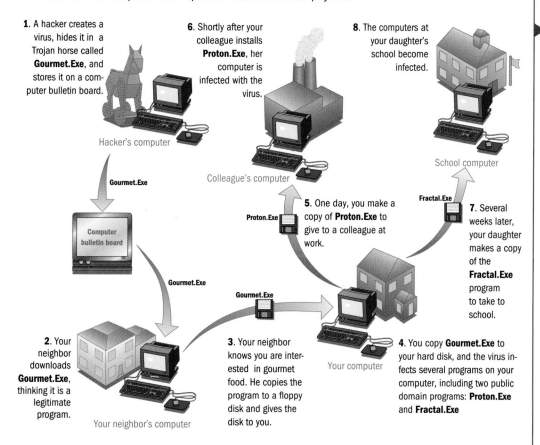

1. A hacker creates a virus, hides it in a Trojan horse called **Gourmet.Exe**, and stores it on a computer bulletin board.

Hacker's computer

Gourmet.Exe

Computer bulletin board

Gourmet.Exe

2. Your neighbor downloads **Gourmet.Exe**, thinking it is a legitimate program.

Your neighbor's computer

3. Your neighbor knows you are interested in gourmet food. He copies the program to a floppy disk and gives the disk to you.

Gourmet.Exe

Your computer

4. You copy **Gourmet.Exe** to your hard disk, and the virus infects several programs on your computer, including two public domain programs: **Proton.Exe** and **Fractal.Exe**

5. One day, you make a copy of **Proton.Exe** to give to a colleague at work.

Proton.Exe

6. Shortly after your colleague installs **Proton.Exe**, her computer is infected with the virus.

Colleague's computer

7. Several weeks later, your daughter makes a copy of the **Fractal.Exe** program to take to school.

Fractal.Exe

8. The computers at your daughter's school become infected.

School computer

Figure 8-6
How a computer virus works

The term "host" has several meanings. It can refer to a computer that has contracted a virus. It can also refer to the main computer in a network.

Most viruses attach themselves to executable files because these are the files that your computer runs. If a virus attaches to an executable file that you rarely use, it might not have an opportunity to spread and do much damage. On the other hand, **boot sector viruses**, which infect the system files your computer uses every time you turn it on, can cause widespread damage and persistent problems. Only a few viruses, such as Cinderella and Frodo, are designed to infect data files. Because a virus needs to be executed to spread, a data file can only be a carrier; it cannot deliver the payload.

Experts say there are over 2,000 viruses. However, 90% of virus damage is caused by fewer than 10 viruses. The extent of damage varies with the virus. Research conducted by Computer Security BBS found that 64% of those surveyed had experienced a computer virus attack in the past 12 months. Forty-nine percent of these cases resulted in damaged or lost data. Figure 8-7 gives you some idea of the financial consequences of virus infections.

Figure 8-7
Impact of virus infections

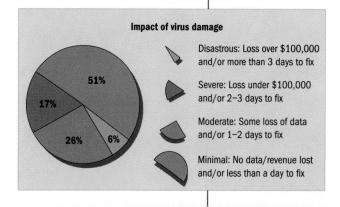

Impact of virus damage

51%

17%

26% 6%

Disastrous: Loss over $100,000 and/or more than 3 days to fix

Severe: Loss under $100,000 and/or 2–3 days to fix

Moderate: Some loss of data and/or 1–2 days to fix

Minimal: No data/revenue lost and/or less than a day to fix

A key point to understand about viruses is that they contain instructions that the computer must perform for the virus to spread or deliver its payload.

The symptoms of a virus infection depend on the virus. The following symptoms *might* indicate that your computer has contracted a virus. However, some of these symptoms can have other causes.

- Your computer displays annoying messages such as "Gotcha! Arf Arf," "You're stoned!," or "I want a cookie."
- Your computer develops unusual visual or sound effects. For example, characters begin to disappear from your screen or the sound of a flushing toilet comes from your computer's speaker.
- You have difficulty saving files.
- Your computer suddenly seems to work very slowly.
- Files are mysteriously missing.
- Your computer reboots unexpectedly.
- Your executable files unaccountably increase in size.

Viruses are just one type of program in a large category of software designed by hackers to disrupt or damage the data on computers. After looking at other software in this category, you'll find out how to avoid and minimize the damage they cause.

A Modern Trojan Horse

How can I avoid being fooled by a Trojan horse?

At the beginning of this chapter, you learned about the legendary Trojan horse. A modern software version waits to surprise unwary computer users. In the context of computing, a **Trojan horse** is a computer program that appears to perform one function while actually doing something else. A Trojan horse sometimes, but not always, harbors a virus. For example, suppose a hacker writes a program to format hard disk drives and embeds this program in a file called **Sched.Exe.** The hacker then distributes disks containing this Trojan horse and posts it on computer bulletin boards where other users are likely to assume it is a free scheduling program. Users who download and run **Sched.Exe** will discover that the program has erased all the files on their hard disk. This Trojan horse does not harbor a virus because it does not replicate itself. Figure 8-8 shows how this type of Trojan horse program works.

Another popular Trojan horse looks just like the login screen on a network. However, as a user logs in, the Trojan horse collects the user's ID and password. These are stored in a file that a hacker can access later. Armed with a valid user ID and password, the hacker can access the data stored on the network. As with the earlier example, this Trojan horse does not harbor a virus. The hacker's program, designed to defeat network security measures, does not replicate itself.

It is easy to be fooled by Trojan horse programs because they are designed to be difficult to detect. Keep your ears open for information about the latest computer pranks circulating in your local area. Also, be suspicious of anything out of the ordinary on your computer system. For example, if your login screen looks a little different one day, check with your technical support person.

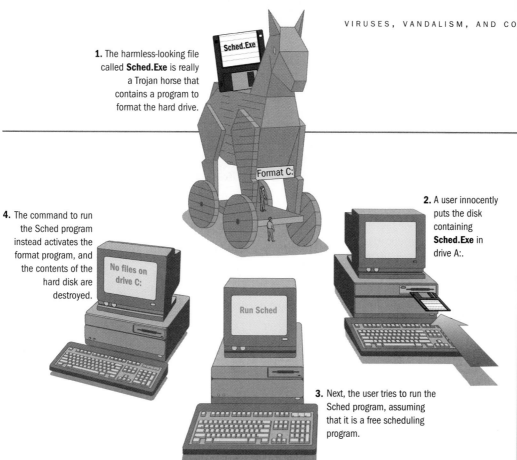

1. The harmless-looking file called **Sched.Exe** is really a Trojan horse that contains a program to format the hard drive.

4. The command to run the Sched program instead activates the format program, and the contents of the hard disk are destroyed.

No files on drive C:

Run Sched

Format C:

2. A user innocently puts the disk containing **Sched.Exe** in drive A:.

3. Next, the user tries to run the Sched program, assuming that it is a free scheduling program.

▶ **Figure 8-8**
How a Trojan horse works

Think of a Trojan horse as a container that hides a secret program. That program might be a virus or a time bomb, or simply a program that, when run, carries out a nasty task such as formatting your hard disk.

Time Bombs and Logic Bombs

Can a virus lurk in my computer system without my knowledge?

Although a virus usually begins to replicate itself immediately when it enters your computer system, it will not necessarily deliver its payload right away. A virus or other unwelcome surprise can lurk in your computer system for days or months without discovery. A **time bomb** is a computer program that stays in your system undetected until it is triggered by a certain event in time, such as when the computer system clock reaches a certain date. A time bomb is usually carried by a virus or Trojan horse. For example, the Michelangelo virus contains a time bomb designed to damage files on your hard disk on March 6, the birthday of artist Michelangelo. March 6 is an odd date for a time bomb attack. Hackers seem to favor dates such as Halloween, Friday the 13th, and April Fool's day for time bomb attacks.

A notorious time bomb appeared in December 1989. Many hospitals and medical clinics received an innocent-looking package containing "AIDS Information" software from a company called PC Cyborg. The process of installing the software also installed a time bomb. After the computer was booted a certain number of times, the time bomb scrambled the data on the hard disk. Next, the bomb displayed an invoice demanding payment before the method for unscrambling the hard disk data was revealed.

A **logic bomb** is a computer program that is triggered by the appearance or disappearance of specific data. A logic bomb can be carried by a virus or Trojan horse. Alternatively, a logic bomb could be a standalone program. For example, suppose a programmer in a large corporation believes that she is on the list of employees to be terminated during the next cost-cutting campaign. Her hostility overcomes her ethical judgment, and she creates a logic bomb program that checks the payroll file every day to make sure her employment status is still active. If the programmer's status changes to "terminated," her logic bomb activates a program that destroys data on the computer.

Worms

Is a worm some type of virus?

"At 2:28 a.m. a besieged Berkeley scientist—like a front-line soldier engulfed by the enemy—sent a bulletin around the nation: *We are currently under attack...* Thus began one of the most harrowing days of the computer age." This lead story in *The Wall Street Journal* reported the now famous Internet worm that spread to more than 6,000 Internet host computers. A software **worm** is a program designed to enter a computer system—usually a network—through security "holes." Like a virus, a worm reproduces itself. Unlike a virus, a worm does not need to be attached to an executable program to reproduce.

The software worm that attacked the Internet entered each computer through security holes in the electronic mail system, then used data stored on the computer to, in effect, mail itself to other computers. The worm spread rapidly, as shown in Figure 8-9.

Figure 8-9 ◀
A worm attacks the
internet

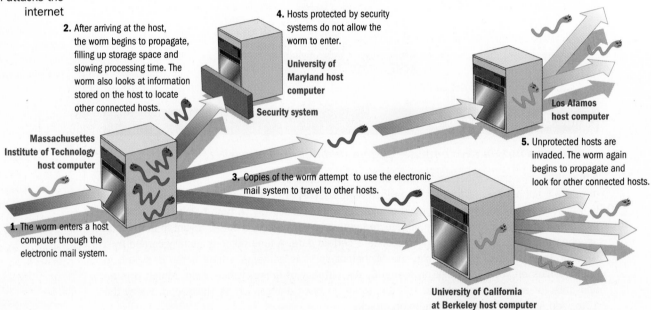

2. After arriving at the host, the worm begins to propagate, filling up storage space and slowing processing time. The worm also looks at information stored on the host to locate other connected hosts.

4. Hosts protected by security systems do not allow the worm to enter.

University of Maryland host computer

Security system

Massachusettes Institute of Technology host computer

3. Copies of the worm attempt to use the electronic mail system to travel to other hosts.

1. The worm enters a host computer through the electronic mail system.

Los Alamos host computer

5. Unprotected hosts are invaded. The worm again begins to propagate and look for other connected hosts.

University of California at Berkeley host computer

The Internet worm was not designed to destroy data. Instead, it filled up storage space and dramatically slowed computer performance. The only way to eradicate the Internet worm was to shut down the electronic mail system on the Internet hosts, then comb through hundreds of programs to find and destroy the worm, a process that took up to eight hours for each host.

You learned in Chapter 3 that a WORM drive is a computer storage device that writes data once, but can read that data many times. A software worm has no relationship to a WORM drive.

Avoidance and Detection

Can I protect my computer from viruses and other types of attacks?

Computer viruses and other types of malicious software typically lurk on disks containing public domain software or shareware and on disks containing illegal copies of computer programs downloaded from bulletin boards. Disks and programs from these sources should be regarded as having a high risk of infection.

You can generally avoid a computer virus if you do not use high-risk disks or programs. If you need to use a disk that you suspect might be infected, you can use a virus detection program to check for viruses before you run any programs from the disk.

A **virus detection program**, or **anti-virus program**, examines the files stored on a disk to determine if they are infected with a virus, then disinfects the disk, if necessary. Virus detection programs use several techniques to find viruses. As you know, a virus attaches itself to an existing program. This often increases the length of the original program. The earliest virus detection software simply examined the programs on a computer and recorded their length. A change in the length of a program from one computing session to the next indicated the possible presence of a virus.

In response to early virus detection programs, hackers became more cunning. They created viruses that insert themselves into unused portions of a program file but do not change its length. Of course, the people who designed virus detection programs fought back. They designed programs that examine the bytes in an uninfected application program and calculate a checksum. A **checksum** is a value that is calculated by combining all the bytes in a file. Each time you run the application program, the virus detection program recalculates the checksum and compares it to the original. If any byte in the application program has been changed, the checksum will be different, and the virus detection program assumes that a virus is present. The checksum approach requires that you start with a copy of the program that is not infected with a virus. If you start with an infected copy, the virus is included in the original checksum, and the virus detection program never detects it.

Another technique used by virus detection programs is to search for a signature A **signature** is a unique series of bytes that can be used to identify a known virus, much as a fingerprint is used to identify an individual. The signature is usually a section of the virus program, such as a unique series of instructions. Most of today's virus detection software scans for virus signatures; for this reason, virus detection software is sometimes referred to as a "scanner."

The signature search technique is fairly quick, but it can identify only those viruses with a known signature. To detect new viruses—and new viruses seem to appear every week—you must obtain regular updates for your virus detection program that include new virus signatures.

Some viruses are specifically designed to avoid detection by one or more of these virus detection methods. For this reason, the most sophisticated virus protection schemes combine elements from each of these methods.

A common misconception is that write protecting your disks prevents virus infection. Although a virus cannot jump onto your disk when it is write protected, you have to remove the write protection each time you save a file on the disk. With the write protection removed, your disk is open to virus attack.

What to Do If You Detect a Computer Virus

What should I do if my computer gets a virus?

If you detect a virus on your computer system, you should immediately take steps to stop the virus from spreading. If you are connected to a network, alert the network administrator that you found a virus on your workstation. The network administrator can then take action to prevent the virus from spreading throughout the network.

If you are using your own computer system and you detect a virus, you should remove it to prevent any further damage. There are two methods for removing a virus. First, you can attempt to restore the infected program to its original condition by deleting the virus with the disinfect function of virus detection software. However, depending on how the virus attached itself to the program, it might not be possible to remove the virus without destroying the program. If the virus cannot be removed successfully, you must use the second method: erase the infected program,

Virus scanners are not the same as flat-bed or handheld scanners. When you see the term "scanner" in the context of computer viruses, it refers to virus detection software that searches or "scans" your files to root out viruses.

Recall from Chapter 3 that you can write-protect your floppy disk by opening the small write-protect window. When the write-protect window is open, the computer cannot save files on your disk.

test the system again to make sure the virus has been eliminated, then reinstall the program from the original disks. In cases where the virus has infected most of the programs on the system, it's often best to make a backup of your data files (which are unlikely to have been infected) reformat the hard disk, and install all the programs again from backup copies of the original disks.

With either method, you must also test and, if necessary, remove the virus from every floppy disk and backup used on your computer system. If you don't remove every copy of the virus, your system will become infected again the next time you use an infected disk or restore data from an infected backup. You should also alert your colleagues, and anyone with whom you shared disks, that a virus might have traveled on those disks and infected their computer system.

Computer Crime

Is it a crime to spread a computer virus?

The accounting firm of Ernst & Young estimates that computer crime costs individuals and organizations in the United States between $3 billion and $5 billion a year. "Old-fashioned" crimes that take a high-tech twist because they involve a computer are often prosecuted using traditional laws. For example, a person who attempts to destroy computer data by setting fire to a computer might be prosecuted under traditional arson laws.

Traditional laws do not, however, cover the range of possibilities for computer crimes. Suppose a person unlawfully enters a computer facility. That person might be prosecuted for breaking and entering. But would breaking and entering laws apply to a person who uses an off-site terminal to "enter" a computer system without authorization? And what about the situation in which a person steals a file by copying it without authorization? Is the file really "stolen" if the original remains on the computer?

Most states have computer crime laws that specifically define computer data and software as personal property. These laws also define as a crime the unauthorized access, use, modification, or disabling of a computer system or data.

In early 1995, cybersleuth Tsutomu Shimomura tracked down a hacker who broke into dozens of corporate, university, government, and personal computers. Before his arrest, the hacker stole thousands of data files and more than 20,000 credit card numbers. "He was clearly the most wanted computer hacker in the world," commented assistant U.S. attorney Kent Walker. The hacker's unauthorized access and use of computer data are explicitly defined as criminal acts by computer crime laws.

Under most state laws, intentionally circulating a destructive virus is a crime. Study the excerpt from a typical computer crime law in Figure 8-10 to see what is specifically defined as illegal.

State authorities have jurisdiction over computer crimes committed in one state, but crimes that occur in more than one state or across state boundaries are under federal jurisdiction. The Computer Fraud and Abuse Act of 1986 makes it a federal crime to access a computer across state lines for

Figure 8-10
Excerpt from a state computer crime law

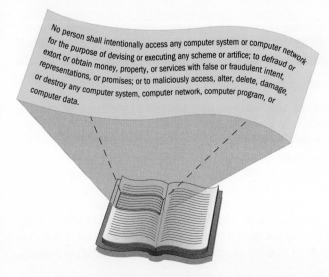

No person shall intentionally access any computer system or computer network for the purpose of devising or executing any scheme or artifice; to defraud or extort or obtain money, property, or services with false or fraudulent intent, representations, or promises; or to maliciously access, alter, delete, damage, or destroy any computer system, computer network, computer program, or computer data.

fraudulent purposes. This act also specifically outlaws the sale of entry pass codes, passwords, and access codes that belong to others.

In a well-publicized espionage case, dramatized in a documentary called *Computers, the KGB, and Me*, hackers used an unclassified military network and the Internet to piece together details on current military research in the United States, which they then sold to the KGB. The hackers, based in Germany, used stolen passwords and telephone access codes to set up communications links from Europe to Virginia, and on to California. The communications crossed state lines, so under the Computer Fraud and Abuse Act the case was placed under federal jurisdiction. With FBI assistance, the case was ultimately cracked by Cliff Stoll, a computer operator of an Internet host computer at the Lawrence Berkeley Laboratory in California.

Laws are made to deter criminals, bring them to trial if they are caught, and punish them if they are convicted. But laws don't actually protect your data. That is something you need to do by making frequent backups and taking steps to prevent unauthorized access to data.

Quick Check

1 A(n) _____ is a program that reproduces itself when the computer executes the file to which it is attached.

2 A(n) _____ is a software container that might contain a virus or time bomb.

3 A(n) _____ is a program that reproduces itself without being attached to an executable file.

4 Suppose that your computer displays a weird message every time you type the word "digital." You might suspect that your computer has contracted a(n) _____ .

5 Three sources of disks that should be considered a high risk of virus infection are _____ , _____ , and _____ .

6 What are three symptoms of a computer virus infection?

7 Many virus detection programs identify viruses by looking for a unique series of bytes called a(n) _____ .

8 Computer crime laws define _____ and _____ as personal property.

Data Security and Risk Management

Data security is the collection of techniques that provide protection for data. Sometimes computer users cite Jeff Richards' Laws of Data security as tongue-in-cheek advice on how to attain foolproof security:

1. Don't buy a computer.

2. If you buy a computer, don't turn it on.

Richards' Laws emphasize the point that it is not practical to totally protect computer data from theft, viruses, and natural disasters. In most situations, providing total security is too time-consuming, too expensive, or too complex. For example, if you are using your computer primarily for word processing, it is too time-consuming to make daily backups, too expensive to keep your data in a fire-proof vault, and too complex to implement password security. On the other hand, if you take no precautions, one day you will be sorry.

In the context of computers, **risk management** is the process of weighing threats to computer data against the amount of data that is expendable and the cost of protecting crucial data. The steps in risk management are as follows:

1. Determine the likely threats to computer data. In the case of individual computer users, the major threats are hardware failure, operator error, and vandalism.

2. Assess the amount of data that is expendable. For this assessment you must ask yourself how much data you would *have* to re-enter if your hard drive was erased and how much of your data would be forever lost because it could not be reconstructed.

3. Determine the cost of protecting all of your data versus protecting some of your data. Costs include time as well as money.

4. Select the protective measures that are affordable, effective against the identified threats, and easy to implement.

If you have your own computer, you can assess your level of risk by doing Project 2 at the end of this chapter.

In the rest of Section 8.3, you'll learn the advantages and disadvantages of the most popular data security techniques that reduce the risk of data loss. These techniques apply to micro, mini, and mainframe computer data. As you read, you'll notice that many of these techniques apply to organizations. This information is also important for you as an individual for three reasons. First, it is likely that you will work with computers within an organization when you graduate, so you will share the responsibility with your coworkers for that organization's data. Second, many organizations maintain data about you such as your credit rating, educational record, and health records. You have a vested interest in the accuracy and the confidentiality of this data. Finally, you currently have data stored on disks that might be time-consuming to reconstruct. You should consider using two of the techniques discussed in this section—backup and virus detection—to secure your own data.

Establish Policies

How can an organization educate its employees on the rules for acceptable computer use?

In a computing environment, **policies** are the rules and regulations that specify how a computer system should be used. Policies are most often determined by management and used by large organizations to stipulate who can access computer data. Policies also help an organization define appropriate uses for its computers and data.

Here are some excerpts from computer policies of private, government, and educational organizations:

- All full-time employees are entitled to an e-mail account, which may be used to exchange messages with other employees on the intercompany network. In the normal course of system maintenance the content of e-mail messages might be read by computer center staff. In addition, management reserves the option to read e-mail messages when there is cause to believe that those messages might be used for illegal or unethical transmission of data.
- Employees are provided with desktop computers to enhance their productivity. These computers may be used for work-related tasks. However, employees are prohibited from using company computers for games, personal financial management, or other activities not related directly to their job description.
- To protect the corporate network from viruses, employees must not install any software that has not been pre-approved by the information systems department. If such software is found on corporate computers, it will be erased immediately and the employee responsible for its installation will be liable for any damages incurred.
- Software piracy is strictly prohibited. Employees who violate this policy will be dismissed.
- The company owns all the data stored on company computers. Unauthorized use or appropriation of data from company computers will be prosecuted to the fullest extent of the law.

The advantages of policies are that they define how a computer system should be used, make users aware of limits and penalties, and provide a framework for legal or job action for individuals who do not follow policies. Policies are an inexpensive building block in the overall structure of data security. Policies do not require any special hardware or software. The cost of policies is the time it takes to compose, update, and publicize them. The disadvantage of policies for data security is that some users disregard policies.

Follow Procedures

What's the difference between policies and procedures?

It might seem that nothing can be done to prevent operator error. After all, mistakes do happen. However, many mistakes can be prevented. Successful computer users develop habits that significantly reduce their chances of making mistakes. These habits, when formalized and adopted by an organization, are referred to as **procedures**. Procedures help reduce human errors that can erase or damage data. Some examples of procedures are these:

- Save your files frequently as you work so you don't lose too much data if the power fails.
- When you format a disk, always view a directory of its contents first to make sure the disk in the drive is the one you want to format.
- Use virus detection software immediately to scan any files that you have downloaded from acomputer bulletin board, commercial information service, or the Internet.
- When entering long columns of data, check off each number as it is entered.
- Before closing out a month, accounting personnel must make a backup.

By now you might have already figured out how policies and procedures differ. Policies are rules and regulations that apply to computer use in a general way. Procedures describe steps or activities that are performed in conjunction with a specific task. Because procedures are more specific, they generally take longer to write than policies, making them somewhat more costly for an organization to create and document.

The major advantage of procedures is reducing operator error. However, procedures have two disadvantages. First, they must be kept up to date as equipment and software change. Second, there is no way to make sure that people follow them.

Use Audit Controls

How can an organization determine if employees are following procedures?

Audit controls monitor the accuracy and efficiency of a computer system. They also track employee activities as well as machine operations to help an organization determine if employees are following procedures. Here are some examples of audit controls:

- A security log audits network usage by recording the time, date, and user ID for each login.
- Audit controls track the time and date each file is opened or modified, as well as the user ID of the person who accesses the file.
- Input data from invoices, receipts, or other paper documents is compared to data stored on the computer system.
- Groupware routes documents for review or approval, tracking the time and date when the document is received in each office.
- Software monitors the number of keystrokes per hour for each data entry operator.

A disadvantage of audit controls is the cost of the software and the time taken by a manager to review the summary reports it produces. Audit controls are sometimes criticized for their "big brother" approach to employee supervision; most employees do not like to have their activities so closely monitored.

Restrict On-line Access to Data

Can people be prevented from accessing data so they can't steal or tamper with it?

The most common way to restrict access to a computer system is with user IDs and passwords. When you work on a multiuser system or network, you generally must have a user ID and password. Data security on a computer system that is guarded by user IDs and passwords depends on password secrecy. If users give out their passwords, choose obvious passwords, or write them down in obvious places, hackers can easily break in. Figure 8-11 shows how the length and composition of passwords affect the chances of unauthorized access.

Figure 8-11
How password length and composition affect the chances of unauthorized access.

	Example	Number of Possibilities	Average Time to Discover
Any short or long name	Ed, Christine	2,000 (a name dictionary)	5 hours
Any short or long word	It, electrocardiogram	60,000 (in a spell checker)	7 days
Two words together	Whiteknight	3,600,000,000	1,140 years
Mix of initials and numbers	JP2C2TP307	3,700,000,000,000,000	1,200,000,000 years
First line of a poem	Onceuponamidnightdreary	10,000,000,000,000, 000,000,000,000,000	3,000,000,000,000,000, 000,000 years
First two letters of each word in a poem	Onupamidr	100,000,000,000,000	32,000,000 years

Passwords are a first line of defense against unauthorized access. What if a hacker breaks in anyway? One way to limit the amount of damage from a break-in is to assign user rights. **User rights** are rules that limit the directories and files that each user can access. When you receive a user ID and password for a password-protected system, the system administrator gives you rights that allow you to access only particular directories and files on the host computer or file server. For example, in your computer lab, you might have only read rights to the directories that contain software. This would prevent you from deleting or changing the programs on lab computers. Most networks and host computers allow the system administrator to assign user rights, such as those shown in Figure 8-12.

Rights	Description
Erase rights	Allow you to erase files
Create rights	Allow you to create new files
Write rights	Allow you to save information in existing files
Read rights	Allow you to open files and read information
File find rights	Allow you to list files with a directory command

▶ **Figure 8-12**
User rights

Granting users only the rights they need helps prevent both accidental and deliberate damage to data. If users are granted limited rights, a hacker who steals someone's password has only those rights granted to the person from whom the password was stolen.

Hackers occasionally gain unauthorized access to computer systems through something called a trap door. A **trap door** is a special set of instructions that allows a user to bypass the normal security precautions and enter the system. Trap doors are often created during development and testing; they should be removed before the system becomes operational.

In the 1983 film *WarGames*, a trap door was the key to preventing widespread nuclear destruction. A young hacker breaks into a secret military computer that has been programmed to deal with enemy nuclear attacks. The hacker begins to play what he thinks is a detailed computer game. The computer, however, thinks it is an actual attack. Soon the computer passes the stage at which it can be stopped from launching nuclear missiles, except by a trap door designed by the reclusive programmer who created the original program. The trap door provides a way for the programmer to bypass official military channels and access the computer's fail-safe program. A special password is required to enter the trap door, and in the exciting climax of the film, the hacker races against time to get the password and gain access to the computer deep within the military installation in Cheyenne Mountain. In this fictional example, a trap door helped save the world. In general, however, if a trap door is not removed, it becomes a possible means of entry for any hacker who discovers it.

Restricting on-line access with passwords and user rights and closing trap doors might discourage some hackers and slow others, but it is possible that some might still slip through.

Encrypt Data

Is there any way to prevent criminals from using stolen data?

When an unauthorized person reads data, the data is no longer confidential. Although password protection and physical security measures are taken to limit access to computer data, hackers and criminals can still access data.

Encryption is the process of scrambling or hiding information so it cannot be understood until it is decrypted, or deciphered, to change it back to its original form. Encryption provides a last line of defense against the unauthorized use of data. If data is encrypted, unauthorized users obtain only scrambled gibberish instead of meaningful information. Edgar Allan Poe, the American writer famous for his tales of horror, was quite interested in secret codes. He was convinced that it was impossible to design an unbreakable method of encryption. You might be familiar with simple encryption and decryption techniques, such as the one shown in Figure 8-13.

Figure 8-13
Encryption by
simple substitution

17 21 15 20 8 20 8 5 18 1 22 5 14 14 5 22 5 18 13 15 18 5

1. This a message encrypted using a simple substitution technique in which the number of each letter's position in the alphabet represents the letter.

2. The key to this encryption looks like this. The 17 in the encrypted message is the "Q," the 21 is the letter "U," and so forth. This is a very simple encryption technique.

A	B	C	D	E	F	G	H	I	J	K	L	M	N	O	P	Q	R	S	T	U	V	W	X	Y	Z
1	2	3	4	5	6	7	8	9	10	11	12	13	14	15	16	17	18	19	20	21	22	23	24	25	26

Quoth the Raven "Nevermore"

3. Once you know the key, you can the decipher the message to see that it is the famous quote from Edgar Allan Poe's poem "The Raven."

Encryption by simple substitution is easy to decipher, but there are many effective encryption techniques that virtually guarantee the security of computer data. This fact worries law enforcement agencies in the U.S. government. Recently, the National Security Agency proposed that something called the Clipper Chip encryption scheme become a standard for all public, private, and government encryption. The **Clipper Chip** is designed to provide secure transmission of voice and data communications while providing a trap door that law enforcement agencies could use to decipher messages. If a law enforcement agency obtained a court order allowing it to tap into encrypted voice or data communications, it could then use its own special key to decipher the messages.

Understandably, a controversy has arisen over the Clipper Chip. Law enforcement agencies say they must have a way to decipher messages; it's not very useful to obtain a search warrant if criminals have encrypted their data with a scheme that could take more than a thousand years to decipher. But opponents of the Clipper Chip maintain that the government has no right to require citizens to use a specific encryption method just so the government can break it. Some people believe that the Clipper Chip is equivalent to the government requiring citizens to use a certain type of lock on their house or business; a lock to which the government holds the master key.

Software is available to encrypt data on micro, mini, and mainframe computers. The cost of this software varies with its sophistication. Regardless of its cost, encryption software is virtually a necessity for some businesses—such as financial institutions that transmit and store funds electronically.

Restrict Physical Access to the Computer System

If it is so easy for hackers to access data from networked computers or terminals, or over phone lines, is there any point to keeping computers locked up?

In 1970, during the Vietnam War, anti-war activists bombed the Army Mathematics Research Center at the University of Wisconsin. A graduate student was killed, the building was damaged, and the computer, along with 20 years of accumulated research data, was destroyed. One of the best ways to prevent people from damaging equipment is to restrict physical access to the computer system. If potential criminals cannot get to a computer or a terminal, stealing or damaging data becomes more difficult. Here are some ways to physically protect computer equipment and data:

- Restrict access to the area surrounding the computer to prevent physical damage to the equipment.
- Keep data backups in a locked vault to prevent theft and to protect against fire or water damage.
- Keep offices containing computers locked to prevent theft and to deter unauthorized users.
- Lock personal computer keyboards in desk drawers at night to prevent access to data on the hard disk drive.
- Lock the computer case to prevent theft of components such as RAM and processors.
- Store floppy disks in a locked cabinet.

You can discuss the pros and cons of the Clipper Chip in Project 4 at the end of this chapter.

Restricting physical access makes it more difficult for unauthorized personnel to destroy equipment and data. You have probably heard about computerized screening techniques that identify people based on voice patterns, finger prints, palm prints, retinal patterns, or handwriting. Researchers are also working on ways to use computers to identify faces as explained in Figure 8-14.

Figure 8-14 ◀
Screening
techniques

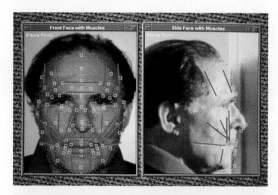

One way for a computer to identify a face is to compare it to a stored photograph on which key reference points, and the distance between them, has been clearly marked. In real life, however, a person might be wearing glasses, eye makeup, or have an injury that would not match the stored reference points.

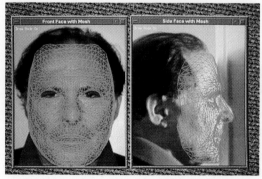

Researchers at MIT are working on a computerized system that would "teach" a computer to recognize a face using a set of generalized characteristics such as a "high forehead" and "thin lips" that the computer generates by comparing the face to a training set of many faces. Using this technique a computer can recognize a face with glasses on or off, with different makeup, or with small injuries.

Restricting physical access to computers has disadvantages. Locks and other screening measures can make it more difficult for authorized users to access the computer system. Also, restricting physical access will not prevent a determined criminal from stealing data. Access from a remote location is more difficult, but it might not be impossible. Finally, although restricting access might deter intentional acts of destruction, it will not prevent accidents.

Provide Redundancy

Can anything be done to minimize the damage from accidents?

Accidents can destroy data and equipment. The result is **downtime**, computer jargon for the time a computer system is not functioning. The most dependable way to minimize downtime is to duplicate data and equipment. You will learn about duplicating data in Section 8.4. Duplicating equipment simply means maintaining equipment that duplicates the functions critical to computing activities. This is sometimes referred to as **hardware redundancy**. Figure 8-15 shows some of the equipment that can be used to provide hardware redundancy.

Hardware redundancy reduces an organization's dependency on outside repair technicians. If it maintains a stock of duplicate parts, an organization can swap parts and be up and running before the manufacturer's repair technician arrives. Duplicate parts are expensive, however, and these costs must be weighed against lost revenue or productivity while repairs are underway.

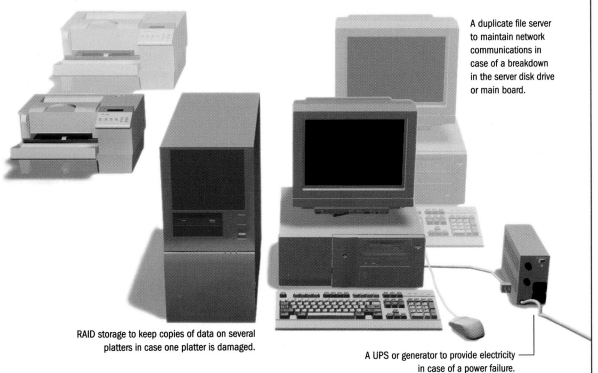

An extra printer in case the main
printer breaks down.

A duplicate file server
to maintain network
communications in
case of a breakdown
in the server disk drive
or main board.

RAID storage to keep copies of data on several
platters in case one platter is damaged.

A UPS or generator to provide electricity
in case of a power failure.

Install and Use Virus Detection Software

How effective is virus detection software?

Virus detection software finds and eradicates many viruses, but it is not 100% reliable. It will fail to detect viruses without a known signature, **polymorphic viruses** that change after they infect your computer, and viruses that use **stealth technology**, to hide from virus detection programs. Virus detection software generally does not detect Trojan horses unless they carry a virus. When virus detection software does not detect a virus in an infected computer, it is called a "false negative report." Sometimes virus detection software tells you that your computer is infected, but a virus is *not* actually present. This is a "false positive report." False negative and false positive reports are infrequent. Virus detection software generally succeeds in detecting and eradicating most widespread viruses, so you should include it in your software collection.

There are many virus detection programs, produced by different software publishers. You can purchase these programs from your local computer dealer or by mail order. Shareware virus detection programs are available from computer bulletin boards and shareware dealers. The cost of a virus detection program for microcomputers is generally less than $100.

Virus detection software can both detect viruses and eradicate them. But this software works only if you use it. You should run your virus detection program periodically to check if any viruses have found their way into your computer system. If viruses are a recurring problem in your computing environment, you might want to configure your virus detection software to continually monitor the behavior of your computer files and alert you if it spots signs of virus-like activity.

*In Project 8 you
have the opportunity
to compare the
price and features
of popular virus
detection software
packages.*

There is no "magic pill" that will protect your computer from hackers, crackers, and cyberpunks. However, you can reduce the risk of infection if you:

- Install and use virus detection software.
- Keep your virus detection software up to date.
- Make frequent backups *after* you use virus detection software to scan your files for viruses.
- Download software only from virus free sources. Use a virus detection program to scan downloaded software before you use it.
- Exercise care with disks that contain shareware or pirated software. Scan them before you run or copy any files from these disks.

Make Backups

If I implement only one security measure, should it be a backup?

A **backup** is a duplicate copy of a file or the contents of a disk drive. If the original file is lost or damaged, you can use the backup copy to restore the data to its original working condition. Backup is probably the best all-round protection for your data. It provides data protection from hardware failures, vandalism, operator error, and natural disasters, as long as you do the following:

- Make frequent backups. You can't restore data that you haven't backed up; so if you wait a month between backups, you could lose a month's worth of data.
- Scan for viruses before you backup. If your computer is infected with a virus when you back up, your backup will also be infected.
- Store your backup away from your computer. If your backup is next to your computer, a fire or flood could also damage your backup.
- Test your backup. Before you depend on your backups, make sure that you can restore data from your backup to your hard disk. You would not want to discover that your backup files were blank because you didn't correctly carry out the backup procedure. The major disadvantage of backups is user forgetfulness and procrastination. You will learn more about backups in Section 8-4.

Quick Check

1 _____ is the process of weighing threats to computer data against the amount of data that is expendable and the cost of protecting crucial data.

2 A(n) _____ is a rule designed to prohibit employees from installing software that has not been pre-approved by the information systems department.

3 Software that monitors the number of keystrokes per hour for each data entry employee would be classified as a(n) _____.

4 Procedures help reduce human errors that can erase or damage data. True or false?

5 If a network administrator assigns _____, users can access only certain programs and files.

6 Hackers sometimes gain unauthorized entry to computer systems through a(n) _____ that is not removed when development and testing are complete.

7 The Clipper Chip is a method of _____ that scrambles data so it cannot be understood until it is decrypted.

8 _____ is computer jargon that refers to the time a computer system is not functioning.

9 If your virus detection software tells you that your computer is infected when it really is not, the software has given you a false _____ report.

User Focus:
Backup

Lab

Data Backup

L osing all your data is one of the most distressing computing experiences. It might be the result of a hardware failure or a virus. Whatever the cause, most users experience only a moment of surprise and disbelief before reaching the depressing realization that they might have to recreate all their data and reinstall all their programs. A backup can pull you through such trying times, making the data loss a minor inconvenience, rather than a major disaster.

Industry experts recommend that all computer users make backups. Sounds simple, right? Unfortunately, this advice tells you what to do, not how to do it. It fails to address some key questions: How often should I make a backup?, What should I back up?, and What should I do with the backups? To keep your data safe, you need a data backup plan, one tailored to your computing needs. To devise your data backup plan, you should consider factors such as the value of your data, the amount of data stored on your computer, the frequency with which your data changes, and the type of backup equipment you have. As these factors change, you need to revise your plan. For example, the backup plan you use while in college is likely to change as you pursue your career. In this section of the chapter you will learn about the advantages and disadvantages of various backup tools and techniques, so you can select those appropriate for your own data backup plan.

Backup Equipment

Does my computer need a tape drive so I can make backups?

Tape backups are the most popular microcomputer backup solution for small businesses, and they are gaining popularity with individuals as the price of tape drives decreases. When you make a tape backup, data from the hard disk is copied to a magnetic tape. If the data on the hard disk is lost, the backup data is restored by copying it from the tape to a functional hard disk drive. Tape backup requires tapes and a tape drive, costing less than $300. However, you can back up your data without a tape drive.

Many microcomputer users back up their data onto floppy disks. This method is unrealistic for backing up the entire contents of today's high-capacity disk drives—a drive with 500 MB capacity would require at least 350 floppy disks for a complete backup! However, backing up every file is not necessary. Many users back up only those directories that contain data files. In the event of a hard disk failure, these users would need to reinstall all their software from original disks, then copy their data files from the backups.

If you use the computers in a college computer lab, your situation is somewhat unique because you store your data on a floppy disk instead of the hard disk. An effective way to back up if you're in this situation is to make a copy of your disk using the Copy Disk utility, described in the next subsection, "Backup Software."

Usually, backups are stored on magnetic media such as disk or tape. However, you can also use a printout of your data for backup purposes. To restore the data from a printout, you can use a scanner or you can retype it. With either restoration method, you can easily introduce errors, so paper backups should be considered only as a last resort.

Backup Software

Do I need special software to make backups?

A backup is essentially a copy of data. You must use software to tell the computer what to copy. There are three types of software you might use: a copy utility, a disk copy program, or backup software.

A **copy utility** is a program that copies one or more files. You can use a copy utility to copy files between a hard disk and a floppy disk, between two floppy disks of any size, from a CD-ROM to a hard disk, or from a CD-ROM to a floppy disk. A copy utility is usually included with a computer operating system. With Windows 3.1, the File Manager includes a copy utility. With Windows 95, the copy utility is available in the Windows Explorer and from the File menu.

The **Copy Disk** utility is a program that duplicates the contents of an entire floppy disk. You can use a Copy Disk utility only to copy all the files from one floppy disk to another floppy disk of the same size. You cannot use the Copy Disk utility for files on a hard disk drive. The Copy Disk utility is provided with most microcomputer operating systems, including DOS and Windows. You can use Windows 95 the procedure shown in Figure 8-16 to duplicate the floppy disk you use for this course.

Figure 8-16
Using Copy Disk
to back up
a floppy

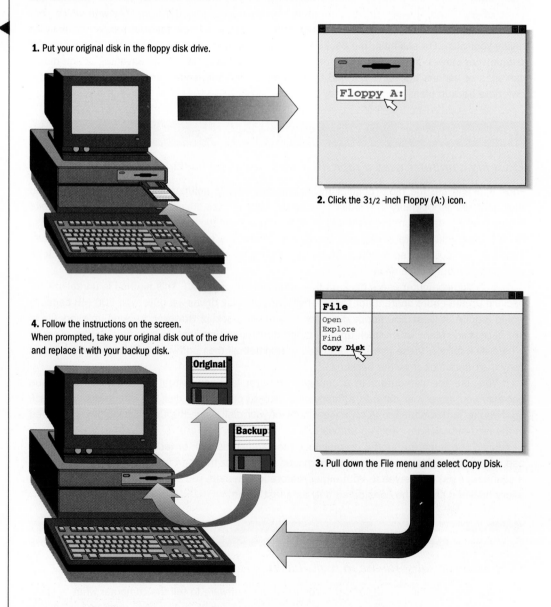

1. Put your original disk in the floppy disk drive.

Floppy A:

2. Click the 3$1/2$ -inch Floppy (A:) icon.

4. Follow the instructions on the screen.
When prompted, take your original disk out of the drive and replace it with your backup disk.

Original

Backup

File
Open
Explore
Find
Copy Disk

3. Pull down the File menu and select Copy Disk.

Backup software is designed to manage hard disk backup to tapes or diskettes. When you use backup software you can select the files you want to back up. Most operating systems include backup software. However, if your tape drive requires special proprietary backup software, you should use the backup software included with the tape drive, instead of the software provided with the operating system. Backup software is becoming quite sophisticated. Many packages offer automated features that allow you to schedule automatic backups and back up only those files that have changed since the last backup.

Types of Backups

Should I back up everything on my disk?

A **full backup** is a copy of all the files on a disk. A full backup is very safe because it ensures that you have a copy of every file on the disk—every program and every data file. Because a full backup includes a copy of every file on a disk, it can take a long time to make one for a hard disk. While the backup is in progress, the computer cannot generally be used for other tasks. Some users consider it worth the time because this type of backup is easy to restore. You simply have the computer copy the files from your backup to the hard disk, as shown in Figure 8-17.

When you use the Copy Disk utility to make a backup of a floppy disk, you are making a full backup of the floppy.

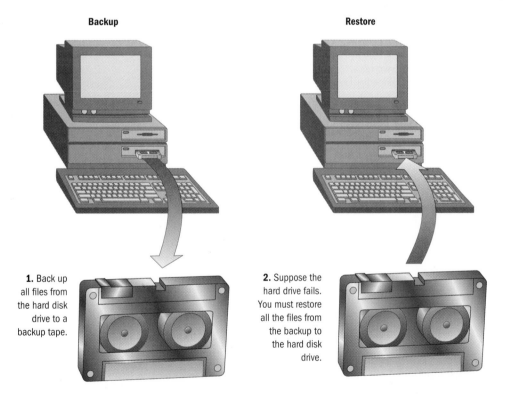

Backup

Restore

1. Back up all files from the hard disk drive to a backup tape.

2. Suppose the hard drive fails. You must restore all the files from the backup to the hard disk drive.

▶ **Figure 8-17**
Full backup

A **differential backup** is a copy of all the files that have changed since the last full backup. You must, therefore, maintain two sets of backups—a full backup that you make infrequently, say once a week, and a differential backup that you make more frequently, say once a day. It takes less time to make a differential backup; than to make a full backup; however, restoring data from a differential backup is a little more complex. To restore your data after a differential backup, you first restore data from the last full backup, then restore the data from the latest differential backup, as shown in Figure 8-18.

Figure 8-18
Differential backup

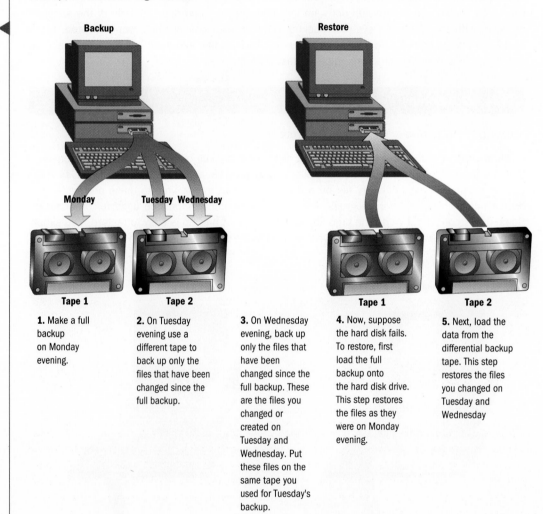

Backup

Restore

Monday   **Tuesday** **Wednesday**

Tape 1   **Tape 2**   **Tape 1**   **Tape 2**

1. Make a full backup on Monday evening.

2. On Tuesday evening use a different tape to back up only the files that have been changed since the full backup.

3. On Wednesday evening, back up only the files that have been changed since the full backup. These are the files you changed or created on Tuesday and Wednesday. Put these files on the same tape you used for Tuesday's backup.

4. Now, suppose the hard disk fails. To restore, first load the full backup onto the hard disk drive. This step restores the files as they were on Monday evening.

5. Next, load the data from the differential backup tape. This step restores the files you changed on Tuesday and Wednesday

An **incremental backup** is a copy of the files that have changed since the last backup. When you use incremental backups, you must have a full backup and you must maintain a series of incremental backups. The incremental backup procedure is similar to the differential backup procedure, but there's a subtle difference. With a differential backup, you maintain one full backup and one differential backup. The differential backup contains any files that were changed since the last full backup. With an incremental backup procedure, you maintain a full backup and a series of incremental backups. Each incremental backup contains only those files that changed since the last incremental backup. To restore the data from a series of incremental backups, you restore the last full backup, then sequentially restore each incremental backup.

Incremental backups take the least time to make and provide a little better protection from viruses than other backup methods because your backup contains a series of copies of your files. However, incremental backups are the most complex type of backup to restore, as shown in Figure 8-19.

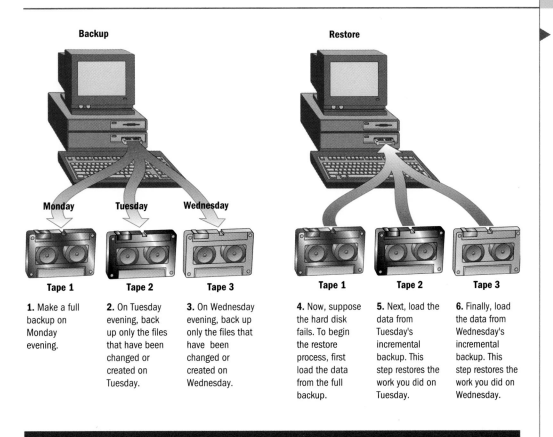

Figure 8-19
Incremental backup

Backup

Restore

| Monday | Tuesday | Wednesday | | Tape 1 | Tape 2 | Tape 3 |

Tape 1   **Tape 2**   **Tape 3**

1. Make a full backup on Monday evening.

2. On Tuesday evening, back up only the files that have been changed or created on Tuesday.

3. On Wednesday evening, back up only the files that have been changed or created on Wednesday.

Tape 1   **Tape 2**   **Tape 3**

4. Now, suppose the hard disk fails. To begin the restore process, first load the data from the full backup.

5. Next, load the data from Tuesday's incremental backup. This step restores the work you did on Tuesday.

6. Finally, load the data from Wednesday's incremental backup. This step restores the work you did on Wednesday.

Backup Schedule

How frequently should I make a backup?

Any data backup plan is a compromise between the level of protection and the amount of time devoted to backup. To be absolutely safe, you would need to back up your data every time you change the contents of a file, which would seriously reduce the amount of work you could complete in a day. Realistically, however, you should make backups at regular intervals. The interval between backups will depend on the value of your data—what that data is worth to you or your employer in terms of time and money.

An individual using a personal computer might not be particularly worried about the consequences of data loss. Data backup for such an individual should be quick and easy to complete and should reduce some of the inconvenience of data loss. However, it would not necessarily restore all data or programs. A backup schedule that offers this minimal amount of protection would require a once-a-week backup of those data files that have changed since the last backup, as shown in Figure 8-20.

In the event of a hard disk drive failure, an individual who uses this backup plan would have to reinstall all software from original disks and restore all the

Figure 8-20
A basic backup plan

			March			
Sun	Mon	Tue	Wed	Thu	Fri	Sat
			1	2	3	4
5	6	7	8	9	10	11
12	13	14	15	16	17	18
19	20	21	22	23	24	25
26	27	28	29	30	31	

data from the backup disks. The data entered or changed since the last backup would be lost. If the last backup was made at the end of the day on Monday and the hard disk failed on Thursday, the data from Tuesday, Wednesday, and Thursday would be lost.

A more rigorous backup plan would be required for more valuable data, particularly if the data was produced by an application, such as an accounting system or payroll program, that operates on a weekly or monthly cycle. Every time you use an accounting system, for example, you do not use all the files that contain your data. Therefore, a file could be damaged by a virus or disk error, but you might not know it for several days or weeks until you try to access the file. In the meantime you might have made backups that contain the damaged file.

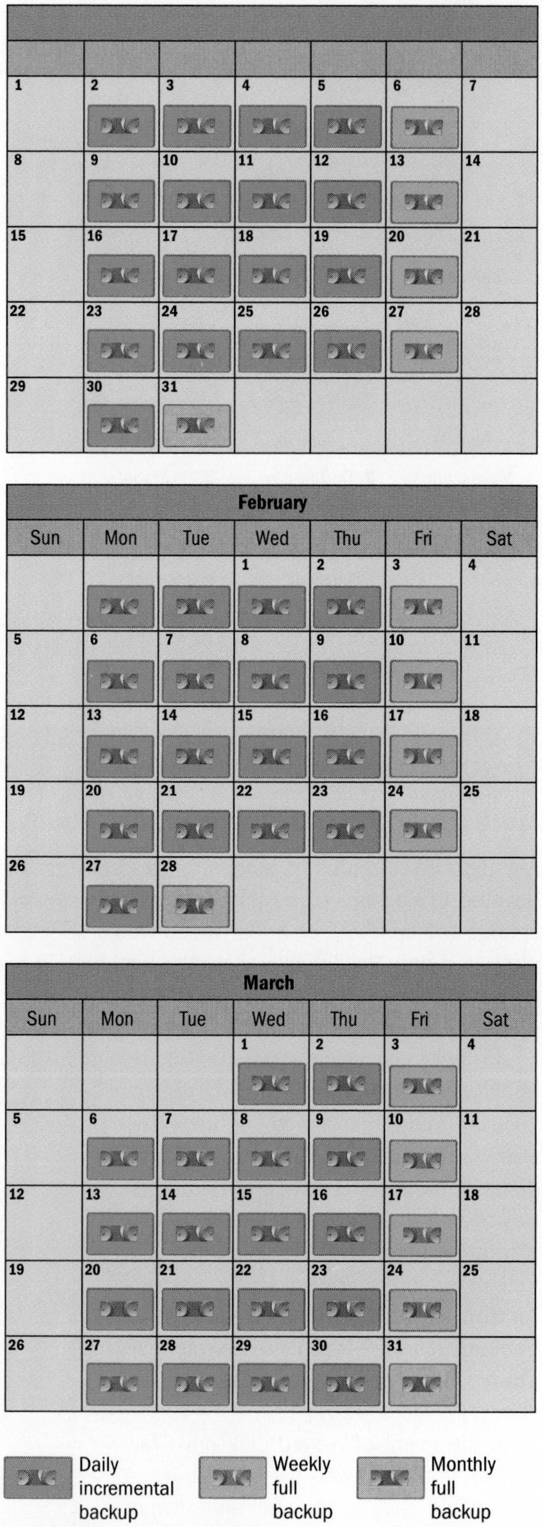

A more sophisticated backup procedure, one that you might use with an accounting system, would typically combine daily, weekly, and monthly backups to allow data to be reconstructed at any point before file damage occurred. The daily backups are incremental backups, one performed each day of the week, except for the day during which the weekly backups are performed. The weekly backups are a series of three full backups, one for each week of the month, except the week when you make the monthly backup. The monthly backups are a series of twelve full backups, each performed just before month-end closing. This backup procedure for an accounting application is illustrated in Figure 8-21.

The data backup plan illustrated in Figure 8-21 is not guaranteed to protect against all data loss. Suppose you were using an accounting system and a virus strikes one of the files in July. You don't notice it until the end of the month. Your last weekly backup contains the virus, but the backup for June does not. You can restore the data for January through June from the June backup. You might have to reenter the July data. However, without your backup you would have to reenter all the data!

Figure 8-21
Backup schedule for an accounting system

Daily incremental backup

Weekly full backup

Monthly full backup

As you can see, a backup does not guarantee data security. However, it does provide a solid level of protection for the problems that are most likely to damage data.

End Note
The amount of data stored on computer systems, combined with the vulnerability of those systems, creates a potentially risky situation. A surprising amount of personal data about you is stored on computers. All of it might not be accurate. It can be accessed and altered by criminals. It can be destroyed by hardware failure, human sabotage, or natural disaster. The same can be said for national security data or the data that keeps the world financial market running smoothly. One of the main issues of the computer age concerns the security and ethical use of computer data. Risk management has, therefore, become a necessity in most organizations.

In the story of the Trojan War, the Trojans seem so naive. Who would be so foolish as to pull such a suspicious horse into the city? But you have learned that today's computer users are often just as naive about modern technology. They install programs on their computers without checking for viruses, they store massive amounts of data without backups, and they transmit sensitive data without first encrypting it. The Trojans fell for the wooden horse trick the first time, but it is a mistake they would be unlikely to repeat. Will modern computer users repeat their mistakes or learn to take precautions? Now that you've read this chapter, what will you do?

Review

1. Use your own words to answer the italicized questions that appear under each section heading in this chapter.

2. List each of the boldface terms used in this chapter, then use your own words to write a short definition of each term.

3. Complete the following chart to review the factors that cause data loss or misuse. List the factors you learned about in this chapter in the first column. Then place an X in the appropriate column to indicate if the factor causes data loss, inaccurate data, stolen data, or intentionally damaged data. Some factors might have more than one X.

Factor	Unintentional data loss	Inaccurate data	Stolen or misused data	Intentional data loss or damage
Operator error				
[You fill in the rest of the factors]				

4. Complete the following chart to summarize what you have learned about Trojan horses, time bombs, logic bombs, and software worms.

Type	Spreads by	Triggered by
Virus		
Trojan horse		
Worm		
Time bomb		
Logic bomb		

5. Make a check list of steps to take if you suspect that your computer is infected with a virus.

6. List the four steps in the risk management process.

7. Make a list of the data security techniques discussed in Section 8.3, Data Security and Risk Management. Then indicate the advantages and disadvantages of each technique.

8. Use your own words to write descriptions of full, incremental, and differential backup procedures. Make sure your descriptions clearly explain the difference between incremental and differential backups.

9. Thinking back over the entire chapter, what was the most useful concept you learned? What questions do you have about data security that still remain unanswered?

10. On a sheet of paper, list all the reasons you can think of for making a backup of computer data.

Projects

1. Lost Data: What's Your Experience? Describe a situation in which you or someone you know lost data stored on a computer. What caused the data loss? What steps could have been taken to prevent the loss? What steps could you or the other person have taken to recover the lost data?

2. Risk Management: A Personal Perspective Assess the risk to the programs and data files stored on the hard disk of your computer by answering the following questions:

    a. What threats are likely to cause your data to be lost, stolen, or damaged?

    b. How many files of data do you have?

    c. If you add up the size of all your files, how many megabytes of data do you have?

    d. How many of these files are critical and would need to be replaced if you lost all your data?

    e. What would you need to do to reconstruct the critical files if the hard disk drive failed and you did not have any backups?

    f. What measures could you use to protect your data from the threats you identified in the first question? What is the cost of each of these measures?

    g. Balancing the threats to your data, the importance of your data, and the cost of protective measures, what do you think is the best plan for the security of your data?

3. Lost Weekend: Full, Incremental, and Differential Backups Assume that your hard disk drive fails on a Friday afternoon. Explain how you would restore your data over the weekend if you had been using each of the following backup systems:

   a. A full backup every Friday evening

   b. A full backup every Friday evening with a differential backup on Wednesday night

   c. A full backup every Friday evening with an incremental backup Monday through Thursday evenings

4. The Clipper Chip Debate In this chapter you learned that the U.S. government wants to standardize all encryption using the Clipper Chip.

   a. Using library or Internet resources, research the controversy surrounding the Clipper Chip.

   b. In a small group, discuss the concerns raised by the plans for the Clipper Chip encryption method. Be sure to discuss whether you think the Clipper Chip is a good idea. Can you or anyone in your group think of any alternative methods that would protect the privacy of individual citizens while providing a way for law enforcement agencies to perform their job effectively?

   c. After you examine the issues, write a two-page paper that is a dialog between two people—one who supports the government's plan for the Clipper Chip and one who doesn't.

5. The Internet Worm The Internet worm created concern about the security of data on military and research computer systems, and it raised ethical questions about the rights and responsibilities of computer users. Select one of the following statements and write a two-page paper that argues for or against the statement. You might want to use the Internet or library resources to learn more about each viewpoint. Be sure you include the resources you used in a bibliography.

   a. People have the "right" to hone their computing skills by breaking into computers. As a computer scientist once said, "The right to hack is held higher than the right of someone to tell you not to. It's an inalienable right."

   b. If problems exist, it is acceptable to use any means to point them out. The computer science student who created the Internet virus was perfectly justified in claiming that he should not be convicted because he was just trying to point out that security holes exist in large computer networks.

   c. Computer crimes are no different from other crimes, and computer criminals should be held responsible for the damage they cause by paying for the time and cost of replacing or restoring data.

6. Understanding an Acceptable Use Policy Obtain a copy of your school's student code or computer use policy, then answer the following questions. If your school does not have such a policy, create one that addresses these questions.

   a. To whom does the policy apply—students, faculty, staff, community members, others?

   b. What types of activities does the policy specifically prohibit?

   c. If a computer crime is committed, would the crime be dealt with by campus authorities or by state law enforcement agents?

   d. Does the policy state the penalties for computer crimes? If so, what are they?

7. You Be the Jury The company that publishes a popular statistical software package leases its software for a one-year period. The software contains a time bomb, set with the lease expiration date. Each day, the time bomb checks the date. When the current date exceeds the date in the time bomb, the leased software stops working. When customers renew the lease, they receive a series of commands that resets the time bomb for the new expiration date.

In a small group discuss the similarities and differences between the time bomb used by the statistical software publishers and that used by PC Cyborg, which was discussed in the "Time Bombs and Logic Bombs" subsection of Section 8.2.

Suppose both of these software publishers were sued by irritated customers. If you were a juror, what would your verdict be in each case?

8. Virus Detection Software If you suspect your computer has become infected, it is useful to immediately activate virus detection software to scan your files for a virus. With the continued spread of viruses, virus detection software has become an essential utility in today's computing environment. Many virus detection software packages are available in computer stores, on computer bulletin boards, and on the Internet. Find information about three virus detection software packages and fill out the following comparison chart.

	Software 1	Software 2	Software 3
Product name			
Publisher			
Price			
Current version			
Update frequency			
Special features			

Resources

- **Cohen, F.** *A Short Course on Computer Viruses*. New York: Wiley & Sons, 1994. Fred Cohen is a guru in computer virus research. He has written this book for the non-technical reader. One of the interesting aspects of this book is Cohen's discussion of "friendly" viruses.

- *comp.risks (risks@csl.sri.com)* comp.risks is an Internet Usenet discussion group on topics related to computer security and risk management. Transcripts of the discussions are available from *http://catless. nci.ac.uk/Risks*.

- *comp.virus (virus-l@lehigh.edu)* comp.virus is a moderated discussion of computer viruses. The site also provides a list of answers to frequently asked questions about viruses.

- **Denning, J.**, ed. *Computers Under Attack: Intruders, Worms and Viruses*. New York, ACM Press, 1990. This book is a collection of papers, some classics, that provide a well-balanced overview of the technical, legal, and ethical issues surrounding network loopholes, computer viruses, and worms.

- **Hrushka, J**. *Computer Viruses and Anti-Virus Warfare*, 2nd ed. New York, Ellis Horwood, 1992. This book is a very clear introduction to computer viruses, worms, and so on. It has several unique features, including screen shots of virus payloads, a profile of virus writers, and the source code for a simple virus detection program.

- *http://www.symantec.com* This is the Web site for the company that publishes Symantec AntiVirus software. At this site you will also find information about Norton AntiVirus software.

- *http://www.mcafee.com* At this Web site, you can find information about the popular MacAfee VirusScan software.

- *http://www.sands.com* This Web site contains information about Dr. Solomon's Anti-Virus Toolkit.

- *http://www-swiss.ai.mit.edu/6095/articles/froomkin-metaphor/text.html* The HTML version of an excellent paper by A. Michael Froomkin on cryptography, the Clipper Ship, and the U.S. Constitution.

- *http://draco.centerline.com:8080/~franl/clipper/about-clipper.html* A Web page that contains links to many sites with information about the Clipper.

- *http://cpsr.org/dox/home.html* The organization, Computer Professionals for Social Responsibility, maintains this Web site where you can find information about computing ethics.

- **Kahn, D**. *The Codebreakers*. New York: Macmillan, 1976. This is one of the classic books on the history of cryptography. The book is huge—over 1,000 pages—and extensively referenced. Don't let that discourage you from checking this book out from your library. It is written in a captivating style, and you can dip in anywhere and sample tales of intrigue—such as how the Greeks established the first system of military cryptography, how the English broke the "unbreakable" German enigma code during World War II, and how to interpret messages from outer space.

- **Linowes, D**. *Privacy in America*. Chicago: University of Illinois Press, 1989. This well-researched book is sure to motivate you to think about the kind of data that government and private computer systems are accumulating about you. The book concludes with a series of guidelines for protecting your personal privacy.

- **Neumann, P.** *Computer Related Risks*. New York: ACM Press, 1995. Peter Neumann is the moderator of the Internet Risks Forum and writes the popular column "Inside Risks" in the professional journal, *Communications of the ACM*. This book is full of documented examples of security breaches. The examples are summarized in table format at the end of each chapter, providing an easy-to-understand overview of the challenge that risk managers face.

- **Slade, R.** *Guide to Computer Viruses*. New York: Springer-Verlag, 1994. Slade's *Guide* is fun to read and packed full of well-researched and accurate accounts of the most widespread PC, Mac, and UNIX viruses. Chapter 5 contains a detailed checklist of the steps that an individual or business should take to protect data from viruses, worms, and other "malware."

- **Stephenson, N.** *Snow Crash*. New York: Bantam Books, 1992. Computer viruses have opened new horizons for science fiction writers, providing good plot twists. In *Snow Crash*, a universal virus spreads to humans as well as computers. Experienced computer hackers are particularly susceptible to one form of this virus, triggered by a particular graphic display on their screens. Although this book is fiction, it shows a good understanding of computers and computer viruses.

- **Stoll, C.** *The Cuckoo's Egg*. New York: Doubleday, 1987. While monitoring user accounts on a large research computer system, the author of this book noticed a $0.75 discrepancy that mushroomed into an international hunt for hackers who were selling U.S. military data to the KGB. This book has all the elements of an espionage thriller, but the story is true and contains a wealth of factual information on computer security. Stoll gave a presentation at Cisco NetWorkers '94 called "Stalking the Wily Hacker." You can access this presentation on the Internet at *http://town.hall.org/university/security/stoll/cliff.html*.

- *Understanding Computers: Computer Security*. Alexandria, VA: Time-Life Books, 1986. A lavishly illustrated, in-depth look at computer security, the methods that hackers use to avoid it, and the improved methods used to foil them. Although written 10 years ago, most of the basic principles of data security presented in this book have not changed, so it is still a good basic reference.

Lab Assignments

Data Backup

 The Data Backup Lab gives you an opportunity to make tape backups on a simulated computer system. Periodically, the hard disk on the simulated computer will fail, which gives you a chance to assess the convenience and efficiency of different backup procedures.

1. Click the Steps button to learn how to use the simulation. As you work through the Steps, answer all of the Quick Check questions that appear. After you complete the Steps, you will see a Summary Report of your Quick Check answers. Follow the directions on the screen to print this report.

2. Click the Explore button. Create a full backup every Friday using only Tape 1. At some point in the simulation, an event will cause data loss on the simulated computer system. Use the simulation to restore as much data as you can. After you restore the data, print the Backup Audit Report.

3. In Explore, create a full backup every Friday on Tape 1 and a differential backup every Wednesday on Tape 2. At some point in the simulation, an event will cause data loss on the simulated computer system. Use the simulation to restore as much data as you can. Print the Backup Audit Report.

4. In Explore, create a full backup on Tape 1 every Monday. Make incremental backups on Tapes 2, 3, 4, and 5 each day for the rest of the week. Continue this cycle, reusing the same tapes each week. At some point in the simulation an event will cause data loss on the simulated computer system. Use the simulation to restore as much data as you can. Print the Backup Audit Report.

5. Photocopy a calendar for next month. On the calendar indicate your best plan for backing up data. In Explore, implement your plan. Print out the Backup Audit Report. Write a paragraph or two discussing the effectiveness of your plan.

Quick Check

Answers

8.1

1. operator error

2. false

3. uninterruptible power supply (UPS)

4. surge protector

5. false

6. false

7. hard disk drive

8. up-to-date backup

8.2

1. virus

2. trojan horse

3. worm

4. virus

5. public domain software, shareware, and illegal copies of computer programs downloaded from bulletin boards

6. weird messages, unusual sound effects, difficulty saving files (or missing files, unexpected reboots, increased executable file size)

7. signature

8. computer data and software

8.3

1. risk management

2. policy

3. audit control

4. true

5. user rights

6. trap door

7. encryption

8. downtime

9. positive

Glossary/Index

Quick Check

Answers

Chapter One

1.1

1. accepts input, processes data, stores data, produces output

2. data

3. process

4. memory

5. storage

1.2

1. keyboard, monitor

2. microcomputer

3. terminal

4. minicomputers, mainframes

5. mainframe

6. compatible

7. network

1.3

1. prompt

2. wizards

3. Enter

4. syntax error

5. submenu, dialog box

6. graphical user interfaces

7. cursor, insertion point

8. Ctrl, Alt

9. Windows

10. character-based

Chapter Two

2.1

1. false

2. data

3. program

4. software

5. shareware

6. license

7. system software

2.2

1. multitasking

2. UNIX

3. micro

4. Utility

5. device driver

6. programming language

2.3

1. word processing, spreadsheet, database management

2. integrated software

3. horizontal market software

4. education software

5. desktop publishing

2.4

1. text, graphics, sound, animation, photo images, video

2. false

3. hypertext, hypermedia

4. MPC

5. speakers, sound card, CD-ROM drive, high-resolution color monitor, fast processor (high memory capacity is also acceptable)

6. multimedia kit

Chapter Three

3.1

1. data, information

2. drive letter, subdirectory, subdirectory, filename, filename extension

3. exe, com

4. Most Windows software automatically adds a specific extension to each file created with it.

5. logical

6. root

7. source

3.2

1. kilobytes(megabytes or gigabytes also acceptable), milliseconds

2. magnetic, optical

3. tracks, sectors

4. random, sequential

5. floppy disk, CD-ROM

6. hard disk drive

7. FAT (File Allocation Table)

8. false

Chapter Four
4.1

1. integrated circuit

2. bit

3. byte

4. ASCII, EBCDIC

5. binary

6. bus (or data bus)

4.2

1. Random access memory (RAM)

2. volatile

3. megabytes

4. capacitors

5. SIMM

6. virtual

7. ROM

8. CMOS

4.3

1. microprocessor

2. ALU

3. Control unit

4. opcode, operand

5. fetch, interpret, execute, increment instruction pointer

6. clock rate, word size, cache, instruction set

4.4

1. expansion bus

2. expansion card

3. slot, port

4. parallel, SCSI, serial, MIDI

Chapter Five
5.1

1. Product development, product announcement, introduction, maintenance, retirement

2. the operating system and application software you intend to use

3. EIDE, SCSI

4. local buses

5. dot pitch

6. 1 MB

7. bps

8. inkjet

5.2

1. PCMCIA

2. active

3. docking station

4. port replicator

5. track point, touch pad, trackball

6. power saving

5.3

1. product announcement, introduction, maintenance, retirement

2. product announcement

3. vaporware

4. plateau

5. version, revision

6. beta

5.4

1. tiers

2. computer retail store, mail-order suppliers, value-added resellers, manufacturer direct

3. trade journal

4. value-added reseller

5. academic journals

Chapter Six
6.1

1. server

2. mapping

3. account (or user account)

4. true

5. false

6. captured, redirected

6.2

1. network interface card

2. non-dedicated server

3. file server

4. true

5. host

6.3

1. network operating

2. true

3. network license

4. groupware

5. document routing

Chapter Seven
7.1

1. cyberspace

2. Internet

3. commercial information service (or on-line service)

4. discussion group

5. chat session

6. downloading

7.2

1. computers, host (mainframe)

2. Prodigy, CompuServe, America Online, Microsoft Network

3. basic services

4. connect time

5. local access number

7.3

1. internet (or internetwork)

2. Internet

3. coco = user ID, @canine = machine name, com = domain name

4. World Wide Web

5. Gopher

6. Anonymous FTP

7. Telnet

8. MOO

9. netiquette

Chapter Eight
8.1

1. operator error

2. false

3. uninterruptible power supply (UPS)

4. surge protector

5. false

6. false

7. hard disk drive

8. up-to-date backup

8.2

1. virus

2. trojan horse

3. worm

4. virus

5. public domain software, shareware, and illegal copies of computer programs downloaded from bulletin boards

6. weird messages, unusual sound effects, difficulty saving files (or missing files, unexpected reboots, increased executable file size)

7. signature

8. computer data and software

8.3

1. risk management

2. policy

3. audit control

4. true

5. user rights

6. trap door

7. encryption

8. downtime

9. positive

Glossary/Index

x86 Family of microprocessors descended from the 8086 micro-processor, used in IBM-compatible computers, 5-4, 5-4–5-5
XENIX, 2-17

Yahoo site, 7-7

Z

zines, 7-7